FOUNDATION PRESS

PROPERTY STORIES

Edited By

GERALD KORNGOLD

Dean and Everett D. and Eugenia S. McCurdy Professor of Law
Case Western Reserve University

and

ANDREW P. MORRISS

Galen J. Roush Professor of Business Law and Regulation
Case Western Reserve University
and Senior Associate, Property and Environment Research Center

FOUNDATION PRESS
New York, New York
2004

THOMSON
WEST

Cover Design: Keith Stout
Photograph: Image of Lucas v. South Carolina Coastal Council, taken from Dartmouth Professor of Economics, William A. Fischel's website http://www.dartmouth.edu/-wfischel/lucasessay.html

© 2004 By FOUNDATION PRESS
   395 Hudson Street
   New York, NY 10014
   Phone Toll Free 1–877–888–1330
   Fax (212) 367–6799
   fdpress.com
Printed in the United States of America

ISBN 1–58778–504–8

 TEXT IS PRINTED ON 10% POST CONSUMER RECYCLED PAPER

PROPERTY STORIES

FOUNDATION PRESS

PROPERTY STORIES

*

Gerald Korngold and Andrew P. Morriss

Introduction: The Story of *Property Stories*

The first-year Property course addresses some of the most weighty concepts in the law and public discourse. Essentially, the law of property and the course are focused on allocating rights and responsibilities of ownership between private parties and between individuals and the collective (perhaps in the form of a governmental entity or through vaguer notions of "the public interest"). While at the risk of appearing to be "property chauvinists," we feel that the course invokes the most complex mix of "big ideas" in the first year curriculum—liberty, responsibility, economic efficiency, redistribution, coercion, reliability, and predictability, among others. The Property course puts a lot on the table.

Moreover, there is a wide range of substantive topics in Property— adverse possession of realty, gifts of personal property, landlord-tenant relations, conveyances of land, easements and covenants, zoning, and regulatory takings to name a few. Sometimes it is hard to see the connections among these various areas—unlike, for example, Contracts where the (albeit slippery) concept of "reasonableness" as a gap filler cuts across many discussions. Much of what goes on in Property is the recognition and allocation of multiple rights in a single piece of property. To develop these ideas, courts and commentators have used a metaphor—thus it is said that owning property is like owning "a bundle of sticks." Each stick represents a right or a privilege, so that when all the sticks are bunched together they comprise complete ownership. And individual sticks can be transferred voluntarily to others (such as an easement or a leasehold) or involuntarily (such as by a taking or regulation). While for at least one self-consciously modern court the bundle of sticks simile is "hoary and simplistic,"[1] the concept continues to provide a way to understand the multiple layers of ownership.

---

[1] International Business Machines Corp. v. Comdisco, Inc., 602 A.2d 74, 76 (Del. 1991).

We offer you here a "bundle of stories"—*Property Stories*—about this "bundle of sticks." The cases described in the following chapters represent the wide range of substantive topics and concepts in the first-year Property course and many of the cases are viewed as "classics" in the field. The chapters provide insights and background into the particular cases and explain why the decisions continue to resonate today with the larger themes of property. Moreover, these chapters remind us of the importance of "stories"—for the root of all of the doctrine, rules, and concepts of property is a dispute between individuals or an individual and the collective. It is out of these conflicts involving real human emotions and desires that our regime of property law emerges and evolves.

Telling *Property Stories* is especially valuable for this generation of Property students and teachers. Traditionally, Property casebooks were very much organized around stories, focusing on the historical development of concepts over time. For example, casebooks of the not-too-distant-past devoted extensive pages to tracing the arcane (and at times bizarre) story of the development of English land law from the Norman Conquest in 1066 to modern day America, complete with the details of property interests (such as the fee tail) that were created to meet new social, economic, and political needs and then abandoned as different demands took precedence. Similarly, these books often examined current issues, such as the warranty of habitability implied into residential leases, by providing a string of cases over the years showing the movement of the law from the absence of an obligation on landlords to the landmark cases finding a warranty. Current casebooks, however, appropriately reflect the modernization of American property law, with an increase of coverage of statutes and regulations,[2] law reform Restatements of the Law,[3] and Uniform Acts[4] in many areas. This modernization has also yielded more uniformity in property law and less focus on the texts of obscure (and obscuring) minority decisions. Finally, first-year law school curricula have changed as well, making room for new subjects and leaving less time for a historical approach to the development of property law. Current property law courses in most schools are semester-long, four credit courses, rather than the traditional, year-long six credit course. These factors, and others, have combined to necessitate

---

[2] See Mary Ann Glendon, The Transformation of American Landlord–Tenant Law, 23 B.C.L. Rev. 503 (1982).

[3] See, e.g., Restatement (Third) of Property: Servitudes (2000); Restatement (Third) of Property: Mortgages (1997); Restatement (Second) of Property: Landlord & Tenant (1977).

[4] See, e.g., Unif. Land Security Interest Act (1985); Unif. Residential Landlord Tenant Act (1972).

reduced coverage of the traditional saga of Property, making the telling of *Property Stories* to the current generation all the more important.

Of the thousands upon thousands of reported appellate decisions dealing with property issues, we—in collaboration with each chapter author—have chosen twelve cases for coverage in this book. Some of these cases were selected because they are widely recognized as breakthrough cases, such as *Javins* or *Euclid*, which continue to resonate to this day. Others were chosen not because they have such marquee value but since they are excellent vehicles to explore a key area of property law. Many were selected since they appear in many first-year Property casebooks, and students would benefit from the in-depth coverage provided in this book. What is common to all of the cases featured here is that they are *great stories* of the interaction of people and the law—some tell of fundamental human aspirations and failings; some tell of cutting-edge scientific developments going to the nature of life; some tell of large social and political movements; some tell of entrepreneurial activities and the regulatory state; and some tell of how we organize and inhabit our country and world.

The initial three chapters of the book consider three leading cases that help define our understanding of the nature of property and ownership. These chapters focus on the social policy underlying property regimes, the types of things that can be subject to ownership, and how ownership can be acquired and lost without the formal consent of the losing party.

Professor A.W. B. Simpson leads off with an examination of the classic English case of *Sturges v. Bridgman*, which Professor Ronald Coase used as the basis of his landmark article, *The Problem of Social Cost*, from which the "Coase Theorem" emerged. That theorem is fundamental to the modern view of property rights and of the law establishing them. Professor Simpson's analysis of *Sturges* is quite different from Professor Coase's. Rethinking *Sturges* raises important questions about the assumptions underlying the Coase Theorem, and this chapter highlights the differences in emphasis between law and law and economics. *Sturgis* dealt with an action by a physician to stop his neighbor—a confectioner—from operating his mortars to grind sugar in a manner that disturbed the physician's work of seeing patients and preparing medical lectures. This chapter tells the story of how the conflict of these competing uses developed and the choices available to resolve it given the factual context. Moreover, Professor Simpson reveals an important lesson that should be kept in mind while reading the other stories in the book and when addressing any property dispute: policy considerations underlie the choices made by many courts in the cases before them. Illustrating this, Professor Simpson questions the use of *efficiency* as a guiding star for decisions and instead supports the *freedom* of owners to do what they like with their property, free of the social engineering by courts.

For millennia, humans have recognized property ownership in real and personal property. The law early on evolved rules for real property (i.e., land and buildings) and tangible personal property (i.e., things we can put our hands on and that carry their value in their physical form). More recently, the law also developed a structure for intangible personal property, such as debts and stock, by extending the concepts first developed for tangible property. Professor Maxwell J. Mehlman's recounting of the story of *Moore v. Regents of the University of California* confronts us with the brave new frontier of property—given that human tissues and other by-products now have commercial value, can these portions of our bodies be owned and transferred like other property interests? This chapter teaches us about the limitations on the property regime, founded in normative values and our notions of what it means to be human, and illustrates the difficulties courts have when wrestling with new factual circumstances.

In the third chapter, Professor R. H. Helmholz tells the story of an oft-cited and taught case on adverse possession, *Van Valkenburgh v. Lutz*. The concept of adverse possession often troubles first-year Property students (and many accomplished lawyers as well!) since it appears to amount to no more than legalized theft—allowing a person to engage in wrongful acts over a period of time thereby acquiring the title of the true owner of land. Courts and commentators have provided various justifications for (rationalizations of?) adverse possession doctrine, suggesting that it helps clear complicated titles by relying on the facts on the ground, represents the societal wish to "let sleeping dogs lie" at a certain point, and yields an efficient allocation of our limited land resources by moving ownership to the person actually utilizing the property. Professor Helmholz adds important considerations to this discussion through his telling of the *Van Valkenburgh* story: adverse possession cases are too often complicated by ambiguous legal standards, harsh personal conflict between the parties, and widely diverging versions of the facts from the parties and other witnesses.

The next four chapters of the book explore the private ordering of property interests. They illustrate the extent of property rights and how the "bundle of sticks" may be shared among parties, and describe how consensual arrangements may be created to share, acquire, and transfer property rights.

What would seem to be a simple matter—a gift of a painting from a father to his son—is the basis of the compelling story of *Gruen v. Gruen*, told by Professor Susan F. French in Chapter 4. This is quite a tale of refugees from Hitler's Europe, family breakups, relationships between parents and children and stepparents and children, and a painting that grew in value from $8,000 to $23.5 million. Professor French shows how the law could put very different spins on the ambiguous, and often emotionally laden, interactions and communications of family life, yielding widely different legal results. Professor French puts this in the context of the rules governing inter vivos gifts of personal property. These standards—requiring donative intent, delivery, and acceptance—sometimes appear to frustrate the wish of the donor to make a gift to the donee, but instead can be viewed as an important construct to ensure that those wishes are clear and fulfilled.

The important case of *Sawada v. Endo* is then reviewed by Professor Patricia A. Cain. This 1977 case took place against the backdrop of advances in the rights of women to own and control property held individually or with their husbands. As Professor Cain explains, at common law, under the doctrine of coverture a married woman could not own property in her own name or even jointly with her husband. While one might expect that the common law tenancy by the entirety suggests real joint ownership between the husband and wife, it was really only one ownership—that of the husband. Early feminist reforms achieved between 1840 and the early 1900s gave married women the right to own property individually, but usually these statutory reforms were silent as to the rights of the wife in property held by a husband and wife as tenants by the entirety. Courts and legislatures spend the next 100 years sorting out the effect of these reforms on tenancies by the entirety, and Hawaii in *Sawada* was late in doing this. Professor Cain shows that even today, issues regarding the tenancy by the entirety estate continue to arise, illustrating that the doctrine of coverture has not been fully erased from the law of real property.

Professor Richard H. Chused then tells the story of a groundbreaking landlord-tenant decision, *Saunders (a.k.a. Javins) v. First National Realty Corporation.* A landlord and a tenant both hold interests in the leased property, with the former owning the reversion (a future interest) and the latter holding a present interest (a term for years, a periodic tenancy, or a tenancy at will.) In this case, the United States Court of Appeals for the District of Columbia reversed centuries-old doctrine and found that landlords owed a warranty of habitability to tenants of urban dwelling units. This decision radically changed the allocation of property rights and responsibilities between landlords and tenants, shifting costs, obligations, and liability to the landlord. This is a tale of the power of the courts to change the rules of ownership (and the questions this raises), the law as an instrument of social reform, the distributive and redistributive effects of judicial decisions on property (and the normative questions this provokes), and the ability of individual lawyers to make a difference in people's lives.

Professor Carol M. Rose's chapter examines the 1948 landmark decision of the Supreme Court of the United States in *Shelley v. Kraemer*. For centuries, parties have made consensual arrangements to share rights in the land of others, primarily through covenants that give the holder veto power over the activities of another owner on his or her land, or through easements where the easement owner has an affirmative right over another property, such as a right of way. Such arrangements serve efficiency concerns, allowing the parties to allocate the bundle of sticks based on market preferences. Covenants and easements are also upheld as they represent the parties' free choice as to how they want their property arranged. Professor Rose tells us of the important lessons of *Shelley*, which held that enforcement of covenants barring non-whites from living on certain properties violated the Equal Protection clause of the Fourteenth Amendment. Professor Rose suggests that while *Shelley* may exceed current notions of state action under constitutional theory, common law property doctrine justifies the result. She argues that property law allows limitations on uses of property but does not question the personal characteristics of the occupants themselves. This chapter also demonstrates the power of an evolving common law.

Professor Peter W. Salsich, Jr., tells the story of *Brown v. Lober*, a case involving the obligations of the seller of a portion of real property. Selling a piece of land worth $100,000 requires a complex transaction with multiple documents and stages, while personal property of the same value can be transferred with a few words and little or no formalities. Some of the reasons for the complexity of realty transfers are good, others reflect history and turf protection (sorry about the pun) by lawyers. Professor Salsich looks at the issue of title covenants in *Brown*. Title covenants create an obligation, which may run to the immediate or future grantees, on the seller as to the quality of the title. Promises made about land are different than those relating to personal property since land lasts forever. Thus agreements made by two consenting parties today may affect and bind future owners, perhaps in perpetuity. Professor Salsich shows that this sometimes means that innocent parties—in *Brown*, this was *both* litigants—are harmed, and suggests that alternative dispute resolution and professionalism by lawyers may provide better solutions at times.

The concluding four chapters of the book deal with the interaction of the individual property owner and the collective. Society's interaction with private property may be manifested in interventions by government, quasi-governmental entities such as homeowners associations, or application by courts of a broad and relatively undefined concept of the "public interest."

The decision of the Supreme Court of the United States in *Lucas v. South Carolina Coastal Commission* is the subject of the chapter by

Professor Vicki L. Been. *Lucas* addresses a fundamental issue in the relationship between individual property rights and the will of the collective—as represented by the government—respecting that property. As Professor Been explains, the difficulty is that the law is unclear when the Fifth Amendment requires compensation to an owner for governmental regulation that reduces the value of property. *Lucas* involved South Carolina legislation designed to prevent beach erosion by creating setback lines. Application of these rules meant that Lucas was unable to build on two lots that he owned. The Supreme Court sided with Lucas, finding that the state's action deprived the owner of all economically beneficial use of the property. Professor Been illuminates the various errors in judgment made by the actors in the course of the story. Moreover, she shows that prior coastal regulation by the state increased the value of Lucas's property, and she cautions against a compensation rule that focuses only on the costs—while ignoring the benefits—of governmental action.

Professor Andrew P. Morriss examines the leading case of *Spur Industries, Inc. v. Del E. Webb Development Co.*, a colorful case involving nuisance doctrine and the clash between a cattle feed lot and a neighboring, major residential subdivision. This case illustrates a large array of forces that can be swept into a dispute about the clash of existing uses with new land development—rapid population growth, a transforming economy, a large scale developer, new homeowners, and vested business interests. Professor Morriss shows how the Arizona Supreme Court resolved this conflict by crafting a creative, practical application of nuisance law that met the public interest, allowed for an evolving and efficient use of land, and placed the legitimate costs on the party most responsible for the problem. This decision, predating some of the most important theoretical work on property law, underscores for Professor Morriss the strength and wisdom of good common law decision making.

Over the past 75 years, a new and powerful collective has arisen in land ownership—community associations and homeowners associations that enforce restrictions applying to homes in a subdivision, provide common facilities (such as recreation and utilities) and services, and promulgate and enforce rules and regulations governing the homeowners. These associations function as private governments, and the law has evolved to articulate the rules pertaining to such entities and their relationship to individual owners. Professor Stewart Sterk examines a trailblazing and still important case in the area, *Neponsit Property Owners' Association v. Emigrant Industrial Savings Bank*. *Neponsit* established the principle that covenants imposing assessments on lot owners bind not only the original purchaser but future owners and are enforceable not only by the original developer but also by a successor association of the owners. This decision opened the way for new types of developments—suburban as well as urban condominiums—that provide housing for many Americans today and which allow owner involvement in a neighborhood private government.

Professor David L. Callies addresses the groundbreaking and still highly potent case, *Village of Euclid v. Ambler Realty Company* decided in 1926. In *Euclid*, the Supreme Court of the United States first upheld large scale zoning for uses by local governments, setting the stage for the comprehensive, public regulation of land use that has developed over the past 75 years. In *Euclid*, the Court found that zoning did not violate the Fourteenth Amendment of the Constitution and permitted the division of municipality into various sectors, each limited to residential, commercial, and industrial uses. Professor Callies examines the legacy of the case, finding that the general upholding of zoning led to the validation of exclusionary zoning—zoning that ostensibly seeks to preserve residential character of areas, but, by providing for large lots and expensive single family homes, in effect bars middle and lower income families from a whole town or village. But Professor Callies asserts that the more egregious forms of exclusion would have been developed without zoning, and concludes that on balance zoning has served people and governments pretty well.

* * *

So, we and our chapter authors present this bundle of *Property Stories*. We hope that they convey to you the vitality, wisdom, and ongoing evolution of this central area of the law.

1

A.W. Brian Simpson

The Story of *Sturges v. Bridgman*: The Resolution of Land Use Disputes Between Neighbors*

Ronald H. Coase's celebrated article, "The Problem of Social Cost",[1] must surely rank as one of the principal foundation documents of the modern law and economics movement, especially in so far as that movement has affected the study of tort law. At the outset Coase explained that "[t]his paper is concerned with those actions of business firms which have harmful effects on others. The standard example is that of a factory, the smoke from which has harmful effects on those occupying neighboring properties."[2] Under the common law this problem, if it is one, was primarily handled by indictments for public nuisance, which Coase does not discuss, by common law tort actions claiming damages for private nuisance, and by suits in equity for injunctions. Criminal proceedings for public nuisance are to be found in medieval law, as are civil proceedings for interference with servitudes by the assize of nuisance, a procedure evolved out of the assize of novel disseisin. In the fifteenth century the courts evolved an action on the case for nuisance, which originally only provided a remedy for interference with servitudes which was not covered by the assize. But in the

---

* Original version published at 25 Journal of Legal Studies 53 (1996), published by The University of Chicago. Copyright 1996 by The University of Chicago. All rights reserved.

[1] First published in 3 *J. Law & Econ.* 1–44 (1960, though actually published in 1961), and reprinted in R.H. Coase, *The Firm, the Market and the Law* 95 (Chicago, 1988). This contains additional "Notes on the Problem of Social Cost" at 157–85. References to "Coase" are to this reprint.

[2] *Id.* at 95.

sixteenth century it came to settled that the action on the case could be
brought when an individual suffered special damage as consequence of a
public nuisance, and that the action might be brought for interference
with the use and enjoyment of land which did not involve a trespass, as
by noise, or smoke, or offensive smells. Suits in equity for injunctions to
restrain occupiers of land from committing private nuisances are not
found before the nineteenth century.[3] Until 1854 an attempt to obtain an
injunction involved litigation both at common law and in the Chancery,
and until the fusion of the courts in 1876 this cumbersome and expensive procedure might still be followed. An example is the leading case of
Tipping v. the St. Helens Smelting Company, which dealt with industrial
pollution from copper smelting, which, after the common law case had
been won in the House of Lords in 1865, was then litigated all over again
in the Court of Chancery, with eventual success in that the defendant
company was induced to relocate.[4] At this period injunctions did not take
the form of orders that the offending factory closed down or relocated,
but only that it should not operate so as to cause a nuisance.

Coase illustrates the problem of social cost and possible reactions to
it by reference to a number of private nuisance cases, several of which
were decided by English courts in the nineteenth century.[5] Both in his
article on social cost, and in his earlier article, "The Federal Communications Commission"[6] Coase makes prominent use of one such case,
Sturges v. Bridgman (1879).[7] This case also makes a cameo appearance
in his *Essays on Economics and Economists.*[8] From the sources available
it is possible to provide a very full account of the dispute which was
litigated in *Sturges v. Bridgman.* I shall proceed by telling the story of
the case, and using it to illustrate some difficulties involved in attending
to the problem of social cost in litigation by way of actions for private
nuisance between neighbors engaged in disputes over conflicting forms
of land use.

The case came before the Master of the Rolls, Sir George Jessel, on
31 May and 3 June 1878, and then went to the Court of Appeal,

---

[3] This is established by J. P. S. McLaren, "Nuisance Law and the Industrial Revolution—Some Lessons from Social History", 3 *Oxford J. Legal Studies* 155 at 186 and ff
(1983). For the early history of nuisance see J.H.Baker, *An Introduction to English Legal
History* (4th. ed. London, 2002) Ch.4.

[4] 4 B. & S. 698, 616, 122 E. R. 588, 591, XI H. L.C. 642, 11 E. R. 1483, fully discussed
in my *Leading Cases in the Common Law* (Oxford, 1995) Ch.7.

[5] See in particular section 5 of "The Problem of Social Cost", *supra* n. 1 at 104–14.

[6] 2 *J. Law and Economics* 1–40 at 27 (1959).

[7] 11 Ch. D. 852.

[8] Chicago (1994) at 121 n.11, in an essay on "Alfred Marshall's Mother and Father".

comprising Lords Justices Thesiger, James and Baggalley, on 13, 14 and 16 June and 1 July of the same year.[9] The rapidity with which the litigation was conducted is striking indeed. It involved a successful suit by a doctor to restrain a confectioner, whose business was conducted in adjacent premises, from using machinery in a way which caused noise and vibration. This interfered with the doctor's use of his consulting room. The plaintiff, Dr. Octavius Sturges, was a medical man of considerable distinction, and a Fellow of the Royal College of Physicians.[10] He was born in London in 1833, and educated at Addiscombe, the military seminary of the East India Company, which at that time governed British India. In 1853 he entered the service of the company as a second lieutenant in the Bombay Artillery. In 1883, with the assistance of his niece, Mary Sturges, he published an autobiographical novel on his experiences, *In the Company's Service: A Reminiscence*. The hero is Norman Farquhar, one of four Addiscombe cadets. One or more of them embody his own experiences. Farquhar is killed in the Indian Mutiny of 1857, in whose suppression Sturges must have been involved. The novel reflects some disgust at the ferocity with which the mutiny was put down, which included such practices as blowing mutineers from the mouths of guns; whether Sturges was present at one of these sanguinary events I do not know. Perhaps because of his unease he resigned his commission and entered St. George's Hospital in London as a medical student. He studied at Emmanuel College in Cambridge, and then returned to London in 1863 to become a medical registrar at St. George's. In 1868 be began to work at the Westminster Hospital, becoming physician there in 1875. From 1878 he was also assistant physician to the Great Ormond Street Hospital for Children. He held these two appointments for the rest of his life. He lectured in the Westminster Medical School, and published extensively, his specialisms being pneumonia and chorea. Until 1965 he lived at 35 Connaught Square in London; he then purchased the lease of 85 Wimpole Street.[11]

---

[9] In addition to the law report, cited above n.7, I have relied on a report in *The Times* for 4 June 1878, and on papers in the Public Record Office, London, comprising J54/80 S.223 (pleadings), C32/322 (cause book), J15/1385, 1386 and 1387 (orders made) and J4/660 (S650–654) and J4/663 (1440–42) (affidavits filed). The case is noted under the title "Quiet Consulting Room" in *The Medical Times and Gazette*, July 20 1878.

[10] What follows is based on Frederic Boase, *Modern English Biography*, Vol.3 (London, 1965), on obituaries in *The Times* (6, 7, 9 November 1894) and *The Lancet* and *The British Medical Journal*, on copies of the annual *London and Provincial Medical Directory*, and on the catalogue of the British Library.

[11] The property had been leased, probably by way of a building lease, by the Duke of Portland at a ground rent of £30 per annum, and in 1865 there were twenty nine years of the leasehold interest to run. If, as was customary, this lease had originally been for 99 years the house would date from the late eighteenth century. In 1873 a reversionary lease

As was the normal practice at this period 85 Wimpole Street was both his home and the place where he saw his fee paying patients when he was not working in the two hospitals with which he was associated.

Dr. Sturges' opponent, Frederick Horatio Bridgman, his second name no doubt reflecting the popularity of Admiral Horatio Nelson at around the time of his birth, was also a person of distinction. He was, by appointment, confectioner to Her Majesty the Queen and to His Royal Highness, the Prince of Wales, a person who would appear, given his girth, to have been better advised to have kept clear of confectioners. In an affidavit Bridgman recounted how he had, in 1830, succeeded his late father John in the business of a cook and confectioner at 30 Wigmore Street: "... my said Father and I have, or one of us, during the last sixty years and upwards, uninterruptedly and in succession to each other carried on the business."[12] So the business had been conducted in the same premises since about the time of battle of Waterloo. Frederick would have started working with his father at some time in the 1820s, being born, one may guess, sometime not long after the date of the battle of Trafalgar in 1805.

No form of municipal zoning existed in nineteenth century London, but individual decisions as to the location of businesses and residences produced much the same effects.[13] Indeed the relative inefficiency of legal remedies relating to interference with land use by neighbors may well have encouraged individuals to avoid trouble by careful choice of location. Thus in the case of residential property the poor lived in stinking hovels because that was all they could afford, and the rich naturally enough chose to live in more salubrious areas. Mid-nineteenth century Wigmore Street, which runs East to West, was predominantly commercial.[14] The principal trade was clothing—there were dressmakers, milliners, lace cleaners and the like. Other business included a bell hanger, wax chandlers and buttermen and, for the medical men of Wimpole Street, a dealer in medical rubber. There were no doctors in Wigmore Street. But in elegant Wimpole Street, which intersects Wigmore Street at right angles, doctors were much in evidence. The street was primarily residential, with professionals like Dr. Sturges conducting their businesses from their homes. The medical profession had been colonizing Wimpole Street for some time. In 1871 there had been only nineteen

---

for 21 years at a ground rent of £50 was negotiated, so that Dr. Sturges had security of tenure until 1923.

[12] Affidavit by F. H. Bridgman, see n. 7 above.

[13] Private nuisance law, which as J. P. McLaren has shown (see n.3 above), was very ineffective indeed, seems to have played virtually no part in establishing informal zones.

[14] What follows is based on the annual volumes of *Kelly's Post Office Directory*. The Guildhall Library in London has a very complete collection of such directories.

physicians there, but in 1878 thirty-eight of the ninety-five properties listed in *Kelly's Post Office Directory* were occupied by physicians or surgeons, and there were some dentists there as well. There was also, according to an advertisement in the *London and Provincial Medical Directory* for 1878, Mrs. Wilson's Institute for Nurses: "For upwards of ten years the most eminent of the medical profession, and the public, have been supplied at a moments notice with my nurses, who reside at 90 Wimpole Street." By 1888 another ancillary trade, that of undertaker, had moved in to 3B Wimpole Street; before this medical failures, or rather their relatives, had to seek this service elsewhere. In 1878, and indeed later, other businesses were conducted from residences there— there was a diamond merchant and a confectioner, and numerous private homes, such as that of William Patchett, Queen's Counsel. Quite recently Sir William Milbourne James, who was to sit in the Court of Appeal in *Sturges v. Bridgman*, had lived there.

So the litigation did not raise what we would think of as a zoning problem: do we want predominantly residential or commercial use in the area? Dr. Sturges had chosen an appropriate location in Wimpole Street, and so had Mr. Bridgman in Wigmore Street. The problem arose because noise and vibration associated with a particular commercial use crossed an informally established boundary; this boundary had been established by individual decisions as to location and land use. The noise and vibration emanating from Wigmore Street affected and interfered with professional and residential use in Wimpole Street. Courts typically have to face the problem of social cost, if they face it at all, only when a stationary or moving informal boundary is involved. The most notable of all Victorian nuisance cases, *Tipping v. St. Helen's Smelting Company*,[15] arose because a gentleman's residence and estate, which Tipping, who was no gentleman but wanted to become one, had bought, was located close to an industrial area which was expanding, and Tipping suffered very damaging pollution from a copper smelting plant which was extending its activities. Tipping was unwilling to relocate; he was very wealthy and able to afford a legal battle, and so he sued. A modern American case, the well known *Spur Industries, Inc. v. Del E. Web Development Co.*, well illustrates the point, adopting an ingenious solution to protect the investment of the party who was first in time, but whose odoriferous commercial activities, harmless when originally located in the country-side, now threatened the health and general welfare of those living in an expanding residential area.[16]

In his affidavit Dr. Sturges explained how the problem had arisen. In 1873, eight years after he first moved into the house, he decided to

---

[15] See n.4 above.

[16] 108 Ariz. 178, 494 P.2d 700 (1972).

have built a consulting room in the very small "yard or garden" at the back of his house. There was no other suitable room; the other ground floor room was used as his dining room, and, after 1873, when the new consulting room came into operation in the autumn, as a waiting room for his patients. Before 1873 his practice was probably carried on entirely in the hospitals with which he was associated. He did, however devote time to writing, and his first book, *An Introduction to the Study of Clinical Medicine,* was published in 1873. His decision to start seeing patients in the new consulting room in 1873 in effect moved the informal boundary between the forms of land use on the two properties. His use of the consulting room was not continuous throughout the day. Between 1873 and late 1875 or early 1876 he saw his private patients from 10 a.m. to 1 p.m. He also used the room at these hours to prepare his lectures before he left for his hospital work. The noise from Mr. Bridgman's kitchen soon began to cause him "great discomfort and annoyance."

The wall which separated the two properties, and which originally had formed the west boundary of the small yard, was also the east wall of Mr. Bridgman's kitchen, which lay at the rear of his property, 30 Wigmore Street. There was a corner building where Wigmore Street intersected Wimpole Street, and Mr. Bridgman's property was the next property located on the north side of the street, and to the west of the intersection. The dividing wall was a party wall, one and a half bricks, that is about fourteen inches, in thickness. The newly built west wall of the consulting room was built directly against this party wall, adding approximately nine inches to its thickness. It was located of course on Dr. Sturges' property, and was not itself a party wall. In the kitchen were two sixteen inch marble mortars, located near the north east corner of the kitchen, close to the south west corner of the consulting room. These mortars were set in brickwork built up against the party wall; presumably the brickwork formed a pedestal for the mortars. They were used for crushing loaf sugar, almonds and indeed meat, and were worked by *lignum vitae* pestles, operated by one of Mr. Bridgman's employees. The affidavit of J. T. Christopher, an architect and surveyor employed by Dr. Sturges for the litigation, explained that the pestles, when in operation: " . . . are each passed through a socket in a bearer secured to a plank bolted onto or as I believe[17] right through the said wall [i.e. the party wall] . . . A more effectual method of communicating or conveying sound and vibration could hardly be devised." Although experts hired by Dr. Bridgman, Robert Reid, a surveyor, and Thomas Harris, an architect and surveyor, disputed the passage of vibration, the latter employing the

---

[17] Christopher would not have been able to check what became of the bolts after they vanished into the wall without engaging in some damaging excavations of the new wall.

unsophisticated egg and tumbler test,[18] there was no conflict over the noise, described by Dr. Sturges as "of a thumping character. Every blow is distinctly heard and felt. The scraping of the handle to the pestle in the socket fixed to the wall is also plainly audible ..." The noise "interfered materially with the comfort of my house as a residence and its use for my professional purposes". In particular "the noise they create seriously disturbs me and by distracting my attention prevents my carrying on any work requiring continuous thought." The noise also interfered with his use of the stethoscope. It also annoyed Dr. Sturges' patients. The doctor's account was supported by other affidavits from colleagues. Dr. John W. Haward, a surgeon working both at St. George's and at the Great Ormond Street Hospital stated:

> The noise was of a kind which would have materially interfered with one's domestic comfort if one was using the room for ordinary purposes and must be particularly disturbing and irritating to a person who engaged in any literary or other work requiring thought or close attention.

Dr. William H. Allchin, a physician who lived at 94 Wimpole Street, thought the thumping, which he had often heard on visits to the house, was enough to stop conversation and was "... exceedingly irritating and troublesome and especially so to a medical man." Dr. Horatio Donkin, a physician from Harley Street, who had been familiar with the house for three years, in substance agreed, though he did not think the noise loud enough to actually drown conversation. Both he and Dr. Haward, made the point that the noise would interfere with the use of the room for ordinary, that is residential, purposes. This the lawyers would have ensured to be put in the affidavit to head off the argument that it was only the peculiar nature of the use to which the room was put which created the problem.

This then was the situation which gave rise, eventually, to the litigation. One point needs however to be understood at the outset. My account of the sources of the dispute is based on the ways in which the lawyers packaged what we call the facts, in the light of their knowledge of the law and of the factors which the law seemed to them to make relevant. Their work survives in the affidavits and pleadings available in the Public Record Office, and placed before the court in the litigation. Now the expression social cost, like so many of the expressions used in the discussion of the relationship between law and economics, is not always, or indeed often, used with any great precision. Coase for example speaks of costs to "neighbors", but if the underlying idea is that of costs to society, or to people generally, then clearly the effects of the thumping

---

[18] Presumably you balance an egg on an inverted tumbler and waited for it to fall off, but this is speculative.

might well impose costs on people who were not neighbors. An example
would be the medical students in the hospital, who might receive ill
prepared lectures, and, I suppose, ultimately their patients who might
receive poor treatment some years later. If the idea of social cost, or for
that matter social gain, has something to do with the effects of the
activities of Mr. Bridgman and Dr. Sturges on society generally, it is
quite clear that the affidavits simply do not address the problem of social
cost at all, or, for that matter, social gain. Clearly all sorts of people
might be indirectly affected by the outcome of the dispute—Her Majesty
the Queen, the Prince of Wales, Mr. Bridgman's employees, Dr. Sturges'
readers, and his publisher. The possible list is endless. But the lawyers
conceived of the dispute as only involving two individuals, unable to
agree on the boundaries of their property rights; the affidavits address
the costs and benefits to Mr. Bridgman and Dr. Sturges and to nobody
else. That the matter should be conceived of in this way was, and is, part
of the conventional ideology of the common law, and of the function of
courts within the legal system. If scholars wish, in the name of economic
rationality, to suggest that such a dispute should be conceived in some
different way, as presenting to the court the problem of social cost, in
the wide sense I have explained, they need to address the consequences
which would have to follow for the way in which the case would need to
be presented to the court for decision. They also need to address how
some limits could be placed on the complexity of the proceedings. So far
as I am aware nobody has even begun to address these questions.

   Let me now turn to the ideas presented in "The Problem of Social
Cost" and, less fully, in "The Federal Communications Commission".
There seem to me to be five.

   The first idea, which runs through all Coase's writings, is a deep
skepticism as to the desirability of government intervention. Various
different expressions are used: "public intervention", "direct government regulation", "governmental administrative regulation", "governmental regulation", "governmental action," "corrective governmental
action," "State action" and "governmental intervention."[19] In fact hostility to this variously described Bad Thing has long been a feature of the
writing of persons interested in political economy, and committed to the
merits of *laissez faire*. Back in the nineteenth century the English judge,
Baron Bramwell, who was a member of the Political Economy Club,
shared Coase's misgivings as to the merits of what he would have
probably called "grandmotherly government". He was a founder member of the Liberty and Property Defence League, formed in 1882 " ... to
uphold the principle of liberty and guard the rights of labour and
property of all kinds against undue interference by the State; and to

---

[19] See Coase, as reprinted, at 22, 117, 199,131, 133, 135.

encourage Self-help versus State-help.... "[20] Richard A Posner, in his *Overcoming* Law,[21] describes hostility to public intervention, except when this will maximize wealth, as a "leitmotif" of Coase's work. In "The Problem of Social Cost" Coase's skepticism is very mildly expressed; he argues that action against a smoke-emitting factory will lead to results which "are not necessarily, *or even usually*, desirable."[22] In *The Firm, the Market and the Law* Coase hardens his position, arguing that whether government intervention is desirable or not is a "factual question", and that economic theory does not support any presumption in its favor. He goes on:

> The ubiquitous nature of "externalities" suggests to me that there is a prima facie case against intervention, and the studies of the effects of regulation which have been made in recent years in the United States, ranging from agriculture to zoning, which indicate that regulation has commonly made matters worse, lend support to this view.[23]

There is a change of emphasis here from the original article, which was more anxious to demonstrate the importance of transaction costs, rather than that of externalities. Indeed although the effect of decisions in cases of conflict on third parties, and on society generally, is mentioned, the expression "externality" is not used, and Coase has explained that his failure to use the term, and his preference for speaking of "harmful effects", was deliberate. Although Coase uses, as I have explained, a variety of expressions, I shall stick to one, "government intervention".

Plainly such intervention might, in the case of a polluting factory, take a wide variety of forms. There might be a pollution tax, or handouts to firms which reduce pollution, or legislation to insist, subject to penalty, or closure, or liability to damages for failure to install and use specified smoke reducing equipment, or legislation might establish some form of institutional licensing, or a system of inspection and administrative control. Given the huge range of choice here, and the widely different circumstances in which harmful and beneficial effects arise, it seems deeply implausible to suppose that much in the way of generalization as to the merits or demerits of government intervention can possibly be made, much less, if made, be substantiated in any rigorous way. And, as we shall see, the analysis as to what counts as government intervention, whatever form it takes, is radically flawed. Here the conception

---

[20] See my *Leading Cases in the Common Law* at 175, citing two pamphlets by Bramwell, published in 1882 and 1883.

[21] (Cambridge, Mass., 1995).

[22] Coase, at 96, emphasis added.

[23] Coase, at 26.

used lacks rigor and precision, and generalizations as to its merits or demerits seem to me to represent declarations of faith, lacking, of their very nature, any conceivable empirical basis.

The second idea is the corollary of the first: since government intervention is suspect, the alternatives to government intervention are viewed sympathetically. An alternative is leaving matters to the market, and the drift of the argument favors this. This possibility is dramatized by the thesis which has come to be called the Coase Theorem: that in the absence of transaction costs the allocation of resources reached by negotiation and bargain, assuming economic rationality, would be unaffected by the rule as to civil legal liability. This is stated in the discussion of *Sturges v. Bridgman* "With costless market transactions, the decision of the courts concerning liability for damage would be without effect on the allocation of resources"[24] This is of course a purely theoretical view as to what would happen in a world which does not exist.

But one of the problems over positing never-never worlds is that we are commonly not told what other features they share with the real world. Thus if we suppose a world in which pigs fly, and then start drawing conclusions as to what that world would be like, we need to know, for example, whether some form of porcine air traffic control exists or not, and whether the pigs wear diapers. Presumably there have to be other assumptions made about the Coasean world before his conclusion follows, for example some sort of embargo on violence, and perhaps, given the marginal utility of income some assumption about relative wealth. In addition there are psychological assumptions about human behavior involved, for apparently in the Coasean world individuals are inspired by the profit motive. I personally find the idea of a world of costless market transactions profoundly unintelligible. This may, I appreciate, be simply a personal failure of imagination. Amongst many obscurities I do not understand what is, for this purpose, meant by, or included in, the conception of a transaction cost. One obvious cost of the transaction we call buying and selling is that the seller has to give up his ownership of the thing sold, which may or may not represent for him a cost, and the buyer has to pay the price. Are these costs included? Or, in a world with no transaction costs, is everything a gift? Or what? Is not making a bargain in itself an activity not free from cost? Are we talking merely of what might be called the incidental expenses of doing business—telephone calls, business lunches, *etcetera*? I have no idea, and whatever may be the case in the heartlands of economics it is idle to seek clarification in writers in the law and economics tradition, who use the expression transaction cost as if it was obvious what it meant.

---

[24] Coase, at 105–6.

Be that as it may Coase relates his thinking to the real world by arguing, surely correctly, that in a case such as *Sturges v. Bridgman* the parties might have reached an economically satisfactory position, or one that seemed to them to be economically satisfactory, by making a bargain, a point which is clear enough without any need for the theory expressed in the Coase Theorem, and quite independent of it.[25] Presumably the reason why they did not do so, *pace* Coase, was either the impediment of transaction costs, or the fact that one or both of them did not behave with economic rationality, or because of differing expectations as to the probable outcome of the litigation. Of course litigation will involve considerable additional costs, as it did in this case. Under the English rule as to costs the winner is entitled to taxed costs from the loser, so the relevance of litigation costs to a decision to litigate, rather than settle by bargain, is bound up with expectations as to the likelihood of success in the action.

Elsewhere Coase gives an account of alternatives to government intervention, which he lists: ". . . inaction, the abandonment of earlier government action, or the facilitation of market transactions."[26] What "inaction" means is unclear and I shall return to the point later. Obviously market transactions might indeed be facilitated by measures taken to reduce costs. There might be, for example, free legal services, or free telephone calls, but this sort of facilitation would surely require either private philanthropy, of an improbable kind, or some sort of government intervention. Other mechanisms for reducing some transaction costs, such as the establishment of a location where trades could take place, could well be the product of private cooperative action. But whatever precisely is intended the implication of Coase's argument is that given such facilitation, leaving the outcome to the market is likely to be the best solution. And so far as the case of *Sturges v. Bridgman* is concerned the resolution of the dispute between Mr. Bridgman and Dr. Sturges was indeed left to the market, in the sense that there was no legal impediment to their reaching an agreement which would have been binding upon them in private law. But though left to the market in this sense, no deal was done.

The third idea is not easy to reproduce accurately; it is most simply put by saying that the problem of social cost is, at least to an economist, a reciprocal problem. This idea, at one level, may be illustrated from *Sturges v. Bridgman*. Alterations in behavior by either Dr. Sturges (giving up the practice of medicine, selling the lease of his house to a

[25] Coase, at 105–6. For an account of what happened in the real nineteenth century world in which the use of the law was very expensive see McLaren, *supra* n.3 and Simpson, *Leading Cases*, Ch.7.

[26] Coase, at 24.

deaf person, writing his lectures elsewhere, *etcetera*) or by Mr. Bridgman (retirement, moving his mortars, using them at a different time of day, relocation, *etcetera*) will cause the problem to go away. For the problem only arises because of the interrelationship between two people and their behavior. Coase however puts this point in two other ways. One of these is negative: it rejects the arrow of causation, which wrongly suggests that Mr. Bridgman's activities were harming Dr. Sturges, with the implication that it is Mr. Bridgman who must be restrained. In one passage Coase says "[i]f we are to discuss the problem in terms of causation, both parties cause the damage."[27] The other is positive: since a decision either way will impose costs on the loser, the real question is: who is to be allowed to harm whom? I am not convinced that the economic argument presented in the positive version of this thesis requires him, in the negative form of the thesis, to do violence to the everyday conception of causation, which distinguishes the necessary conditions for harm to occur from the cause or causes of that harm. Nor does it seem to me to be necessary to reject the evaluative distinction which everyday thought makes between harms and costs. If I buy a pint of beer I do not think of the price of the beer as a harm inflicted on me by the publican; perhaps some economists do, but I do not. Be that as it may his view certainly sets Coase apart from lawyers, who everywhere make use of causal notions, and do not treat harms and costs as equivalent. But a more worrying implication of Coase's insistence on the reciprocal nature of the problem of social cost is that it suggests that, from an economist's point of view, deciding a case such as *Sturges v. Bridgman* ought to involve evaluating a wide and, so far as I can see, unlimited range of alternative courses of action, any one of which would solve the problem. There is a tendency to discuss the reciprocal character of the problem of social cost, as Coase himself does, in terms of just two activities: growing crops or running railways, making cakes or seeing patients. But this is misleading. For once the reciprocal nature of the problem is conceded, there is just no end to the possibilities; they include the mutual suicide of Mr. Bridgman and Dr. Sturges. The implications of this for private law litigation are problematic, and nowhere addressed by Coase.[28] Or by anyone else.

The fourth idea is much less easy to state with any precision, perhaps because it involves a number of intimately related ideas. It concerns the role of law. In the real world, with which Coase was, as he has insisted, primarily concerned, as opposed to some ideal world in

---

[27] *Id.* at 112.

[28] The reciprocal nature of human interaction can raise other problems, as for example when women object to the idea that the way to stop sexual assaults on the streets at night is for them to stay at home. Even if, for the sake of argument, they are the cheapest cost avoiders, whatever that is made to mean, ought this fact to be conclusive?

which there were no transaction costs, there is, as Coase himself has emphasized, an important role for law.[29] One reason is that, in his view, rights have to be defined or allocated before you can have bargains about them. Coase further argues that because transactions are not costless: "The initial delimitation of legal rights does have an effect on the efficiency with which the economic system operates."[30] Those of more left wing sympathies often make a similar point by saying that in a world in which, wherever you start, property rights are very unequally allocated, assets will not necessarily end up in the hands of those who can make the best use of them; this seems to me at least to be self evidently true. It is not simply a consequence of the imperfection of markets, but of the initial distribution of entitlements, which the market does not necessarily correct over time. Coase's conclusion is that: "Even when it is possible to change the legal delimitation of rights through market transactions, it is obviously desirable to reduce the need for such transactions and thus reduce the employment of resources in carrying them out."[31] So the law should tend to allocate rights in the way in which they would be allocated by the market in a world in which the costs of market transaction, and presumably other imperfections, were not an impediment. This is a somewhat startling thesis unless it is assumed that the law should somehow both exhibit this tendency, and yet, at the same time, not upset the existing unequal allocation of property rights. Coase does not address this point. And although skeptical he concedes that there may be some situations, for example smoke nuisance affecting a large number of people, where transaction costs are likely to be large, in which government intervention is appropriate: "There is no reason why, on occasion, such governmental administrative regulation should not lead to an improvement in economic efficiency."[32] It all depends on the circumstances.

What is somewhat curious is that Coase, who on questions of allocation and delimitation of property rights has in mind private law, nowhere treats judicial decisions by the courts of the state as a form of governmental intervention or action. Thus the common law, evolving through judicial decisions, is, for reasons never explained, privileged against the criticisms he directs at government intervention. This seems to me to be a radical flaw in the whole argument. When Coase instances "inaction", an idea captured for some by the expression *laissez-faire*, as one possible reaction to the problem of social cost, what he must really mean is leaving the matter to the common law. But since courts of first

---

[29] Coase only considers private law, and has nothing to say on the role of criminal law.

[30] *Id.* at 115.

[31] *Id.* at 119.

[32] *Id.* at 118.

instance are not allowed to simply wash their hands of disputes, this never means doing nothing.[33] In the case of an allegation of nuisance caused by the emission of smoke the court may impose strict liability, or liability for negligence, or rule that there is no liability at all; there are indeed other possibilities. But whatever decision is taken the court is bound to take sides. Coase is critical of others for discussing the problem of social cost without specifying the institutional context, as by discussing, for example, *laissez-faire* without telling the reader what monetary, legal or political system is assumed to be in force.[34] But he does not fully specify what other assumptions he is making about the state of the law, and this makes it difficult to be entirely clear as to what he does have in mind. For example in *Sturges v. Bridgman*, given a state of nature, Dr. Sturges might have solved the problem by using his military skills and bayoneting Mr. Bridgman, or Mr. Bridgman might have crowned the good doctor with one of his *lignum vitae* pestles. Doing nothing about the problem of social cost might or might not mean that the state would intervene in such circumstances. Of course in the real world such activities are discouraged by the provisions of the criminal law, as well as by civil law, which provides remedies for violent assaults.

It is probably possible to divine why Coase is sympathetic to leaving matters to the common law from the doubts he expresses about governmental intervention, which he takes to involve some sort of legislative authorization or scheme. Writing of "restrictive or zoning regulations" as a possible mechanism he says of such regulations: "... there is no reason to suppose that [such regulations], made by a fallible administration subject to political pressures and operating without any competitive check, will necessarily always be those which increase the efficiency with which the economic system operates."[35] So judicial decisions, though presumably made by fallible judges, and not obviously subject to competitive checks either,[36] are better because they are apolitical. This view is of course highly controversial. Another possible reason for leaving the

---

[33] Appellate courts can, under some systems of procedure, simply decline to adjudicate, as is frequently the case with the U.S. Supreme Court. Under other systems, such as that established by the *European Convention on Human Rights*, certain disputes may not be adjudicated on the ground that an application to the Court is inadmissible. So there may be barriers to entry into the adjudicative system.

[34] *Id.* at 154.

[35] *Id.* at 117–8.

[36] It has been suggested that there is a form of competitive check on judicial decisions in that those thought by some actor to be unsatisfactory can be appealed, or challenged in subsequent litigation. But the hypothesis that there exists something in the nature of a market in legal doctrine seems to me to require much more elaboration than it has ever received to rank as more than a far fetched analogy, and the empirical basis for the claim is, currently, non-existent.

matter to the common law is that parties can contract out of a common law ruling, whereas they normally cannot do this where there is regulatory control, such as zoning, at least if they want their agreement to be legally binding. If you believe that the operation of the market will tend to produce economic efficiency and operate to correct misallocations of rights, whether by the government or by the courts, this will seem an advantage.

The fifth idea may perhaps be intimately connected with Coase's view as to the role of private law. It is that the right way to decide cases involving the problem of social cost, and he has in mind here private nuisance cases in which an injunction is sought, is to ask: ". . . whether the gain from preventing the harm is greater than the loss which would be suffered elsewhere as a result of stopping the action which produced the harm."[37] This view is put forward in a number of passages: "The solution to the problem depends essentially on whether the continued use of the machinery adds more to the confectioner's income than it subtracts from the doctor's"[38] Sometimes the emphasis is slightly different:

> "And it would be desirable to preserve the areas [Wimpole Street] for residential or professional use [by giving non industrial users the right to stop the noise etc. by injunction] only if the value of the additional residential facilities obtained was greater than the value of cakes . . . lost."[39]

In his article on the Federal Communications Commission he wrote:

> What the courts had, in fact, to decide was whether the doctor had the right to impose additional costs on the confectioner through compelling him to install new machinery, or move to a new location, or whether the confectioner had the right to impose additional costs on the doctor through compelling him to do his consulting somewhere else on his premises or at another location.

Later on the same page, linking his discussion to idea of reciprocity, he adds: ". . . the suppression of the harm which A inflicts on B inevitably inflicts harm on A. The problem is to avoid the more serious harm."[40] And in a striking footnote which brings out the gulf which separates Coase's economic analysis from legal analysis, he applies it to hypotheti-

---

[37] *Id.* at 132.

[38] *Id.* at 106.

[39] *Id.* at 107. I have omitted reference to a hypothetical case mentioned in *Sturges v. Bridgman* and discussed by Coase.

[40] *Id.* at 26.

cal litigation between Dr. Sturges and Mr. Bridgman, not over an alleged nuisance, but as to title to land itself:

> In the case of Sturges v. Bridgman, the situation would not have been analytically different had the dispute concerned the ownership of a piece of land lying between the two premises on which either the doctor could have installed his laboratory[41] or the confectioner could have installed his machinery.

So the conception is that in such a case the real issue which confronts the court is to assign the piece of land so as to inflict the least harm on the losing party. This is, by any account, a startling proposal, if, that is, it is intended either to describe what courts do in land disputes, or what they ought to do. It is of course the case that virtually all[42] decisions in litigated cases are good for one party and bad for the other, but a legal system premised on the assumption that the right decision is the one which generates the least harm or cost to the losing party would be weirdly different from any system of civil adjudication which has ever existed.

Coase's skeptical attitude towards the merits of government intervention, as expressed in "The Problem of Social Cost," and, though much less pervasively, in The "Federal Communications Commission," is developed around a criticism of views on social policy which are attributed in the main to Arthur C. Pigou. Pigou, who was born in 1877 and died on7 March 1959, succeeded Alfred Marshall as Professor of Political Economy in Cambridge in 1908, and held the chair until 1943.[43] He was an undergraduate at Kings College, where he was a pupil of Oscar Browning, and, apart from non-combatant service as a stretcher bearer in the First World War, for he was a conscientious objector, he spent his whole adult life in King's. A mountaineer of considerable ability he had, on occasion, climbed with George Mallory, rendered immortal by death in 1924 on Everest, which he may conceivably have climbed.[44] In 1927 Pigou suffered a severe breakdown in health which

---

[41] This is a slip for consulting room.

[42] I say "virtually all" to reflect the possibility that the loss of a law suit is sometimes a blessing in disguise as, for all we know, it may have been in *Sturges v. Bridgman*.

[43] Biographical information based on correspondence with the late Sir Austin Robinson and Sir Noel Annan, obituary attributed to Robinson in *The Times*, 9 March 1959, article by Robinson in *The Dictionary of National Biography* 814–17 (volume for 1951–60), article by J. de V. Graaf in *The New Dictionary of Economics* 876 (J. Eatwell, M. Milgate and P, Newman, eds. 1994) and an article by R. Skidelsky on J. M. Keynes at 282, 286–7, 387, 702, and R. H. Coase, *Essays on Economics and Economists* Ch. 10. His name was of Huguenot extraction.

[44] P. and L. Gillman, *The Wildest Dream. The Biography of George Mallory* (Seattle, 2000) at 159. The unidentified person seated in the front row of the picture of the Pen y

affected his heart; thereafter he was a shadow of his former athletic self, becoming increasingly eccentric and reclusive. He was an example of a type of Oxbridge don once common but now almost extinct: a lifelong bachelor, petrified of women, who enjoyed the company of young men but who never, so far as this is known, was involved in any close emotional much less physical relationship, though he did develop romantic attachments to young adult men. There are many stories about his peculiarities. Over time his misogyny became grotesque; thus when dictating to a female secretary he would insist on locating her in an adjoining room, with the connecting door only slightly ajar to enable her to hear him. It is said that he never once was in the same room as Barbara Wootton, one of his more distinguished graduate students. In recent times he has achieved an undeserved notoriety, the late John Costello in his *Mask of Treachery* having presented him as one of the Cambridge soviet spies, having sinister Russian contacts, as well as enjoying a knighthood, which I fear he neither received nor ever could have received because of his objection to military service.[45] All this is nonsense; Pigou merely held mildly left wing views.

His most radical political view as an economist, a view not original to himself, was that because of the marginal utility of income wealth transfers from rich to poor would in general enhance utility.[46] He strongly disliked discussing economics, either with colleagues or anyone else; he thus differed from the type of Oxbridge don, such as Ludwig Wittgenstein, or J. L. Austin, whose ideas were principally disseminated orally through seminars and private discussions. He was a rather uncritical follower of the views of his predecessor, Marshall, and the late Sir Austen Robinson told me that he tended to be intolerant of anyone who presumed to criticize the views of the master. He published extensively,[47] and delivered formal lectures somewhat repetitively in a style which was then quite normal in academia.

As an economist: "... he set out to investigate the full conditions for maximum satisfaction, the conditions in which private and social net product (as he called them) might diverge, and the measures which could

---

Pass climbing party, Easter 1919, between pp.128–9, is, I think, Pigou. See also J. Hemleb, L. A. Johnson, E. R. Simonson, *Ghosts of Everest. The Search for Mallory and Irvine* (Seattle 1999).

[45] J. Costello, *The Mask of Treachery* (New York, 1988) at 149, 176, 181.

[46] Coase does not discuss this view, which is not significant for his thesis as to social cost.

[47] *Industrial Fluctuations* (1927), *Public Finance* (1928), *Employment and Equilibrium* (1941), *Socialism versus Capitalism* (1937), *Lapses from Full Employment*, and *Income* (1945) are listed in the *Times* obituary.

be taken to bring them into equality, and maximise satisfaction."[48] In his *Wealth and Welfare* Pigou gave examples of such divergences. Some arose from the form of contracts, for example when leases provided no incentive for the tenant to maintain the future fertility of the land, or improve it. Or they might arise when services of social utility went uncompensated, as when a lamp put up by a householder at the entrance to his house threw light onto the street, to the general benefit of the public users of the highway. He also gave illustrations of situations where the social net product falls short of the private net product, as when motor cars wear out roads.[49]

The views criticized by Coase are principally to be found in his *The Economics of Welfare*, first published in 1920, a textbook developed out of his earlier *Wealth and Welfare* (1912).[50] Coase presented Pigou as influencing a school of economists: "Some fifteen or twenty years ago economists, under the influence of Pigou and others, thought of government as waiting beneficently to put things right whenever the hidden hand pointed in the wrong direction."[51] I have argued elsewhere, at somewhat tedious length, this being necessary to establish the point in a rigorous way, that Pigou did not in fact hold the view attributed to him by Coase. His view as to the desirability of government intervention did not differ much from that of Coase, though he was marginally less skeptical about the merits of government intervention; it all depended on the facts of particular cases. Coase is better understood not so much as attacking the ghost of Pigou, but as attacking a tradition in academic circles which he had met in his youth, and which can be called the Pigovian tradition, since it was apparently fathered on Pigou.

Pigou's attitude was in fact much the same as that of Henry Sidgwick, whose lectures he attended. Sidgwick made the point that utility to the individual and utility to society might diverge. He concluded therefore that there was, in consequence, a case for state intervention when this occurred, but added a caution lest it be thought to necessarily be a compelling case: "It does not of course follow that whenever laisser faire falls short of government interference is expedient: since the inevitable drawbacks and disadvantages of the latter may, in any particular case, be worse than the shortcomings of private industry."[52] Pigou's

---

[48] Robinson in *Dictionary of National Biography*, cited n. 43 above.

[49] *Wealth and Welfare* at 148–71.

[50] Coase gives references to the fourth edition of 1932, and I shall do the same. There were other editions in 1924, and 1929, and reprints in 1938, 1946, 1948, 1950 and 1952 (with appendices).

[51] Coase, at 30.

[52] H. Sidgwick, *The Principles of Political Economy*, (London, 1883) Bk.3 Ch.2 419.

view is summed up in one of his books, *Economics in Practice: Six Lectures on Current Issues*, published in 1935:

> The issue about which popular writers argue—the principle of laissez-faire *versus* the principle of state action—is not an issue at all. There is no principle involved on either side. Each particular case must be considered on its merits in all the detail of its concrete circumstance.[53]

The "state action" which Pigou seems principally to have had in mind was the imposition of taxes or the provision of bounties. He explains that:

> ... it sometimes happens that only a portion of the benefit or damage due to a person's private action is reflected in the reward that person received; and, consequently, that he tends to carry that action less far or further than the general interests of society requires.[54]

Thus in the case of a factory emitting polluting smoke the public interest may require the use of smoke prevention devices even though it does not pay the factory to install them. The factory might be given an incentive to install such devices by the imposition of a smoke pollution tax. Where an action would not pay a private individual, but would nevertheless be desirable in the public interest, the private individual might be encouraged to take the action by the provision of a bounty; obviously this could be done to encourage the use of smoke prevention devices as an alternative to the imposition of a tax. Pigou appears to have had virtually no knowledge of, or interest in, private tort law, and it is quite impossible to form any view as to how he would think that a case like *Sturges v. Bridgman* should be approached or decided. Coase in his article made much of the fact that Pigou used the example of uncompensated damage caused by the emission of sparks from steam locomotives as an example of a possible divergence between his "private net product" and "public net product", but Pigou nowhere gives any indication as to what, if anything, should be done about this.[55]

His moderate commitment to socialism is set out in a declaration of faith in the conclusion to his *Socialism versus Capitalism* (1937), which he concedes to be based on inadequate data, and to be "crude and tentative". So far as industry is concerned he wrote:

---

[53] A.C. Pigou, *Economics in Practice: Six Lectures on Current Issues* 127–8 (1935).

[54] Pigou, *Economics in Practice* at 77 and ff.

[55] Coase supposed that the fact that some such damage was uncompensated was the consequence of a legislative decision, but this is incorrect. The law on the subject was common law.

All industries affected with a public interest, or capable of wielding monopoly power, he would subject at least to public supervision and control. Some of them, certainly the manufacture of armaments, probably the coal industry, possibly the railways, he would national- ise, not of course on the pattern of the Post Office, but through public boards or commissions. The Bank of England he would make in name—what it already is in effect—a public institution....[56]

This confession of faith has nothing to say about the forms of govern- ment intervention, taxes and bounties, which Pigou thought might in some circumstances be desirable to deal with the problem of social cost, much less about any modification of private tort law.[57] Pigou's latest expression of view on the merits and demerits of government interven- tion in the economy are set out in a review of L. Robbins, *Central Planning in Peace and War*. Here he discusses what he calls primary planning, which is concerned with decisions as to when government should intervene in the economic system order to affect the distribution of resources amongst different productive uses, and the distribution of outputs, and secondary planning, which was concerned with the choice of differing mechanisms intended to achieve ends determined by primary planning. The manipulation of taxes and bounties, called financial policy, features in his account of secondary planning, and the general tone of the review is to argue for extreme caution, and to argue that in general financial policy is likely to be preferable to "direction" of resources, as by conscription, commandeering, granting licenses, assigning priorities and rationing, together with price control. Tort law nowhere features in the discussion, though it seems obvious enough that it is capable of acting as a mechanism to encourage the direction of resources one way or the other, as the medical profession in the U.S.A regularly complains. Although there are some earlier examples, Coase was the first economist whose work directed serious attention towards the economic significance of tort law; the legal world has never been quite the same since. Pigou, by way of contrast, had nothing whatever to say on the matter, and the same is true of most earlier economists.

Elsewhere in *Socialism versus Capitalism* Pigou expressed consider- able doubt as to the practicality of his idea of using taxes and bounties in situations in which there was a divergence between private net product and social net product. The problem was, as he saw it, that although economists had suggested the use of these devices, no government had ever tried to use them, and economists: "... have never attempted the

---

[56] A fuller quotation will be found in Coase, "Law and Economics and A.W. Brian Simpson" XXV J.Legal.Studies 103, 114–5.

[57] (London, 1947), reprinted as "Central Planning" as Chapter XVI of his *Essays in Economics* (London, 1952).

quantitative study that would be necessary before the suggestion could be applied in practice."[58] His idea was that such study would be needed to settle the level of taxation; ignorance of the facts militated against the use of these remedies.[59] Earlier, in his *The Economics of Welfare*, he had argued that in assessing the economic effects of an activity, such as running a railway, all consequences, good or bad, must be placed on the scales.[60] This was clearly essential under his theory in order to tell whether private net product was greater or less than public net product. Put simply you have to consider all the consequence of the operation of a smoking factory, good or bad, before you can tell what is best to do about it. Later, in his *Socialism versus Capitalism*[61] he showed a realization that making up such a balance sheet might be an extremely difficult operation, if indeed possible at all. It raises both analytical questions—how do you identify the relevant consequences?—and a practical problem,-how you find out the facts, and do the calculations? Pigou therefore grasped the fact that the application of his economic theory to the real world might be, to put it no stronger, very difficult indeed. In many contexts in which economic ideas are currently applied to legal issues of the type which come before courts for decision this problem is, I fear, simply ignored.

Let us now turn from economic theory to the mundane world of legal decision, as exemplified in the story of *Sturges v. Bridgman*. The case certainly illustrates the reciprocal nature of the problem of social cost, in that the dispute only arose because of the manner in which the working practices of the doctor and the confectioner were so organized that the noise and vibration originating in the confectioner's property interfered with the work of the doctor. It is also clear that the parties could perfectly well have avoided litigation by reaching some mutually acceptable bargain, and this will always be possible in principle in private nuisance disputes, though a bargain by itself will not necessarily solve a public nuisance case.[62] In law school jargon such bargains are commonly called Coasean bargains. The sort of bargain which Coase seems to have in mind involves a one way payment, based on a rational calculation of respective alternatives and costs:

> The doctor would have been willing to waive his right and allow the machinery to continue in operation if the confectioner would have

---

[58] Pigou, *Socialism versus Capitalism* at 42–44.

[59] His view is similar to that set out by Coase at 184.

[60] *The Economics of Welfare* at 134.

[61] Pigou, *Economics of Welfare*, at 31–46.

[62] It would if the bargain involved the cessation of the activities constituting a public nuisance.

paid him a sum of money which was greater than the loss of income which he would suffer from having to move to a more costly or less convenient location or (and this was suggested as a possibility) from having to build a separate wall which would deaden the noise and vibration.... The solution of the problem depends essentially on whether the continued use of the machinery adds more to the confectioner's income than it subtracts from the doctor's.

Here Coase is talking about a bargain concluded after the decision in the case, but his reasoning would apply to one preceding litigation just as well.

In fact Dr. Sturges did try negotiation, first complaining personally and then, in the spring of 1876, through his solicitor. The precise form of the negotiations is unrecorded, but from what Mr. Bridgman said in reply we may guess that there was some suggestion that he might arrange to use his mortars at times when the consulting room was not in use. Apparently the noise was at its worst during the London season, that is from May until the end of July, when the upper classes repaired to London to engage in conspicuous consumption. The defendant's trade therefore increased at this time. Dr. Sturges thought that the problem had progressively worsened over the years. There are hints in the affidavits of deteriorating personal relations. Thus Dr. Sturges' surveyor was refused access to Mr. Bridgman's property on the second occasion on which he tried to carry out an inspection.

In his affidavit Mr. Bridgman, as if he had read Coase, indeed made the point that the problem was a reciprocal one, and he took the line that it was all the fault of Dr. Sturges. He pointed out that Dr. Sturges had "... instead of building a separate and distinct wall utilized the North Wall[63] of my said kitchen." He went on to state the length of time the mortars had been in use, and the fact that there had previously only been one complaint, in 1848. An invalid lady then living at number 85 had asked him not to use his mortars before 8 a.m.. He explained to her that in his business this was impossible, and she never complained again. Nor had there been any complaints for eighteen months after the consulting room was built. In response to Dr. Sturges' complaint he had done what he could to confine the use of the mortars to times which did not trouble the doctor. Since July 1876 all sugar had been pounded between 11 a.m. and 1 p.m.. He could do no more if he was to run his business.

So it was that little was achieved in the negotiations, and the dispute came to litigation, presumably at considerable cost, much greater, in all probability though we cannot be certain of this, than those eventually incurred by Mr. Bridgman in conforming to the court's order.

---

[63] North that is from Wimpole Street.

And, since he lost the action, Mr. Bridgman would have had to pay Dr. Sturges' legal costs as well as his own. What the effect of conforming to the order of the court was on Mr. Bridgman's income we today can have no idea; all that we know is that he thought that a change in his working schedule would be costly. Whether this view was based on any precise exercise in quantification we may well doubt.

Negotiation will normally precede litigation in nuisance cases of this kind. The story which emerges from the affidavits is a very everyday account of a dispute between neighbors, here both engaged in commercial activity, with an attempt to work things out amicably. Although we do not know the details it would be quite astonishing if Dr. Sturges considered for one moment the possibility of paying Mr. Bridgman money to change his ways, much less that Mr. Bridgman would have considered offering Dr. Sturges money to change his, for example by reducing the number of patients he saw, or seeing them in his dining room, or wherever. Much less is there any suggestion that either of the parties ever considered moving elsewhere, or changing their employment. It would also be quite astonishing if the doctor and the confectioner approached the matter by supposing that: "The solution of the problem depends essentially on whether the continued use of the machinery adds more to the confectioner's income than it subtracts from the doctor's."[64] Nor is there any support in the affidavits for thinking that the parties engaged in some elaborate cost benefit analysis of the infinite range of alternative courses of action open to them. The calculations required would have included an assessment, by both of them of course, of the potential loss of income which the doctor would suffer: "... from having to move to a more costly or less convenient location, from having to curtail his activities at this location or (and this was suggested as a possibility) from having to build a separate wall which would deaden the noise and vibration."[65] In fact nobody suggested building a separate wall. The function of the reference to such a wall was purely argumentative: Mr. Bridgman was making the point that the trouble was not his fault, but arose because the doctor's builder did not do a good job. But it is correct to say that a comprehensive cost benefit analysis would have to include this, and endless other, possibilities and cost them all. Something a little closer to the elaborate calculations envisaged may perhaps take place in situations in which two forms of land use are, in practical terms, suspected of being quite incompatible. There may be situations in which relocation turns out to be the only viable solution. Given the costs of litigation, and the English rule as to responsibility for them there must, in the nineteenth century, have been

---

[64] Coase, at 106.

[65] Coase, at 106.

many situations in which the victim of pollution relocated, but they do not feature in the law reports.[66]

Coasean cost benefit analysis bears no relationship at all to how neighbors behave in real life situations where the situation is not so intolerable as to present the stark choice between litigation and relocation. It may be that in some imagined world such analysis would take place, but lawyers are concerned with the real world. Law involves practical reason. It is unclear to me what lawyers can learn from an imagined world. If neighbors are trying to resolve a dispute they will normally have to accept the broad outlines of the situation: the confectioner's kitchen is going to remain in operation, and the consulting room will continue to be used for consulting. To reach an amicable arrangement they will have to accept each other's rights, broadly defined, and concentrate their attention on some simple or cheap method whereby the exercise of these rights can be mutually accommodated. No doubt Mr. Bridgman thought he had a perfect right to go on using his mortars as he and his father had done in the past, and you do not offer to pay people money for a right you believe you already possess. He was, to his own way of thinking, prepared to be reasonable and make some adjustments, and he thought he had already done so. Anyway the trouble was all Dr. Sturges' fault. And no doubt Dr. Sturges, perhaps after taking advice from his lawyer, thought that he had a right to peace and quiet in his home, so that he could see his patients and write his lectures, and again you do not offer to pay people money for what is yours already. It was all Mr. Bridgman's fault; all he had to do was to employ an engineer to come up with a new way of arranging his machinery, or perhaps alter his working schedule. In short I doubt if either of the two men questioned for one moment the right of the other to continue to pursue their business on their property.

The reason why a market transaction in the sense of a purchase and sale of rights is usually not possible in such situations is that the parties are not willing to place their rights in the market. Once this is understood it becomes offensive not to respect their unwillingness. There is of course a sense in which every asset which is legally capable of sale is always in the market, but this is merely an uninteresting tautology: what is legally capable of sale is legally capable of sale. Markets in a non-tautological sense have elaborate boundaries, sometimes imposed by formal law, sometimes imposed by consensual arrangements which may not be legally binding but which are sanctioned through other institutional mechanisms, and sometimes imposed by a variety of constraints of the type that have recently been rediscovered in the legal academy, and

---

[66] For nineteenth century examples of the few known instances in which litigation in private or public nuisance induced a polluting enterprise to relocate see my *Leading Cases* Ch.7.

called social norms. Life would be quite intolerable if individuals did not in general respect social limits to the market; in most cultures, though not apparently all,[67] when invited to a dinner party it is unacceptable for a guest to make offers for the silverware, or the wine, or the pictures which adorn the dining room, or offer to tell a good joke for $50, or try to sell life insurance to fellow guests. Engaging in market transactions is just one form of human activity, and without such boundaries life would dissolve into unstructured chaos, in which it would be impossible to distinguish going shopping, from going out to dinner, or from going mountain climbing, or from going fishing with a friend. In the situation which confronted the doctor and the confectioner an offer of money by Dr. Sturges to help over any costs involved in moving or insulating the mortars might well have been socially acceptable, and would not, except to a certain type of economist anxious to assimilate all human interaction to market transactions, be thought of as a sale, but rather as a contribution to the cost of action from which he would be the principal beneficiary and from which he would otherwise be unjustly enriched.[68] Anything more than such an offer would surely have bordered on the offensive.

Hence solving a conflict of this character in a particular case does not entail attempting to reach an economically efficient solution to the general question of how two tracts of land should be used. Nor does it mean agreeing to a market transaction whose paradigm is a sale. It means agreeing on some form of mutual accommodation which brings the dispute to an end, and if this is achieved it is wholly irrelevant that this mutual accommodation does not constitute an efficient solution, or the efficient solution (assuming there was any way of telling this) or maximizes the gross national product, or whatever. Such an accommodation will usually be marginal in character. The process resembles the manner in which large numbers of people contrive, by a process of cooperative and marginal adjustment of speed and direction, to use a sidewalk without colliding with each other. The aim of negotiations is not to maximise the value of production; it is, more modestly, to avoid the costs, in particular legal costs, though other costs are involved, which will be imposed on both parties if the dispute is not resolved. Economic considerations enter into the matter because if what is perceived as expenditure is needed to achieve an agreed solution, then the smaller the expenditure the better the chances of a solution being agreed. Less costly solutions, that is to say accommodations which end the dispute, will tend

---

[67] I am told that in some American contexts the social rules are different.

[68] I recently agreed with a neighbor that I should carry the cost of felling a tree which was shading the lawn behind my home in England. There was no suggestion that the shading constituted an actionable nuisance, and as it turned out my neighbor disliked the tree in question and was happy to have it felled and removed.

to be preferred to more costly solutions, though this will not always be so. The cheapest solution may not appear to the parties to be the best solution.

The possibility of reaching some form of marginal accommodation certainly entails accepting the idea that the problem is a reciprocal one, but only in a weak sense, and one which severely limits the range of optional adjustments the parties will be prepared to consider. I would imagine that if Mr. Bridgman had suggested to Dr. Sturges that he move his practice elsewhere negotiations would have come to an abrupt halt.

Coase argues that the essential prerequisite for the sort of market transaction he has in mind is that the rights of the parties must be settled, or at least well defined. This is no doubt why he envisages a Coasean bargain *after* the case has been decided. Thus he says: "It is necessary to know whether the damaging business is liable or not for damage caused, since without the establishment of this initial delineation of rights there can be no market transactions to transfer or combine them."[69] This is incorrect. Even if it is true, which I doubt, over all cases of buying and selling,[70] it is certainly not true over negotiated settlements of problems of conflicting land use between neighbors. Even if Dr. Sturges and Mr. Bridgman agreed to differ as to whether or not Mr. Bridgman had a right to make the noise complained of, they could perfectly well reach an agreement which resolved any dispute about it, and do so before there was a decision in litigation. The significance of a clear allocation of rights in such a case is surely that it allocates power in the negotiations, not that it makes them possible. Thus if Dr. Sturges is legally in a position to stop Mr. Bridgman using his mortars in the way in which he has been using them, he does not have to bargain with him at all, and he can reject offers from Mr. Bridgman which, if he was *homo economicus*, he would accept. This last possibility is often called the *problem* of holdout, but this characterization is a mistake. In a society which accepts the notion of private property it is not a problem at all. It is, instead, quite central to the institution itself. Long ago Sir William Blackstone explained this:

> There is nothing which so generally strikes the imagination, and engages the affections of mankind, as the right of property; or that sole and despotic dominion which one man claims and exercises over

---

[69] Coase, at 104. Cf. *Id.* at 158 "the delimitation of rights is an essential prelude to market transaction ... the ultimate result (which maximizes the value of production) is independent of the legal decision".

[70] The idea that, to use the example of land, there must be recognition of private property rights in land, rules of some kind to allocate such rights, and some system for resolving disputes, before you can have buying and selling of land, seems obviously true in general, but it does not follow from this that purchase and sale of land may not take place in situations in which the allocation of the property right in the land may be uncertain.

the external things of the world, in total exclusion of the right of any other individual in the universe.[71]

Despotic dominion is what the right of private property is all about, and it includes the right to behave in ways which make no contribution whatever to the national wealth. If I own a Renoir or a Picasso I may refuse every offer to purchase it and do so since I have decided to burn it.[72] It may well be that in general a system of private property rights, allied to a system of free contract, has a tendency to maximise aggregate wealth. But such systems presuppose a respect for private autonomy in relation to decisions as to land use, and the formation of contracts, in particular cases, even though the exercise of that autonomy is capricious, irrational or inspired by motives which have nothing to do with the maximizing of aggregate or even individual wealth.

In the event, the negotiations failed, and the case came to court. The judge was Sir George Jessel, the Master of the Rolls, and the evidence made it pretty clear, and indeed there was really no dispute, that Mr. Bridgman's activities were seriously interfering with Dr. Sturges' enjoyment of his property. There were no suggestions that Dr. Sturges' activities were causing any problem for Mr. Bridgman. So from a legal point of view the first question to settle was whether Mr. Bridgman was, as he claimed, entitled to continue his noisy activities, through having, over the years, acquired a right to do so under the fictitious doctrine of lost modern grant. It was more or less conceded that unless Mr. Bridgman could show that he had acquired such a right he had invaded the rights of the doctor. The judge ruled that no such right had been acquired. It is possible in English law to acquire such a right by long use and acquiescence, but the judge took the view that until the consulting room came into use the noise was not causing any problem, and was thus not actionable, nor was Dr. Sturges or his predecessors in a position to stop it. Hence it would have been wrong to infer that the doctor and previous occupiers of 85 Wimpole Street had acquiesced in the noise.

So Mr. Bridgman had not acquired a right to make the noise, and Dr. Sturges got his injunction. Plainly the issue in the case, as seen by Sir George Jessel, had nothing whatever to do with the question—"whether the continued use of the machinery adds more to the confectioner's income than it subtracts from the doctor's."[73] In the legal scheme of things that was not a matter which had to be decided, or

---

[71] Blackstone, *Commentaries on the Laws of England*, Vol. II at 2.

[72] This example is not fanciful. Winston Churchill so disliked a portrait painted by Graham Sutherland, which had been presented to him, that his wife had the gardener burn it. Only by sophistry could it be argued that this action maximized aggregate wealth or welfare.

[73] Coase, at 106.

indeed had any relevance to the outcome. The injunction did not go into specifics as to what should be done; it maximized the liberty of the defendant property owner by merely requiring him not to use his pestles and mortars "in such a manner or at such times as to be a nuisance to the plaintiff". There was no suggestion that the business should be closed down or relocated. Indeed the judge gave time to Mr. Bridgman "to make the necessary alterations to his premises; and no doubt he would find some skillful mechanic in London who would tell him how to work these machines without making any noise at all". So the injunction was not enforceable until 1 August 1878. This was to reduce the cost of making the accommodation required, and minimize the risk of further costly proceedings. So here economic consideration were important, but only at the margins, and not in relation to the principal issue which the court had to decide.

The case was then taken on appeal, and the main issue ventilated was the same—had Mr. Bridgman acquired a right to make the noise? The judges thought he had not. An analogy was offered with a hypothetical case: a noisy blacksmith's forge situated in what had long been a barren moor, near which a residence had recently been built. This hypothetical case involves of course the problem of the moving boundary between land uses, to which I have already referred.

> As regards the blacksmith's forge, this is really an *idem per idem* case with the present. It would be on the one hand in a very high degree unreasonable and undesirable that there should be a right of action for acts which are not in the present condition of the adjoining land, and possible never will be any annoyance or inconvenience to either its owner or occupier; and it would be on the other hand in an equal degree unjust, and from a public point of view, inexpedient, that the use and value of adjoining land should, for all times and under all circumstances, be restricted or diminished by reason of the continuance of acts incapable of physical interruption, and which the law gives no power to prevent. The smith in the case supposed might protect himself by taking a sufficient curtilage to ensure what he does from being at any time an annoyance to his neighbour, but the neighbour himself would be powerless in the matter.

The opinion of Lord Justice Thesiger claims that any other principle would "produce a prejudicial effect on the development of land for residential purposes."[74] To this extent the general principle adopted by the court may be thought to attend to economic considerations, or alternatively to a respect for the despotic dominion or liberty of the property owner, the value to which Blackstone referred. But the particu-

---

[74] *Sturges v. Bridgman*, 11 Ch.D. at 865–6.

lar decision pays not the least attention to the relative economic value of the two conflicting forms of land use.

So it is that the judicial opinions in the case, like the affidavits on which they are based, make not the least attempt to investigate the economic or social value of the activities of either confectioner or doctor. It would be idle to claim that views on such matters do not have, in practice, any effect on the outcome of cases; the legal doctrines involved are malleable, and impressionistic views as to social welfare or ethical standing may influence the way they are applied. Good guys tend to win, and bad guys to lose. But legally speaking notions of economic or social value are wholly irrelevant. They must be in a capitalist system which respects the right of private property, for it is not the business of the courts to substitute their despotic dominion to that of the litigants. As owners or occupiers of property the parties must be treated equally, with respect for their rights to do what they like on their property, however inefficient, so long as this does not violate some legal prohibition. The whole point of the law of nuisance is to protect that equality, and in consequence the law intervenes when either party engages in activities which significantly abridge the freedom of their neighbor.

Valuable though the distinction is, confusion can be caused here by contrasting entitlements protected by property rules from entitlements protected by liability rules, or property *rights* with liability *rules*.[75] The statement of a property right is the statement of an entitlement which the law protects; in a sense it is the statement of an ideal. The mechanisms whereby such an entitlement is protected are quite distinct, and usually complex. They may involve both the civil and the criminal law. These mechanisms represent the outworks of rights, not their substance. A landowner's property rights are protected by criminal law, by property rules, and by liability rules, not to mention such institutions as that of testamentary succession, contract law and the law of gifts. The enthusiasm or intensity of protection varies, so that in relation to personal property, much of which is fungible, orders for specific restitution are commonly not available. To view this as a legal recognition that people can take other people's personal property so long as they pay for it seems to me to be profoundly mistaken. In the world we live in, which is partly structured by law, that is not the understanding. To do so will usually, but not always, constitute a criminal offence. With rights in land, specific recovery in cases of dispossession is available partly because it is more practicable, and partly because land is not treated as fungible. For interference involving entry but no dispossession there may be in some situations criminal sanctions as well as the civil action for

---

[75] See W. E. Landes and R. A. Posner, *The Economic Structure of Tort Law* (Cambridge 1987) 29, based on G. Calabresi and A. D. Melamed, "Property Rules, Liability Rules and Inalienability: One View of the Cathedral," 85 *Harv. L.R.* 1089 (1972).

trespass. But the protection provided by such criminal sanctions, and by the action of trespass, would in some contexts be quite inadequate unless less tangible interference was remedied, and the law of private nuisance offers a remedy where there has been significant interference. After some controversy it came to be settled in mid-nineteenth century common law that this basic principle was not to be displaced by the public interest in economic development.[76] So, to use the modern catch phrase, the common law rejected the idea of permitting the economically efficient level of pollution. However the judges, and no doubt juries, in determining what is to count as an actionable nuisance, which is bound to involve questions of degree, have no doubt always accepted the idea that some level of mutual tolerance and adjustment between landowners is necessary if life is to go on, given the fact that the effects of land use are bound to cross territorial boundaries, and no doubt too a rough and ready economic calculus has been significant at the margins. To this weak extent the reciprocal nature of the problems of conflicting land use has been accepted by the oracles of the law, and presumably by members of juries too. But in so far as economic considerations have been taken into consideration this does not mean that a rigorous system of analysis has replaced a less rigorous legal analysis; economic arguments, in so far as they feature in legal decisions, have been impressionistic only. If the realist movement has left us with an awareness of the inherent malleability of legal rules, we should also be aware of the fact that economic analysis is just as malleable, most obviously in situations in which hard data simply does not exist.

In modern American law such decisions as that in the well known and controversial case of *Boomer v. Atlantic Cement Company*[77] have retreated from an enthusiastic protection of property rights by refusing injunctions in situations in which, although there is substantial interference, the cost of abating a nuisance is thought to be much greater than the damage caused by allowing it to continue. Given certain arrangements about the recovery of damages, this may allow a polluting landowner to acquire a right to pollute without the consent of the victim on payment of a price fixed by the court, a bizarre state of affairs in a capitalist society. But even today, and certainly not in the nineteenth century, courts do not enter into open-ended investigations as to the efficient use of adjacent tracts of land, and allocate rights accordingly. To do that would be the end of the right of private property. The decision in the *Boomer* case certainly weakens the protection of that right. It may well be that the institution of private property, coupled with the institu-

---

[76] See my discussion in *Leading Cases* of *Tipping v. St. Helen's Smelting Co.*, 4 B. & S. 608, 616, 122 E. R. 588, 591, 11 H. L. C. 642, 11 E. R. 1483, 1 Ch. App. Cas. 66 (1865).

[77] *Boomer v. Atlantic Cement Company*, 26 N.Y.2d 219, 257 N.E.2d 870, 309 N.Y.S.2d 312 (1970).

tion of contract, has, in general, a tendency to encourage and facilitate the creation of wealth. In some schemes of thought this tendency may be regarded as providing a utilitarian justification for the institution, a justification which is only be thought necessary because there are obviously problematic aspects of the institution, such as the fact that some people have too much property, and others to have too little. It does not in the least follow that in particular cases property rights should be allocated to those who will produce the most wealth even if it was possible to tell. So it is that the law allows gifts to be made to the feckless and improvident, and testamentary dispositions too. Nincompoops may inherit, and contracts of sale are in no way affected by the fact that the purchaser is a shopaholic who has not the least use for the goods he purchases.

In nineteenth century law tort law economic considerations played a role, but operated only at the margins, and then impressionistically only, as when Sir George Jessel in *Sturges v. Bridgman* guessed that Mr. Bridgman would find some fairly cheap way of dealing with the problem caused by his use of the mortars.

The judge seems to have been right, for Mr. Bridgman, somehow or other, dealt with the problem. His business did not move as a result of the litigation, and in due course his son, whose name was James, joined him, appearing for example in *Kelly's Directory* for 1888 and 1889. But in 1891 James is in business at 792 Old Kent Road, and the Bridgmans do not feature at all in the directory for 1890, so we may assume that Frederick died or retired in that year. Figures produced for the litigation, designed to rebut the argument that the nuisance was increasing, indicated that in 1878 the gross income of the business had been falling for some years. In 1852 it had been £9,416, but in 1876–7 it was only £5,340. Presumably it eventually became unprofitable. At about the turn of the century 28–34 Wigmore Street was redeveloped and became Norfolk Mansions, the building which today stands upon the site.

And as for Dr. Sturges he practiced medicine from 85 Wimpole Street until his death. In spite of the success of the action he became rather deaf, and he did not hear the approach of a rubber tired hansom cab, which knocked him down in Cavendish Square on 16 October 1894. He died of internal injuries at his home on 3 November. The premises at 85 Wimpole Street remain, however, just as they were at the time of the litigation, and are now occupied by Adlers, a firm of Surveyors, Estate Agents, and Property Development Consultants. They use the consulting room for their meetings. If you visit there you will see the original roof light, installed no doubt to enable the doctor the more easily to examine his patients, and indicating to this day the original medical function of the room.

How ought cases like *Sturges v. Bridgman* be handled by courts? The idea that they could enter into open ended cost benefit analysis in pursuit of the economically efficient solution is simply fanciful; the litigation would never end. Indeed the whole idea of an ideally efficient solution is it itself, from a practical point of view, vacuous. There is absolutely no way in which we can ever say that this or that land use represents the ideal, because to establish that this was so would involve just such an open ended cost benefit analysis. So whatever the theoretical utility of the ideal conception of economic efficiency may be, it is devoid of empirical or practical significance. It is the crock of gold at the end of a rainbow. Furthermore if courts were to attempt to apply such a notion to litigation the outcome of each case would of necessity depend upon its own special facts; there could be no general rule except to pursue the goal of maximizing economic efficiency, which would require an attempt to reach the end of the rainbow and find the crock of gold in every litigated case. That could not be a new and better way to decide nuisance cases.[78]

---

[78] This essay is based on an article, "Coase v. Pigou Reexamined", which originally appeared in the *Journal of Legal Studies* Vol. XXV at 53.

2

Maxwell J. Mehlman

Moore v. Regents of the University of California

There is a truism in the fields of law dealing with science that the law is constantly having to play catch-up with scientific advances. The *Moore* case is an apt illustration. In one sense, the case is about what is termed "surgical waste." This is what is left over after an operation, in particular the tissues and fluids that are removed from the patient's body. In John Moore's case, it was his spleen, which was removed to slow down the progress of a disease called hairy-cell leukemia.[1] Historically, no one much cared about what happened to this stuff, at least in terms of to whom it belonged. It had little if any commercial value. If it had a use, it was only as research or training material for physicians and medical students, and the law concerned itself only with making sure that it was disposed of in such a way as to protect the public health. California, for example, had a law requiring it to be buried, incinerated, or disposed of according to the rules of the state health department.[2] As Justice Broussard notes in his concurring and dissenting opinion, a person is prohibited from "taking the removed part home and keeping it on his mantel."[3]

But science marches on. The first major development that challenged the way the law thought about excised body parts was organ transplantation. In 1954, physicians performed the first successful kidney transplant, which was followed in 1967 by the first successful heart and liver transplants. In the 1980's, researchers developed effective drugs to suppress the body's immune reaction to foreign tissue, thereby

---

[1] The facts described in the *Moore* case, of course, are merely the allegations of the complaint, since the case was never tried.

[2] (Cal. Health & Safety Code § 7054.4).

[3] 793 P.2d at 503.

reducing the risk of rejection. Human organs now had the ability to save lives, and it became necessary for the law to figure out how they should be obtained and distributed. They had significant commercial potential. But should they be treated as someone's property? In particular, could they be bought and sold?

In the meantime, other scientific advances were taking place. Researchers had developed the technique of DNA recombination, permitting them to produce new forms of life. A question immediately arose whether these life forms were a form of intellectual property that could be patented to increase their commercial value. The same issue arose later in regard to genetic sequences and other discoveries resulting from the Human Genome Project, which resulted in the decoding of the human genetic code. Could someone own the genetic blueprints for life itself?

Physicians also were developing techniques to overcome infertility. Some of these, like artificial insemination and surrogacy, involved transferring human biological materials, such as eggs, sperm, or fertilized embryos, from one individual to another. Should the law treat them as property, and if so, could these biological materials be traded on the open market?

It was against this background of scientific progress and legal uncertainty that John Moore's spleen was removed in 1976. But instead of discarding the tissue as surgical waste, the physicians allegedly kept it and worked on it and eventually developed a cell line, a highly valuable research tool that they patented in 1984 and licensed for commercial development. According to Moore's complaint, the physicians had received hundreds of thousands of dollars for their efforts, and the cell line had a potential value in the billions. His splenetic tissues were hardly "waste," and when Moore found out about it, he wanted a piece of the pie.

Moore filed suit, alleging a number of causes of action. The trial judge only focused on one of them—"conversion"—and dismissed the case on the ground that Moore had failed to state a cause of action for conversion. Conversion is a type of intentional tort. It grew out of the old common law remedy of trover, which was an action against the finder of lost goods who failed to return them to the rightful owner. Gradually, the courts extended trover to include cases in which the losing and finding was merely fictional, and the real injury was being dispossessed of a chattel in a manner that seriously interfered with the owner's right to control it.[4] The Supreme Court of California agreed with the lower court that Moore could not sue for conversion, since he lacked a

---

[4] See Restatement (Second) of Torts § 222 cmt. a (1965).

sufficient ownership interest in his spleen cells.[5] However, the court held that Moore could proceed with an action for breach of fiduciary duty or failure to obtain his informed consent to a medical procedure.

The Contextual Framework of the Case

It is interesting to compare the decision in the *Moore* case with the way the law has dealt with property issues in other contexts involving excised human tissues. In connection with transplant organs, the National Conference of Commissioners on Uniform State Laws drafted a Uniform Anatomical Gift Act (UAGA) that all states had adopted by 1972, and Congress stepped in with the National Organ Transplant Act of 1984 (NOTA). While these laws do not directly address the question of whether transplant organs are property, they prohibit buying and selling them. Section 10 of the UAGA states that "[a] person may not knowingly, for valuable consideration, purchase or sell a part for transplantation or therapy, if removal of the part is intended to occur after the death of the decedent." NOTA makes it unlawful "for any person to knowingly acquire, receive, or otherwise transfer any human organ for valuable consideration for use in human transplantation if the transfer affects interstate commerce."[6] The organ procurement system is premised on the notion that organs are "donated," that they are "gifts," as the name of the uniform state law indicates. While the UAGA only applies to organs from deceased persons, NOTA prohibits the sale of organs from living donors as well.

Unfortunately, the voluntary, altruistically-based organ procurement system established by NOTA and the UAGA has not produced nearly enough organs for transplantation. According to data from the United Network for Organ Sharing, the nonprofit organization that administers the national organ transplantation program, over 50,000 people currently are waiting for kidneys alone, yet in 2001 only 14,152 kidneys were transplanted. Approximately 3,000 people die every year while waiting for a kidney. Others die waiting for hearts, livers, and other organs. This has prompted the transplant community to search for ways to increase the number of organs available for transplantation. One suggestion is that the provisions in the UAGA and NOTA that prohibit the sale of organs be repealed. Commentators have devised various schemes for facilitating a market in organs. One of the boldest is that individuals be allowed to sell future interests in their organs to would-be recipients.[7] Critics respond that creating a market for organs would treat

---

[5] 793 P.2d at 488–89.

[6] 42 U.S.C. § 274e(a).

[7] See, e.g., James F. Blumstein, The Use of Financial Incentives in Medical Care: The Case of Commerce in Transplantable Organs, 3 Health Matrix 1 (1993).

the body as a mere commodity; that it would prey on the poor, who would feel pressure to sell their organs to raise money for basic necessities; and that paying for organs would deny people the opportunity to act altruistically. The critics also argue that the legal rules that would be necessary to govern the market would be complicated and distasteful. For example, could someone who had purchased a future interest in an organ control the seller's lifestyle to help maintain the quality of the organ, avoiding the deterioration caused by excessive alcohol consumption and other destructive behaviors? If the seller reneged on the agreement, could the buyer require specific performance? Many of these issues would become even more problematic in the case of organs and tissues procured from living donors, as opposed to from cadavers.

The irony, however, is that, notwithstanding the prohibition on buying and selling organs, organ transplantation is big business. As Professor Linda Fentiman points out: "... the transplant surgeons receive ego gratification, prestige, and money for their labor on the transplant team; the transplant center and its workers gain both an enhanced reputation and income; the nonprofit organ procurement organization maintains its raison d'etre–the business of organ procurement and allocation ...."[8] Indeed, as she notes, "under the current organ transplantation system, everyone profits except the organ donors ...." Moreover, the law has carved out exceptions for limited amounts of human blood and blood products, as well as for hair and other materials that, unlike organs, can be replenished by the body and that can be removed without physiological injury. As Justice Mosk notes in his dissent, these materials can be bought and sold. An argument can be made that, since the removal of Moore's cancerous spleen cells was not injurious to his health but rather beneficial, the cells should be regarded as more akin to blood and hair than to organs like kidneys.

The continuing shortage of transplant organs has kept alive the idea of paying people for their organs. The most popular proposal falls short of allowing a free market, but instead allows the families of donors to receive a modest sum of money to help defray burial expenses. The Pennsylvania legislature in fact has authorized a pilot program that would pay funeral homes $300 to bury a person who had agreed to be an organ donor, with funding provided by a voluntary $1 donation on state tax returns, drivers license applications and automobile registrations.[9] This program has not yet been implemented, however, apparently be-

---

[8] Linda C. Fentiman, Legislative Model: Organ Donation as National Service: A Proposed Federal Organ Donation Law, 27 Suffolk U. L. Rev. 1593, 1601 (1993).

[9] See Peter A. Ubel et al., Pennsylvania's Voluntary Benefits Program, Health Affairs, Sept.-Oct. 2000.

cause of fears that it would violate NOTA's prohibition against transferring organs for value.

Of course, as the justices in *Moore* acknowledged, just because people cannot legally sell something does not mean that they have no property rights in it, or that they cannot bring an action for conversion. As section 222A of the Restatement of Torts (Second) acknowledges, the key element of conversion is interference with a person's right of control over tangible items. As Justice Broussard points out,[10] the California Supreme Court's views on Moore's right to control his spleen cells seems to depend largely on timing. The majority acknowledges that Moore has a right to control what happens to his cells *before* they are removed, but believes that this right adequately can be protected by holding the defendants liable for breach of fiduciary duty or failing to obtain Moore's informed consent. The majority feels that, *after* the cells are removed, he loses whatever ownership rights he may once have had since he no longer desires to possess the cells. Yet a cause of action for conversion clearly will lie even though a person no longer desires to possess an item, so long as he once had the right to control it. The Restatement, for example, gives numerous illustrations of conversions involving property that the owner no longer can have returned and no longer controls, such as property that has been destroyed (illustrations ##7, 17, 20) or that has been forfeited to the government after illegal use (illustration #23).

The right of control also is a troublesome issue for organ donation. Biomedical ethicists and legal scholars have struggled with the question of who should control the disposition of a person's organs following death. The obvious answer might seem to be the donor, and this is the approach taken by the UAGA.[11] Potential donors can declare their intent on their drivers' licenses, or in living wills and other forms of advanced health care directives. But there is no effective registry where these intentions are recorded, so that the information often is not readily available to physicians and hospitals. In some cases, moreover, the wishes of donors conflict with those of the next-of-kin. Despite the UAGA, hospitals typically follow the directions of the family to avoid upsetting them further. (A more cynical viewpoint is that, unlike the decedent, the survivors can sue the hospital.) In an effort to increase the supply of transplant organs, a bill was introduced in the Ohio legislature in 2000 that would give organ procurement organizations the right to sue families who tried to block donation contrary to the decedent's wishes. Then there are the numerous instances in which decedents have not expressed their preferences. The UAGA establishes a presumption that they do not intend to donate their organs unless they have ex-

---

[10] 793 P.2d at 501.

[11] UAGA § 2(h) (1987).

pressed a willingness to do so, but the act permits organs to be removed with the consent of the family in the absence of an express refusal by the decedent.

The shortage of organs for transplantation even has led some policy-makers to consider permitting doctors or hospitals to remove organs without the decedent's permission unless the decedent has expressly refused, thus flipping the current presumption.[12] In fact, the UAGA permits a coroner to remove organs and corneas unless the coroner is aware of a refusal by the decedent or the family or has failed to make a reasonable effort to determine their wishes.[13] In a number of cases, however, family members have sued coroners' offices for removing corneas and other organs for transplantation despite the wishes of the family or the decedent, claiming that this deprives them of a property right without due process of law. This right is often called a "quasi-property" right because of the legal limitations on the family's ability to dispose of the organs; as noted earlier, they cannot sell them, and they cannot take them home and place them on the mantelpiece.

The most celebrated case, Brotherton v. Cleveland,[14] involved a family that had made clear to the hospital its opposition to the removal of corneas, only to discover later that the coroner had removed them anyway because he had not reviewed the hospital records, where the refusal had been recorded. (The coroner's failure to review the hospital records was deliberate and routine, however, so that the coroner's determination of the cause of death would not be biased by the hospital's own conclusions.) The Sixth Circuit held that the family had a property interest in the decedent's organs, and that they were entitled to due process before the organs could be removed. While the court did not specify what would satisfy due process, it suggested that, at a minimum, the family was due some sort of hearing.

No case so far has held that the family can bring an action for conversion when organs are removed without consent. But cases recognizing a property right in someone else's organs seem to conflict with the majority position in *Moore*: If a family member can assert a sufficient property right in a decedent's body parts to compel due process, a living person might seem to have the right to control the disposition of his own body parts after they are removed, including the right to bring an action for conversion. Interestingly, the Ninth Circuit recently followed the

---

[12] See, e.,g., Maxwell Mehlman, Presumed Consent to Organ Donation: A Reevaluation, 1 Health Matrix 31 (1991).

[13] UAGA § 4(a) (1987).

[14] 923 F.2d 477 (6th Cir. 1991).

holding in *Brotherton* in Newman v. Sathyavaglswaran,[15] but did so without any mention of *Moore*.

Property Rights in Other Biological Materials

Similar property questions have arisen in connection with whether patents could be issued for living organisms and for the building blocks of life–genes and their constituents. For years, the law took the view that living organisms could not be patented because they were "products of nature." Thus, you could not patent a tiger, or even a previously-unknown plant species that you had discovered in the jungles of South America. The courts even went so far as to hold that manmade organisms—such as strains of bacteria that did not occur naturally and therefore hardly seemed "products of nature"—could not be patented.[16]

This changed with the landmark case of Diamond v. Chakrabarty,[17] in which the Supreme Court upheld the plaintiff's right to obtain a patent on bacteria that he had genetically engineered to consume oil spills. Subsequently, the Patent Office issued a patent for a genetically-engineered mouse that is susceptible to human cancers.

The bacteria in the *Chakrabarty* case were engineered using a gene-splicing technique called recombinant DNA. This same technique can be used to induce microorganisms to produce substances that occur naturally in the human body, like human growth hormone. In Amgen, Inc. v. Chugai Pharmaceutical Co., Ltd.,[18] the court held that the recombinant DNA process for producing erythropoeitin, a naturally-occurring substance in the body that stimulates the production of red blood cells, was patentable, even though the substance itself was a product of nature. One of the important ramifications of this decision involved the fact that the recombinant DNA process included the process of isolating and purifying–that is, decoding—the human erythropoeitin gene itself. Genes are regions of the DNA molecule that contain the instructions for the production of proteins, which in turn produce the structural and function aspects of the organism, or phenotype, that are genetically-inspired. The genes are made up of sequences of chemicals called nucleotides. To program a microorganism to produce human erythropoeitin, researchers had to unravel the nucleotide sequence that codes for that substance. Starting in 1990, the government poured billions of dollars into the Human Genome Project, the aim of which was to sequence the entire

---

[15] 287 F.3d 786 (9th Cir. 2002).

[16] Funk v. Kalo, 333 U.S. 127 (1948).

[17] 477 U.S. 303 (1980).

[18] 927 F.2d 1200 (Fed. Cir. 1991).

sequence of the human gene. By 2000, the project basically had been completed. The *Amgen* decision meant that patents in effect could be issued on the genetic sequences themselves. In short, human genetic sequences could be someone's property. This has led to a number of concerns. One is that, by requiring expensive licenses in order to employ their patented discoveries, the patent-holders would hamper further genetic research or the medical application of their discoveries. Yet to date, researchers have submitted thousands of patent applications for genes and gene fragments.

Another biomedical realm that has raised property issues is assisted reproduction. A number of the methods for overcoming infertility involve the use of eggs, sperm, and even the wombs of persons other than the would-be parent(s). The question is whether the persons whose eggs, sperm, and wombs are used can sell them. State laws generally prohibit the sale of the products, but permit payment for the "service" of providing the product. In some cases, the payments in question can be substantial. For example, newspapers on college campuses occasionally feature advertisements like the following: "Egg Donor Needed. Large Financial Incentive. Intelligent, athletic egg donor needed for loving family. You must be at least 5–10. Have a 1400+ SAT score. Possess no major family medical issues. $50,000. Free medical screening. All Expenses Paid."[19]

Why did the Court in *Moore* Reject a Property Claim?

This brings us back to Moore's complaint. The law clearly gives individuals a limited right to control whether or not their organs will be used for transplantation or research following their deaths. Some courts have recognized that families have a limited property right in the organs of their loved ones. Where there is no legal prohibition against commercialization, these property rights are even more clear cut: People can buy and sell their blood and hair, as well as, in effect, their eggs and sperm. Finally, by allowing them to be patented, the law regards living organisms and their underlying structures as someone's property. An action for conversion might well lie if a fertility clinic walked off with and sold someone's eggs or sperm, or if someone stole a bacterium that someone had patented. The question, then, is why the majority in *Moore* took such a dim view of the plaintiff's cause of action for conversion.

One answer is the majority's fear that allowing Moore to bring an action for conversion would disrupt the fledgling biotechnology industry. For example, the majority expresses its concern that granting individuals like Moore a property right sufficient to sustain an action for conversion

---

[19] Kenneth R. Weiss, The Egg Brokers, Los Angeles Times, May 27, 2001, at A1.

would cast a cloud over all the research that was performed using the derivatives from their cells. Not only the physicians who had removed his spleen and begun the process of creating the cell line but all downstream researchers who used the cell line might be liable for the tort, which would decrease their readiness to use the material. To understand the majority's concern, it is important to be aware of what was going on at the time the complaint was filed (1984) and at the time the case was decided (1990). What was happening was that the biotechnology industry was getting off the ground nationally, and especially in California. One of the earliest biotech companies, Genentech, was founded in San Francisco in 1976, went public in 1980, and licensed the first drug made with recombinant DNA technology, synthetic insulin, in 1982. That same year, the company received marketing approval from the U.S. Food and Drug Administration for its own recombinant DNA form of human growth hormone. Another biotech start-up, Amgen, opened for business in Sherman Oaks, California, in 1980. The Human Genome Project, a $3 billion federal project to issue grants to private researchers to map and sequence the human genetic code, began in 1990. The California biotechnology industry was poised to be in the front ranks of what Time Magazine in 1981, quoting the British publication The Economist, called "one of the biggest industrial opportunities of the late 20th century." The California Supreme Court definitely did not want to rock that boat.

On a more philosophical level, the concurrence by Justice Arabian reflects a concern that the human body is sacrosanct and should not be commodified–i.e., treated like any other type of property. This view has garnered widespread support from medical ethicists. Liberals object to the commercialization of medicine in general, while conservatives worry that commodifying the body would weaken opposition to abortion and to fetal and embryo experimentation. But Justice Mosk makes the interesting counter-argument that giving Moore a property right in his cells would enhance rather than decrease respect for the body.[20]

Conflicts of Interest in Medicine

Apart from the question of whether Moore had a property right in his cells, the case raises the issue of how economic self-interest may affect physician behavior toward patients. In theory, physicians are supposed to act as fiduciaries for their patients, placing their patients' interests foremost. But the patient-physician relationship is fraught with circumstances that create conflicts of interest, tempting physicians to sacrifice patient interests for their own self-interest. One context is

---

[20] 793 P.2d at 515–16.

medical research. Physicians can obtain significant financial rewards for conducting medical research, ranging from payments from corporate and government sponsors for enrolling patients in studies to lucrative equity interests in the commercialized results of their research. This has led to fears that physicians will compromise the welfare of their patients for economic gain. The majority opinion in *Moore* notes, for example, that a physician "may be tempted to order a scientifically useful procedure that offers marginal, or no, benefits to the patient."[21] In *Moore*, there was little doubt that the removal of Moore's spleen itself was beneficial and appropriate, but Moore did complain that his repeated postoperative trips to the defendants' hospital where blood and other substances were withdrawn were not for his benefit but to further the defendants' research program.[22]

The majority's concern over physician/researcher conflicts of interest is part of a larger set of problems created by managed care and other efforts to reduce health care spending. Managed care uses a number of techniques to encourage physicians to limit the amount of care that they provide patients. These techniques include profit-sharing and year-end bonuses; withholding a percentage of the physician's fee that is returned to the physicians only if they hold down expensive services like inpatient hospital admissions; and the threat of terminating the physician's membership in the managed care network. The concern is that physicians will respond to these incentives by denying patients access to medically-necessary care.

The question of what to do about these economic conflicts of interest is troubling for lawmakers, judges, and legal scholars. Some commentators urge that the law should prohibit physicians from placing themselves in situations in which these conflict can arise. Professor George Annas, for example, notes that ethical norms prohibit a transplant surgeon from pronouncing the death of a patient who might be an organ donor, so that the physician is not tempted to pronounce death prematurely in order to obtain the organs, and that physicians who perform abortions are not supposed to participate in medical research using aborted fetuses.[23] (As Annas points out, however, these are ethical norms that have not been embodied formally in the law.) Medicare prohibits physicians from entering into managed care arrangements in which a substantial portion of their earnings is based on how economically they care for their patients. But it would be impossible to prevent all conflicts

---

[21] 793 P.2d at 484.

[22] 793 P.2d at 484, n. 8.

[23] George Annas, Outrageous Fortune, Selling Other People's Cells, Hastings Ctr. Rep. Nov/Dec 1990 at 36, 38, cited in Judith Areen et al., Law Science, and Medicine, at 911–12, n. 2 (2d ed. 1996).

of interest between physicians and patients. After all, even before the rise of managed care when physicians were paid a separate fee for each service they provided, thereby giving them no economic motivation to withhold medically necessary services, physicians still faced a conflict of interest: They had an incentive to do too much for their patients in order to increase their revenues, including providing services that had little or no marginal value. Furthermore, prohibiting physicians from engaging in certain behavior that creates conflicts has its own social costs. For example, the law might be changed to prohibit Moore's physicians from having their patients participate in research, or from commercializing the results, but patients are a critical source of subjects, and denying physicians a right to enjoy the fruits of their research labors will hinder socially beneficial research.

Recognizing that conflicts of interest are inherent in the patient-physician relationship and that the circumstances in which they arise can provide significant social benefit, other commentators argue that patients simply need to protect themselves by looking out for their own interests. This view is put forward by a curious mixture of market and consumer advocates; the former believe that a market free of government intervention and legal rules will produce the most efficient results, while the latter want patients to play a greater role in medical decision-making. But this position assumes that patients will be able to spot a situation in which they need to protect themselves or to assert decision-making authority, and that they will have the ability to do so–that they will know what is in their best interest and have the bargaining power to make physicians act that way.

This has led to an intermediate approach which requires physicians to alert their patients to the presence of a conflict, instead of relying on patients to detect these situations themselves. This is the approach taken by the majority in *Moore*: "a physician must disclose personal interests unrelated to the patient's health, whether research or economic, that may affect the physician's professional judgment."[24] But this approach is by no means universally endorsed by the courts. In Neade v. Portes,[25] for example, the Illinois Supreme Court held that a patient does not have a cause of action against a physician for breach of fiduciary duty for failing to disclose economic incentives to limit care created by managed care. The majority opinion distinguished *Moore* on the basis that the alleged behavior of Moore's physicians was more egregious and that, unless Moore's doctors had disclosed their intent to commercialize his spleen cells, Moore would have no way to find this out, while under Illinois law, patients can obtain information about physician incentive

---

[24] 793 P.2d at 483.

[25] 193 Ill.2d 433, 250 Ill.Dec. 733, 739 N.E.2d 496 (2000).

arrangements by contacting managed care plans.[26] The Illinois court thus places the burden on patients to uncover the conflicts of interest, while the California court places an affirmative burden of disclosure on physicians. But under either approach, how realistic is it to expect patients to be able to look out for their own interests and protect themselves? How realistic is it, for example, to expect a patient like Moore, suffering from a form of cancer, to stand up to his surgeons and conduct hard-headed negotiations over the commercial value of his cells? If the surgeons had refused to give him a stake in the commercial venture, how likely is it that he would have delayed the operation while he sought the surgery from another set of physicians who were not planning to commercialize his cells? Who even wants to think about things like this when they are seriously ill?

Moore's Remedies

A final interesting point about the *Moore* case relates to the measure of damages.

If he had won his cause of action for conversion, what damages would he have been entitled to?

The general measure of damages for conversion is the value of the plaintiff's property at the time of conversion, plus the plaintiff's cost of pursuing the case. The difficulty in Moore's situation is deciding when the conversion took place and evaluating the value of his cells at that point. If the conversion took place when the cells were first removed, it can be argued that they had hardly any value because their eventual transformation into a lucrative line of immortal research cells was highly speculative. On the other hand, if the conversion is deemed to have taken place after the defendants had successfully commercialized the cell line, including obtaining a patent and entering into commercialization agreements with Genetic Institute and Sandoz, the value of the cells would be enormous.

Another problem with establishing the value of the cells is how to factor in the efforts of the defendants. When property is converted and then significantly altered by the efforts of another party, the law invokes the doctrine of "accession." Title to the property actually can transfer to the converting party if they make substantial improvements, in which case the original owner only receives the value of the property at the time of conversion. However, title would only transfer in this fashion if the conversion were innocent–in *Moore*, for example, if the defendants had acted in the good-faith belief that they owned the cells after they were removed from Moore's body. On the other hand, if the conversion is

---

[26] 739 N.E.2d at 505.

willful, the original owner will be awarded the enhanced value of the property, even though the value was enhanced by the efforts of others.[27] In addition, if the conversion is deemed to be willful, the plaintiff also might be awarded punitive damages.

In short, it is conceivable that, even if Moore had prevailed on a theory of conversion, he might have received little compensation beyond token payment for his cells and reimbursement for the costs of the litigation. On the other hand, if the court felt that the conversion was willful, Moore might have won a substantial award, an award that might have equaled or, thanks to punitive damages, even exceeded the value of the commercialized cell line.

What will Moore's damages be under the majority's theory of the case? The majority holds that he is entitled to damages for breach of fiduciary duty or for failure to obtain a patient's informed consent. Many commentators on the case interpret these causes of action essentially as a medical malpractice claim: a claim that the defendants negligently failed to act the way reasonable physicians should under the circumstances. In this instance, they point out, Moore's claim would be subsumed under California's medical malpractice reform law, MICRA, which limits damages to actual losses plus a maximum of $250,000 for pain and suffering. But if the defendants are deemed to have acted intentionally, a plaintiff in California also can recover punitive damages, notwithstanding MICRA.[28]

Interestingly, failure to obtain a patient's consent to treatment traditionally was considered an intentional tort of battery, since the defendant intentionally contacted the patient in a harmful or offensive manner without permission. With the rise of the doctrine of *informed* consent, however, courts by and large have transformed the failure to obtain a patient's consent into an action for negligence. Physicians not only are required to obtain their patient's permission to proceed with treatment, but to give patients the information necessary for the patient to make an informed decision. It is unlikely that Moore could have asserted a successful claim for battery under the traditional approach. He did, after all, consent to the surgery. Under the modern rules of informed consent, however, he could complain that the defendants had failed to inform him that they intended to commercialize his cells. As discussed earlier, the majority believes that this information was crucial for Moore because it would enable him to protect himself against the impairment of his physicians' medical judgment.

---

[27] See generally, Roy Hardiman, Comment: Toward the Right of Commerciality: Recognizing Propety Rights in The Commercial Value of Human Tissue, 34 UCLA L. Rev. 207, 253 (1986).

[28] See, e.g., Perry v. Shaw, 88 Cal.App.4th 658, 106 Cal.Rptr.2d 70 (2001).

One consequence of the transformation of the failure to obtain a patient's consent to treatment from a battery action to negligence is pointed out by Judge Mosk in his dissent: to prevail in an action for lack of informed consent, patients must prove "causation" just like in any other negligence action–namely, that had they been given the missing information, they would not have agreed to proceed with the recommended course of action.[29] As noted earlier, it is difficult to believe that Moore would have refused to have his cancerous spleen removed because his physicians were planning on commercializing his cells.

But the majority opinion not only allows Moore to proceed with a cause of action for failure to obtain his informed consent, but with an action for "breach of fiduciary duty." The majority seems to regard these as separate causes of action, but never makes clear whether there is a separate remedy for the latter. Historically, a breach of fiduciary duty gave rise to an action in equity. If property held in trust was misappropriated by the fiduciary for the fiduciary's own benefit, the court would impose a constructive trust on the property for the benefit of the beneficiary of the trust. Any value added to the property by the acts of the fiduciary were forfeit; it was as if the fiduciary had added the value for the benefit of the beneficiary. According to this approach, Moore would be entitled to the full value of his commercialized cells. The only deduction might be for value added by innocent third parties, and even then, the courts favor the interests of the beneficiary, and may relegate the innocent third party to recover its losses solely from the fiduciary.

It is curious that the majority opinion does not discuss these implications of its position. This omission has led some commentators to question whether the majority intended for the breach of fiduciary duty to constitute a separate cause of action, rather than just being another way of describing the failure to obtain Moore's informed consent as a simple negligence action for medical malpractice. In fact, courts increasingly are taking the view that there is no separate cause of action against physicians for breach of fiduciary duty to their patients, but instead, only an action for malpractice. The U.S. Supreme Court in Pegram v. Herdrich,[30] for example, opined that an accusation against an HMO for breaching its fiduciary duty to patients by failing to disclose financial incentives to limit care was nothing more than an allegation of medical malpractice, a view followed by the Illinois Supreme Court in Neade v. Portes, mentioned earlier.

In view of the likelihood that the majority did not contemplate a separate cause of action for breach of fiduciary duty, and given that Moore might well be unable to prevail in an action for failure to obtain

---

[29] 793 P.2d at 519.

[30] 530 U.S. 211 (2000).

informed consent because he would not be able to prove causation–
namely, that he would have refused to allow his spleen to be removed if
he had known that the surgeons were planning to commercialize it—
some commentators join Judge Mosk in describing the majority's remedy
as "unidirectional." The majority grants Moore the right to refuse to
permit the defendants to commercialize his cells, they point out, but he
is left with no meaningful remedy if they went ahead and did so anyway.

Judge Mosk goes even further, though. He asserts that the law gives
Moore no right to grant permission to commercialize his cells on the
condition that he share in the profits. This aspects of Mosk's view is
perplexing. If informed that his physicians proposed to commercialize his
cells, Moore in theory at least could refuse to allow them to remove his
spleen unless they agreed to give him a piece of the action. In an
analogous situation, a group of patients suffering from a rare disorder
called pseudoxanthoma elasticum established a tissue bank and permitted researchers to gain access to it only on condition that they signed a
contract giving the patients a share of any profits from their research.[31]
If the physicians refused, Moore in theory could seek the surgery
elsewhere. And if Moore did not have this alternative–for example, if his
condition were too advanced to permit him to find other surgeons–he
could argue that his consent was ineffective due to duress, an argument
that the California Supreme Court would be likely to uphold based on an
earlier decision, Tunkl v. Regents of the University of California.[32]

Conclusion

The issues raised by the *Moore* case continue to plague biomedicine.
An interesting illustration is a case filed by Washington University in
August 2003 against a former member of its faculty, William Catalano,
seeking to maintain possession of a repository containing thousands of
samples of human tissue and blood. Catalano collected the samples from
patients over a number of years in connection with his research on
prostate cancer. In February, 2003, he quit his position at Washington
University and joined the faculty at Northwestern University School of
Medicine. When Catalano sent letters to his former patients seeking
permission to take the samples with him, Washington University sued,
claiming that the samples, which have substantial value for research into
the genetic causes of cancer, were university property.[33]

---

[31] See Lori Andrews et al., Genetics: Ethics, Law and Policy 218, n.13 (2002).

[32] 60 Cal.2d 92, 32 Cal.Rptr. 33, 383 P.2d 441 (1963).

[33] Peter Shinkle, WU, Researcher Are Fighting Over Study Samples, St. Louis Post–
Dispatch, August 7, 2003, at A1.

The Catalano case pits the two theories of the *Moore* case squarely against each other. On the one hand, the university argues that the samples are its *property*: it owns the samples since they were collected as part of research conducted under its auspices. But Dr. Catalano asserts that, since he obtained the samples from his patients, the material should be treated like any other confidential patient data, and that patients have the right to protect their privacy by controlling what happens to that information, including after the ending of relationships with physicians. Therefore, Catalano insists, he can ask his former patients for *informed consent* to take the samples with him when he leaves. If the case is resolved under a property approach, then the university may prevail. But if the court decides the case under the informed consent doctrine that the majority of the court embraced in *Moore*, Dr. Catalano may have the better argument.

As this case demonstrates, conflicts over the control of potentially valuable biological material will continue to arise. If the law regards the material as property, it will have to decide to whom it belongs and what they can and cannot do with it. The same issues will be presented if the courts follow the approach in the *Moore* case, except that the question of control will be decided on the basis of privacy and autonomy rather than property considerations.

3

R.H. Helmholz

The Saga of *Van Valkenburgh v. Lutz*: Animosity and Adverse Possession in Yonkers

Adverse possession spawns litigation–too much litigation. The number of contested cases is quite considerable, even judging by the imperfect measure of appellate decisions. Very often the economic stakes are small and the costs of litigation are large. Relatively insignificant plots of land have been at issue. The odor of personal animosity between the parties all but rises from the pages of the printed reports. Something seems to be wrong. The law on the subject is old, but antiquity has not led to stability in the decisions.

The bitter contest over a small piece of land in Yonkers, New York, one that was fought out as part of a long-running quarrel between members of the Van Valkenburgh and Lutz families from 1947 until 1968, provides a good example of some of the factors that lie behind this unhappy state of affairs. The litigation between these parties also illustrates many of the things that have long bedeviled this area of the law–uncertain legal standards in the courts, deep personal animosity between the litigants, and relevant facts the parties and witnesses remember and characterize very differently.

This particular dispute is well known to students of the law of real property from the opinion rendered by the New York Court of Appeals in 1952.[1] The opinion has been included in the best selling Casebook currently used in First Year Property courses and has also attracted the attention of several commentators.[2] All credit to the Casebook editors.

---

[1] Van Valkenburgh v. Lutz, 304 N.Y. 95, 106 N.E.2d 28 (1952).

[2] Jesse Dukeminier and James E. Krier, *Property* 129 (5th ed. 2002). It is also printed in Patrick Rohan, *Real Property: Practice and Procedure* § 2.06[1] (1981) and described in

They have picked a case that is as interesting in human terms as it is illuminating of the dilemmas involved in the law of adverse possession. They have not been deterred by academic criticism that describes the case as "notorious" and holds that it is in urgent need of overruling.[3] The case is illuminating. Not all of the complications are apparent in the opinion itself. However, some of them are stated; others are at least hinted at; and examination of the circumstances that lay behind the case brings still others to the surface.[4] In a fuller look at them lies a lesson about the law of adverse possession. In the cases, the facts are often complex and disputed. The legal merits and the equities are often clouded. The decisions are not easy to reconcile.

The Place

Map A, prepared for purposes of municipal taxation in 1984, provides a one-dimensional view of the land that was the subject of *Van Valkenburgh v. Lutz*. It shows the taxable lots in this part of Yonkers, essentially as they were laid out in 1912. The area in dispute in the litigation is the six-sided, but roughly triangular, lot at the bottom of the Map. Hereafter referred to as "the triangular parcel," it is marked by crosses. It measures from 150 to 126 feet by 170 feet.

Map B, prepared by the U. S. Army Corps of Engineers in the late 1940s, gives a quite different, and more realistic, view of the same land at the time of the lawsuit. Gibson Place was not actually connected with Leroy Avenue, as it is shown to do on Map A. Nor did the row of suburban houses suggested by the orderly lots laid out along Leroy Avenue exist. The small black areas represent buildings (not necessarily to scale). There was thus a considerable area of vacant land behind the Lutz house. It extended to Courter Avenue, the street at the left, that runs roughly parallel to McLean Avenue, the curving street at the bottom.

The Land

The City of Yonkers lies along the Hudson River in Westchester County, just north of the border with New York City. It has a proud

---

James Winokur, R. Wilson Freyermuth, and Jerome Organ, *Property and Lawyering* 180 (2002).

[3] Lila Perelson, *New York Adverse Possession Law as a Conspiracy of Forgetting: Van Valkenburgh v. Lutz and the Examination of Intent*, 14 Cordozo L. Rev. 1089, 1091 (1993) (hereinafter cited as Perelson, *Intent*). It is described as a "good case to avoid" by Roger Bernhardt, *Teaching Real Property Law as Real Estate Lawyering*, 23 Pepperdine L. Rev. 1099, 1118, no. 67 (1996). *See also* Charles Callahan, *Adverse Possession* 3–11 (1961).

[4] Perelson, *Intent*, supra note 3, at 1098–1104.

history. In 1900, it was "unapproached by any other municipality of
[Westchester] county."[5] Today, Yonkers has its share of the many
problems that plague many medium sized American cities.[6] But neither
civic pride nor municipal problems come much into the quarrel that led
to *Van Valkenburgh v. Lutz*. The quarrel that led finally to the New York
Court of Appeals was one between neighbors–neighbors who had come to
hate each other.

As far as the participants were concerned, the events that led to the
quarrel began early in the twentieth century. Before then the triangular
parcel, located in the very southern part of the village, had been part of
what was known as "The Murray Estate". The term "Estate" almost
certainly gave too grand a name to the reality, however, even then. For
one thing, although one of the briefs to the case described it as including
467 acres, an 1881 Atlas listed the lands owned by the Murray family as
including twenty acres or less.[7] For another, the land involved was (and
is) exceedingly hilly and rocky. In the words of a description of the time,
it was "a piece of rugged wilderness" and indeed "one of the wildest
spots in the city."[8] Only in some parts could it have been used for any
kind of agriculture, still less for activities appropriate to the tastes of a
leisured class. The triangular parcel that would figure in litigation was
covered with trees and outcroppings. It was difficult of access from
outside. Even when the construction of houses began, it was never on
the scale or with the same opulence that marked the land to the
immediate north known as the Park Hill District. The Park Hill District
is now applying for designation as an historical landmark site; its
application states diplomatically that the area to its south "differ[s] from
the character of the historic district."[9] A conversation with the authorities at the Yonkers Historical Society confirms that this is no idle claim.

In fact it is only in recent years that several parts of the area
surrounding the triangular parcel have been developed at all. Single

---

[5] Frederic Shonnard and W. W. Spooner, *History of Westchester County, New York* 559
(1900); Charles Elmer Allison, *The History of Yonkers from the Earliest Times to the
Present* (Introduction) (1896).

[6] On the present problems, see, e.g., George Raymond, Rebuilding our Cities: Urban
Renewal in Westchester County, in: *Westchester County: The Past Hundred Yeas 1883–
1983*, 250–51 (Marilyn Weigold, ed. 1983).

[7] *Atlas of Westchester County New York from Actual Surveys and Official Records* [by
G. W. Bromley & Co.] 22–23 (1881).

[8] *See* Application, Park Hill Historic District, Yonkers, NY (Application of Residents'
Association and Park Hill Land Conservancy submitted to the City of Yonkers Landmarks
Preservation Board), at http://www.parkhillyonkers.org/hd_web.html (last visited June 17,
2003), at 13.

[9] Ibid., at 3.

family residences were built on Gibson Place north of the land in question during the 1990s, but only a few were there before that date. At the time of the start of the dispute in the 1940s, the Lutz house was still the only dwelling house west of Leroy Avenue in its immediate vicinity, although there were houses farther north and some to the west. The land just behind the house to the west, including the triangular parcel, was wooded and rocky. And no residence had been built there or on many of the other lots shown in Map A. Thus, although the land at issue in *Van Valkenburgh v. Lutz* was within a few hundred feet of the northern border of New York City, it was essentially unoccupied at the time Lutz began the activities that would give rise to his claim of adverse possession. For many years, the Lutz family was its only serious users.

More active settlement of all the land had, however, been envisioned from an earlier time. In 1912, the lots on Map A taken from "The Murray Estate" were divided as shown. They were offered for sale to the public. William and Mary Lutz bought lots 14 and 15. The other lots attracted buyers too, but no residents. Perhaps because of the absence of access–the roads came later–only the Lutz family built a house there. The land to the west of that house was partly flat, however, and Eugene Lutz used it to gain access to his own house in preference to the difficult ascent from what became Leroy Avenue. He chose a route at the north end of the triangular parcel, referred to as "the traveled way" by those who lived nearby. This long continued usage is the source of the prescriptive easement he was held to have acquired in subsequent litigation with the Van Valkenburghs.

The land in dispute is now occupied by a parking lot (capacity 75 cars) for worshippers at the Greek Orthodox Church of the Prophet Elias. The church eventually purchased the land from the litigants in the case and is now the largest landowner in the immediate vicinity. According to the Church's pastor, even that uncomplicated use of the triangular parcel required something like two tons of dynamite to prepare. The parking lot also had to be constructed on two distinct levels because of the difficulty of the terrain. To the east, a steep hill precluded easy access to Leroy Avenue, even after the road was paved (as it was not at the time of Lutz's purchase). The route is usable today, but particularly in the winter when it snows, access remains challenging. The incline was steep enough that the house in which the Lutz family lived was barely visible from Leroy Avenue.

The People

William Lutz and his wife, Mary, bought lots 14 and 15 at the initial sale of the Murray Estate in 1912. They were newly married at the time, and William gradually built a house for his family on the land, aided by his brother, Charlie. It had been completed by 1920, and the family (the couple had had five children by 1921) moved into the house. William, who was employed in New York City as an electrician at the time, left his job in 1928 in order to repair a broken pipeline that supplied water to the house. He did not return to the City. Whether he would have been welcomed back is not clear in the record, but whatever the reality, he chose to remain in Yonkers, earning a living by a succession of odd jobs and the revenue he was able to raise by selling produce from a garden. During these years, he and the rest of his family made regular use of "the traveled way" to reach their house. They also made at least intermittent use of the rest of triangular parcel. What that usage amounted to in the eyes of the community and the law turned out to be a crucial question. It will be discussed in due course, but it was admitted by all concerned that William had cleared at least parts of the area and made use of it.

William died in 1948, soon after the beginning of the feud with the Van Valkenburghs in 1946. By that time, he had made his opposition to them and their claims to the land clear enough. He had argued heatedly about it with Joseph Van Valkenburgh, and he had chased one of Joseph's children off the triangular parcel, threatening (according to one account) to kill the child with an iron pipe he held in his hand. Van Valkenburgh had him arrested for criminal assault in 1947, a time when William must have been a tired man, for he died the next year. William devised all his land (and the on-going litigation that went with it) to his wife, Mary, who herself later transferred all her interest in both to Eugene Lutz, the only one of their children to remain in Yonkers. By then, Eugene had himself purchased other lots in block 54, including lots 17 and 18, the southernmost tracts in Map A. He carried on the dispute with the Van Valkenburghs, with the spirit of persistence and animosity he shared with his father.

The Lutz family members were thus long-time residents of the neighborhood and have remained so. They have never been well-to-do, that seems clear from the record. William eked out a living in unpromising circumstances. He supported his family as best he might, and his son Eugene owned and operated a filling station in the community. However, the Lutz family seem to have won the friendship and support of most of their neighbors. Several of them testified on their behalf in his dispute with the Van Valkenburghs.

It is true that the dispute embittered the Lutz family. It left scars and made them edgy. When Lila Perelson, then a student at Cardozo Law School, contacted Eugene in preparing her study of the case, she found him to be a decidedly "hostile man". He refused even to speak with her. His reception of Father Nicholas Palavas, pastor of the nearby church, was similarly unfriendly when the priest first knocked at the door of the Lutz house.[10] As the years went on, however, the two men established better relations, and Father Palavas recently described their relationship as "excellent" up to Eugene's death just a few years ago.

Father Palavas is not so complimentary about Joseph D. Van Valkenburgh, whom he had come to know at the time of the adverse possession litigation. Describing him as "a tough guy", the priest remembered him without fondness. A man of ability, no doubt, but no friend. The two managed to establish at least a half-way decent relationship. The priest was able to purchase the Van Valkenburghs' land for the expansion of his church, and Joseph was willing to haggle with his buyer over the price, substantially reducing it in the course of negotiations. But the relationship lacked mutual cordiality.

The Van Valkenburghs themselves belonged to a different level of society than the Lutz family (and probably the Greek Orthodox priest). The family maintains an extensive web-site, complete with an elegant family coat-of-arms.[11] The site traces the ancestry and accomplishments of the descendants of Lambert of Valkenburgh, who came to the New World with his wife, Annetie Jacobs, in 1644 and settled in Manhattan. Members of the family hold periodic reunions and publish at least an occasional newsletter. They keep meticulous genealogical records. Nothing like that can be said of the Lutz family.

Joseph D. Van Valkenburgh himself seems not to have been a particularly prominent member of the family. He was associated with the family publishing firm in New York City, and was described by those who knew him in Yonkers as "well off", but he earned no place in *Who's Who*, and it has been impossible to find an obituary for him in the *New York Times*. In April, 1947, his wife, Marion, was chosen to be executive director of the now defunct American Woman's Association,[12] a women's club organized "to advance the economic, the cultural and social interests [of women] in their chosen fields of endeavor."[13] It was a public honor indicative of the family's status in society as well as her own public spirit. By contrast, Joseph, though not a diffident man, seems to have been content to remain outside the spotlights of public life.

The Disputes

The Lutz family had been making use of the triangular parcel between their house and Courter Avenue for twenty-five years when the

---

[10] Perelson, *Intent, supra* note 3, at 1106–07.

[11] http//www.vanvalkenburg.org

[12] *See* N.Y. Times, April 1, 1947, at 34, col. 2.

[13] *See The A.W.A. Bulletin*, May 1, 1930, at 3.

dispute with the Van Valkenburghs first broke out. Access to their house via "the traveled way" had long been their main purpose. But it was not the only one. The Lutz family would later claim that they made regular and adverse use of the parcel, plowing it and exploiting it to raise fruits and vegetables. They also employed it as a kind of general repository for household purposes. Dump might be the right word. Used cars, old furniture, and other debris were left there. Lutz built a small shack on the property at some point, although how substantial it was is now difficult to ascertain. No enclosure of the land or permanent change to the land's character is mentioned in the evidence, however, and some of their neighbors said that most of it had remained wild and uncultivated. In any event, the Lutz family made no formal claim to the land, and they paid no taxes on it. They did make some use of it. One could see that much. But the triangular parcel cannot have been an ornament to the neighborhood, if indeed anyone cared.

The Van Valkenburghs did care. Joseph D. and Marion Van Valkenburgh purchased land and built a house on Courter Avenue in December, 1937. They could see the Lutz house from their own and obviously they had a good view of the triangular parcel that separated them. At first there could have been no dispute involving land itself, however, since they had as yet no interest in it. Moreover, they did not actually live in the house they had constructed. Exactly why they thought it was a good idea to own it is not now evident in the record. Perhaps they expected their children to live there. According to Father Palavas, they themselves lived elsewhere, probably in New York City. They came to the Yonkers property from time to time to keep things in decent order. Joseph obviously cared about his investment in the house and grounds, and it does not require a leap of the imagination to suppose that he would have found the triangular parcel to the east of his house something of an eyesore when he did come.

The Van Valkenburghs allowed their children to play on the triangular parcel. Out of one such incident arose the first recorded "run-in" between the two families. It happened in April of 1946. Again, there were two different versions of exactly what took place, but it was common ground at the time that William Lutz had chased the Van Valkenburgh children off the lot, and that he and Joseph exchanged hard words in consequence. Lutz was not all words either. He must have struck Van Valkenburgh's son as part of the incident, since he was arrested and ultimately convicted of criminal assault at the instigation of Van Valkenburgh. Someone, probably Lutz, later attempted to have Joseph arrested for criminal trespass. From that point, it must have been obvious that the two would not be good neighbors. Things got worse.

The next year brought opportunity for the Van Valkenburghs and trouble for the Lutz family. The owners of the triangular parcel (whoever they were) had not kept up payment of their property taxes, and the City of Yonkers held a tax sale to clear the back taxes. Van Valkenburgh bought the tax title, paying $379.50 and receiving a deed from the City dated April 14, 1947. He quickly conveyed the land to his wife, Marion. His reasons for the conveyance are still not clear; he certainly did not withdraw from the fray. Lutz himself had not been notified of the tax sale. Perhaps straitened financial circumstances would have kept him from taking part in any event, and he may not have cared. At least there was no record of an objection to the lack of notice before the sale in the abundant litigation that followed.

Having made the purchase, Van Valkenburgh was determined to assert his rights. He had his lawyer send Lutz a registered letter, informing Lutz that he (and his wife) were now owners of the triangular parcel and meant to occupy it. He had the land surveyed, determining that Lutz's garage encroached slightly on the area they owned. He insisted that this mistake be rectified on the ground. He visited Lutz personally, coming in the company of two policemen and demanding that Lutz remove the garden, the chicken coop, and whatever other debris Lutz had been accustomed to leaving on the land. Van Valkenburgh also erected two fences across the traveled way, blocking Lutz's access to his house from the west.

These aggressive actions provoked a response from Lutz. He found a lawyer, and with his help Lutz brought suit against the Van Valkenburghs to establish his right to an easement over the traveled way. Access would have been his most immediate problem. Without it, his house was hard to reach from outside and he had employed it since his house had been there. A trial before an Official Referee ended in a judgment in Lutz's favor, and this was affirmed, unanimously but without opinion, by the Appellate Division on June 21, 1948.[14]

This suit turned out to have been a tactical mistake on Lutz's part. It would later be used against him. In law, it amounted to an admission that title to the triangular parcel lay in the Van Valkenburghs. Asserting a prescriptive easement impliedly conceded the title to the land in holder of the servient tenement; it was thus an admission on the record that Lutz recognized he held no title to the land and that Van Valkenburgh did. Similar admissions, even if made informally, have long been troubling in adverse possession cases. When made after the statute of limitations has run (as could be argued in this case), the claimant can argue that his admission of lack of title was merely a mistaken statement about who owned the land and of no legal relevance. However, they

---

[14] Lutz v. Van Valkenburgh, 274 A.D. 813, 81 N.Y.S.2d 161 (1948).

often harm the adverse possessor's case, because they tend to negative the "claim of right" that is required in many jurisdictions for title to ripen. They can be used to describe the character of the claimant's possession as lacking the requisite intent to establish a right to the land while the statue was running. Moreover, Lutz had agreed to remove his personal property from the triangular parcel in response to Van Valkenburgh's earlier demand. This too was an admission that he recognized his own lack of title. He may have been confused, of course. He may have known nothing whatsoever about adverse possession. Perhaps he thought Van Valkenburgh would be satisfied by a show of good will.

If this was Lutz's reaction, he was to be disappointed. Only his death on August 28, 1948, saved him from the indignities of further litigation. He died knowing what was coming, however. Process in the next suit was served against him about four months before he died. It was the opening of a suit in ejectment brought by the Van Valkenburghs. Apparently Lutz had not fully removed "the garage, shed, shack, hut, chicken coop, and other structures" he had placed on the triangular parcel.[15] At least that was what the complaint alleged. The successor defendant, Mary Lutz, who was the widow, executrix, and sole legatee of William, carried on in his place, assisted by a new lawyer and their son Eugene. They responded by a counterclaim of their own, asserting title to the triangular parcel based on adverse possession of more than thirty years. Only fifteen was required at the time. The stage was set for resolution of what one commentator would later describe as a "Dickensian adverse possession struggle over ownership of two rather dismal lots in Yonkers."[16]

The Decision

The Van Valkenburghs were the ultimate victors in the ensuing litigation. Most aspects of the road to a decision in their favor are stated clearly enough in the decision of the New York Court of Appeals. Judge Dye wrote the opinion and Judge Fuld the dissent. The points raised by the case and found to be legally determinative need not be rehearsed here at any length. It is worth noting, however, that the result was far from foreordained. The Lutzes were successful in the first instance. A trial held before Judge Frederick Close of the Supreme Court for Westchester County came out in their favor.[17] The Supreme Court,

---

[15] Perelson, *Intent, supra* note 3, at 1103.

[16] Joseph Rand, *Understanding why Good Lawyers Go Bad: using case studies in teaching cognitive bias in legal Decision–Making*, 9 Clinical L. Rev. 731, 732 (2003).

[17] Van Valkenburgh v. Lutz, 125 *N.Y.L.J.* 770, col. 3 (March 2, 1951).

Appellate Division, affirmed in a brief, four to one opinion.[18] The initial result was thus to vest Mary Lutz with fee title to the triangular parcel. The Van Valkenburghs were undeterred by initial failure. They again appealed, and they prevailed before the New York Court of Appeals.

The majority opinion in that Court held: 1) Lutz had not adequately proved that the family's use of the land was substantial enough to meet the law of adverse possession's requirement of actuality; 2) Lutz had not shown the requisite "claim of title" because he merely used the triangular parcel intermittently, all the while knowing that it belonged to someone else; and 3) Lutz, having succeeded in establishing an easement, could not later disavow the effect of a judgment favorable to himself by claiming title in the land itself. A strong dissent, joined by two other judges, insisted there had been "ample evidence to sustain the [trial court's] finding that William Lutz actually occupied the property in suit for over fifteen years under a claim of title," and found fault with the majority's opinion for violating the court's "constitutional provision that limits our jurisdiction to the review of questions of law."[19]

Whatever one thinks of the outcome, the 1952 decision should have brought an end to the litigation. In fact it did not. Eugene Lutz quickly made a motion for re-argument, which was denied.[20] Still unwilling to let the matter drop, by 1960 he had began again, bringing suit in the name and as guardian *ad litem* for his uncle, Charles Lutz, who had occupied some of the same property. The new action described the Van Valkenburghs as "squatters or intruders, licensees, no long entitled to possession."[21] The contentions and issues were virtually identical to the earlier litigation, however, and this new effort also failed. But the end did not come until the spring of 1968, again by a decision of the New York Court of Appeals.[22]

Commentary

Academic commentary on *Van Valkenburgh v. Lutz* has not been kind to the opinion. It is true that the decision has lately been cited as providing an example of a "pliability rule" that serves several goals in the law,[23] but most comments have gone the other way. The law reviews

---

[18] Van Valkenburgh v. Lutz, 278 A.D. 983, 105 N.Y.S.2d 1003 (1951).

[19] Van Valkenburgh v. Lutz, 304 N.Y. 95, 105, 106 N.E.2d 28, 33 (1952).

[20] Van Valkenburgh v. Lutz, 304 N.Y. 590, 107 N.E.2d 82 (1952).

[21] Matter of Lutz, 11 A.D.2d 746, 205 N.Y.S.2d 956 (1960).

[22] Lutz v. Van Valkenburgh, 52 Misc.2d 935, 277 N.Y.S.2d 42 (1967), affirmed, 21 N.Y.2d 937, 237 N.E.2d 84, 289 N.Y.S.2d 767 (1968).

[23] Abraham Bell and Gideon Parchomovsky, *Pliability Rules*, 101 Mich. L. Rev. 1, 55 (2002).

of four New York State law schools took note of the case at the time, and they did so unfavorably. One of them concluded that the Court of Appeal had left the jurisdiction "without a workable criterion of what constitutes adverse possession."[24] The editors of one casebook, which describes the case briefly, use it as an example of "the confusion to which some courts have fallen prey."[25] The most extensive discussion of the case concluded ruefully that the opinion was "so contradictory in terms of the hostility requirement that it cannot be used as a precedent."[26] Commentators have sought to marginalize the case as standing by itself.[27]

All the same, the decision has not been overruled. Indeed it continues to be cited with apparent approval in New York cases, some of them in situations remarkably like those which gave rise to the earlier case.[28] The most recent assessment of the situation found just as much confusion in the current New York case law of adverse possession as had been there in the aftermath of *Van Valkenburgh v. Lutz*.[29]

It will not be the object of the remainder of this account to argue that the critics of the case's holding are wrong and the Court of Appeals was right. Doing so would only lead the author into more hot water. It is true that the law of the case leads to uncertainty in the law and unpredictability in the outcome of litigation. It is also undeniable that there are cases that go the other way, cases which state that the mental state of the user of land is quite irrelevant in determining whether or not he has possessed the land adversely. There are, however, three more general points about the case and the law of adverse possession that may usefully be made in any discussion of the cases and its implications.

First, *Van Valkenburgh v. Lutz* does not stand alone, in New York or elsewhere. Pretending it does is an exercise in wishful thinking. In many cases, what a user of land has known about the title of the land has affected the character of his possession. It has swayed the opinions of many (but not all) judges. One way or another, claimants like the Lutzes,

---

[24] Note, 27 St. John's L. Rev. 151, 153 (1952). *See also* Note, 17 Alb. L. Rev. 181 (1953); Note, 19 Brooklyn L. Rev. 145 (1952). A measured assessment was given by Elmer Million, *Real and Personal Property*, 27 N.Y.U.L. Rev. 1067, 1068–71 (1952).

[25] *See* Winokur, Freyermuth, and Organ, *Property and Lawyering*, *supra* note 00, at 180. *See also* Lawrence Berger, *Unificataion of the Doctrines of Adverse Possession and Practical Local in the Establishment of Boundaries*, 78 Neb. L. Rev. 1, 4–5 (1999).

[26] Perelson, *Intent*, *supra* note 3, at 1104.

[27] *See, e.g.*, Robert Parella, *Real Property*, 47 Syr. L. Rev. 681, at 705–06, n. 216 (1997).

[28] *See, e.g.*, DaCostafaro v. DeVito, 289 A.D.2d 765, 766, 733 N.Y.S.2d 817, 818 (2001); Weinstein Enterprises, Inc. v. Pesso, 231 A.D.2d 516, 517, 647 N.Y.S.2d 260, 261 (1996); Yamin v. Daly, 205 A.D.2d 870, 871, 613 N.Y.S.2d 300, 301 (1994).

[29] Robert Parella, *Real Property*, 51 Syr. L. Rev. 703, 716–22 (2001).

who are aware they have no right to be on the land they occupied, have been held to lack the requisite hostility or claim of right. Call them "squatters" or call them something more polite, they are attempting to take advantage of consciously wrongful acts, and not all judges are willing to treat that conduct as equivalent to an honest mistake. This may be contrary to the better view. It does lead to inconsistency in the law. But it is the fact. Students of the law may legitimately ask what the proper course should be for a lawyer dealing with an adverse possession claim. Law professors have the luxury of proclaiming which rule is right; lawyers in practice usually do not.

Second, in considering the merits of the case, one might take notice of what appears to be a more general movement turning away from adverse possession. Cases like *Van Valkenburgh v. Lutz* may be considered as part of this broader movement of opinion. Adverse possession has always fit awkwardly together with Recording Acts and Marketable Title Acts. It is thus settled law that statutes allowing it are to be strictly construed because they deprive record owners of their land.[30] But today there is also criticism coming from other directions. It is said that restricting the scope of the doctrine will further the goals of the environmental movement by protecting wild lands from encroachment.[31] It is said that an expansive notion of adverse possession is inconsistent with goals of economic rationality.[32] It is said that adverse possession may have been suitable for a society where the supply of land was ample, but in modern conditions it is "succumbing to new priorities."[33] And even committed advocates of the rights of the poor recognize that "squatting" is a problematic response to the urban housing shortage.[34]

---

[30] *See, e.g.*, Peters v. Smuggler–Durant Mining Corp., 930 P.2d 575, 580 (Colo. 1997).

[31] John Sprankling, *An Environmental Critique of Adverse Possession*, 79 Cornell L. Rev. 816 (1994); William Ackerman and Shane Johnson, Comment, *Outlaws of the Past: A Western Perspective on Prescription and Adverse Possession*, 31 Land & Water L. Rev. 79 (1996); Shane Raley, Legislative Note, *Color of Title and Payment of Taxes: the New Requirements under Arkansas Adverse Possession Law*, 50 Ark. L. Rev. 489, 518–20 (1997).

[32] Jeffrey Stake, *The Uneasy Case for Adverse Possession*, 89 Geo. L.J. 2419 (2001); Thomas S. and C. F. Sirman, *An Economic Theory of Adverse Possession*, 15 Int'l Rev. L. & Econ. 161 (1995); Noel Elfant, Comment, *Compensation for the Involuntary Transfer of Property between Private Parties: Application of a Liability Rule to the Law of Adverse Possession*, 78 Nw. U.L. Rev. 758 (1984).

[33] Warsaw v. Chicago Metallic Ceilings, Inc., 35 Cal.3d 564, 575, 676 P.2d 584, 590, 199 Cal.Rptr. 773, 779 (1984); Finley v. Yuba County Water Dist., 99 Cal.App.3d 691, 697, 160 Cal.Rptr. 423, 427 (1979); Swan v. Seton, 629 So.2d 935, 938 (Fla. Ct. App. 1993); Meyer v. Law, 287 So.2d 37, 41 (Fla. 1973).

[34] Eric Hirsch and Peter Wood, *Squatting in New York City: Justification and Strategy*, N.Y.U. Rev. L & Soc. Change 605 (1987); Brian Gardiner, Comment, *Squatters' Rights and*

Adverse possession is not on the verge of disappearance, one may say. It serves a vital function in our law. However, those among academic commentators who take a strictly "internalist" view of the doctrine (and the author of this chapter admits he probably belongs to this group) may be swimming against the tide.

Third, there is the nagging question of what, if anything, could have been done about the hatred between the Van Valkenburgh and the Lutz families. Their mutual animosity was long-running. It was intense. It is only half-hidden in the judicial opinions, and it must stand out in any exploration of the dispute that led to the litigation. Historians say that litigation was originally an alternative to the feud.[35] In this situation, litigation was one means of carrying on a feud. Bargaining between them in order to reach the socially optimal result did not come within the picture.[36] It could not have.

Recognizing this, one still cannot be certain that the courts could have done much better. Litigation is an imperfect means of composing differences. But it is also hard not to wonder whether more creative solutions might have played a larger part in bringing such disputes to a happier conclusion. Professor Merrill has endorsed one such possibility, and there may well be more ways of restoring a modicum of peace between the parties.[37] Otherwise, *Van Valkenburgh v. Lutz* may be an edifying saga, but it is a sad one.

Adverse Possession: a Search for Equitable Application of Property Laws, Ind. Int'l & Comp. L. Rev. 119 (1997).

[35] *See, e.g.*, 2 William Holdsworth, *A History of English Law* 43 (4th ed. 1936).

[36] *See* Ward Farnsworth, *Do Parties to Nuisance Cases Bargain after Judgment? A Glimpse inside the Cathedral*, 66 U. Chi. L. Rev. 373 (1999).

[37] Thomas Merrill, *Property Rules, Liability Rules, and Adverse Possession*, 79 Nw. U.L. Rev. 1122 (1984–1985).

*

4

Susan F. French*

Gruen v. Gruen: A Tale of Two Stories

Like much litigation over gifts, *Gruen v. Gruen*[1] arose after the purported donor's death and pitted a child of a former marriage against the widow. Unlike most such litigation, however, there was no doubt that Victor Gruen really did intend to give the painting to his son, Michael, and there was no suggestion that in doing so he treated his widow, Kemija, unfairly. Why, then, did it take a seven-day trial and two appeals to establish Michael's ownership of the painting? Ah, therein lies a tale, a tale of two stories. First, there is the family story and, then, there is the legal story. Both are interesting. Sit back, relax, and I'll tell you the tale.[2]

---

* Professor of Law, UCLA Law School.

[1] 68 N.Y.2d 48, 505 N.Y.S.2d 849, 496 N.E.2d 869 (1986).

[2] I obtained the information I am about to share with you from the legal record, the internet, newspaper archives, and telephone conversations with three of the four lawyers involved in the case, one of whom was Michael Gruen, the plaintiff. The legal record I consulted consisted of the three briefs filed in the Appellate Division of the New York Supreme Court, respondent's brief in the New York Court of Appeals (appellant's brief was not available to the retrieval service I used), the Appellate Division's opinion, 488 N.Y.S.2d 401 (1984), and the Court of Appeals' opinion, 496 N.E.2d 869 (1986). The internet sources I used were sites maintained by the Austrian Press & Information Service in Washington, D.C., www.austria.org/oldsite/jul00/exile.html; the American Heritage Center of the University of Wyoming, http://ahc.uwyo.edu/digital/gruen/intro.htm, Gruen Associates, the firm Victor founded in Los Angeles, www.gruenassociates.com; the Artnet Research Library, http://www.artnet.com/library/; the Klimt museum maintained by Expo–Shop.Com at http://www.expo-klimt.com/; the site maintained by Michael Gruen's firm, Vandenberg & Feliu, www.vanfeliu.com/bio_gruen.htm; and the Martindale–Hubbell Law Directory on Lexis. Where I have referred to Web sites in the footnotes, these are the sites to which I refer if nothing more specific appears. Newspaper articles I used are cited at appropriate places in the text. The telephone conversations I had were as follows: Victor Muskin, lawyer for plaintiff, Michael Gruen, on March 22, 2003; Michael Gruen, who appeared pro se in the

I.   The Family Story, or "A Famous Man and a Fabulous Painting"

Victor Gruen, born Viktor Grünbaum in Vienna, Austria, on July 18, 1903, became a famous and successful architect and urban designer, but not without struggle. During his training as an architect at the Akademie der Bildenden Künste in Vienna, he was subjected to anti-Semitic harassment, but managed to complete his training and opened his first architectural office in 1932. He worked on projects rebuilding shops and apartments in downtown Vienna. As a young man in Vienna, he was active on the cultural scene, collaborating on plays with Jura Soyfer, a leftist playwright, and founding a political cabaret where he performed regularly in anti-Nazi satirical revues.[3] One day, sometime after Hitler annexed Austria in 1938, Viktor arrived at his office to find his erstwhile clerk, dressed in a high-ranking Nazi officer's uniform, sitting at his (Viktor's) desk. The firm had been "aryanized" and Viktor was now the employee. Viktor rushed out of the office, found a telephone, and called home. His wife, Litzi, told him that he must not come home—the Gestapo was there. Fearing for his life, he went to the cabaret and donned a German officer's uniform used in one of its revues. Back in the street, he was able to hitch a ride with some unsuspecting German recruits to an airfield and managed to fly out to freedom.[4]

Viktor made his way to New York where he found work as an architect and changed his name to Victor Gruen. He soon formed a partnership with Elsie Krummeck, a native New Yorker and industrial designer who had studied at the Parsons School of Design. The firm designed specialty shops in New York until the department-store magnate, Joseph Magnin, lured them to Los Angeles in 1940.[5] Victor and Elsie married in 1941 and had two children, Michael and Peggy. The Gruen & Krummeck firm broke up in 1948 and Elsie and Victor divorced in 1951, but they both stayed in Los Angeles.[6] In 1949, Victor and Rudolf

---

New York Court of Appeals, on March 27, 2003; and Paul S. Whitby, lawyer for defendant, Kemija Gruen, on April 7, 2003.

[3] See www.austria.org/oldsite/jul00/exile.html.

[4] Susanna Baird, "Victor Gruen's Return Home to Vienna" http://ahc.uwyo.edu/digital/gruen/return.htm. Susanna Baird was Michael Gruen's first wife. The account on the Austria Web site is somewhat less dramatic. It suggests that Victor worked as an employee in his old office for a while, saying that he was assigned by his former clerk to work on "designing buildings and interiors for 'Strength through Joy,' the Nazi sports and tourism scheme for the masses. But he did not stay on that job very long, for soon he managed to emigrate."

[5] See Myrna Oliver, *Elsie Krummeck Crawford: Artistic Industrial Designer*, (obituary),Los Angeles Times, June 3, 1999, Part A, p. 26,•Metro Desk, and the Austria Web site.

[6] After the divorce, Elsie married architect Neil Crawford and continued designing—everything from toys to fabrics to planters for airport parking lots. LA Times, *supra*, note 5.

Baumfeld, another Austrian émigré and classmate of Victor's from architecture school, founded Victor Gruen Associates in Los Angeles. The firm became highly successful and opened additional offices in New York and Washington, D.C. It remains successful to this day.[7] Victor became famous as the inventor of the suburban shopping mall,[8] and went on to establish a reputation as a major urban planner and designer.[9]

After his divorce from Elsie, Victor married Lazette Van Houten.[10] They maintained a house in Los Angeles, an apartment in New York, and a pied-à-terre in Vienna. Although Victor's son Michael grew up in Los Angeles living with his mother, he also spent so much time in New York that he says on his Web page[11] that "he thinks of himself almost as a native."

1959 was an important year in this story. Michael finished high school that spring, having spent his last year at the Lycée Jaccard in Lausanne, Switzerland,[12] and then, during the summer, vacationed with Victor and Lazette in Austria. During that vacation, the three of them met Kemija, who was later to become Victor's fourth wife. She was working as a maid in a hotel where they stayed.[13] During that same year, the Gallerie St. Etienne in New York put on the first one-man show of Gustav Klimt's work in America, and Victor and Lazette bought his "Schloss Kammer am Attersee II" for $8,000.

Gustav Klimt (1862–1918) was a well-known Austrian artist who worked in Vienna in the late 1800s and early 1900s. The Schloss Kammer am Attersee II, an oil on canvas painted in 1909 or 1910 and measuring 110 x 110 centimeters (a little more than 43 x 43 inches), is

---

[7] See www.gruenassociates.com. Current firm projects range from an interior design for a restaurant to master plans for Pusan, South Korea, and Valencia, California.

[8] Northland, near Detroit, opened in 1954; Southdale, the first enclosed mall, opened near Minneapolis in 1956. His concept of the suburban mall was that it should function as a town center with cultural and civic activities as well as shopping and entertainment.

[9] Wolf Von Eckardt, *The Urban Liberator: Victor Gruen and the Pedestrian Oasis*, Washington Post, Feb. 23, 1980. This article written shortly after Victor's death, describes him as "one of the most important architect-planners of our time" and said that he was "the first architect-planner, as distinct from an urban philosopher such as Lewis Mumford, to stem the tide of the new technocratic vision of the human habitat, the calamitous 'City of Tomorrow' with its Autobahnen and glass towers, that Mies, Gropius and the Swiss-born Frenchman Le Corbusier, had in store for us."

[10] Respondent's Brief in the Court of Appeals p. 5 [hereafter Respondent's Brief, Ct App.]. Paul Whitby, Kemija's lawyer, says that Victor was "crazy about" Lazette.

[11] See www.vanfeliu.com/bio_gruen.htm.

[12] *Id.*

[13] Respondent's Brief, Ct. App. pp. 3, 6.

one of five that Klimt painted of the Schloss Kammer. Located on the Attersee, a lake near Salzburg, Austria, Schloss Kammer was Klimt's favorite vacation spot. Victor and Lazette had the painting delivered to their New York apartment, where it hung until the summer of 1963. You can see an image of the painting at http://www.expo-klimt.com/1_3.cfm?ID=-335260456.

Schloss Kammer am Attersee II[14]

---

[14] This image reprinted by permission, Christie's Images Ltd. (2004). To see other works by this artist, visit the www.expoklimt.com website.

Michael Gruen entered Harvard in the fall of 1959 as a member of the class of 1963. Three years later, in July, 1962, Lazette died. Sometime before Lazette's death, Kemija had come to work as a maid for Victor and Lazette in their Vienna household. After Lazette's death, Kemija offered to come to the United States with Victor.[15] Seven months later, on Feb. 28, 1963, Victor and Kemija were married[16] and we come to a critical point in the story. On March 13, 1963, Victor wrote a letter to Michael from Los Angeles[17] noting Michael's approaching 21st birthday and "announcing that he intended to give him an important present worthy of the occasion."[18] The next day, March 14, 1963, Victor's lawyer, Ralph Erickson, wrote the following internal memo:[19]

> VG is making present gifts of all his art objects to Peggy and Michael. Gift tax returns will be filed and each object tagged or identified in some manner as belonging to one of the children.
>
> The amount of the gifts will exceed the annual exclusions but the returns will be filed claiming some of the specific exemption so no federal gift tax will be payable. A small state gift tax will be payable in each instance, however.
>
> VG is also giving the Hillman-Minx outright to Peggy. It is of no significant value.

On March 25, 1963, Victor spent Michael's twenty-first birthday with him in Boston. A few days later, Michael received a letter from Victor sent from Los Angeles.[20] Dated April 1, 1963 the letter said: "I am sending enclosed a written confirmation of your most important birthday present. I hope that it will take a long time before you can enjoy it."

A few weeks later Michael received two more letters from Victor.

---

[15] Conversation with Paul Whitby. He suggested that Victor was devastated by Lazette's death and was not going to return from Vienna to the U.S. until Kemija assured him that she would return with him and take care of him.

[16] Respondent's Brief, Ct App. p. 6.

[17] Appellant's Brief, Appellate Division p. 8 [hereafter Appellant's Brief, App. Div.].

[18] Respondent's Brief, Ct. App. p. 6.

[19] *Id*. p. 19; Respondent's Brief, App. Div. p. 18.

[20] Appellant's Brief, App. Div. p. 8–9.

May 22, 1963

Dear Michael:

I wrote you at the time of your birthday about the gift of the painting by Klimt.

Now my lawyer tells me that because of the existing tax laws, it was wrong to mention in that letter that I want to use the painting as long as I live. Though I still want to use it, this should not appear in the letter. I am enclosing, therefore, a new letter and I ask you to send the old one back to me so that it can be destroyed.

I know this is all very silly, but the lawyer and our accountant insist that they must have in their possession copies of a letter which will serve the purpose of making it possible for you, once I die, to get this picture without having to pay inheritance taxes on it.

Love,
Victor

Beverly Hills, California
April 1, 1963

Dear Michael:

The 21st birthday, being an important event in life, should be celebrated accordingly, I therefore wish to give you as a present the oil painting by Gustav Klimt of Schloss Kammer which now hangs in the New York living room. You know that Lazette and I bought it 5 or 6 years ago, and you always told us how much you liked it.

Happy birthday, again.

Love,
Victor

As requested, Michael returned the original gift letter to Victor on May 24 and kept the others. Shortly thereafter, he graduated from Harvard and returned to Los Angeles to go to UCLA Law School. He showed the gift letter to his mother, Elsie, who later testified in the trial that he had "exhibited great pleasure" at the gift.[21] Sometime in that same spring or summer of 1963, Victor gave up the New York apartment and shipped the painting to his home in Los Angeles.[22]

---

[21] Appellant's Brief, App. Div. p. 34.

[22] Appellant's Brief, App. Div. footnote* p. 9.

The painting remained in Victor's possession until his death in 1980, except for a period in 1964 and 1965 when he loaned it to the Baltimore and Guggenheim Museums for an exhibition. Victor took complete responsibility for the painting during his life, paying for the insurance, authorizing restoration work, deciding whether to allow others to use it, and deciding when and how to ship it when he moved it from New York to Los Angeles, and later to Vienna. He never physically handed over the painting to Michael and never tagged the painting to show Michael's interest or ownership;[23] nor did he list Michael as an owner when he loaned the picture to the museums. The catalog of the exhibition simply said the painting was "from the collection of Victor Gruen." Finally, Victor did not file a gift tax return even though the value of the painting exceeded the threshold amount required for filing a return. However, Victor repeatedly told people that he had given the painting to Michael, and in his letter authorizing restoration work, he stated that the authorization was given on Michael's behalf.

Victor retired from his U.S. practice sometime in the late 1960s and he and Kemija moved back to Vienna, where he opened a new office. A story written by Michael's first wife, Susanna Baird,[24] tells of a visit she and Michael, and their baby daughter, made to Vienna in 1968 or 1969 at the time Victor opened his new office there. The night before the opening festivities, Victor took them for a tour of the new office building. Just as they were leaving, a black Mercedes limousine pulled up and out jumped a fellow who greeted Victor expansively. Victor recoiled and ordered him to leave at once, threatening to call the police. It turned out the man was Victor's former Nazi clerk and "Aryan overseer" who had taken the office from him in 1938. Much shaken, Victor abandoned his plans to have dinner with them that evening and returned home.

In 1972, the painting was shipped from Los Angeles to Victor and Kemija's home in Vienna, where it remained until he died. In Vienna, Victor continued to show visitors the painting and tell them that it belonged to Michael. There is no doubt that Kemija knew about Victor's gift of the painting to Michael. In addition to showing that she had filled out the papers for shipping the painting to Vienna, which showed Michael as the owner, Michael testified that on several occasions Kemija tried to persuade him to exchange the Klimt for one of her own paintings.[25] Before Victor died, she even asked Michael to give her the

---

[23] Michael claimed that the trial court's finding on this point was not supported by the evidence, which showed only that there was no tag visible on the front of the painting. Appellant's Brief, App. Div. p. Addendum 1.

[24] The story can be found in the Gruen archives at the University of Wyoming Web site, www.uwadmnweb.uwyo.edu/AHC/digital/gruen/return.htm.

[25] Appellant's Brief, App. Div. pp. 6–7.

name of a warehouse to which she should ship the painting because she did not want to "baby-sit" his Klimt after Victor's death.

In the year before Victor died, Michael tried to persuade Victor to allow the painting to leave Austria for an exhibition in London. Victor applied for an export permit stating on the application that he owned the painting and had bequeathed it to his heirs on his death.[26] However, Victor was much opposed to letting the painting travel, and it remained in the Vienna apartment until he died in February, 1980. After Victor's death, Michael attempted to collect the painting, but Kemija refused. Interestingly, at that time she did not deny that Victor had made the gift to Michael or claim that the gift was invalid. Instead, she claimed that the painting in the apartment was a copy, not the original. She claimed variously that Victor had sold the original to buy jewelry for her, that Victor had willed the painting to her, that the original had been stolen, and that she had cut the painting out of its frame, rolled it up, and taken it to Switzerland in a suitcase.[27]

Failing to persuade Kemija to turn the painting over to him, Michael called in the law. He was by then an experienced litigator. At UCLA Law School Michael was not only editor of the school newspaper, but he was also a member of a championship moot court team. After graduation in 1966, he was admitted first to the bar of California in 1966, and then to the New York bar in 1967. He went to work in New York as an associate at Paul, Weiss, Rifkind, Wharton & Garrison. After three years there, he moved on to several different firms, including opening his own office in 1975.[28] In the early 1980s he was practicing in partnership with Victor Muskin at Gruen, Muskin & Thau.[29]

Michael first sued Kemija in Austria. Under Austrian law, Victor's gift of the painting would apparently have been ineffective because the gift letter was not sufficiently formal—it had not been executed before a notary and lacked necessary stamps. However, an expert opinion letter

---

[26] This permit application figured prominently at the trial as part of Kemija's argument that Victor had not relinquished control of the painting before his death. It may not have been related to Michael's desire to send the painting to London for an exhibition, however, but to Victor's concern that Michael might not be able to get the painting out of the country after his death. Victor apparently had not notified the Austrian government when he brought the painting into the country. See Appellant's Brief, App. Div. pp. 49–50. Since it was by a famous Austrian painter, was regarded as a national treasure. Conversation with Victor Muskin.

[27] Michael's lawyer, Victor Muskin says that they never seriously believed that she had cut it out of the frame because of the effect that would have had on its value. Telephone conversation with Victor Muskin.

[28] See www.vanfeliu.com/bio_gruen.htm.

[29] See the briefs filed on appeal in the *Gruen* case.

from a California lawyer persuaded the court that title to the painting had passed to Michael under California law.[30] While the Austrian case was pending on appeal, Kemija made a trip to New York. Tipped off by an old friend that she was in town, Michael stayed up all night preparing papers to start a lawsuit in New York. Early the next morning, an associate from his firm served Kemija at her hotel and *Gruen v. Gruen* was under way.

Michael enlisted his then partner, Victor Muskin to represent him in the case. Born in 1942 like Michael, Victor graduated from Oberlin College in 1963 and received his J.D. from New York University Law School in 1966. Victor handled the case at trial and argued the first appeal to the Appellate Division of the New York Supreme Court. Although Victor appeared on the brief at the Court of Appeals, Michael also appeared pro se and argued the case himself. Property buffs will be interested to learn that in about the same period that *Gruen v. Gruen* was getting under way, Michael was representing the plaintiff in the famous takings case, *Loretto v. Teleprompter Manhattan CATV Corp.*[31]

Kemija was represented by Paul S. Whitby, then a partner at Hall, Dickler, Lawler, Kent & Howley. Born in 1947, Paul was five years younger than Michael and Victor Muskin, and had spent five fewer years at the bar. Paul received his B.A. from the University of Utah and his J.D. from Columbia Law School. He was admitted to practice in 1972. Paul was assisted in the case by his associate, Wendy Williamson, who had just graduated from Columbia Law School in 1981.[32] She obtained her B.A. at Princeton in 1977. Kemija found her way to Paul Whitby through Michael's first wife, Susanna Baird, who had retained Paul in connection with some post-divorce issues regarding Michael's obligations

---

[30] Telephone conversation with Michael Gruen.

[31] 458 U.S. 419 (1982). Michael won in the U.S. Supreme Court. Reported opinions in the case begin with a New York trial court order denying the plaintiff's claim, entered March 14, 1979, and include two unsuccessful appeals in the New York state courts, the successful appeal to the United States Supreme Court decided in 1982, an opinion of the New York Court of Appeals after remand on Feb. 17, 1983, and a denial of a motion for reargument on April 28, 1983. See Westlaw Keycite tab. The case, which appears in most property casebooks, held that legislation authorizing a permanent physical invasion of property by a third party is a "per se" taking. The importance and social utility of the purpose are irrelevant, as is the lack of economic harm to the landowner.

[32] Wendy was the only lawyer involved in the case I did not talk to. Despite sending a letter and an email, and leaving a telephone message explaining the purpose of this project, I was never able to reach her. A 1981 graduate of the Columbia University School of Law, she is now a corporate attorney with Anderson Kill & Olick in New York. Her bio on the firm's Web page says that she has "extensive experience litigating in both federal and state courts." See www.andersonkill.com/Bios/williamsonh.asp. *Gruen v. Gruen* must have been one of the first cases she was involved in.

to pay child support.[33] This connection was to prove critically important for the trial, as you will see.

As Michael and Kemija prepared for the showdown over the painting, both had able champions. Looking at their educational backgrounds, it should come as no surprise that the fight was a good one.

II. The Legal Story, Part I: The Trial

At first glance, gift law looks pretty simple. All it takes to make a gift is intent, delivery, and acceptance—and acceptance is presumed if the gift is beneficial to the donee. But looks can be deceiving. There is actually quite a bit of doctrinal complexity in both the intent and delivery requirements and, even when the rules are clear, there is considerable room for judges to determine outcomes by their interpretation of the facts. As one recent commentator observed "[A] close examination of the cases leaves a reader with the sense that ad hoc considerations of fairness and justice or propriety do much of the work in leading judges to decisions."[34]

A. Doctrinal Complexity

As a preliminary note, one of the complicating factors in the *Gruen* case was the question whether California or New York law governed the validity of Victor's attempted gift to Michael. In 1963, at the time of the gift, Victor and Michael were both domiciled in California and Victor sent the gift letters from California, but the painting was located in Victor's apartment in New York. At the time of trial, it appeared that the choice of law could make a big difference because California's law was both clearer than New York's and appeared to be much more favorable to Michael.

1. Intent

Beyond the very basic question whether the donor intended to make a gift at all, gift cases often present the question whether the donor intended to make an inter vivos gift or a testamentary gift. Inter vivos gifts may be made by delivery of the property or by delivery of a deed to the property, but testamentary gifts must be made by will. Deeds and wills are both written instruments signed by the transferor, but they differ in the time at which the transfer of the property takes place and in the formalities that are required. A deed transfers an interest in property to the grantee when it is delivered; a will does not transfer a property interest to the beneficiary until the testator's death. Until modern times,

---

[33] Telephone conversation with Paul Whitby.

[34] Roy Kreitner, *The Gift Beyond the Grave: Revising the Question of Consideration*, 101 Colum. L. Rev. 1876, 1906 (2001).

a deed required a seal, but today may require nothing more than the grantor's signature. A will requires the signatures of two witnesses in addition to that of the testator. Some states, like California, also recognize holographic wills, which do not require witnesses, but must be in the testator's handwriting. At the time of the *Gruen* case, neither New York nor California required that a deed or other instrument of gift be sealed.

When the donor retains possession or use of the property for his lifetime, as Victor Gruen did, the heirs or devisees often argue, as Kemija did, that the intended gift was testamentary, and therefore void because not made by a will. An inter vivos transfer gives the donee rights with respect to the property during the transferor's lifetime. A will, however, has no effect until the testator's death—the beneficiary has no rights in the property until the testator dies. When the donor retains possession or use of the gift property, a court might reach any one of three possible conclusions as to the donor's intent: (1) the donor intended to transfer full title to the donee immediately and then kept possession with the donee's consent or acquiescence (the donor became a bailee of the property); (2) the donor intended to transfer a future interest to the donee which gave the donee the right to possession at the donor's death (the donor became a life tenant); or (3) the donor did not intend to transfer anything to the donee until the donor's death (donor remains full owner; donee has a "mere expectancy"). If the court reaches either of the first two conclusions, the gift is inter vivos and may be made by delivery. If it reaches the third conclusion, the gift is testamentary and is invalid unless made by will.

In thinking about what Victor Gruen might have intended, it is helpful to look at the practical consequences of these three different gifts. If Victor intended to give Michael full title to the Schloss Kammer painting in 1963, for example, he would have given up any right to do anything with the painting thereafter without Michael's permission. He would not have had the right to allow others to exhibit it or do restoration work on it, and Michael could have claimed possession at any time. When Michael wanted to send the painting to London for an exhibition in 1979, he would not have needed Victor's consent.[35] If Victor intended to give Michael only a remainder, however, retaining a life estate for himself, Victor would have retained the right to use and possess the painting, and allow others to do so, during his lifetime. Michael would have had no right to possession until Victor's death and could not have loaned the painting out without Victor's consent. Any income produced by the painting during his life would have belonged to

---

[35] This is not to say that he might not have wanted to get Victor's agreement for other reasons, like family harmony, respect for his father's wishes, or the like.

Victor. As life tenant, it would be normal for Victor to pay for insurance on the painting and to make necessary repairs. He would have had a life tenant's duty not to commit waste. By contrast to the two inter vivos gifts, if Victor intended to make a testamentary gift to Michael, no property rights would have passed to Michael until Victor's death. Until then, Michael would have had a "mere expectancy," which receives little or no legal protection.[36] While Victor was alive, he could have sold the painting, given it away, pledged it to secure a loan, damaged it, or changed his mind and given it to Kemija in his will, and Michael would have had no legal grounds for complaint.

The legal consequences that flow from the court's choice of the possible interpretations of such a gift are usually dramatic. If the court finds that a testamentary gift was intended, the gift fails if the donor did not use a written instrument that can be admitted to probate as a will. In the *Gruen* case, for example, Victor's letters could not have qualified as a will in either New York or California because they were neither witnessed nor in Victor's handwriting. Thus, if Kemija could persuade the court that Victor did not intend to give Michael any rights in the painting until after his death, she would win on that ground alone. Even if the court finds that an inter vivos gift was intended, however, the choice between finding that the donor intended to give a present or a future interest may have dramatic consequences. Under the federal estate tax law,[37] the full value of the gift property at the donor's death will be included in calculating the amount of taxes due at the donor's death if the donor retained a life estate. By contrast, if the donor transferred the full title to the donee when the gift was made, the gift property is not included in the donor's taxable estate. A gift tax may have been due when the gift was made, but the amount of tax is based on the value of the property at that time. In the *Gruen* case, the difference was significant. We know that the painting was worth $8,000 in 1959 and over $5,000,000 in 1987. We don't know exactly what it was worth in 1963, but it surely was a lot less than it was worth when Victor died in 1980. Michael argued vigorously that Victor intended to transfer full title to him in 1963.

Under New York law, although not under California law, it was possible that additional consequences might flow from determining that Victor intended to retain a life estate, rather than to transfer full title to Michael at the time of the gift. Two New York cases, discussed in the next section, suggested that an attempt to give away a remainder interest in the painting while retaining a life estate was void.

---

[36] His expectancy might be protected against tortious interference by a third party, but would not be protected against a change of heart by Victor.

[37] Internal Revenue Code § 2036.

2. Delivery

Under California law it was clear that delivery of the letters to Michael was effective to make the gift so long as Victor intended to make an immediate transfer either of full title or a remainder interest in the painting.[38] Under New York law, however, there were two potential delivery problems. First, there was a question whether a donor who retained possession for life could make an effective gift of tangible personal property at all; and second, there was the question whether, even if such a gift was allowed, it could be made without physically handing over the property.

Two New York cases addressed the question whether a gift of a remainder was valid if the donor retained a life estate. In *Young v. Young*, decided in 1880, the decedent had put envelopes containing bonds into a safe which both he and one of his sons used. On the envelopes, which he signed, decedent noted that a certain number of the bonds belonged to one son and the rest to his other son, but that the interest on the bonds was "owned and reserved" by him during his lifetime and that, at his death, "they belong absolutely and entirely to them and their heirs." The decedent did not hand the envelopes to his son, but simply placed them in the part of the safe where his son's papers were kept. During his life, decedent clipped the coupons from the bonds and collected the interest. After his death, his heirs claimed the bonds belonged to his estate and the court agreed.

The court recognized that the purpose of such a gift (retaining the interest for life) could "undoubtedly be accomplished by a proper transfer to a trustee and perhaps by a written transfer delivered to the donee," but decedent had neither created a trust nor delivered a written transfer to his son. Without a written transfer, the court said that the only way the gift could have been made would have been by an absolute delivery of the bonds to the donee "vesting the entire legal title and possession in him, on his undertaking to account to the donor for the interest which he may collect thereon." The court went on to say: "But if the donor retains the instrument under his own control, though he do so merely for the purpose of collecting the interest, there is an absence of the complete delivery which is absolutely essential to the validity of a gift."[39] Since Victor did deliver a written transfer to Michael, this case

---

[38] Failure to deliver the painting could be used to argue that Victor intended to make a testamentary rather than an inter vivos gift, but if the court found he intended to make an inter vivos gift, delivery of the letters was all that was required. See Calif. Civ. Code § 1147; Gordon v. Barr, 13 Cal.2d 596, 91 P.2d 101 (1939); Driscoll v. Driscoll, 143 Cal. 528, 77 P. 471 (1904).

[39] Young v. Young, 80 N.Y. 422, 431 (1880).

would not have been dangerous to Michael's claim, except that the court did not stop there. It went on to say:[40]

> [D]elivery is essential to gifts of chattels *inter vivos*. It is an elementary rule that such a gift cannot be made to take effect in possession in *futuro*. Such a transaction amounts only to a promise to make a gift, which is *nudum pactum* . . . . There must be a delivery of possession with a view to pass a present right of property. "Any gift of chattels which expressly reserves the use of the property to the donor for a certain period, or (as commonly appears in the cases which the courts have had occasion to pass upon) as long as the donor shall live, is ineffectual." (Schouler on Pers. Prop. Vol. 2, p. 118, and cases cited; Vass v. Hicks, 3 Murphy [N.C.], 494.[41]) *This rule has been applied even where the gift was made by a written instrument or deed purporting to transfer the title, but containing the reservation.*

The other New York case that posed potential danger for Michael was *In re Ramsey's Estate*,[42] a 1950 Surrogate's Court opinion. In that case, Milton Ramsey Sr., age 67, married Ruby Cabe, age 26, in 1938. Just before his marriage Milton Sr., executed and recorded a deed conveying a 7.5 acre farm to his son, Milton Jr., together with the "household furniture . . . , all farm tools, equipment, including butchering tools, trucks and personal property used in connection with said premises . . . subject to the rights of the life use of the above premises and the personal property," which were reserved to the grantor. After delivering the deed to his son, and before his death in 1944, Milton Sr. sold some of the personal property and moved most of the rest of it to another farm he owned. There some of it was destroyed in a fire. Milton Sr.'s will left all his household furniture to Ruby and the balance of his estate to his infant son, a child of his marriage to Ruby. After Milton Sr. died, Milton Jr. filed a claim against the estate for some of the missing items.

The court declared the gift of the personal property void on the ground that there was no delivery of the personal property to Milton,

---

[40] *Id.* at 435–436 (emphasis added).

[41] The citation of a North Carolina case is interesting because North Carolina seems to be the only state that follows the English common law rule that legal future interests in personal property cannot be created at all. See Woodard v. Clark, 236 N.C. 190, 72 S.E.2d 433 (1952). If you are interested in how the English reached that result, see 7 William S. Holdsworth, *History of English Law* 470–71 (1926); and if you are interested in how North Carolina, alone among the states, came to follow it, see John Chipman Gray, *The Rule Against Perpetuities* 75–78 (3d ed. 1915).

[42] 98 N.Y.S.2d 918 (Surrogate's Court, Lewis County, 1950).

Jr.,[43] but it also quoted the statement from *Young v. Young* to the effect that no gift with a retained life estate was valid. The court in *Ramsey* reached the curious result that delivery of the deed was effective to make a gift of the real property with a retained life estate, but ineffective as to the personal property. As a practical matter, the decision allowed the court to avoid the messy problem of determining whether Milton Sr. really intended to give up the right to sell or dispose of the personal property during his lifetime. As a doctrinal matter, however, the decision rests on the ground that a gift of tangible personal property cannot be made by delivery of a deed.[44]

Even though the English common law had moved beyond the seemingly primitive idea that ownership of property can only be transferred by physical delivery of the property as early as 1468,[45] the idea cropped up again in the United States. At the time of the *Gruen* case, New York was not the only state in which there were doubts about whether gifts of tangible chattels could be made by delivery of a written instrument. A 1956 A.L.R. annotation, "Delivery as Essential to Gift of Tangible Chattels or Securities by Written Instrument,"[46] concludes that:

> [N]o general rule that an informal instrument will or will not sufficiently substitute for delivery of the gift can be stated with any degree of assurance since while, in a substantial majority of the cases where the question has been presented it has been held that there was no sufficient showing of a gift, it is frequently not clear whether the court was relying upon the absence of delivery of the subject of the gift, or had decided adversely to the donee upon other grounds, such as that the instrument insufficiently evidenced the donor's donative intent or that the instrument itself had not been effectively delivered.[47]

In her arguments, Kemija also quoted another statement from the New York Court of Appeals on the delivery requirement. Although this

---

[43] As an alternate ground, the court found that Milton Sr. revoked the gift by executing his will leaving the same property to his wife and infant son before Milton Jr. had accepted the gift. Since Milton Jr. accepted the deed, the court again seems to be saying that the personal property could be transferred only by physical delivery, not by deed.

[44] By this time, the New York courts had recognized that gifts of intangible property could be made by written instrument, so this decision, if good law, meant that there was a different rule for tangible and intangible property. See discussion by the Appellate Division in *Gruen*, 488 N.Y.S.2d at 406.

[45] Harlan F. Stone, *Delivery in Gifts of Personal Property*, 20 Colum. L. Rev. 196, 199 (1920).

[46] 48 A.L.R.2d 1405.

[47] *Id.* at § 2.

case, like *Young v. Young*, did not involve a written instrument of gift, the statement does not caution the reader to limit the doctrine stated to oral gifts:[48]

> The delivery necessary to consummate a gift must be as perfect as the nature of the property and the circumstances and surroundings of the parties will reasonably permit.... There was in the case now before us no possible reason for a symbolical delivery.... It is true that the old rule requiring an actual delivery of the thing given has been very largely relaxed, but a symbolical delivery is sufficient only when the conditions are so adverse to actual delivery as to make a symbolical delivery as nearly perfect and complete as the circumstances will allow.

Under California law, Michael's only problem at trial was to convince the court that Victor intended to make an inter vivos rather than a testamentary gift—that his retention of possession of the painting did not negate an intention to make a present gift. Under New York law, Michael faced the additional problems that the court might apply these old delivery cases either to hold that no gift of a remainder with retained interest was valid, or that such a gift could not be made without physical delivery of the painting.[49] However, these cases were old and the two Court of Appeals opinions were distinguishable because the cases did not involve gifts attempted by delivery of a written instrument of transfer. The *Ramsey* case, which did say a gift of a chattel could not be made by delivery of a deed had little precedential value since it was not an appellate decision.

3. Acceptance

A transfer of an interest in property is not complete until the transferee accepts the property, but if the transfer is beneficial to the transferee, acceptance is presumed. Michael might have anticipated a little difficulty in persuading the court that Victor had intended to make an inter vivos, rather than a testamentary, gift, and some greater difficulty in showing that the delivery requirement had been met; but if those two problems were overcome, acceptance should have followed as a matter of course. Surprisingly, it did not turn out that way.

B. The Trial: Strategy and Tactics

Going into the case, all the equities were with Michael. It was clear that Kemija had no moral claim to the painting and that Victor had

---

[48] In re Van Alstyne, 207 N.Y. 298, 100 N.E. 802, 806 (1913)

[49] Although neither Michael nor his father was in physical proximity to the painting when the gift was made, a court so inclined might conceivably have decided that Victor should have physically delivered the painting to Michael when they were all back in Los Angeles after the summer of 1963.

wanted Michael to have it. Victor and his third wife, Lazette, bought the painting. Kemija knew about the gift to Michael. There was no evidence that Victor had not provided for Kemija. Indeed, she must have been the residuary beneficiary under his will because she claimed that she took the painting under it. In this contest between the stepmother—a fourth wife—and the decedent's son, the stepmother must have looked greedy and unsympathetic. For a court sympathetic to carrying out Victor's wishes, it would have been easy to find the gift valid. The language of Victor's letters and his subsequent statements that he had given the painting to Michael provided a sound basis for concluding that he intended an inter vivos gift. Delivery of the letters clearly satisfied California requirements for such a gift. Even if the court concluded that New York law applied, the authorities against Michael's position were old and ill suited to the modern world. What court in the 1980s would want to hold that a gift of a valuable painting could not be made by delivery of a written instrument, or that—using a writing—it was not possible to make a gift while retaining a life estate? Paul Whitby, Kemija's lawyer, had a difficult case.[50]

At the outset, it must have appeared to Michael and his lawyer, Victor Muskin, that their most difficult problems would be getting past the New York Deadman Statute[51] and persuading the court that Victor had intended to transfer full title to Michael in 1963, rather than retaining a life estate for himself, in order to avoid potential estate or inheritance tax problems. For Paul Whitby, his problem was to persuade the court that it should disregard the language of the gift letter to find that Victor did not intend to make a present gift, or to take an archaic position with respect to delivery or creation of future interests in chattels, or to overcome the strong presumption in favor of acceptance of the gift. Whitby's problem would be nearly insurmountable if the judge was the least bit progressive or analytical in his approach to gift law and was sympathetic to the idea that Victor's wishes should be carried out if possible. After a seven-day trial, the judge issued a lengthy opinion[52] in

---

[50] Even he says that everybody knew Victor intended Michael to have the painting. Telephone conversation with Paul Whitby, supra.

[51] The Dead Man Statute made testimony of a party about a personal transaction or communication with the decedent inadmissible. Michael was thus prevented from testifying about the letter he wrote Victor thanking him for the gift and other communications he had with Victor. Testimony Michael claimed was improperly excluded is described in Appellant's Brief, App. Div. pp. 49–52 and in Appellant's Reply Brief, App. Div. pp. 27–28. There is a copy of the Dead Man Statute in Appellant's Brief, App. Div. p. Addendum 6.

[52] I have not seen the trial court opinion, but Paul Whitby says it was 70 or 80 pages long and tracked quite closely the analysis presented in his post-trial brief. Conversation with Paul Whitby.

which he ruled for Kemija on every substantive issue.[53] The trial judge ruled that New York law applied and that the gift failed because Victor did not deliver physical possession of the painting to Michael, because Victor intended to and did retain full rights of control for his lifetime, and did not intend the gift to become effective until his death. He also ruled that the gift failed for lack of acceptance. How did this happen? Through four brilliant tactical legal maneuvers by Whitby.

First, Whitby successfully moved to bifurcate the trial so that the question whether Michael had title to the painting was tried first.[54] Only if Michael succeeded in establishing the validity of the gift would the court proceed to the question of remedy. Bifurcation allowed Paul to keep out evidence about what Kemija might have said or done with the painting after Victor's death. The only relevant evidence was that bearing on the question whether Victor had made a valid gift to Michael, which was important because Whitby did not want evidence of Kemija's behavior after Victor's death to prejudice the proceedings. She did not even come to New York for the trial.

Second, Whitby was able to build a stealth case for applying New York law. To avoid calling attention to his intentions, he did not file a pre-trial brief. Instead he prepared separate briefs on each question he anticipated might come up during the trial, and used them when appropriate. At the end, he filed a post-trial brief laying out all Kemija's arguments. In cross examining Michael's witnesses, Whitby was careful to avoid questions about anything that might have transpired in California. Instead, he asked lots of questions about time they had spent with Victor in New York, Victor's activities in New York, and Victor's New York apartment. According to Whitby, by the time the plaintiff's case rested, there was lots of evidence in the record about Victor's ties to New York and very little about his ties to California.[55]

Third, Whitby argued that Victor's motivation was to avoid estate and inheritance taxes on the painting when he died, rather than to give Michael any present interest in the painting. The statement in Victor's

---

[53] He ruled against Kemija on some of her attempts to exclude testimony by various people that Victor had told them he had given the painting to Michael.

[54] Michael initially opposed the motion, but then agreed to severing the issue of title to the painting. He appealed denial of his motion for a new trial, which was based on a claimed misunderstanding about the scope of the issues to the tried first—particularly whether Kemija's affirmative defense that Michael had released his interest in the painting back to his father in exchange for some later gifts could be tried in a later phase. See Appellant's Brief, App. Div. p. 56, Respondent's Brief, App. Div. p. 66. Kemija does not appear to have pursued the issue of release after Michael's win on appeal.

[55] There may have been more evidence of Victor's contacts in California than Whitby suggested in his conversation with me, but it failed to persuade the trial court. See Appellant's Brief, App. Div. pp. 7–9.

letter of May 22 that the purpose of the letter was "making it possible for you, once I die, to get this picture without having to pay inheritance taxes on it" coupled with his failure to show Michael's interest by tagging the painting or listing him in the exhibition catalog when the painting was loaned to a museum provided a basis for this argument. He also argued that Victor's retention of possession, his payment of insurance premiums, his refusal to agree to allow Michael to send the painting to London for an exhibition, and his statement on the application for an export permit that he had given the painting to his heirs by his will showed that he really did not intend to give up control of the painting until he died. In addition, Victor's failure to file a gift tax return, or to follow his lawyer's advice about how to make the gift, allowed Whitby to paint a picture of Victor as a tax evader who believed he could do things his own way rather than as required by the law.[56]

Finally, Whitby had a surprise up his sleeve. He called Michael to the stand and presented him with affidavits from the file of the proceedings for dissolution of his marriage to his first wife, Susanna, and subsequent proceedings with respect to child support.[57] In none of the affidavits was the painting listed as one of Michael's assets. Although Michael objected strenuously[58] that use of the affidavits was improper, the judge let some of the them in. The affidavits apparently put Michael in a bad light with the court, which called them "damning evidence"[59] and provided the basis for the finding that Michael had not accepted the gift. Michael's lawyer, Victor Muskin, is convinced that they lost at trial because of those affidavits.[60]

And, so, the mystery is solved. By keeping Kemija out of the courtroom, and focusing on the apparent moral failings of the father and son, Whitby was able to shift the emotional balance of the case. The trial judge went right down the line with him in adopting the interpretation of the facts most favorable to Kemija and deciding to follow the archaic doctrines of the old New York cases. But what happened on appeal? Did the appellate judges defer to the trial court's determination of Victor's intent or its reading of the law? You probably know the answer, but

---

[56] Appellant's brief in the Appellate Division argued at p. 12 that "Trial Term's intimations that Victor intended no gift at all but only a tax evasion scheme runs afoul of the rule that 'Intention is presumed, unless the inference of innocence is belied with a reasonable certainty, to be conformable to the law.' . . . [citation omitted]."

[57] The affidavits are described in Respondent's Brief in the Appellate Division at pp. 38–42.

[58] See Appellant's Brief in the Appellate Division at pp. 34–43.

[59] See quotation at note 66, *infra*.

[60] Telephone conversation with Victor Muskin.

indulge me a bit longer. I may have learned some things you will find interesting.

III. The Legal Story, Part II: The Appeals

Michael appealed the decision to the Second Department of the Appellate Division of the New York Supreme Court. During oral argument, the four judges grilled Victor Muskin about Michael's affidavits. He argued strenuously that the affidavits should not be dispositive of the case—they were filed seven to ten years after the gift was made, and there was other evidence that Michael had gladly accepted the gift. Responding to the judges' concerns about the fact that Michael, a lawyer, appeared to have filed misleading affidavits in a court proceeding, Muskin assured the court that he had had a "heart to heart" talk with his client, who fully understood the seriousness of the matter. Apparently satisfied with the response, the Appellate Division unanimously reversed the trial court, finding as a fact that Victor intended to make a present gift to Michael while reserving a life estate.

Interestingly, the Appellate Division decided that the choice of law question, which had been given such extensive attention by the trial court, was irrelevant. Despite *In re Ramsey* and *Young v. Young*, the judges concluded that New York's law was in fact the same as California's. Going straight to the question whether delivery of the letters was effective to make a gift, the court readily concluded that at common law a gift could be effected by delivery of a writing to the donee evidencing the gift,[61] and that New York law was well settled that a valid gift inter vivos could be made by written instrument. It noted that even though there might be reservations about claims of oral gifts against the estates of decedents, no such reservations should apply when the gift was made in writing.[62] The court rejected the statements from *Young v. Young* as dictum and characterized the holding of *In re Ramsey* as "an anomaly." Based on other cases, the court concluded that in New York, gifts of future interests in chattels can be made. The distinction between gifts of intangibles and gifts of chattels, argued by Whitby on Kemija's behalf,[63] made no sense to this court.

The court regarded the letters as incontrovertibly establishing Victor's intent to make a present gift of a remainder to Michael. The language of the letters, coupled with Victor's subsequent declarations that he had given the painting to his son, led the judges to the

---

[61] This, of course, had been the rule in England since 1468. See Stone, *supra* note 45, at 199.

[62] 488 N.Y.S.2d at 404. See text at note 70, *infra*, for a quotation of the court's full treatment of the issue.

[63] Respondent's Brief, App. Div. p. 38.

conclusion that he clearly intended a present transfer of a future interest, rather than a future transfer. Victor's failure to file a gift tax return, regarded as "highly significant" by the trial court, was, in the Appellate Division's view, only of "marginal significance."[64] Since the stated purpose of the gift was to avoid estate taxes, inferring lack of donative intent from failure to file the gift tax return did not make much sense. Victor's intention to avoid estate taxes, in the Appellate Division's view, buttressed the conclusion that he intended to make an inter vivos gift—otherwise his objective could not have been accomplished. Of course, by finding that Victor retained a life estate, the Appellate Division effectively sabotaged Victor's plan to escape estate taxation.[65]

The Appellate Division also dismissed as without importance Victor's statement on the 1979 export permit application that he had willed the painting to his heirs. The statement was made 16 years after the gift letters, and was inconsistent with the many statements he had made over the years, both orally and in writing, that he had given the painting to Michael. Finally, the court also rejected the trial court's conclusion that Michael did not accept the gift. It said:[66]

> In the instant case, delivery was effectuated via delivery of the gift letters, and there is no substantive evidence that the donee ever rejected or repudiated these instruments.... In this regard, we cannot ascribe to Trial Term's conclusion that plaintiff's failure to include his interest in the painting in financial affidavits which he submitted in connection with his matrimonial action is "damning evidence" of nonacceptance. In fact, assuming, *arguendo*, the admissibility of this evidence, we fail to see how it can reasonably be given such weight.... [T]he failure to include his remainder interest in the painting in his financial affidavits in the matrimonial action does not reasonably support the inference that plaintiff never accepted the gift. Its omission from the marital affidavits clearly admits of other, more reasonable inferences....

---

[64] 488 N.Y.S.2d at 407.

[65] Retention of a life estate by the donor results in inclusion of the entire gift asset in the donor's estate under § 2036 of the Internal Revenue Code. Paul Whitby believes this result was the Appellate Division's punishment for Michael's transgressions with the affidavit. Telephone conversation with Paul Whitby. Victor Muskin characterized the court's judgment as "Solomonic" because it both gave Michael the painting and made it financially impossible for him to keep it because of the taxes that would be payable. Telephone conversation with Victor Muskin.

Michael, however, told me that no estate or inheritance taxes were in fact paid with respect to the painting, and that the insurance and security costs made it infeasible for him to keep the painting. The fact that the painting left the country in 1972 and never returned may explain why he did not end up having to pay taxes on it.

[66] 488 N.Y.S.2d at 407–08.

Thus the Appellate Division ruled right down the line for Michael, as thoroughly as the trial court had ruled for Kemija. Away from the emotional atmosphere of the trial, the judges were able to see past the claims of tax evasion and misleading affidavits to carry out Victor's clear intent to give the painting to his son. On remand to the trial court, judgment was entered against Kemija for $2,500,000, the estimated value of the painting. She then appealed to the New York Court of Appeals.[67]

At the Court of Appeals, although Victor Muskin appeared on the brief, Michael appeared pro se and argued the case himself. Paul Whitby recounts that when he arrived in Albany to argue the case, he was puzzled to find great numbers of the press swarming outside the court. Even though the Klimt was a valuable painting, he thought it unlikely that the case could have generated so much interest from the press. As it turned out, he was right. The *Gruen* case, which had been scheduled first on the calendar, had been pushed back to make room for an argument in the Bernhard Goetz case. Goetz, in case you don't remember, was the guy who shot four black teenagers on a Manhattan subway on December 24, 1984, claiming that he acted in self-defense when they tried to shake him down for $5.[68] The press did not stick around for the *Gruen* arguments, which were apparently uneventful.[69] The Court of Appeals unanimously affirmed the Appellate Division.

The only respect in which the Court of Appeals appears to have disagreed with the Appellate Division is over the question whether delivery of a written instrument can always be used to make a gift. The Appellate Division wholeheartedly accepted the idea that delivery of a written instrument with intent to make a present gift is effective, saying:[70]

> At common law, a gift of property could be effected by the delivery of a writing to the donee evidencing the gift.... When property is conveyed in this manner, it is the delivery of the instrument itself which fulfills the "delivery" requirement ... and duplicative manual delivery is unnecessary.... [I]n the case of an oral gift, the fact of delivery serves to assist, in an evidentiary manner, to confirm the

---

[67] She was able to appeal of right at that time, something which would not be possible today. Conversation with Paul Whitby.

[68] See www.courttv.com/archive/verdicts/goetz.html for a story about the civil case brought by one of the teenagers who was paralyzed by Goetz (he won a $43 million verdict), and www.s-t.com/daily/05–96/05–03–96/2goetz.htm for a story on Goetz's move away from New York City.

[69] Paul Whitby says that everything he had to say was in his brief; he was there primarily to answer the Court's questions. Conversation with Paul Whitby.

[70] 488 N.Y.S.2d 401 at 403–04.

intent of the donor, and to prevent the assertion of fraudulent claims.... No such policy considerations are applicable to a gift made in writing, for, as one commentator has noted, "the delivery of a written conveyance * * * requires a high degree of deliberation on the part of the donor, substantially higher than a manual delivery, and affords the clearest and most convincing evidence of the fact that a gift has taken place" (Mechem, The Requirement of Delivery in Gifts of Chattels, 21 Ill. L. Rev. 568, 586).

The Court of Appeals was more cautious. It said:[71]

... [W]hat is sufficient to constitute delivery "must be tailored to suit the circumstances of the case".... The rule requires that " '[t]he delivery necessary to consummate a gift must be as perfect as the nature of the property and the circumstances and surroundings of the parties will reasonably permit.' " ...

Defendant contends that when a tangible piece of personal property such as a painting is the subject of a gift, physical delivery of the painting itself is the best form of delivery and should be required. Here, of course, we have only delivery of Victor Gruen's letters which serve as instruments of gift. Defendant's statement of the rule as applied *may be generally true*, but it ignores the fact that what Victor Gruen gave plaintiff was not all rights to the Klimt painting, but only title to it with no right of possession until his death. Under the circumstances, it would be illogical for the law to require the donor to part with possession of the painting when that is exactly what he intends to retain.

Does the New York Court of Appeals really believe that "it is generally true" that a person, intending to make a gift of personal property, who delivers a written instrument to the donee that clearly states it is intended to pass title to the property to the donee fails to make an effective gift if the property could easily be handed over instead? I would hope not, but only time will tell.

IV. Epilogue

The appellate courts vindicated Michael's claim to the painting, but would it do him any good? Kemija was not in the U.S. and had not been forthcoming as to the whereabouts of the painting. But, one day, out of the blue, Michael received an envelope in the mail with a brief note saying something like "OK, here's your painting." A bank vault receipt from a Swiss bank was enclosed. He flew immediately to Zurich, Switzerland, presented the receipt and was given possession of the painting.[72]

---

[71] 496 N.E.2d at 874 (emphasis added).

[72] Whitby says he wrote Kemija after the Court of Appeals opinion came down saying that he had done all he could for her and telling her that she should give Michael the painting. He does not know whether this accounts for her capitulation or not.

Instead of bringing the painting home, however, he arranged for it to be sold by Sotheby's at auction in London.[73] Sotheby's sold the painting on June 30, 1987 for £3,300,000 (approximately $5,336,000). The buyer was a London dealer, Marlborough Fine Art, and the sale set a record price for Klimt's work.[74] The buyer made a good investment. Ten years later, in October, 1997, the painting was sold again at auction in London, this time by Christie's, for £14,500,000 (approximately $23,500,000).[75] This sale not only set a record price for a Klimt, but was almost one-half higher than any previously paid for a painting of the 19th and 20th century Germanic schools.[76] The painting, at that time the only one of the five Schloss Kammer paintings which was not already in a museum,[77] ended up in the Galleria Nazionale d'Arte Moderna in Rome.[78]

Kemija died in Vienna in 1994 at age 57.[79] Michael remains a practicing lawyer in New York. He moved, in 2002, to a new firm where he continues his involvement in land-use issues. In 2000, he was representing neighbors of the Museum of Modern Art who objected to expansion plans that included building a movie theater, restaurant, educational wing, several new galleries, and a new entrance on West 53rd Street.[80] Michael and his wife Vanessa are both members of the Municipal Art Society and have been actively involved in the fight to control the newspaper boxes that clutter the sidewalks of New York.[81]

Paul Whitby has moved from the private practice of law, which he

---

[73] Michael says the painting was too valuable to keep. The problems and expense of insurance and security were too great. Conversation with Michael Gruen.

[74] The Financial Times (London), July 1, 1987, Section 1; The Arts, p. 21.

[75] Id., Oct. 10, 1997, Section News–UK, p. 9.

[76] International Herald Tribune (Neuilly-sur-Seine, France), Oct. 25, 1997, Section Special Report, p. 10. It was also the third highest price that had been paid at that time for any painting at a London salesroom.

[77] The Financial Times (London) Oct. 10, 1997, Section News–UK, p. 9.

[78] http://www.expo-klimt.com/1_3.cfm?ID=-334260456.

[79] Social Security Death Index, http://ssdi.genealogy.rootsweb.com/cgi-bin/ssdi.cgi.

[80] New York Times, Sept. 3, 2000, Section 1, Page 38, Col. 4: "Neighbors say the plans ... would bring an unbearable amount of traffic to the area and would block spectacular views of the stained-glass windows of St. Thomas Church, a New York City landmark."

[81] Clyde Haberman, Foot Traffic Blocked by the Box, New York Times, Dec. 9, 2000, Section B, Page 1, Col. 1; Boxes are Only One Way to Distribute a Paper (letter from Michael S. Gruen), New York Times, Dec. 30, 2001, Sec. 14, p. 13, col. 1. Wedding announcements for two of their children appear in the New York Times of June 11, 2000 and Jan. 20, 2002 and state that Michael is the founder of the New York Landmarks Conservancy Society and member of the legal committee of the Municipal Art Society; Vanessa is the director of special projects for the Municipal Art Society.

had come to find increasingly disagreeable,[82] into a position as house counsel with Van Wagner Communications, LLC, which he very much enjoys. By contrast with his previous litigation practice, where he found people at their worst, he now works on interesting deals with "brilliant and honest people."[83] Victor Muskin and Paul Whitby have become friends since the *Gruen* trial, and Victor occasionally handles matters referred to him by Paul. Victor has recently moved from a solo practice to become of counsel to Scheichet & Davis, P.C. in New York City.

And now you know most of what I can tell you about *Gruen v. Gruen*. I hope you have enjoyed the tale. If you are interested in more detail, you can read the appellate briefs on the Web site created to accompany this book and follow the links to view the famous Schloss Kammer am Attersee II and other Web sites I found in my research.

---

[82] After the Gruen trial, Michael filed a complaint with the bar association seeking to have Paul Whitby disciplined for what he claimed was improper use of the affidavits from Michael's matrimonial proceedings file. Whitby said the complaint was dismissed after about two years, but that having it hanging over his head was very unpleasant even though he believed it was without foundation. Telephone conversation with Paul Whitby.

[83] Telephone conversation with Paul Whitby.

5

Pat Cain

Two Sisters vs. A Father and Two Sons: The Story of *Sawado v. Endo*

Introduction

In 1892, the territory of Hawaii through its legislature officially adopted the common law. In 1959, Hawaii became the 50th state. Connecting with the number 50, television producers aired the first Hawaii Five–O segment in September of 1968, filmed on location in Oahu. Just two months later, in a cross walk on the island of Oahu, in the town of Wahiawa, Masako Sawado and her sister, Helen, were struck by an automobile driven by 82 year old Kokichi Endo. And thus began a simple tort case that turned into one of the most important common law property cases in the history of the state.

The torts cases

Masako and Helen Sawado were sisters. Masako lived on the island of Maui and Helen lived in Honolulu, on the island of Oahu. On November 30, 1968, the two sisters were in the town of Wahiawa, about 25 miles north of Honolulu. The briefs do not disclose what attracted them to Wahiawa. In the 1960s, Wahiawa was a small rural town in the middle of the island, bordered on the east and west by the Schofield Army Barracks (seen in the film "From Here to Eternity"). The Dole Pineapple Plantation lay to the north.

On November 30, 1968, Kokichi Endo was also in Wahiawa. He lived there, with his wife Ume, at 14 Wilikina Drive. Kokichi was 82 years old and his wife was 75. They had very few assets and no liability insurance. But they did own their home and held title as tenants by the entirety.

As the sisters, Masako and Helen, were crossing a street in Wahia-wa, Kokichi drove his car into the pedestrian crosswalk and hit them both. They were seriously injured and suffered permanent damage.

Helen Sawada filed suit against Kokichi Endo in June of 1969. Her sister, Masako, filed a similar suit two months later, on August 13, 1969. For some unknown reason, the complaints were not served on the defendant until October 29, 1969. The cases went to trial and on January 19. 1971, judgments were entered in favor of both sisters ($8,846.46 for Helen and $16,199.28 for Masako). Ten days later, Ume Endo, the wife of Kokichi Endo, died.

The property case

The property case arose because Kokichi Endo had no assets with which to pay the judgments entered in the torts cases. On July 26, 1969, just one month after Helen Sawada had filed her tort claim, Kokichi and Ume deeded their home as a gift to their two sons, Samuel and Toru. Shortly thereafter they transferred all monies on deposit in two bank accounts to their sons and a third person named Frances S. Todani. All members of the Endo family were aware of the automobile accident at the time these transfers were made.

Having transferred all his available assets to his sons, Kokichi Endo was unable to satisfy the tort judgments. The Sawada sisters then filed an action against Endo and his two sons, asking the court to set aside the conveyance of the real property as a transfer in fraud of their rights.

Summary of Plaintiffs' argument

Plaintiffs claimed that they were creditors of Kokichi Endo at the time he and his wife transferred their home to their sons. Prior to the conveyance, the spouses held the property as tenants by the entirety. Thus, prior to the conveyance, both husband and wife had an interest in the property. The plaintiffs' claim was solely against the husband and so only his interest in the property could be attached. When spouses hold property as tenants by the entirety, each spouse has the right to use the property during their joint lives and at the death of the first spouse, the survivor owns the property in fee. Had the spouses not conveyed the property to their sons and had the wife survived the husband, her survivorship rights would have taken effect and plaintiffs' liens as creditors would have been unenforceable against the realty. However, since in fact the husband survived the wife, *but for* the conveyance to the sons, the plaintiffs' claim against the husband's interest in the property could have been enforced against his survivorship interest in fee. Therefore, the plaintiffs argued, the conveyance should be set aside as fraudulent and the plaintiffs should be allowed to enforce their claims against Mr. Endo's survivorship interest in fee.

Summary of Defendants' argument

Defendants argued that when spouses own property as tenants by the entirety, they not only have survivorship rights that are protected from the creditors of the other spouse, but they also have lifetime rights that are protected from such creditors. Hawaii's Married Women's Act of 1888 provided that a married woman's property should be held free from the debts of her husband.[1] If the husband's creditors could attach the husband's interest in entireties property at any time during the wife's life, even if the lien were not currently enforced, then "the wife's right would be diminished and drastically impaired."[2] Specifically, "she would be deprived of the right to sell, mortgage or otherwise convey the property with her husband's consent"[3] during their joint lifetimes. The defendants argued that, in order to protect the married woman from her husband's creditors, her *full* interest in the entirety property, including her right to convey her interest during her lifetime, must be absolutely protected from the husband's creditors. (And presumably, in the interest of equality, the husband should be similarly protected from the wife's creditors, although that was not the issue in this case.) Finally, since the property itself could not be attached by the husband's creditors at the time of the joint conveyance, the defendants argued that the conveyance was not fraudulent and should not be set aside. As a result, the argument continued, the sons owned the realty free of the claims of the Sawada sisters.

The trial court's opinion

On July 16, 1973, trial judge Yasutaka Fukushima ruled against the sisters and refused to set the conveyance aside. Judge Fukushima agreed with the defendants about the nature of a tenancy by the entirety. He reasoned that creditors should not be able to reach property held by husband and wife as tenants by the entirety during their lives and thus a husband and wife should be able to transfer entireties property jointly as a legitimate exercise of their ownership rights. Under this view, transfers of entireties property *ipso facto* could not be in fraud of the creditors' rights. In other words, if the Sawada sisters could not enforce

---

[1] Hawaii Revised Statutes § 573–1.

[2] Answering Brief of Defendants–Appellees at 17.

[3] Id.

a judgment lien against the property in the first place, they could not be harmed by the conveyance to the sons. The trial judge noted in open court that, given the ages of the Endo parents, it was about time for them to start giving their property to their children.[4]

The trial judge emphasized that the right to convey property was an important incident of ownership. And while conveyances that defeat creditors' claims may be set aside as a general rule, it was his opinion that tenancies by the entirety were unique. A spouse who is not at fault should not lose her right to convey her interest in the entirety property during her lifetime, albeit only jointly with her husband's consent. "This is one area that you are going to have a unit," explained Judge Fukushima. "That's their residence held in tenancy by the entirety. No one is going to take that right away."[5]

The case on appeal

The Sawada sisters appealed to the Hawaii Supreme Court. Their lawyer, Andrew S. Hartnett, who had offices in both Honolulu and Wailuku, Maui, filed an "opening brief" on November 26, 1973. George M. Takane, representing the Endos, filed his "answering brief" on April 8, 1974, and Hartnett filed a "reply brief" in July. The focus of both sides' briefs was the effect of Hawaii's Married Women's Property Act on tenancies by the entirety. The Married Women's Property Act had been passed by the Hawaii legislature in 1888, but no court had ever had to rule on its effect on estates held as tenants by the entirety. Now, almost 90 years after its enactment, "Drew" Hartnett, in his 7th year of legal practice, was preparing to argue his case before the Hawaii Supreme Court. The question presented to the court was: "Whether the interest of one party in property held in tenancy by the entireties is subject to attachment and/or execution by the separate creditors of such party."[6]

Tenancy by the Entirety under English Common Law

At common law, under the doctrine of coverture, married women had no legal existence. They could not enter into contracts or incur debts. They could not own property. Only the husband could own and manage property. Husband and wife could not contract with each other, for, as Blackstone explained, they were one person rather than two. Upon marriage, the wife's personal property became the absolute proper-

---

[4] Sawada v. Endo, Answering Brief at 6.

[5] Id.

[6] Opening Brief at 1.

ty of her husband. A husband might gift certain items of personal use to his wife, such as jewelry and clothing, but he retained the right to make lifetime dispositions of these chattels without her consent. (He could not, however, will them away at death.)

While the wife's real property did not become the absolute property of her husband upon marriage, the husband had broad rights over the wife's real property. He could manage, control, and encumber it. He could take the profits from the property and use them for himself without accounting for them. Since the husband could appropriate the realty to himself, his creditors could also reach it. If he took no action during the marriage to appropriate the realty to himself and if the wife survived,[7] she would regain ownership. If the wife died first, the husband typically enjoyed a life estate in the realty in the form of a tenancy by the curtesy, provided issue were born of the marriage.[8]

If husband and wife were one, as Blackstone explained it, then joint ownership of property by husband and wife would not have been possible. Coverture would have transformed the husband into the sole owner because the wife's separate existence was not possible. Indeed, Blackstone's early writings appear to omit any reference to the joint spousal estate known as the tenancy by the entirety. Not until the publication of a posthumous edition of his *Commentaries* does any reference to this particular common law estate occur. In the ninth edition of the *Commentaries*, edited by Richard Burn, and based on Blackstone's handwritten comments to an earlier edition, one finds the following insert at the end of Blackstone's discussion of joint tenancy:

> And therefore, if an estate in fee be given to a man and his wife, they are neither properly joint-tenants, nor tenants in common: for husband and wife being considered as one person in law, they cannot take the estate by moieties, but both are seised of the entirety, *per tout et non per my*; the consequence of which is, that neither the husband nor the wife can dispose of any part without the assent of the other, but the whole must remain to the survivor.[9]

---

[7] A marriage might also end by divorce but divorce was generally unknown in England until 1857. See Lawrence Friedman, A History of American Law, 204 (2d ed. 1985). Hawaii began to adopt common law principles after the arrival of Christian missionaries in 1820. In 1853, jurisdiction over the granting of divorces moved from the King to the courts. Fault was required. See generally Calvin G.C. Pang, *Slow-Baked, Flash-Fried, Not To Be Devoured: Development Of The Partnership Model Of Property Division In Hawai'i And Beyond*, 20 U. Hawaii L. Rev. 1 at 15, n 47 (1998).

[8] See George L. Haskins, Curtesy in the United States, Penn. L. Rev. 196 (1951). See also Cornelius J. Mohnihan, Introduction to the Law of Real Property at 52–55 (1962).

[9] Quoted in John V. Orth, Tenancy by the Entirety: The Strange Career of the Common Law Marital Estate, 1997 BYU L. Rev. 35 at 38. Note: "per tout et not per my"

Thus, rather than treat husband and wife as mere joint tenants or co-tenants, the common law presumed that joint estates in spouses were tenancies by the entirety. In a sense, the entirety was the couple (ruled, of course, by the husband) and the entirety, so long as it existed, owned the property. As with joint tenancy property, the tenancy by the entirety carried with it the right of survivorship. Yet, because the owner of the property was the "entirety" and not the two individuals, no unilateral severance of the unities of ownership was possible. As a result, the right of survivorship was indestructible.

Under the common law, a wife who owned property as a tenant by the entirety with her husband would have the same rights that a wife had in her separately owned real property. She would have the right, in effect, to a remainder interest in fee should she survive her husband and, during her lifetime, he would have full management and control over the property. All of the wife's real estate, whether separately owned or jointly owned with her husband, would therefore be available to satisfy claims of the husband's creditors, subject to the wife's survivorship interest in the property should she survive her husband.

Common Law in the United States

All of the states, other than Louisiana, adopted or "received" the common law as part of their own law. Sometimes the common law was adopted by statute and sometimes it was adopted (or "received") by judicial decree. Thus, in all states (other than Louisiana), even in community property states, the basic principles of common law coverture became an operative part of state law.[10] As a result, most states would have recognized the tenancy by the entirety as part of the common law, provided there was no statute abolishing the estate. If recognized, the common law estate would contain the primary attributes that it did under English common law. It would provide each spouse with an indefeasible right of survivorship, and the property would be reachable by the husband's creditors during the joint lives of the spouses.

In the community property states, which followed European civil law traditions rather than English common law, property acquired during marriage was generally held by the community of husband and

roughly translates as "held as a unity and not in shares." The ninth edition of *Blackstone's Commentaries* was published in 1783.

[10] Although Louisiana never adopted English common law, the civil law conventions that accompanied community property closely resembled the rules of coverture. For example, until the United States Supreme Court declared the state law unconstitutional, Louisiana law gave the husband full control over the community property. See Kirchberg v. Feenstra, 450 U.S. 455 (1981).

wife. Wives in community property states were thought to be more protected because their rights in the community property were more vested than the rights that wives had in common law property states. Yet, as with tenancies by the entirety, community property rules gave the husband full control over all community property. In community property states, as well as in common law property states, the husband's creditors could reach the entire property. Some community property states enacted laws that protected the wife's interest in separate property from the claims of her husband's creditors. Community property, however, remained available to satisfy the husband's debts.

Married Women's Property Acts

In the middle of the nineteenth century, early feminists campaigned to end the legal disabilities experienced by married women under the doctrine of coverture. At the First National Woman's Rights Convention held in 1850 at Worcester, Massachusetts, the delegates adopted the following resolution:

> That the laws of property, as affecting married parties, demand a thorough revisal, so that all rights may be equal between them;— that the wife may have, during life, an equal control over the property gained by their mutual toil and sacrifices, be heir to her husband precisely to the extent that he is heir to her, and entitled, at her death, to dispose by will of the same share of the joint property as he is.[11]

States did not respond to feminist demands by enacting new marital property regimes. Community property states remained community property states and common law states retained much of the common law doctrine of coverture. In community property states, some minor reforms occurred during the last half of the nineteenth century that protected a wife's separate property from the husband's creditors. Property owned by the community, however, remained under the sole control of the husband for another century.[12] In common law states, feminists were successful during the last half of the nineteenth century in persuading state legislatures to enact laws that that gave married women

---

[11] Quoted in Reva Siegel, Home as Work: The First Woman's Rights Claims Concerning Wives' Household Labor, 1850–1880, 103 Yale L. J. 1073 (1994).

[12] Texas did not give wives meaningful control over community property until 1967. See Joseph W. McKnight, "Texas Community Property Law–Its Course of Development and Reform," 8 Calif. Western L. Rev. 117 (1971). Louisiana did not abandon the rule the husband was "head and master" of the community estate until 1980. See discussion in Kirchberg v. Feenstra, 450 U.S. 455 (1981) (holding pre–1980 Louisiana law violated the equal protection clause).

limited control over their own earnings and such property that might come into their hands by gift or devise.

Hawaii's statute from 1888 is typical. It provides:

> Separate Property: The real and personal property of a woman shall, upon her marriage, remain her separate property, free from the management, control debts, and obligations of her husband; and a married woman may receive, receipt for, hold, manage, and dispose of property, real and personal, in the same manner as if she were sole.[13]

All such statutes were in derogation of the common law. As a matter of statutory construction, the applicable rules commanded that these statutes be narrowly construed.

In no state was the doctrine of coverture completely repealed. As one commentator observed, the statutory language necessary to effectuate a complete repeal is difficult to imagine. Perhaps a complete repeal would have been accomplished if a state legislature had enacted a provision stating that the property rights of husbands and wives should be determined as though they had never been married. But that was not the case. The Married Women's Property Acts began with the assumption that marriage affected the wife's property rights and specified some narrow changes in the common law rules of coverture that affected those rights. Thus, for example, a statute that enabled a married woman to acquire property in her own name by *gift* did not sufficiently repeal coverture so as to enable her to acquire property in her own name by *purchase*. Nor would such a statute convert her earnings, owned by her husband under coverture, into her own separately-owned property.[14]

Married Women's Property Acts and the Abolition of Tenancies by the Entirety

In most states with common law property regimes, the enactment of Married Women's Property Acts enabled married women to hold property in their own names as separate property and to own property jointly with their husbands as tenants in common or as joint tenants. Before these Married Women's Property Statutes took effect, the primary form of joint spousal ownership in common law states had been the tenancy by the entirety and it was based on the legal fiction that the husband and wife were one, the very concept that the Married Women's Property Acts were aimed at abolishing. Not surprisingly, in the decades immediately following passage of these Married Women's Property Acts, states

---

[13] Hawaii Stat. § 573–1.

[14] See, e.g., H. Apple & Co. v. Ganong, 47 Miss. 189 (1872).

in which the tenancy by the entirety had been recognized were now faced with the question of whether the estate, based as it was on the legal fiction that husband and wife were one in the law, should continue to be recognized.

Of the 50 states, there are 42 common law property states and 8 community property states. Community property states would not have recognized the tenancy by the entirety as part of their common law since property acquired by husband and wife was usually presumed to be community property. Because community property did not include survivorship rights, the tenancy by the entirety with its irrevocable right of survivorship would have been contrary to basic notions about marital property. Although several community property states do mention the tenancy by the entirety in their statutes and case law, none appear to have recognized the estate as it existed at common law. Indeed, the community property regime of Texas seemed so inconsistent with spousal rights of survivorship that until recently the Probate Code included a statute that claimed: "Joint Tenancies Abolished."[15]

Most common law property states, by contrast, had recognized the tenancy by the entirety as an estate that was consistent with their "reception" of the common law of England. Some, however, did not, on the theory that joint tenancies with survivorship were not favored by American law, in large part because the survivorship feature affected the free alienability of the land. And, since the tenancy by the entirety created an indefeasible right of survivorship, it should have been even more strongly disfavored than a mere joint tenancy which could be severed or partitioned.[16]

With the passage of the Married Women's Property Acts, there was even more cause to disfavor the tenancy by the entirety. Not only was it inconsistent with the country's need to have estates vest early and be freely alienable to support economic development, the tenancy now conflicted in principle with the core message of feminists who were

---

[15] But see Chandler v. Kountze, 130 S.W.2d 327 (Tex. Civ. App. 1939), writ refused (holding that although the common law estate known as joint tenancy was abolished by the statute, rights of survivorship could be created by contract or by intent of the parties). Spousal estates with rights of survivorship have experienced a tortured history under Texas law. See Joseph W. McKnight, 1988 Annual Survey of Texas Law: Family Law: Husband and Wife, 42 Sw L.J. 1, 10–13 (1988).

[16] Most American states by statute abolished the joint tenancy as it was known at common law, i.e., as an estate that arose automatically if the four unities were met. Instead, joint ownership was presumed to create a tenancy in common. One might think that it would require a similar statute to eliminate the common law estate of tenancy by the entirety. But at least three state courts were willing to rule that the estate was not part of their common law, even though coverture was. See, e.g., Iowa, Conn. Ohio. See Sergeant v. Steinberger, 2 Ohio 305 (1826); Whittlesey v. Fuller, 11 Conn. 337 (1836); Hoffman v. Stigers, 28 Iowa 302 (1869).

fighting for the reform of property regimes: that a wife is her own separate person.

Surprisingly, in most feminist histories of marital property reform, there is virtually no mention of the tenancy by the entirety. Thus, it does not appear that this particular estate with its understanding of the unity of husband and wife was a primary target of early feminists. Nonetheless, as questions about the validity of the tenancy by the entirety arose in courts and legislatures across the country after passage of the Married Women's Property Acts, courts and legislatures often provided feminist-inspired justifications for refusing to recognize the estate.

The Supreme Court of Alabama, for example, reasoned as follows: "By this legislation, the one legal person of the common law has been resolved into two distinct persons, so far at least as the capacity of taking separate estates is concerned. ... Both of the grantees being capable of taking separately, it is impossible that they should take by entireties, as if they constituted a single person."[17]

Nebraska had by statute adopted the common law of England to the extent it was not inconsistent with the existing organic law of the territory. The Nebraska Supreme Court held that the tenancy by the entirety was inconsistent with the institution of marriage as it was understood in 1900 and thus was never part of the common law of Nebraska.[18] The court explained: "The old common-law idea of the oneness in the relation of husband and wife is fast disappearing. The identity of the woman is not lost in her husband. She is no longer under his dominion or control. On the contrary, in law, husband and wife are now considered as equals..."

Despite the argument that the unity of husband and wife was an archaic notion, approximately half the common law property states continued to recognize the tenancy by the entireties estate after the passage of Married Women's Property Statutes. For example, the Pennsylvania Supreme Court proclaimed: "The design of the legislature was single. It was not to destroy the oneness of husband and wife, but to protect the wife's property, by removing it from under the dominion of the husband." Under this view, the Married Women's Property Acts said nothing about what sort of estate a married woman might enjoy with her husband. Rather, their sole concern was that, whatever the estate, it would be protected from the husband's creditors.

Some states continued the tenancy by the entirety by statutorily declaring it to be one of the forms of joint ownership permissible under

---

[17] Walthall v. Goree, 36 Ala. 728, 735 (1860).

[18] Kerner v. McDonald, 60 Neb. 663, 84 N.W. 92 (1900). See also Whyman v. Johnston, 62 Colo. 461, 163 P. 76 (1917).

state law. Hawaii falls into this latter group. In 1903, the state legislature adopted what is now Section 509–1 of the Hawaii Statutes. This statute has never been amended. It provides quite simply:

> All grants, conveyances, and devises of land, or of any interest therein, made to two or more persons, shall be construed to create estates in common and not in joint tenancy or by entirety, unless it manifestly appears from the tenor of the instrument that it was intended to create an estate in joint tenancy or by entirety; provided that this section shall not apply to grants, conveyances, or devises to personal representatives or trustees.

The statute does not purport to define a tenancy by the entirety or describe any of its attributes. All it does is provide the requirements for creating the estate: a clear manifestation of intent.

Married Women's Property Acts and the New Definition of Tenancy by the Entirety

In the absence of a statutory definition of the tenancy by the entirety, courts willing to recognize the existence of the estate were faced with the further question of what the essential attributes of the tenancy were. The indestructibility of the survivorship feature was the primary defining attribute at common law. All states agreed that this feature remained after Married Women's Property Acts were passed. Thus, neither spouse could unilaterally convey any interest in the entireties property that would defeat the other spouse's survivorship right. Furthermore, each spouse should be viewed as having at least two identifiable interests in the property: (1) the present right to the shared use or profits from the property, and (2) the right to enjoy the entire property in the future should that spouse survive.

The question that divided the states was whether either spouse could unilaterally convey one or both of these two interests. The answer to this question is an important first step in determining whether a spouse's creditors can reach the entireties property. Whatever interest an individual can convey is the interest that the individual's creditors should be able to reach. At the time of the *Sawada* appeal, four possibilities existed:

> *Rule #1 (three states)*: Under the traditional common law rule granting the husband the right to the use and profits of all property owned by the wife, the husband would be able to convey that interest as well as his contingent survival interest. His creditors therefore could reach the entireties property subject only to the wife's contingent claim to a survivorship interest. Massachusetts

initially followed this rule.[19]

Rule #2 (five states): Because the Married Women's Property Acts were supposed to equalize the rights of the spouses, the wife's creditors should be able to reach the wife's interest in entireties property to the same extent that the husband's creditors could. Each spouse should be viewed as having two interests in entireties property, a present right to share either the use or the profits and a future contingent survivorship right to own the property in fee. Thus, the creditor of one spouse should be able to reach that spouse's two interests in the property, subject to the rights of the non-debtor spouse. Arkansas appears to have followed this rule as early as 1895.[20]

Rule #3 (ten states and the District of Columbia): This rule created an absolute bar to creditors. They could not attach any interest of the debtor spouse unless the other spouse had joined in the conveyance or agreed to the transaction. The theory underlying this approach was that neither spouse could unilaterally convey his or her interest. As a result, so long as the marriage existed, no creditor could reach the entireties property. Florida has followed this rule since at least 1920.[21]

Rule #4 (two states): In two states, creditors could not reach any of the current profits of the property, but instead were limited to attaching the survivorship rights of the debtor spouse. If the non-

---

[19] See Oval A. Phipps, "Tenancy by Entireties," 25 Temple L.Q. 24 (1951) (relied on heavily by the attorneys for both plaintiffs and defendants in *Sawada*). The three states Phipps identified as following this rule were Massachusetts, North Carolina, and Michigan. Massachusetts has more recently equalized the rights of the spouses by statute so that creditors of either spouse can reach that spouse's interest subject to the rights of the non-debtor spouse. In effect the creditor takes only a defeasible interest and will take nothing unless the debtor spouse survives For a good discussion of the history of the tenancy by the entirety in Massachusetts and the effect of the new statute see Coraccio v. Lowell Five Cents Saving Bank, 415 Mass. 145, 612 N.E.2d 650 (1993). North Carolina has equalized spousal rights by statute so that entireties property is equally protected from the creditors of both spouses. While an early Michigan case recognized the husband's right at common law to manage the profits of entireties property, Michigan law has never recognized the right of one spouse to convey an interest in entireties property. Thus, Michigan, like North Carolina, effectively bars the creditors of both spouses from reaching entireties property.

[20] See Branch v. Polk, 61 Ark. 388, 33 S.W. 424 (1895). Phipps also lists New Jersey, New York, and Oregon in this category. Alaska has joined this group, as has Massachusetts. See note 18.

[21] Ohio Butterine Co. v. Hargrave, 79 Fla. 458, 84 So. 376 (1920). In addition to Florida and the District of Columbia, according to Phipps, this group of states included Delaware, Indiana, Maryland, Missouri, Pennsylvania, Rhode Island, Vermont, Virginia, and Wyoming.

debtor spouse survived, the creditor would take nothing.[22]

These four alternative approaches were described in detail in an article written by St. Louis University Law School Dean Oval A. Phipps in the Temple Law Quarterly.[23] He listed nineteen states as states that recognized the entireties estate and classified them according to the four rules described above. Twenty-nine states were identified as not recognizing the entireties estate.[24] Lawyers for both plaintiffs and defendants relied heavily on this article and argued that the law in other states supported their clients' competing positions.

Arguments by Plaintiff on Appeal

Of the four rules described by Dean Phipps, three (i.e, rules 1, 2 and 4) would have supported the outcome that the plaintiffs were seeking. Rule #1, allowing creditors of the husband to reach the entireties property would not have been available in Hawaii, however, because it would have conflicted with the language of Hawaii's Married Women's Statute which provided that the wife's property should be free from the control and the debts of the husband. The plaintiffs, Masako and Helen Sawada, argued that Hawaii should follow rule #2. In truth, either rule #2 or rule #4 would have done the trick for the sisters, because, as it turned out, Mrs. Endo had predeceased Mr. Endo. No one was claiming a right to current profits. Only Mr. Endo's survivorship interest was at stake.

As counsel for the Sawada sisters counted the states, he had not only the seven states that allowed creditors to reach entireties property on his side[25] but also the 21 common law states that had abolished or failed to recognize the tenancy by the entirety because it was inconsistent with the post-Married Women's Property Acts view of the marital unit. By his count, at least 28 states of out 41[26] were on his side, thereby

---

[22] The two states listed by Phipps were Kentucky and Tennessee. See, e.g., Cochran v. Kerney, 72 Ky. 199 (Ky. App. 1872) (indicating that allowing a husband's creditors to reach the profits during the lifetime of the wife would be to defeat her present rights, but holding that his survivorship rights could be reached).

[23] Oval A. Phipps, "Tenancy by Entireties," 25 Temple L.Q. 24 (1951).

[24] At the time Dean Phipps did the research for his article, neither Hawaii nor Alaska were states. Thus they were not included in his analysis. As the *Sawada* court points out, however, Alaska ultimately joined those states following rule #2. The 29 states included the 8 community property states.

[25] I.e., the rule #2 and rule #4 states.

[26] The 41 states include all states other than the 8 community property states and Hawaii. Counsel for plaintiff in fact lumped the community property and common law property states together, claiming 29 jurisdictions had abolished the tenancy by the

placing his position in line with the clear majority.[27]

Arguments by Defendant on Appeal

Defendant's counsel by contrast focused on the 20 states that continued to recognize the tenancy by the entirety.[28] Under his count, the "decided weight of authority" was on his side. Ten states out of twenty, plus the District of Columbia, followed Rule #3. Rule #1 was unavailable because it maintained the common law rule of allowing only the husband's creditors to reach the property. Furthermore, states that followed rules #2 and #4 had, according to defendant, transformed the tenancy by the entireties estates into something else: a joint tenancy with an indestructible survivorship feature. If the Hawaii Supreme Court were to adopt that approach, defendant argued, it would in effect be creating a new form of ownership unheard of at common law. Such changes in the law were for the legislature to make, not the courts. Furthermore, this approach would fail to protect all of Mrs. Endo's rights. She, as well as all married women who owned entireties property, had a fully vested right to convey the property jointly with her husband during her lifetime. The Married Women's Property Statute protected *all* of her rights from her husband's creditors. Thus she had an absolute right to make the joint conveyance to their sons, free of the claims of the Sawada sisters.

Defendant made two additional arguments:

(1) Under Hawaii law, "the right of survivorship is merely an incident of the estate and does not constitute a remainder, either vested or contingent."[29] As such, it is a "mere possibility" and thus, it is not alienable. If it is not alienable, then it is not a property right that creditors could attach.

---

entirety. Reply Brief at 13. This statement is somewhat misleading because it includes the 8 community property states (California, Arizona, Texas, Louisiana, Washington, Idaho, Nevada, and New Mexico) in addition to three common law states (Connecticut, Ohio, and Iowa), which in fact had never recognized the tenancy the entirety.

[27] And arguably, he could also have relied on the three states that followed rule #1 for the proposition that since creditors of the husband could reach the property under the common law rule, they should still be able to reach the property under the modern rule provided the wife's interest was sufficiently protected. Once the wife predeceased the husband, there would be no interest to protect.

[28] "We will not be concerned on this appeal with the twenty-nine states which do not recognize tenancies by the entireties but only with the jurisdictions which do." Answering Brief at 29.

[29] Answering Brief at 34.

(2) Hawaii's statutory homestead exemption buttresses the defendant's argument for "family solidarity" because it protects the husband and wife's interest in the homestead from creditors in much the same way as the tenancy by the entirety does. The exemption is evidence that the state has a strong public policy favoring family solidarity at the expense of creditors.

Plaintiffs' Reply

Plaintiffs responded to defendant's arguments by explaining that the court was not being asked to create a new estate. Rather, the court was being asked to construe the Married Women's Act, as applied to the tenancy by the entirety. Furthermore, the effect of Hawaii's Married Women's Act was not to prevent creditors of both spouses from ever reaching the estate, but rather to prevent the husband's creditors from reaching the wife's interest in the property. By protecting her survivorship interest, the court could carry out the intent of the Married Women's Act. By contrast, those cases relied upon by the defendants, in fact, created a "radical alteration of the incidents of tenancy by the entirety from what it was at common law."

Plaintiff's counsel did not directly counter the argument that the survivorship interest alone could not be alienated because it was a mere expectancy. Instead, counsel argued that the fraudulent transfer at the heart of this transaction was Mr. Endo's transfer of *all* his interest, which included his right to the present use of the property as well as his survivorship right.

As to the argument based on the interest in "family solidarity," plaintiffs countered that the "effect of this argument is to convert tenancy by the entirety into a kind of sweeping homestead exemption, without limitation as to the extent or value. It permits a husband and wife to hold *all* of their property free from the claims of their respective creditors..."[30]

The Court's Ruling

The court ruled in favor of the defendants, in favor of the unity of husband and wife. The court thereby created a "super homestead" exemption for all property held by spouses as tenancies by the entirety. Today, Mr. Hartnett, counsel for the Sawada sisters, remembers the case primarily for the principal of family solidarity that it created.

---

[30] Reply Brief at 19.

Observations

If one looks at the comments made by the trial court (e.g., "That's their residence... No one is going to take that right away."), it appears that the judge might have been unduly swayed by the fact that this property was the Endo's homestead. Hawaii law at the time exempted homesteads at a very low value, "not in excess of $2,750." In 1972, after the accident and before the final ruling in the case, that limit was increased to $20,000. While the 1972 increase in the homestead exemption would likely have provided adequate protection for the Endos, the statute in effect at the time the Sawada sisters made their claim was clearly inadequate. At all times, according to the record, the value of the Endo home exceeded $2,750. The effect of the court's decision was to give the Endos the benefit of the increased homestead exemption. The Endos got to keep their homestead. Mr. Endo continued to live in the homestead even after the transfer to his sons and after the death of his wife.

In response to plaintiffs' concerns about the creation of a "super-homestead" exemption available for all tenancy by the entirety property, the court explained weakly that "creditors are not entitled to special consideration."[31] After all, creditors can inform themselves about what property the debtor owns and whether the property is or is not reachable if the debtor defaults. True enough for banks who lend money and apprise themselves in advance of the borrower's creditworthiness. But the Sawada sisters were hardly in the same position as commercial lenders. They were tort victims with no opportunity to review the tortfeasor's creditworthiness before the accident.

If a person, wishing to avoid potential future creditors, were to place all his assets in trust with an instruction that the trustee pay the income out to the creator of the trust, but in no event allow the creator's creditors to reach the trust, we'd call that a spendthrift trust. And while a valid spendthrift trust can be created for the benefit of third parties, American courts have fairly uniformly held that the creation of a spendthrift trust for the benefit of the creator is against public policy.[32] As one Pennsylvania court put it: "This would be a startling proposition to affirm. It would revolutionize the credit system entirely, destroy all faith in the apparent ownership of property, and repeal all our statutes and decisions against frauds."[33] In other words, it is against public policy to allow someone to transform property ownership so as to continue enjoying the property, while keeping it free from creditors. And yet, that is exactly what the tenancy by the entirety estate accomplishes.

---

[31] Sawada at 616, quoting from a Delaware case.

[32] See, e.g., Petty v. Moores Brook Sanitarium, 110 Va. 815, 67 S.E. 355 (1910).

[33] Mackason's Appeal, 42 Pa. 330 (1862).

Under state law, some property is uniformly exempted from creditors' claims. Homestead laws protecting the owner and the owner's family exist in all states. Small items like tools of the trade, clothing, and other personal items are similarly exempted from creditor's claims under state law. But typically these statutes deal with specific types of property and contain limits. The "super-homestead" exemption for tenancy by the entirety property, created by the *Sawada* court, includes all types of property that can be held as tenants by the entirety. While only real estate qualified for this form of ownership at common law, modern law recognizes the estate in personalty, which may include bank accounts, as well as stocks and bonds of any value.

Thus, in states like Hawaii, which provide an absolute bar to creditors when the debtor is one spouse who holds property as a tenancy by the entirety, this joint form of ownership provides incredibly valuable benefits. Of course, to reap the benefits, the debtor generally must be married and willing to share the property with a spouse. As a means to avoid creditors, perhaps this principle of family unity, of sharing, is sufficient to distinguish the tenancy by the entirety from a self-created spendthrift trust. But it seems, to this author at least, a pretty slim reed.

Current State of the Law

Currently, twenty-five states recognize the tenancy by the entirety.[34] The other twenty-five states do not.[35] Fourteen states protect the tenancy from all claims by creditors.[36] If there is a trend, slight though it may be, it is in favor of recognizing the tenancy and protecting it from the claims of creditors.

The original common law estate was created only when the property was owned by husband and wife. Yet, in two of the states that offer some

[34] Those states are: Alaska, Arkansas, Delaware, Florida, Hawaii, Illinois, Indiana, Kentucky, Maryland, Massachusetts, Michigan, Mississippi, Missouri, New Jersey, New York, North Carolina, Oklahoma, Ohio, Oregon, Pennsylvania, Rhode Island, Tennessee, Vermont, Virginia, Wyoming. Note this is 6 states more than the number listed by Dean Phipps in his article. Alaska and Hawaii account for two of the six. Illinois, Ohio, and Oklahoma have enacted statutes that authorize creation of tenancy by the entirety estates. Mississippi appears to have recognized the common law tenancy all along.

[35] The 25 states not recognizing tenancy by the entirety include the 8 community property states (Arizona, California, Idaho, Louisiana, Nevada, New Mexico, Texas, and Washington). Some of these states have distanced themselves substantially from their civil law origins and all but Louisiana have adopted the common law in some form or other. Some of them have statutes that mention the tenancy by the entirety estate, but none of them have court decisions specifically recognizing the estate.

[36] In addition to the ten states identified by Phipps, the following states belong in this group: Hawaii, Illinois, Michigan, and North Carolina.

of the strongest protection against creditors, the estate has been extended to nonmarital units. In Vermont, same-sex couples are authorized by statute to enter into "civil unions." Civil unions are treated like marriages and one of the benefits available under state law is property ownership in the form of a tenancy by the entirety estate, fully protected from creditors. Hawaii, in response to litigation over the recognition of same-sex marriages in the mid 1990s, enacted legislation that recognized certain unmarried couples as "reciprocal beneficiaries," who are entitled to a handful of the rights married couples enjoy. One of the few benefits offered "reciprocal beneficiaries" is the tenancy by the entirety estate,[37] which post-*Sawada* is fully protected from creditor claims based on the debts of one spouse.

The Supreme Court of Massachusetts has recently ruled that barring same-sex couples from the state institution of marriage violates the Massachusetts constitution. When that decision takes full effect, married same-sex couples will enjoy the same right to hold property as a tenancy by the entirety. Thus, the trend in favor of tenancy by the entirety not only includes new states, it also includes new types of couples.

But there is one fly in the ointment. Even in those fourteen states that fully protect tenancy by the entirety property from the claims of creditors, there is one creditor who can reach the property: the IRS. In 2002, the United States Supreme Court held in *United States v. Craft*[38] that a husband's rights in Michigan tenancy by the entireties property constituted "property" to which a federal tax lien could attach. Remember that Michigan law bars the creditors of one spouse from reaching any interest in tenancy by the entirety property.[39] Note also that federal tax law looks to state property law to determine what rights a taxpayer has in property.

Using the "bundle of sticks" metaphor, Justice O'Connor noted that the husband had a number of rights (or "sticks") in the entireties property:

> According to Michigan law, respondent's husband had, among other rights, the following rights with respect to the entireties property: the right to use the property, the right to exclude third parties from it, the right to a share of income produced from it, the right of survivorship, the right to become a tenant in common with equal shares upon divorce, the right to sell the property with the respondent's consent and to receive half the proceeds from such a sale, the right to place an encumbrance on the property with the respon-

---

[37] See Hawaii Stat. 509–2.

[38] 535 U.S. 274 (2002).

[39] See note 19 supra.

dent's consent, and the right to block respondent from selling or encumbering the property unilaterally.[40]

There was, however, one "stick" that he didn't have–the "right of unilateral alienation." All in all, held the Court, there were enough "sticks" in the bundle to constitute "property" for purposes of the federal tax lien statute. In other words, "unilateral alienation" was not viewed as an essential stick in the bundle.[41]

Michigan courts, recognizing these limits on the husband's rights, would say that the husband had no separate "property interest" to which a creditor's lien could attach. The Supreme Court, also recognizing these limits on the husband's rights, said that the husband did have a separate "property interest" to which a federal tax lien could attach. The difference in outcome can be explained by the fact that the *Craft* Court was construing a federal statute, which provided that any amount a taxpayer owed in delinquent taxes "shall be a lien in favor of the United States upon all property and rights to property, whether real or personal, belonging to such person."[42] The tax lien attached to the "property" or "rights to property" that belonged to the husband, and not to the real estate itself owned by the spouses as a tenancy by the entirety. Because the real property had been sold, the lien then attached to the sales proceeds and the IRS was entitled to recover the portion of the proceeds allocable to the husband's interest in the property. The Supreme Court remanded the case for a determination of what that amount should be.

One can only wonder what the Sawada sisters would think about this turn of events. Mr. Endo was a tortfeasor, a wrongdoer. He owed them compensation and he owned a property interest in entireties property from which he could have paid their claim. He was the spouse who survived. Using the property to pay the claim after her death would not have taken away her Mrs. Endo's survivorship rights. Nonetheless, the Hawaii Supreme Court said the sisters could not recover from Mr. Endo. Twenty-five years later, the United States Supreme Court, relying on the same sort of property arguments set forth by the Sawada sisters, i.e., that a lien could attach to the husband's interest in the property, has ruled that the IRS could have recovered if it had been the creditor of Mr. Endo. Innocent tort victims lose; the Internal Revenue Service wins. What policy arguments support this difference?[43]

---

[40] Craft at 282.

[41] Its absence would of course affect the value of the husband's property interest. How much would you want to pay for property that you could not sell without Mrs. Craft's consent?

[42] Section 6321 Internal Revenue Code.

[43] The question is not merely rhetorical. The reader is encouraged to identify competing policy arguments. E.g., the *Sawada* court ruled in favor of a policy that favored family

Conclusion

Tenancy by the entirety began in England as a special joint estate between husband and wife, necessitated by the common law disabilities of the wife under the doctrine of coverture. Coverture crossed the Atlantic and took hold in the United States, but was greatly modified in the mid-nineteenth century. Once the wife's legal disabilities were removed (primarily through the enactment of state Married Women's Property Statutes, but sometimes also through state constitutional provisions), there was no strong need to retain the estate. Some state courts recognized this and ruled that the estate was no longer part of the common law. Courts in other states continued to recognize the estate, often ruling that their Married Women's Property Act was silent about the estate and thus had no effect on its existence. In addition, some state legislatures passed statutes after the Married Women's Statutes were enacted that specifically listed the entireties estate as a permissible form of joint estate. None of these statutes, however, explained how a tenancy by the entirety differed from a joint tenancy. Nor did they explain what effect the Married Women's Property Acts had on the attributes of the entireties estate.

As courts in those states that retained the estate struggled with the question of how to define the tenancy by the entirety, they uniformly held that the estate's survivorship feature was inviolate. As a result, in those states, the creditors of one spouse can never attach the property so as to destroy the survivorship rights of the other spouse.

While these states agree that the non-debtor spouse's survivorship rights are fully protected, they differ on a host of subsidiary questions dealing with creditor's rights in entireties property. Some states allow creditors to attach the survivorship rights, some allow attachment of the current income interests, and some allow attachment of no interests in entireties property whatsoever.

The indestructibility of the survivorship right can be traced to the common law roots of the tenancy by the entirety. The notion that such property is totally immune from the claims of creditors so long as it remains a tenancy by the entirety, however, is a creature of modern law. It is this "asset protection" aspect of the entireties estate that makes it attractive to some modern spouses. But note that once the marriage ends, the protection from creditors also ends. Upon divorce, for example, if the debtor spouse retains any interest in the property, that interest

---

solidarity and protected married women from the creditors of their husbands. The *Craft* Court's decision supported a policy in favor of uniform tax collection processes, regardless of the variations in state law.

can be attached at that time.[44]

The *Sawada* court identified four different rules affecting creditors' rights in tenancy by the entireties property. Today, those rules have been collapsed into the following three categories:

Category one: highest level of protection. Some states, including Hawaii, provide an absolute bar to creditors of one spouse as long as the property is held by the spouses as a tenancy by the entirety. Under this rule, the spouses have the right to convey the property jointly free from the creditors claims.

Category two: intermediate level of protection. At least two states (Kentucky and Tennessee[45]) protect the tenancy by the entirety during the joint lives of the spouses, but do allow creditors to reach the debtor spouse's contingent survivorship interest. Under this rule, if a creditor has attached the debtor spouse's survivorship interest, any joint conveyance by the spouses will be subject to the creditor's claim to the property in the event the debtor spouse survives.

Category three: minimal protection. A minority of states allow creditors to attach the lifetime interest in profits of the debtor spouse as well as the contingent survivorship right, while fully protecting the survivorship right of the non-debtor spouse. In these states, a joint conveyance by both spouses will be subject to the creditor's lien against the interest of the debtor spouse. If the conveyance is a sale producing cash proceeds, the creditor should be entitled to the portion of the proceeds attributable to the debtor spouse. But, if the non-debtor spouse retains her survivorship interest, and if she survives, then the creditor's lien should be worthless.[46]

The question yet to be determined is whether the federal rule announced in *Craft* fits within category three or whether the federal rule allows the IRS as creditor to force a sale of the entireties property thereby destroying the non-debtor spouse's survival right. That specific issue did not arise in *Craft* because Mrs. Craft, the non-debtor spouse,

---

[44] See, for example, Corey v. Jonathan Manor, Inc., 59 Haw. 277, 580 P.2d 843 at 844 (1978). At divorce, wife was entitled to 100% interest in the property for life and a survivorship right. Husband, who was the debtor also had a survivorship right. The court held that the husband's contingent survivorship right was subject to levy and execution for his debts.

[45] See Robinson v. Trousdale County, 516 S.W.2d 626 (Tenn. 1974).

[46] Massachusetts clearly follows this rule. In *Coraccio*, supra note 19, the court declared that Massachusetts law did not "require the consent of both spouses before a mortgage may encumber the property, and that the bank, if it foreclosed, could acquire Stephen Coraccio's interest in the property, namely a right wholly defeasible should the plaintiff, the nondebtor spouse, survive him . . " 612 N.E.2d at 655.

had agreed to a sale. The only question in that case was whether the IRS could assert its lien against the portion of the proceeds of the sale that were allocable to the husband's interest. The Supreme Court held that the IRS could claim that portion allocable to the husband and remanded for a determination of how to make that allocation. Mrs. Craft, having agreed to the sale, effectively transferred her lifetime rights along with her contingent survival right to the purchaser and was entitled to full compensation for her rights out of the sales proceeds. The IRS was entitled to the balance.

It is quite a different question whether the IRS has the power to force a sale of entireties property when the non-debtor spouse does not agree to the sale. Being paid the fair market value of one's survival right is simply not the same thing as knowing that if you are the spouse who survives, you will take fee title to the entire property. The guarantee of ownership upon survival is especially important to some spouses when the property is the homestead, a favorite vacation home, a particularly loved piece of artwork, or some other form of unique or constitutive property that is not fungible.

Absent a specific statutory authorization to foreclose against the property itself, creditors, under state law, should only be able to foreclose (i.e., enforce a lien by a forced sale) against the husband's interest in the property. Since *Craft* merely stands for the proposition that the husband's interest in the entireties property constituted "property" for purposes of the lien, it does not tell us that the IRS can foreclose its lien against the husband's property interest by forcing a sale of entireties property itself.

Only one case post-*Craft* has considered this issue. In June of 2003, the Court of Appeals for the Sixth Circuit ruled in favor of the IRS and held that a non-debtor spouse's interest in entireties property, including her survival rights, could be subjected to a forced sale in order to pay back taxes owed by the debtor spouse.[47] The court found that the foreclosure was authorized under a federal tax statute which empowered the IRS to force a sale of any property against which it had a tax lien. Section 6335(c) of the Internal Revenue Code provides that "if any property liable to levy is not divisible, so as to enable the [government] by sale of a part thereof to raise the whole amount of the tax and expenses, the whole of such property shall be sold." To be consistent with the holding in *Craft*, it would seem that the court should have held that the only "property liable to levy" was the bundle of sticks held by the husband and not the real estate itself.[48]

---

[47] Hatchett v. U.S., 330 F.3d 875 (6th Cir. 2003).

[48] The court's opinion seems clearly wrong. At the time of this writing, the case was still before the Sixth Circuit and the court was considering whether to amend its opinion. The taxpayer is prepared to petition the Supreme Court for review if necessary.

There is, however, an alternative method available to the IRS to enforce it tax lien. This alternative method would allow the government to force a sale of the real estate, even though the delinquent taxpayer had only a partial interest in the property. Under Section 7403 of the Internal Revenue Code, the government can ask for a foreclosure sale of the entire property. The federal district court, however, has discretion and can consider the rights of the other property owners before ordering the sale. This alternative offers some protection of the non-debtor spouse, while balancing the rights of the creditors.[49]

Correctly applying the federal tax law provisions, a fourth category of protection for spousal interests in entireties property is created:

Category four: equitable protection. By statute, a creditor (e.g., the IRS) can request foreclosure of a lien against the debtor spouse's interest in the entireties property. The court may decide to grant the request or not. In exercising its discretion, the court might look to such factors as: (1) the extent to which the creditor's financial interests would be harmed by restricting the creditor to a sale of the partial interest, (2) the reasonable expectations of the non-debtor spouse, (3) the costs to the non-debtor spouse that would occur if she or he were forced to sell the property, and (4) the relative values of the interests in the property.[50]

Given the fact that there are competing values in all cases in which a creditor asserts a claim against one spouse who owns property with a non-debtor spouse as tenancy by the entirety, the rule in category four offers a possibility for balancing those values. Those tenancy by the entirety states that have not fully worked out the details of how to deal with the competing claims of spouses and creditors might consider this possibility. Indeed, all tenancy by entireties states might be well advised to consider this possibility. By enacting a state statute modeled on Section 7403 of the Internal Revenue Code, states could continue to offer some protection to spouses who own entireties property without creating the "super-homestead" complained about by the Sawada sisters.

The underlying policy question is how best to balance the interests of spouses and creditors. The modern estate of tenancy by the entirety should be constructed using modern techniques. Statutorily empowering courts to balance the interests of modern-day spouses against various

---

[49] See, e.g., United States v. Rodgers, 461 U.S. 677 (1983)(holding that a district court may under Section 7403 order the sale of home even when the wife owes no taxes and has homestead rights in the property). See also Steve R. Johnson," Fog, Fairness, and the Federal Fisc: Tenancy-by-the-Entireties Interests and the Federal Tax Lien," 60 Mo. L. Rev. 839 (1995).

[50] These factors are similar to ones suggested by the U.S. Supreme Court in the *Rodgers* case, supra.

types of creditors is a more attractive approach than blindly applying rules that date back to coverture and the early Married Women's Property Statutes.

6

Richard H. Chused*

Saunders (a.k.a. Javins) v. First National Realty Corporation

Introduction

The clerk for Judge Austin Fickling called *First National Realty Corporation v. Saunders* for trial on June 17, 1966.[1] It must have been quite a scene. As Gene Fleming, the tenants' lawyer, tells the story, the tenants living in the Clifton Terrace Apartments who had refused to pay their rent because of the terrible conditions in the three building complex, were asked to collect evidence of housing code violations and bring their exhibits to court. They brought bags of mouse feces, dead mice, roaches and pictures of their apartments to the courtroom, which was filled with tenants from the buildings. A housing inspector was also there, carrying a pile of paper that, according to Fleming, "stood at least one and one-half feet high," memorializing well over one thousand citations for code violations. Herman Miller, the lawyer for Sidney Brown's First National Realty Corporation which owned Clifton Terrace, moved to bar the introduction of any evidence of code violations on the ground that it would inflame the jury. Fleming, of course, vehemently

---

* A longer, fully documented version of this article will be published in volume 11, issue 2 of the Georgetown Journal on Poverty Law and Policy (Winter 2004). At the editors' insistence, the full documentation and citations were removed to accommodate the book's format.

[1] Actions for possession for non-payment of rent are typically called for their first hearing about ten days after the complaint is served. In these cases, Fleming filed answers and requested jury trials. This later became routine in cases with tenants represented by counsel.

opposed Miller's motion.[2] Judge Fickling, in accordance with the long-standing refusal of courts to allow tenants to raise defenses in eviction cases, then barred introduction of the evidence, entered judgments for possession as a matter of law and dismissed the jury.[3]

These events formed the beginning of what turned out to be a very long saga. Eventually, in *Javins v. First National Realty Corporation*,[4] the United States Circuit Court of Appeals for the District of Columbia Circuit became the first tribunal to unequivocally hold that a warranty of habitability was implied in all residential leases and that tenants could set off damages for violation of that warranty defensively in eviction cases. But the propriety of Judge Fickling's decision took four years to resolve. During that time Clifton Terrace became the object of enormous coverage in the press, City Hall politicians took center stage in the controversy for a time, plans to sell the building to a non-profit corporation for remodeling emerged, collapsed and reemerged, Sidney Brown was sent to jail for a brief period, the city erupted in major civil disturbances and the tenants continued to suffer under terrible living conditions.

The acrimonious quality of the trial between Brown and his tenants typified many of the events surrounding the litigation of *Javins*, arguably the most influential landlord-tenant case of the twentieth century. The tenants were largely poor and black residents of Washington, D.C.— a city rife with racial unrest and protest. The efforts of some tenants living in Clifton Terrace to alleviate hundreds of housing code violations in their apartments included sit-ins at the offices of Corporation Counsel of the city and of the Secretary of the Department of Housing and Urban Development, as well as a rent strike. It was the rent strike, and the resulting actions brought by the landlord to obtain possession of the apartments from the non-paying tenants that eventually led to the *Javins* decision.

---

[2] In addition to arguing that he should be able to introduce evidence of 1500 housing code violations at Clifton Terrace, Fleming also wanted to use the testimony of Robert Gold, Chief of Research for the National Capital Planning Commission to show that low income families—especially black families—in the District of Columbia had great difficulty finding housing that met code standards. A summary of Fleming's offer of proof may be found in Settled Statement of Proceedings and Evidence, *First National Realty Corp. v. Saunders*, et al., filed in the District of Columbia Court of Appeals on Aug. 18, 1966.

[3] Since no facts were left to be determined—everyone agreed that rent had not been paid—there was nothing for the jury to do. Traditionally, the court decides legal issues and the jury resolves factual disputes.

[4] 428 F.2d 1071, 138 U.S. App. D.C. 369 (D.C. Cir. 1970), rev'g Saunders v. First National Realty Corp., 245 A.2d 836 (D.C.App. 1968). The proceeding in the Landlord and Tenant Division of the D.C. Court of General Sessions resulted in no published opinion.

Protest and unrest in this epoch went far beyond sit-ins and rent strikes. June 17, 1966, the date the striking tenants' efforts to avoid eviction from the Clifton Terrace Apartments were first frustrated in Landlord and Tenant Court, was only ten months after the Watts area of Los Angeles went up in flames in an outburst of black anger,[5] ten days after civil rights worker James Meredith was shot by a sniper in a failed assassination attempt while on a "March Against Fear" from Memphis to Jackson, five days after the start of the first of two civil disturbances that summer in Chicago, and the same day Stokely Carmichael, chairman of the Student Non–Violent Coordinating Committee, made his famous "Black Power" speech in Greenwood, Mississippi. And these same tenants lost their appeal before the District of Columbia Court of Appeals on September 23, 1968,[6] only a few months after Dr. Martin Luther King, Jr. was assassinated and parts of Washington, D.C., including areas on 14th Street north and south of Clifton Terrace, went up in flames. By the time the United States Circuit Court of Appeals issued its now famous decision in 1970, old downtown Washington had begun a steady decline from which it is only now recovering.

The *Javins* story, therefore, is full of the raw passion of actors convinced of the righteousness of their positions. Reconstructing the tale requires more than a review of the changes *Javins* made in landlord-tenant law, though that material will be covered. The meaning and impact of the case can be grasped only if some of the emotions of its actors and the passions of their historical moment can be recaptured in these pages.

I. In the Beginning

A. *The Apartment Buildings*

Harry Wardman, with the help of his architects Frank Russell White and A. M. Schneider, constructed the three Clifton Terrace Apartments at 1308, 1312 and 1350 Clifton Street, NW, originally called Wardman Courts, between 1914 and 1915. Wardman, "who often appears to have

---

[5] The civil unrest in Watts, the first of what became a series of disturbances that affected many major American cities, began on August 11, 1965.

[6] At the time of this litigation, Washington, D.C. had a two level local court system. The trial level court was the Court of General Sessions and the appellate court was the District of Columbia Court of Appeals. For the most part citizens of the city did not control or elect those who governed them. The lack of self-governance was manifested in the court system by the existence of a right to apply for review of a local appellate decision by the United States Court of Appeals for the District of Columbia Circuit. Ironically, that right of review is what led to the *Javins* opinion read in most first year property course. Legislation ending the system of federal review of local court decisions was adopted in 1970, the same year *Javins* was decided by the federal circuit court. District of Columbia Court Reform and Criminal Procedure Act of 1970, Pub. L. 91–358, 84 Stat. 473 (1970)

built Washington single-handedly, is known to have developed over 200 apartment buildings as well as hundreds of houses, 'flat' units, commercial spaces and office buildings.''[7] Wardman Courts was one of many middle class apartment complexes constructed in Washington between 1910 and the Great Depression. Located on the crest of a hill adjacent to a major streetcar line running up and down 14th Street, many of the apartments had spectacular views of downtown Washington. They were the largest buildings in the area and, therefore took on enormous importance as the symbolic center of the neighborhood.

The buildings were part of a major shift in urban planning and architectural design. As noted in the narrative supporting the 2001 certification of Clifton Terrace for listing in the National Register of Historic Places:

> The use of modern styles for Washington apartment buildings between the 1920s and the 1930s stands out as the single most significant change during those years. As visually striking as was the contrast of the light stone of the classically derived styles of the early twentieth century against the dark red brick of the Victorian era, so was the impact of the styles associated with the Modern Movement. Clifton Terrace is a significant example of apartment building design influenced by the Garden City Movement in the 1920s[.] * * * [E]ncouraged by a desire for healthful living and suburban interest, [architects integrated] * * * more green space into urban living and apartment design, dispensing with many of the stigmas associated with urban living. The new "garden" apartments offered superior air circulation, more pleasing views, the inclusion of balconies, and enhanced light in each apartment—all at a moderate price.[8]

The Garden City Movement and the related City Beautiful Movement probably began with publication in 1898 of a thin volume entitled *To-morrow: A Peaceful Path to Real Reform*, by Ebenezer Howard. Reissued under the more propitious title *Garden Cities of To-morrow* in 1902, the book advocated a combined use of modern urban architecture and countryside landscaping to create a wholesome and healthy environment for city dwellers.[9] Like many other planners of his time, Howard

---

[7] National Park Service, Department of the Interior, National Register of Historic Places Registration Form, Sec. 8, p. 9 (Nov. 7, 2001). [Hereinafter cited as Historic Registration.] A long feature article published in the Washington Post also headlined Wardman's impact on the city. Deborah K. Dietsch, *The Man Who Built Washington*, Washington Post (Sep. 5, 2002) at H1.

[8] Id. at Section 8, p. 4.

[9] For more on these movements, see Peter Hall, Cities of Tomorrow 86–135, 174–202 (Blackwell, 1988).

believed that the moral and civic fiber of urban society could be improved by altering the physical settings of city life.[10] While many contemporary planners view the Garden City Movement as a bit romantic and naïve, residents of Washington found developments like Wardman Courts quite attractive. Through the 1950s the buildings were almost always full of middle class tenants.

B. Pre–Reform Eviction Law

At the time Wardman Courts was constructed, landlord-tenant law in Washington, D.C. and most of the rest of the country was based on a fairly simple and already old-fashioned set of property norms. The norms rested upon an English tenurial notion that in return for a grant of permission to use land, a tenant agreed to pay rent, maintain the land and return the land when the lease expired. It was a simple contract exchanging some form of payment in cash, service or kind for the right to possess land. Granting the tenant the right to take possession fulfilled all of the responsibilities of the landlord. After gaining the right to take possession, the tenant was obligated to pay the rent and return the land to the landlord at the termination of the lease. The customary view was that a lease gave the tenant virtually complete control over the use of the rented property for the lease term.[11] If, therefore, the tenant vacated the land before the end of the lease, the obligation to pay rent did not end. Since, the reasoning went, the landlord had transferred the entire rental term by granting possession to the tenant, there was no obligation to take it back before the end of the lease.[12] For similar reasons a tenant injured because of some flaw on the leased property was unable to obtain compensation from the landlord. The obligation to keep the land safe for use and occupancy fell upon tenants.[13] And, of course, the landlord could reclaim possession if the tenant did not pay rent.

Nineteenth century civil procedure in the United States reemphasized the notion that leases were straightforward exchanges of posses-

---

[10] The positive environmentalists—believers in the ability of architecture and design to enhance civic responsibility—are discussed in Paul Boyer, Urban Masses and Moral Order in America: 1820–1920, at 220–283 (Harvard Univ. Press, 1978).

[11] In many ways this vision was false. If, for example, rent was paid in kind, the landlord might take large portions of the tenant's crops as payment. The terms of the lease could easily leave a tenant as a serf—a servant of the landlord.

[12] The common law rules went so far as to hold a tenant responsible for rent even after the building was destroyed by fire, storm, or other natural cause. That result was altered by statute throughout the United States in the nineteenth century. For a case on this issue in Washington, D.C., see Schmidt v. Pettit, 8 D.C. 179 (Sup. Ct. 1873).

[13] This was the rule in the District of Columbia. In Howell v. Schneider, 24 App. D.C. 532 (1905), the landlord was not responsible for personal injuries to a tenant resulting from a toilet flush tank falling off the bathroom wall.

sion for payment. American judicial procedures, also based in many ways on English precedents, were often as narrow in their vision as a standard lease. Litigation began by the filing of a writ, usually limited to the statement of a single legal theory. There were certain defenses to each kind of writ, but merger of claims and parties, and the use of counter-claims were not nearly as extensive as today.[14] Thus, when a landlord sought to evict a tenant for non-payment of rent, the tenant could not respond by asserting that the leased property was unusable for agricul-ture, even if the landlord had warranted that the land was a farmer's delight. To raise the warranty issue, the tenant had to file a new breach of contract case. Similarly, if a landlord sued a tenant for unpaid rent after the lessee abandoned the property, the tenant could not assert that her departure was partially or totally excused because of personal injuries suffered as a result of the landlord's negligent behavior. Again, the tenants had to file a separate tort claim.

Combining the law of leases with the limitations of nineteenth century procedural systems established a regime in which suits against tenants for either possession or unpaid rent were treated as independent from each other and from suits for breaches of other contracts or tort duties of care.[15] The basic lease—the exchange of possession for rent—was both substantively and procedurally independent from other con-tractual terms. Since each covenant in a lease was said to be indepen-dent, breach of one covenant by the landlord—such as a warranty of fitness—could not be used to defend a claim that the tenant breached a different covenant—like the obligation to pay rent for possession. In-deed, the independence of covenants construct governed not only the law of leases but also much of nineteenth century contract law. As a result, a suit for unpaid rent was defendable only by a claim of accord and satisfaction (payment), constructive eviction (an action by the landlord so disturbing to the tenant's right to possess the property that the rent for land exchange was deemed void for failure of consideration) or

---

[14] Today, a plaintiff suing in a standard civil forum may join all his or her claims against the defendant in the same case, including all those arising out of the same facts. Fed .R. Civ. P. 18. Defendants may respond to a plaintiff's case by asserting all available claims against the plaintiff. Fed. R. Civ. P. 13. Claims arising out of the facts giving rise to the plaintiff's case must be asserted. Fed. R. Civ. P. 13. In most cases, all the parties involved in the claims may be joined in the same case. Fed. R. Civ. P. 20.

[15] A related body of rules was used to limit the ability of tenants to defend eviction actions brought when they held over beyond the end of their terms. At common law, a landlord, without stating any reasons, could terminate a periodic tenancy upon the giving of appropriately timed notice, even if he breached another standard of care by seeking the tenant's eviction. Landlords, therefore, could retaliate and seek the eviction of tenants who complained about housing code violations to public authorities. That was the rule in Washington, D.C. until 1968. Edwards v. Habib, 227 A.2d 388 (D.C.App. 1967), reversed by Edwards v. Habib, 397 F.2d 687 (D.C. Cir. 1968).

perhaps fraud in the inducement (fraud that induced the tenant to agree to a contract he would otherwise have eschewed).

For American residential tenants, the most serious consequence of this vision of landlord-tenant law was the ability of landlords to speedily evict non-paying tenants. Indeed, American practice "purified" the early English law by getting rid of some impediments to the use of ejectment law to evict non-paying tenants. Early ejectment law often contained a number of technical constraints on the ability of landlords to remove tenants quickly. For example, common law ejectment rules required a property owner to prove that a right to reenter the premises in case of the tenant's breach of a covenant was reserved in the lease. Some statutes, including those in Washington, D.C. and New York, also limited the eviction of tenants to cases where rent was more than six months in arrears. These sorts of constraints on eviction made some sense in pre-industrial England where leasehold arrangements formed the backbone of much of early English property law and embodied a large set of cultural norms and interlocking chains of human relationships. In such a world it was rational to provide for some limits on ejectment. Removal of a tenant could cause a drastic change in social status and class. It served to protect not only the lower classes, but also those in the upper ranks of society who fell upon hard times.

This system came under enormous strain in the United States as towns and cities blossomed during the nineteenth century. The strain arose not out of a perceived need to safeguard the well being of an increasingly large number of poor urban tenants, but from a desire to protect the financial security of property owners. Early nineteenth century New York City, for example, had a large number of residential tenants. Many of them were immigrants occupying apartments and houses under oral, periodic leases that could be terminated on a month's notice. Use of the ejectment process made it difficult to evict those tenants not paying their rent. Landlords using oral leases could not always prove to the satisfaction of ejectment court judges that they had reserved a right to reenter the premises. But, most importantly, landlords viewed the six-month waiting period as a major hardship. In 1820, the New York General Assembly rewrote the eviction statute, allowing a tenant to be summarily removed after holding over past the end of the lease term or defaulting in the payment of rent. This statute did away with some of the traditional limitations on ejectment and, more significantly, shifted the proceedings to a different court for speedier action. In case of a rent default after the legislative changes, the landlord had to show that the rent was due, that a right to reenter the property was reserved,[16] and that a written demand for the rent was served on the

---

[16] Once the eviction cases were shifted to a specialized, speedy court, handling a large volume of cases, this requirement became a formality fulfilled by appropriate statements from the landlord that the re-entry right had been reserved in oral undertakings.

tenant at least three days before the judicial proceeding was filed. Statutes similar to New York's appeared all across the United States, including in Washington, D.C., during the nineteenth century.[17]

II. As Wardman Courts Aged . . .

A. *Precursors to Reform*

Though there were a few changes in landlord-tenant law during the first half of the twentieth century, they had virtually no impact on the procedures used to evict non-paying tenants. The most significant shifts relevant to our story actually occurred in other areas of consumer law and in civil procedure. By the time the myriad "movements" of the late 1960s and early 1970s arose, it was palpably obvious that change in eviction law was long overdue. Cultural shifts also began to have an impact on Wardman Courts. Through the 1950s, Wardman Courts, by then called Clifton Terrace, was occupied by mostly white middle class tenants. But by the 1960s, Sidney Brown's First National Realty Corporation owned the complex, the occupants were largely black and the buildings had fallen into disrepair. These legal, demographic and structural shifts laid part of the groundwork for major controversy.

Contract and consumer law underwent a major transformation between 1900 and 1970. The independent covenant notion, to whatever degree it controlled the contours of nineteenth century law and judicial procedure, disappeared from standard contract law by the early twentieth century. Its demise actually began in the late eighteenth century with an opinion by Lord Mansfield in *Kingston v. Preston*.[18] Justice Cardozo put the lid on the coffin in the United States in the early twentieth century.[19] In addition, nineteenth century rules favoring freedom of contract and *caveat emptor* gave way either to judicially enforced limitations on bargains or to legislatively imposed regulatory regimes. Grant Gilmore, one of the most trenchant chroniclers of twentieth century contract law, nicely described the contours of the transformation in 1957:

> It has been a commonplace of legal scholarship that one of the great ground-swells of movement in the nineteenth century was from status to contract—from the protection of rights of property and ownership to the protection of rights of contract. It is easy to see how this should have happened as wealth multiplied and an aristocratic society gave way to its pushing, aggressive, dynamic successor. I suggest that the ground-swell carried an undercurrent

---

[17] Many states adopted summary eviction remedies prior to 1850.

[18] 2 Doug. 689 (1773).

[19] Jacob & Youngs v. Kent, 230 N.Y. 239, 129 N.E. 889 (1921).

with it and that, as the great wave recedes, we are being caught in the undertow. The next half century may well record a reverse movement.

In the crucial business of allocating commercial and social risks we have already gone a long way toward reversing the nineteenth century. In tort we follow a banner which bears the strange device: liability without fault—though we soften the impact on the innocent tortfeasor by various schemes of insurance and compensation. In contract we have broken decisively with the nineteenth century theory that breach of contract was not very serious and not very reprehensible—as Justice Holmes once put it: every man is 'free to break his contract if he chooses'—from which it followed that damages for breach should be held to a minimum. Today we look on breach of contract as a very serious and immoral thing indeed: never, I dare say, in our history have the remedies for breach been so easily available to the victim, or the sanctions for breach so heavy against the violator * * *. The continuing increase in seller's warranty liability is merely one illustration of what has been going on all along the contract front.[20]

The contracts and torts textbooks used by first year law students are littered with famous opinions exemplifying the shifts described by Gilmore.[21] But these at times dramatic shifts in consumer law had quite limited effects on landlord tenant law. The notion of independent covenants continued to govern suits by landlords for rent or possession. Only the rules on the liability of owners for tenant injuries were swept along with the general tide of reform.

Recall that at common law, landlords were not responsible for any injuries suffered by tenants on rented property. Once landlords transferred possession to tenants, they were relieved of further responsibility. Two developments caused the common law rule to erode. First, the growth of apartment living led to a number of cases in which injuries occurred in building areas left in the control of landlords. Just before Wardman Court was constructed, the Court of Appeals for the District of Columbia followed a national trend in holding a landlord responsible for

---

[20] Grant Gilmore, *Law, Logic and Experience*, 3 How. L.J. 40–41 (1957).

[21] Among the best known are Justice Cardozo writing on products liability in MacPherson v. Buick Motor Co., 217 N.Y. 382, 111 N.E. 1050 (1916), Justice Francis limiting the validity of form contracts disclaiming warranties in Henningsen v. Bloomfield Motors, Inc., 32 N.J. 358, 161 A.2d 69 (1960), Judge Traynor opining on products liability in Escola v. Coca Cola Bottling Co., 24 Cal.2d 453, 150 P.2d 436 (1944) and on strict liability in Greenman v. Yuba Power Products, Inc., 59 Cal.2d 57, 377 P.2d 897, 27 Cal.Rptr. 697 (1963), and Judge Wright exploring unconscionable sales contracts under Uniform Commercial Code § 2–302 in Williams v. Walker–Thomas Furniture Co., 350 F.2d 445 (D.C. Cir. 1965).

property damage caused by steam escaping from a heating pipe. Recognizing that apartment living was "a class of tenancy of comparatively recent origin" and that it was not reasonable "to suppose that the [landlord] * * * intended to permit the plaintiff to exercise any control over the main steam pipes in his apartment" the court placed a duty on landlords to properly maintain stairways, common areas and other facilities under their control.[22] The same result was reached a short time after Wardman Courts was completed in a case against Wardman himself.[23]

The other major impetus for changes in landlord liability was the adoption of housing and building codes, beginning in New York around the turn of the twentieth century. Eventually, courts looked to the codes to establish duties of care in tort cases. Justice Benjamin Cardozo was among the first to take this step, holding in the famous case of *Altz v. Leiberson*[24] that a landlord was responsible for injuries caused to a tenant when a bedroom ceiling collapsed. Reform of this sort was much slower in coming to Washington, D.C. The city did not adopt a comprehensive housing code until 1955. A few years after the code went into effect, Judge Bazelon, explicitly relying in *Whetzel v. Jess Fisher Management Company*[25] on the ground broken by Justice Cardozo in *Altz*, used the newly adopted regulations to impose a duty on landlords to safely maintain their premises.

At the same time that consumer and tort law reforms were altering the obligations of product manufacturers and vendors, civil procedure reforms were altering the face of American litigation. The Federal Rules of Civil Procedure were promulgated in 1938, enhancing the ability to litigate all issues arising out of the same situation at one time. Party joinder, counterclaims and cross-claims became routine. Within a fairly short time, most states emulated the federal system in their own procedural rules.

Despite these reforms in both law and procedure, the day-to-day relationships between landlords and tenants in Washington, D.C. and elsewhere did not change very much. The parties most commonly met in summary dispossess court when the landlord sued for possession of an apartment. In this setting the old common law regimes continued to operate largely unchanged and unchallenged. A tenant could still move out and claim constructive eviction if the premises were "unfit for the

---

[22] Iowa Apartment House Co. v. Herschel, 36 App.D.C. 457 (Ct. App. D.C. 1911).

[23] Wardman v. Hanlon, 280 F. 988, 52 App. D.C. 14 (Ct. App. D.C. 1922).

[24] 233 N.Y. 16, 134 N.E. 703 (1922).

[25] 282 F.2d 943, 108 U.S. App. D.C. 385 (1960).

purpose for which they were rented."[26] This standard, worded much like an implied warranty of fitness for use, was more lenient than the common law rule.[27] But residential tenants rarely took advantage of the opening. It was risky for tenants to move out and claim constructive eviction. If tenants lost their claim they were still responsible for paying rent. Most judicial proceedings, then and now, were simple actions brought by landlords for possession, either because rent was due or because tenants stayed over beyond the end of their terms. In these actions, courts still routinely applied the old common law rules—covenants were independent, no warranties were implied and, save for accord and satisfaction, no defenses were available to an action for possession for non-payment. The lack of lawyers willing to represent tenants exacerbated the problem. Tort lawyers sometimes were willing to take on the personal injury cases of poor injured tenants in the hopes of obtaining a contingent fee, but virtually no lawyers were willing to take on the eviction problems of a poor non-paying tenant. Until legal services programs arrived in the late 1960s, lawyers rarely challenged the operation of summary dispossess proceedings in residential lease disputes.

The real historical mystery in all of this is why the treatment of eviction cases in landlord-tenant court remained in this nineteenth century mode until the late 1960s and early 1970s. Progressives spent enormous amounts of time and energy during the late nineteenth and early twentieth centuries on tenement house reforms, City Beautiful buildings and parks, sanitation systems, and zoning. The social work and settlement house movements knew well the plight of immigrant and black tenants. Yet the most common assistance given to poor tenants about to be evicted was to urge summary dispossess court judges to delay the eviction of "good" tenants a few days so they could find another place to live. Blaming the poor for their plight was endemic even among the most forward looking activists of the day. They could not get beyond the notion that the payment of rent was an unchallengeable obligation.

Perhaps the explanation can be found in the hearts and souls of those in the middle and upper classes who drove the Progressive Movement. For the most part they were reacting to the chaos and disorganization of urban life at the turn of the twentieth century. The various crusades to clean up cities focused on the ways urbanization lowered the virtue and health of the impoverished and tempted children of all classes to misbehave. Structural reforms thought likely to make city life safer,

---

[26] Ackerhalt v. Smith, 141 A.2d 187 (Mun. Ct. App. D.C. 1958).

[27] The earlier standard was that the "landlord must have done, or be responsible for, some act of a permanent character with the intention and effect of depriving the tenant of the enjoyment of the demised premises." Hughes v. Westchester Development Corporation, 77 F.2d 550, 64 App. D.C. 292 (1935).

poor people more virtuous and urban cacophony less threatening to the better off dominated the agenda. Many accepted the notion that improving the physical surroundings of the poor strengthened their moral backbone. Tenement house reforms, housing codes, creation of parks, improving sanitation systems and zoning fit naturally into the progressive mix, even for many conservatives. Each focused on the physical surroundings in which the poor lived and promised to protect those living in nearby middle and upper class neighborhoods. Reconstructing summary dispossess court, however, met few if any of the progressives' goals. Indeed, providing tenants with the ability to remain in unhealthy tenement house apartments only exacerbated the problem. And for those—progressive and otherwise—motivated by nativism and racism, the very idea of helping the immigrant and black residents of the slums was anathema.

Many of the same basic trends continued to dominate urban reforms after World War II. As those perceiving themselves as artificially suppressed members of the middle class left the slums during the post-war recovery from The Great Depression, the poor population of urban America became largely black. During the late 1940s and early 1950s, vast resources were focused on assisting veterans, meeting pent up demand for middle class housing, constructing the interstate highway system and opening suburbs for development. Blacks were systematically excluded from most of these resources as public antipathy to those left behind in the cities grew. Summary dispossess court did not become a focus of public attention until black Americans began to claim their full citizenship rights and to gain access to legal services.

Regardless of the reasons for the long delay in eviction court reforms, Sidney Brown hardly could have anticipated that either the tenants or the city would cause him legal troubles when he purchased Clifton Terrace in 1963 It was easy to remove non-paying residents and the city's code enforcement system was largely ineffectual. By the early 1960s the landlord-tenant court was processing tens of thousands of cases per year. Handling this enormous load was relatively simple. Landlords quickly obtained judgments for possession from a court that refused to allow non-paying tenants to raise any warranty or other consumer defenses. Most cases took only moments to hear. For those tenants who bothered to show up,[28] the proceedings went something like this:

---

[28] Even today, a large proportion of the tenant-defendants in urban dispossess courts do not show up for their hearings. This occurs for a variety of reasons. Some move out after receiving a complaint and summons and never bother to go to court. Others never receive notice or ignore it. And some pay their rent after receiving legal papers and assume they don't have to go. If a tenant fails to appear a default judgment is entered for the landlord, who can then seek to have the tenant's possessions removed from the apartment.

The Clerk calls the parties to stand before the judge:

Landlord's Lawyer: (After introducing his rent payment records into evidence.) My records show that Tom and Teresa Tenant have not paid the rent for the past month. I rest.

Court (speaking to the unrepresented tenant): Have you paid the rent?

Tenant: No, but . . .

Court: Judgment for landlord. Call the next case.[29]

Tension was the result. Such hearings were out of sync with the widely publicized arrival of consumer remedies in other judicial settings. Racial friction and urban unrest were exacerbated as thousands of tenants—mostly black by the 1960s—were dragged through urban landlord tenant courts. Housing conditions, thought by many to be on the decline in black urban neighborhoods, created additional disaffection. It was inevitable that, at some point, eviction courts would become the focus of public attention. For Washington, D.C., that point arrived not too long after 1965 when a program offering legal services for the poor—created with funds from a federal grant from the Office of Economic Opportunity—opened an office in the basement of the Clifton Terrace Apartments.

B. Rent Strike

Columbia Heights, the neighborhood in which Clifton Terrace is located, was a logical spot to place a legal services office. Though housing quality may well have been improving across income and racial lines nationally and in the District of Columbia, Columbia Heights was an exception to the general trend. "[B]etween 1950 and 1970, the proportion of the nation's housing stock characterized as 'dilapidated' decreased by more than 50 percent; the proportion not having complete plumbing facilities decreased by more than 80 percent; the proportion that was overcrowded fell almost 50 percent."[30] Housing even improved for those in the lowest third of the income distribution. The number of units without complete plumbing facilities fell by more than 80 percent and the percentage of overcrowded units dropped by more than half.

---

[29] This is my version of what these "trials" were like based on my own visits to landlord-tenant courts in Chicago while in law school between 1965 and 1968 and in Newark while teaching at Rutgers Law School between 1968 and 1973. A very similar version was given by Gene Fleming, the legal services attorney who represented the Clifton Terrace tenants in court, when he was interviewed for Some Are More Equal Than Others, Part I of the three part series Justice in America moderated by Eric Sevareid and televised by CBS News Reports in 1971.

[30] Housing in the Seventies: A Report of the National Housing Policy Review 165–182 (1974) at 165.

Some of the same general trends appear in the data for Washington, D.C. By 1970, only 2.3 percent of all the housing units in the city lacked some basic plumbing facilities. Overcrowding also declined, though not as fast as the national rate. But in the census tract containing Clifton Terrace, some major trends were flowing in the opposite direction. While plumbing became more ubiquitous, serious overcrowding almost doubled and the number of owner occupied units fell dramatically. And, not surprisingly, the census tract flipped from an almost completely white to an almost completely black neighborhood between 1950 and 1970. Similar trends existed in other impoverished urban neighborhoods as the number of non-whites living in substandard housing increased from 1.4 to 1.8 million during the 1950s alone.

Edmund "Gene" Fleming, a 1961 law school graduate of George Washington University Law School, was among the first lawyers hired by the Neighborhood Legal Services Program in Washington. He sought out the job after part-time work with a firm while in school and a couple years of practice after graduation convinced him that people "without funds or sophistication" caught up in the legal system were "cheated most of the time."[31] He saw an announcement about the establishment of the neighborhood legal services program in Washington, called Julian Riley Dugas, the director, and was hired. Shortly after Fleming joined the organization, Dugas asked him to run the Clifton Terrace office. When he arrived, Fleming had two other lawyers on the staff, along with two neighborhood workers[32] and a secretary named Ruth Bradley.[33]

In January, 1966, not too long after Fleming arrived at the Clifton Terrace office, Pat Garris walked in, asked to speak with a lawyer and was taken to see Fleming.[34] Garris was a neighborhood organizer for the War on Poverty and a resident, along with her two children, of the apartment complex. She told Fleming that Clifton Terrace was a mess— no heat in the buildings for the past six weeks together with a host of other maintenance and vermin problems. "Something," Garris said, "had to be done."

---

[31] Email from Gene Fleming to the author (Aug. 19, 2002).

[32] These workers were hired from the community with funds from the Office of Economic Opportunity.

[33] Gene Fleming says she played an "essential" role in the case, "keeping track of everything, keeping things in order amid the chaos, talking to the tenants, answering their questions." She did "everything you would hope a very good secretary would do, including taking the initiative when needed." Email from Gene Fleming to the author (Nov. 17, 2002).

[34] The narrative that follows in the text, unless otherwise noted, comes from a telephone interview of Gene Fleming by the author on May 29, 2002.

Fleming visited her apartment. He found a washtub in the middle of the living room floor collecting water dripping from the light fixture and discovered that she was trying to heat her apartment with the kitchen stove. After some discussion Garris and Fleming agreed that a rent strike was the best strategy. Fleming promised to provide legal assistance—though he confided in a recent interview that "I was dreaming up the legal solutions as I went along." Garris agreed to help organize the strike.

Garris found twenty-nine tenants willing to withhold rent.[35] Each sent the landlord a letter drafted by Fleming stating that rent would be withheld until repairs listed in each letter were made.[36] Sidney Brown, according to Fleming, responded to the letters with a series of steps designed to reduce the impact of the planned strike. First, he complained to the Director of the Legal Services Program about Fleming's support for the Clifton Terrace tenants. A little "hearing" was held in the program offices on the matter. Though he was allowed to continue his work, Fleming is still miffed about being called in to explain his actions. Brown also visited the United States Marshal and alleged that Fleming had stolen money from the tenants. Nothing came of it. In addition, tenants told Fleming that Brown went around Clifton Terrace "talking" with the rent-striking tenants and "threatening" them with eviction and other acts of reprisal. The pressure led some of the strikers to back out and pay their rent.

Finally, one of the tenants in the group of strikers, who was behind in rent before the letters announcing the rent strike were distributed, was approached by the landlord and agreed to submit an affidavit accusing Garris and Fleming of wrong-doing in the hope of getting a break on his overdue rent. But Brown went ahead and sued for possession of his apartment anyway. The tenant—thinking no help would be provided after he agreed to cooperate with the owner—never brought his court papers to Fleming's attention. As a result, no answer or other pleading was filed to protect him from eviction. Brown proceeded with this case as quickly as he could. A judgment for possession was obtained and the tenant's belongings were put on the street. These events were the subject of widespread discussion among the tenants and caused some of those who had initially agreed to strike to fold their tents. Rent

---

[35] Rent strikes occurred in many cities across the country during the late 1960s and early 1970s. For a description of one of the largest, see Frances Fox Piven & Richard A. Cloward, *Rent Strike: Disrupting the System*, New Republic (Dec. 2, 1967).

[36] The wisdom of this strategy was revealed later. Virtually all implied warranty cases, including *Saunders*, require the tenant to give notice of housing defects to the landlord in order to defend any later action for rent or possession based on housing code violations. Fleming made the logical assumption that this sort of rule would emerge if he ever managed to alter then extant legal norms.

withholding began in April, 1966. Almost immediately after those still willing to strike followed through by refusing to pay rent, actions were filed seeking to evict them from their apartments.[37] By the time the trial rolled around, only six tenants remained as defendants. And so the stage finally was set for the legal drama that would alter the contours of landlord-tenant law.

III. The Local Appeal: From Rent Strike to Civil Disorder

A. The "Trial"

The attorney for the First National Realty Corporation was Herman Miller. He was a courthouse fixture who represented numerous landlords for many years in eviction actions. During the early part of his career he represented tenants seeking relief under the rent control statutes adopted during World War II. He also helped train legal services lawyers in landlord-tenant law. But by the late 1960s, the bulk of his clients were landlords. Miller, it is said, used to announce "God bless the person who sues my clients!" He also was "very proud of the fact that he had represented tenants" during the war.

In preparation for trial, Fleming took the then unusual step of filing answers to the complaints for possession filed by First National Realty Corporation. Normally tenants were told to show up about ten days after being served with the complaint and summons. The cases then went forward in quick succession without further procedural ado.[38] The format for raising defenses in eviction cases was far from well established. Only one fairly obscure case suggested the availability of an implied warranty defense in eviction actions.[39] Law review literature on tenant defenses was barely extant. The Clearinghouse Review, a newsletter published by the National Clearinghouse for Legal Services which became a major resource for poverty lawyers, and the CCH Poverty Law Reporter did not appear until 1967 and 1968 respectively. So when Fleming said he was making up things as he went along, there is every reason to believe him. Under the circumstances, he did very well indeed, anticipating exactly the sort of remedy that was put into effect when *Javins* was finally resolved. In each answer he claimed:

> That as and from April the 1st, 1966, the premises occupied by the Defendant have been in an uninhabitable condition and in violation of the Housing Regulations of the District of Columbia. Plaintiff has failed and/or refused to maintain a habitable dwelling for Defendant and others according to their agreement. This failure and/or refusal has occurred in spite of repeated complaints by and/or

---

[37] The eviction actions were filed on April 8, 1966.

[38] Recall the "transcript" of a typical hearing *supra* at pp. 18–19.

[39] Pines v. Perssion, 14 Wis.2d 590, 111 N.W.2d 409 (1961).

on behalf of the Defendant and others of these conditions to the proper authorities of the District of Columbia. All to the damage of the Defendant in an amount equal to that otherwise due as rent payment for the month of April had the premises been in a habitable condition under the Housing Regulations of the District of Columbia.[40]

As noted at the beginning of this essay, Judge Austin Fickling heard the cases—bags of mouse feces, dead mice, roaches and all—on June 17, 1966. Notices of appeal were filed immediately after judgment was entered for the landlord.

B.   Appellate Briefs

Of the six tenants involved in the landlord-tenant court hearing, four participated in the appeal to the District of Columbia Court of Appeals—Rudolph Saunders, Ethel Javins, Gladys Grant and Stanley Gross. Saunders, according to Fleming, was the central figure among the rent strikers—"staunch, 30'ish, slender, quiet and determined." When the appeal was filed, Fleming made sure to have him listed first so the case would be named after him. That worked in the District of Columbia Court of Appeals,[41] but not in the federal Court of Appeals, which listed Ethel Javins first in the opinion even though the first round of briefs filed in the case styled it in the name of Saunders. To this day, Fleming does not know why the name switch occurred. Perhaps authors of first year property textbooks should rename the case in Saunder's honor as will be done in the rest of this essay.[42]

The dispute was ready for argument in the District of Columbia Court of Appeals fairly quickly. Some minor delays in the submission of briefs were occasioned by one "curious" event. Fleming arrived at his legal services office in Clifton Terrace one morning to find that "shit had fallen on my desk during the night and ruined the papers I was working on."[43] He asked for a continuance and finally filed his brief for the

---

[40] Answer in First National Realty Corporation v. Saunders, Civil Action No. LT 28968–66 (April 22, 1966). Fleming also included a paragraph asking the Court to hold rent payments pending the outcome of the action. This was probably a wise strategic step for it insured that if the tenant defenses were found wanting, the landlord would still get his rent money. It also according to Fleming, was designed to make it easier to stay evictions during the appeal he assumed would be necessary. Email from Gene Fleming to the author (Nov. 17, 2002).

[41] The decision in that forum is Saunders v. First National Realty Corp., 245 A.2d 836 (D.C.App. 1968)

[42] Except when citing to the official case report, I will refer to the case by Saunders' name in the rest of this tale.

[43] Interview with Gene Fleming (May 29, 2002). Remember that this occurred in pre-computer days. Typed documents with errors, or in this case stains, had to be re-typed.

tenants on November 4, 1966. The landlord's brief was filed only twelve days later and the tenants' reply a week after that. By Thanksgiving the case was ready to be heard. Oral arguments, however, did not occur until March 11, 1968, almost one and one-half years after the briefs were all submitted. The appellate decision was not rendered until September 23, 1968, well over two years after Judge Fickling's original order was entered.

The arguments in the briefs were fairly straightforward. Much of Fleming's argument was similar to the contents of the first major law review article on the implied warranty of habitability.[44] Written by Professor Robert Schoshinski of Georgetown and full of information about District of Columbia case law and regulations, it was published just before the trial. He and Fleming drew upon recent changes in consumer law, especially tort cases like *Whetzel v. Jess Fisher Management Co.*[45] finding that housing code regulations created a duty of care for landlords.[46] Their argument also relied upon constructive eviction cases, trying to make the claim that the underlying rule had long ago undermined the notion of independent covenants[47] and to convince the court to modify constructive eviction theory for use in eviction cases. Finally, relying upon a court rule that allowed tenants in eviction cases to "set up an equitable defense or claim by way of recoupment or set-off in an amount equal to the rent claim," Fleming argued that Judge Fickling's refusal to hear any evidence of housing code violations or to allow recoupment of rent as damages for housing code violations was erroneous.[48]

Miller's brief for the landlord responded that enforcement of the housing regulations was strictly a matter between the city and the

---

[44] Robert Schoshinski, *Remedies of the Indigent Tenant: Proposal for Change*, 54 Geo. L.J. 519 (1966). Though quite familiar with the article by the time he composed his arguments for the United States Court of Appeals, Fleming isn't sure if he read it for the District of Columbia Court of Appeals brief. Emails from Gene Fleming to the author (Nov. 5 and 19, 2002). The similarities between Schshinski's and Fleming's arguments suggest it was used for both briefs.

[45] *Supra* note 25.

[46] Brief for Appellants (November 4, 1966), Saunders v. First National Realty Corp., 245 A.2d 836 (D.C.App. 1968).

[47] This was a pretty dubious claim. Constructive eviction traditionally was limited to those cases in which the entire possession of the tenant was unavailable due to actions of the landlord. In such settings, the basic rent for possession exchange—the single most central covenant of a lease—was rendered null. In most cases, no other covenant was involved; dependency, therefore, usually was irrelevant.

[48] The fairly long brief also contained quite a bit of material on the difficulties confronting poor urban tenants, the deteriorating condition of housing in much of Washington, DC, and the need for judicial remedies.

building owner. The landlord, he argued, was not an insurer of his tenants' well being. Nor, he claimed, did constructive eviction rules provide any basis for granting the tenants relief. Rescission of a lease because of constructive eviction required the tenants to return to the pre-contract situation by relinquishing possession back to the landlord.[49] The brief also contained quite a bit of language that some tenants and many legal services lawyers viewed as gratuitously nasty.[50] At one point, for example, Miller wrote:

> There are many instances where landlords expend large sums of money to come into compliance [with housing codes], and just as soon as he is finished, the tenant's use, his carelessness, the ignoring of his obligations, and his lack of care creates the same violations and in addition to others. Is it fair to require the landlord to keep an armed guard present to prevent the tenants' continued abuse of the property, and constantly damage the premises, over and over again, and then complain that the landlord is in violation and although the tenant continues to occupy, assert that no rent is due or payable?[51]

The written arguments were closed with a very short Reply Brief in which Fleming made an emotional plea for the application of contract law to eviction law.

> It is patently unsupportable that a person renting an apartment in this city does so in disregard of his dependence on the landlord to provide * * * [basic services], or that he would knowingly and willingly agree to do without or get them only at the landlord's whim. The principle of Contract law which provides for dependency, mutuality and consideration, and provides remedies for aggrieved parties to the contract, are much more appropriate than ancient doctrines which purport to recognize no relationship between the obligations of the parties.[52]

C. *Waiting Amid Major Public Controversy*

The somewhat muted fervor of the briefs gave way to outbursts of passion long before the District of Columbia Court of Appeals actually

---

[49] Brief of Appellee (Nov. 16, 1966), Saunders v. First National Realty Corp., 245 A.2d 836 (D.C.App. 1968).

[50] From my own experience handling landlord-tenant issues in the late 1960s and early 1970s, it was a common landlord litany that the tenants caused most or all of the problems. Tenants, when confronted with such talk, uniformly castigated their landlord's indifference to their plight. The differences in perception, accentuated by racial and other tensions of the day, sometimes were remarkably stark.

[51] *Id.* at 2. Pardon the bad English, but a quote is a quote.

[52] Reply Brief 2 (Nov.23, 1966), Saunders v. First National Realty Corp., 245 A.2d 836 (D.C.App. 1968).

heard oral arguments in the case. Indeed, the court waited so long to calendar the case for oral argument that Fleming took the unusual step of filing a motion requesting the court to do so. Claiming that "the time which has elapsed since the filing of the briefs * * * is well beyond the normal lapse of time within which this case would ordinarily have been scheduled for oral argument"[53] he asked that the case be heard at "the earliest practicable time." The motion didn't seem to make a lot of difference; arguments were not held until March, 1968.

During the wait, the tenants and their advocates were not idle. In June of 1967, the Housing Development Corporation (HDC), a non-profit group set up with a grant from the Office of Economic Opportunity to develop low cost housing, revealed plans to purchase the notorious buildings at Clifton Terrace. By October, the plans were in jeopardy. The Federal Housing Administration, claiming that it would be cheaper to tear the buildings down and start from scratch and that the rent levels proposed by HDC would support only a $3.8 million dollar project, refused to provide a loan for the $4.8 million dollars HDC wanted for the proposed project. HDC and city officials responded that the FHA "is shunning the central city ghettos and appears unable and unwilling to do the low-cost housing job Congress assigned."[54] This was the first volley in a continuing stream of criticism of the city and the federal government over the course of the next thirty-five years as Clifton Terrace repeatedly roller-coasted from acceptable to unacceptable housing. The prominence of the complex in the Columbia Heights neighborhood of Washington made it a symbol of both the possibilities for developing housing for the less well off and the difficulties of bring those possibilities to fruition.

The Washington Post starkly described conditions in the building during the controversy over HDC's plans:

> Broken glass and trash litter the walks, alleys, grounds and the large patch of sand and dirt out back called the play area.

> Boarded windows deface the spacious entrance lobbies, which hark back to their better days with well-worn marble stairs, carved pillars and high ceiling with elaborate moldings. All upper story apartments have their own balconies, many of them festooned with drying laundry, airing rugs and junk.

> * * *

> Rain damage and leaking pipes have buckled the floors and collapsed water-logged ceilings in at least 18 apartments.

---

[53] Motion to Calendar for Argument (Dec. 19, 1967), Saunders v. First National Realty Corp., 245 A.2d 836 (D.C.App. 1968).

[54] Carol Honsa, *Slum Fighters are Stymied*, Washington Post, (Oct. 2, 1967) at B1.

The central heating system, a coal burning furnace that con-
sumes 13 tons of fuel a day, breaks down from five to ten times a
month during the winter * * *.[55]

Even a local community organization with its offices in the basement of
the complex was forced to move out because the conditions were unacceptable.

While the various parties to the proposed transaction dickered over
the terms of the proposed sale and rehabilitation of the apartments, the
city began to respond to tenant pressure and pressed Brown to reduce
his asking price for the building to enhance the project's feasibility. The
story unfolded in a series of Washington Post articles by Carl Bernstein—later to become famous as part of the Woodward and Bernstein
investigative reporting team during the Watergate Era. Although housing code violations at Clifton Terrace going back at least three years had
been filed with the city's Department of Licenses and Inspection, no
enforcement actions had been taken. Late in October, 1967, shortly after
another blast of criticism from officials at HDC, Robert Campbell, an
assistant Corporation Counsel for the city, announced he was going to
haul Sidney Brown into court to enforce the code violations, and Robert
Weaver, Secretary of the Department of Housing and Urban Development, announced he had reopened negotiations for FHA support of the
Clifton Terrace redevelopment project. Campbell claimed he could not
understand why the case had never been turned over to the Corporation
Counsel for enforcement action, though at least some of the charges
against Brown had been held in abeyance at the city's request during
negotiations over sale of the buildings.

A few days later "a delegation of angry tenants visited Corporation
Counsel Charles T. Duncan" demanding that heat be provided at Clifton
Terrace immediately. Duncan dispatched a member of his staff and a
housing inspector to the apartments, documented the continuing violations and directed that Brown be ordered to provide heat by the
following day. Despite the order, heat did not percolate through the old,
broken down steam pipes. The next day Brown was brought into court,
forced to go to trial immediately, found guilty by Judge Milton Kronheim
for heating system code violations and sentenced on the spot to a sixty-
day term in jail. Clifton Terrace made the front page for the first time:

As the judge pronounced the sentence, which court officials said
represented the first time in their memory that a landlord has been
ordered jailed on housing code violation charges, a cheer went up
from more than 50 Clifton Terrace tenants in the room.

---

[55] Id.

Brown, who is yet to be tried for another 1200 violations at Clifton Terrace cited by housing inspectors, was visibly stunned by the sentence.

As he was led away to the court's basement cellblock, the landlord, his hands visibly shaking, did not appear to be the defendant who moments before had told the Judge from the witness box that the District government was responsible for the lack of heat at Clifton Terrace.

After remaining in the cell block for about 45 minutes, Brown's attorney, George E. C. Hayes, filed notice of appeal in the case and the landlord was released after posting $2000 bond.[56]

Though heat apparently returned to the apartments for a time, the situation did not cool off. Tenants, along with some legal services attorneys, Paul Fred Cohen and Florence Wagman Roisman, visited Mayor Walter Washington's office demanding that the city make basic repairs and bill the costs to the owner. Roisman made several visits with tenants to the District Building (Washington's city hall) demanding action on Clifton Terrace. Charles Duncan witnessed one. His main assistant was a gentleman named Hubert Pair. "Pair," Duncan reports, "was a very proper and old school lawyer."[57] Duncan recalls walking into Pair's office one day to find Florence Roisman speaking to a group of tenants from Clifton Terrace while standing behind the desk of a perplexed Mr. Pair. Roisman had pulled a copy of the D.C. Code off the shelf and "was reading to the tenants the sections from the code saying the city had the authority to help out." His relationship with Roisman, Duncan says, was a bit "stormy" in those days, but "we later became good friends."

Sidney Brown responded to the swelling controversy by threatening to close down the entire complex and evict everyone.[58] This may have been a reaction not only to pressure from city authorities, but also to his failure to obtain an occupancy permit for Clifton Terrace after he purchased the buildings. Carl Bernstein revealed the lack of a permit after an unnamed reporter for the Washington Post made inquiries

---

[56] Carl Bernstein, *Landlord is Given Jail Term*, Washington Post (Nov. 8, 1967) at A1.

[57] This little story comes from an Interview with Charles Duncan by the Author (May 27, 2002). The exact timing is not clear. Roisman thinks it might have occurred before the city criminally prosecuted Brown and that the prosecution was, in part, a result of this event. Duncan recalled the event, but not its exact historical moment. Roisman also insists she was never behind Pair's desk. Duncan's recollection is different.

[58] Most tenants were on month-to-month leases. At common law, landlords could evict such tenants on one month's notice. In some areas now, a good cause must be posited in order to terminate month-to-month tenancies.

about it with city authorities. Perhaps Bernstein was in training for his later Watergate exploits.

This chapter of the conflict came to a head just before Thanksgiving. On the morning of November 16, Corporation Counsel Charles Duncan visited Clifton Terrace. "I've never seen," he has said, "a more appalling place where people lived." The conditions were "subhuman." Later that day he took Mayor Washington for a look—a step that led to a story on the front page of the Washington Post with a large photo and a large headline. On the day of the Mayor's visit tenants of Clifton Terrace filed suit in federal court seeking to require the city and Sidney Brown to make repairs. On Thanksgiving Day, it was reported that "60 percent of the units were without heat." In early December, amid talk of landlords and tenants being "at war,"[59] legal services lawyers partly reconstructed their litigation by filing an amended complaint seeking to bar Brown from evicting the tenants from Clifton Terrace.

The entire ruckus, which also included sit-ins by tenants in the offices of Robert Weaver, Secretary of the Department of Housing and Urban Development, designed to convince him to fund the Clifton Terrace project, finally led to the signing of agreements calling for the sale of the buildings to HDC. Sidney Brown obtained $1.4 million dollars for the complex, $400,000 less than his initial demand. Brown later claimed that the price was $200,000 below what he paid for the buildings and $250,000 less than the mortgage encumbering the complex. The second criminal trial of Sidney Brown and his First National Realty Corporation for violating the housing code began on December 15,[60] almost immediately after Brown turned over operation of Clifton Terrace to HDC. Like the first trial, this proceeding must have been quite a scene. In addition to Brown, tenants and all the regular lawyers, Washington Post reporter Carl Bernstein showed up. Though author of many of the stories most damaging to his cause, Brown subpoenaed him.[61] The Washington Post, of course, sent along lawyers to protect the paper's interests. Adding to the theatrics, Brown's lawyer moved for a change of venue, claiming that a fair trial was impossible in the District of Columbia. Drama aside, the case was continued.

Fleming filed his motion to calendar the *Saunders* case for oral argument in the District of Columbia Court of Appeals the following week. Early in 1968 all the remaining criminal charges for housing code

---

[59] Jack White, Jr., *Landlords, Tenants at War*, Washington Post (Nov. 25, 1967) at B1.

[60] The first trial was the "hurry up" proceeding during the public controversy about heating Clifton Terrace. *See supra* pp. 32–33.

[61] It is not clear why he did. Maybe he thought it would help delay things. Or maybe his lawyer hoped to impeach his articles and reduce their impact on the judicial proceedings.

violations were settled. First National Realty Corporation pled no-contest in return for the dismissal of all charges leveled personally against Sidney Brown. The corporation was sentenced to pay a fine of $5000, "one of the largest imposed in a local housing case."[62] Judge Tim Murphy, when announcing his sentence, said that the corporation's misconduct "reaches incredible proportions." But he also castigated the city, saying that "the delay and neglect by District officials" helped cause the problems the code was designed to prevent. Brown's sentence to serve 60 days in jail in the earlier trial was still on appeal. Brown did not pay the $5,000 fine until May, 1971.[63] The affirmative litigation against Brown and the city brought by the tenants of Clifton Terrace was dismissed after HDC took over the complex. And the oral arguments in *Saunders* finally occurred on March 11, 1968.

D. Oral Arguments and . . . Assassination

As the attorneys gathered to argue *Saunders*, each side had some developments to ponder. Three of the four tenants appealing their eviction from Clifton Terrace no longer lived in the complex. The fourth—Gladys Grant—had paid her rent to HDC after the buildings were sold. The case, perhaps, was moot. In addition, the District of Columbia Court of Appeals had rendered a decision just five weeks earlier invalidating a residential lease entered into in contravention of the housing code.[64] Section 2304 of the District of Columbia Housing Regulations provided that:

> No persons shall rent or offer to rent any habitation * * * unless such habitation * * * [is] in a clean, safe and sanitary condition, in repair, and free from rodents or vermin.

The court read this regulation to specifically bar the creation of leases in buildings violating the housing code and ruled that the presence of conditions violating the code at the inception of the tenancy made the lease illegal. As a result, a judgment of eviction was reversed.

Fleming opened the arguments, returning to Washington, DC for the occasion from Des Moines, Iowa, his hometown, where he had moved in 1967 to direct a newly funded OEO funded legal services program.

---

[62] William Schumann, *Ex-Landlord Of Clifton Fined $5000*, Washington Post (Jan. 27, 1968) at A1.

[63] *Landlord Finally Pays Fine*, Washington Post (May 22, 1971) at B1. This occurred only after Monroe Freedman, who represented Florence Roisman in her tussle with the Committee on Admissions and Grievances, sought the appointment of a special prosecutor to complete the prosecution of Brown. Letter from Florence Roisman to the author (Oct. 18, 2002).

[64] Brown v. Southall Realty Company, 237 A.2d 834 (D.C.App. 1968). The opinion in this case, argued by Florence Roisman, came down on February 7, 1968.

Hopeful that the results of the *Brown* litigation would be useful in his cases, he made sure to raise illegality as an issue for the court to resolve.[65] He, of course, also contended that the old independent covenant rules were no longer valid and that tenants should have a right to recoup damages for the existence of code violations by reducing their rents. Herman Miller responded with a strong attack on *Brown* and on the city for failing to enforce housing codes. *Brown*, he contended, allowed tenants to create violations and then refuse to pay their rent. And, he continued, the existence of a criminal penalty for code violations strongly suggested that only the city should be able to enforce housing regulations.

Both sides could claim some moral support for their positions from the difficulties encountered by HDC after it gained control of Clifton Terrace from Sidney Brown. Brown may have taken perverse delight in the heating problems that continued to plague the complex. It was impossible to replace the old system in a short time. Similarly, the new owners were forced to take steps to control vandalism by tenants and outsiders. Brown constantly complained about misbehaving tenants. On the other hand, HDC's rehabilitation plan began under an unusual arrangement giving the tenants' association the legal authority to patrol the buildings, collect rents and seek the eviction of any people misbehaving or failing to pay. In addition, HDC contracted with Pride, Inc., a nonprofit community organization, to arrange to hire tenants and other nearby residents to clean and maintain the buildings. Marion Barry, Jr., later to be Mayor of Washington, D.C., was a high official in Pride. These actions began the process of cleaning up the complex in ways that Fleming and some tenants might have found quite acceptable. Nonetheless, conditions in the buildings were so bad that a significant number of tenants moved out. By the middle of 1968 only 121 of the 275 units were occupied. Those tenants remaining were moved into the east and south buildings to allow for reconstruction to begin first in the western most structure. After a few snags, the project formally began on August 13, 1968.[66]

The ground breaking was one of the few bright moments for downtown Washington, D.C. during the summer of 1968. The black communities of Washington, D.C. and most other areas of the country were still trying to recover from the events that unfolded after the assassination of the Reverend Martin Luther King, Jr. in Memphis,

---

[65] If you read the pleadings carefully, it had been raised below. But not much attention had been paid to at trial or in preparation of the briefs many months before. The court read his arguments about *Brown* as raising the issue for the first time. Saunders v. First National Realty, 245 A.2d 836, 837 (D.C.App. 1968).

[66] Rehabilitation Begins (Photo and Caption Only), Washington Post (Aug. 14, 1968) at B1.

Tennessee on the evening of Thursday, April 4—about three weeks after the oral arguments in *Saunders*. Within hours, a twenty-block stretch of 14th Street, NW stretching north and south from Clifton Terrace was engulfed in civil disturbances. Similarly long stretches of 7th Street, NW from E Street in downtown Washington on the south to W Street on the north and of H Street, N.E. running East from Union Station were also involved, as were stretches of 8th Street, S.E. through the heart of Capitol Hill and other areas in Southeast and Northeast Washington. According to one report, seven people died, 1,166 were injured, 7,370 people were arrested, and 711 fires were set. Over eleven thousand troops were called out to restore order. Calm began to descend on the smoky city by Monday, April 8. Like Los Angeles, Newark, Detroit and other cities hit by major disturbances between 1965 and 1967, Washington faced the grim task of making sense out of the racial tension that inflamed the city.

No one knows why Washington exploded after King's assassination while some other cities remained relatively calm.[67] The final report of the Kerner Commission, assembled by President Johnson to investigate the causes of earlier racial disturbances, issued its famous explanation in 1968: "Our Nation is moving toward two societies, one black, one white—separate and unequal."[68] Perhaps the uproar surrounding Clifton Terrace—which sat right in the middle of an impoverished black neighborhood devastated by destruction after the death of Martin Luther King—exemplified the inequalities the Kerner Commission saw as a primary cause of the unrest.

E. *Decision*

Not quite six months after large areas of Washington went up in smoke, just over three months after Robert F. Kennedy was assassinated immediately after declaring victory in the 1968 California presidential primary election[69] and just weeks after both the tumultuous Democratic Party Convention in Chicago and the Prague Spring ended the District

---

[67] One survey of the literature suggests that those most likely to participate in the disturbances were part of an "ambitious, hard working, but intensely dissatisfied group of working class and lower middle class blacks who feel deprived and excluded from what they feel are justified expectations." John S. Adams, *The Geography of Riots and Civil Disorders in the 1960s*, 48 Ec. Geography 24, 30 (1972). And the areas most likely to explode were black neighborhoods "midway between ancient, emptying ghetto cores, and youthful, prosperous, advancing ghetto margins. Trapped in these middle zones were people with intense expectations who found the relative deprivation gap widening when it should have diminished." *Id*. at 35. The Clifton Terrace area may well have fallen within this description. Wealthier black areas of town were just to the northwest.

[68] Report of the National Advisory Commission on Civil Disorders 1 (1968).

[69] The killing took place on June 5, 1968.

of Columbia Court of Appeals rendered its decision in *Saunders*. Unmoved by either its own decision in *Brown*,[70] the tumult surrounding the Clifton Terrace complex or the disturbances following Martin Luther King's death, the court affirmed the eviction judgments. The court agreed to decide the merits of the case even though the appealing tenants had left Clifton Terrace or paid the back rent.[71] But the illegality holding of *Brown* was said to be inapplicable because the tenants never claimed that violations of the housing code existed at the *inception* of their tenancies—the moment the contracts were created. And the broader claim of the tenants that standard consumer oriented contract defenses should be available in eviction cases was brushed aside on the ground that enforcement of the housing code regulations rested solely with the government. "We cannot believe," the court wrote, "that the Commissioners intended that the single violation of any of the Regulations for any length of time would give ground for defending against payment of rent in whole or in part." In addition, the tort cases imposing a duty of care based upon the housing code were different, the court wrote opaquely, because those results "did not hold that the Housing Regulations enlarge the contractual duties of a landlord."[72] The judges did not discuss the potential contradiction between allowing the illegality defense in *Brown* or the use of housing codes to establish duties of care in tort while refusing to allow use of contract defenses in *Saunders*.

The District of Columbia Court of Appeals might also have decided *Saunders* differently if it had paid attention to actions taken by the United States Court of Appeals. Between the oral argument and decision in *Saunders,* the federal court reversed the local judges in another famous landlord-tenant case, *Edwards v. Habib*.[73] Judges Wright and McGowan, both of whom would shortly sit on the panel deciding *Saunders*, issued a strongly worded rebuke of the District of Columbia Court of Appeals' refusal to recognize a "retaliatory eviction" defense when a landlord attempted to terminate a periodic tenancy in response to tenant complaints about housing code violations to public authorities. With a sense of annoyance, Judge Wright noted:

---

[70] Two of the three judges in *Saunders* were the same as in *Brown*—Andrew Hood and Frank Myers.

[71] The court's willingness to hear the cases was based on the same ground as in *Brown*—that resolution of the dispute would bind the parties on the question of how much rent was due for the months in question.

[72] Saunders v. First National Realty Corp., 245 A.2d at 839.

[73] 397 F.2d 687 (D.C. Cir. 1968), rev'g Edwards v. Habib, 227 A.2d 388 (D.C.App. 1967). The Circuit Court issued its opinion on May 17, 1968 and declined an invitation to rehear the case en banc on July 11, 1968.

[A]s a court of equity we have the responsibility to consider the social context in which our decisions will have operational effect. In light of the appalling condition and shortage of housing in Washington, the expense of moving, the inequality of bargaining power between tenant and landlord, and the social and economic importance of assuring at least minimum standards in housing conditions, we do not hesitate to declare that retaliatory eviction cannot be tolerated.[74]

The refusal of the District of Columbia Court of Appeals to recognize a retaliatory eviction defense in *Edwards* was even more remarkable than the chiding language of the federal court suggests. For this same case had come before the Circuit Court previously. After the landlord-tenant court refused to allow the defense at trial, the District of Columbia Court of Appeals refused to stay the eviction pending review. A petition for a stay was then taken before the Circuit Court and granted[75]—surely a strong signal that future actions in the case were going to be watched. These two courts, however, were beating to different drummers.

Prior to the adoption by Congress in 1970 of legislation creating a local court system in the District of Columbia that looks much like those in the various states, the President appointed judges of the District of Columbia Court of Appeals, subject to confirmation in the Senate. As a practical matter, the Chair of the Senate subcommittee overseeing the District of Columbia had substantial input into the selection of local judges. In contrast to appointments to the federal courts in the District of Columbia, nominations to the city's tribunals usually raised few eyebrows and drew little attention from either the President or the Senate as a whole. Chief Judge Andrew Hood, the author of the District of Columbia Court of Appeals' opinions in both *Edwards v. Habib* and *Saunders*, was an interesting example of the problem. President Franklin Roosevelt originally appointed him for a ten-year term on the old Municipal Court of Appeals, a tribunal established by Congress in 1942 to handle minor criminal and juvenile cases. At that time, major civil and criminal matters were all handled by the federal district and circuit courts. Presidents Truman, Eisenhower, Kennedy, who named him Chief Judge, and Johnson, all reappointed him. Hood served on the court until his death at the age of 78 in 1979. His service, therefore, overlapped the transition of the court from a minor appellate tribunal to the court of last resort for the District of Columbia. In his obituary in the Washington Post, it was reported that he said his court was "more of a traditionalist than an activist" tribunal. Because of the review function

---

[74] 397 F.2d at 701.

[75] Edwards v. Habib, 366 F.2d 628 (D.C. Cir. 1965).

of the federal courts, he thought, "we were never free to indulge in activism, although I don't say that we wanted to." Important matters, he believed, should be left to the legislature rather than be resolved by the courts. It is now much less likely that a person with such views would either be appointed to the court or retain a seat for multiple terms. But in the days of *Edwards* and *Saunders,* Hood spoke for the court. It should have surprised no one, including Judge Hood himself, that the *Saunders* case ended up on the Circuit Court of Appeal's docket.

IV.   The Federal Appeal: The Wright Stuff

A.   The Briefs

On October 1, 1968 the tenants filed a petition asking the United States Court of Appeal for the District of Columbia Circuit to review the *Saunders* case. On January 16, 1969, the Circuit Court agreed to allow the appeal.[76] In reality, this was all quite odd. In the normal course of events, the federal appellate courts lack authority to review decisions of the highest courts of a state on matters of local law. The District of Columbia, however, has always been a legally strange place—neither fish nor fowl. It was established by act of Congress. Many of its executive, legislative and judicial actions appear state-like but its entire structure, including its courts, are creatures of federal law. At the time *Saunders* was decided by the District of Columbia Court of Appeals, the court of last resort for matters of District of Columbia law was the United States Court of Appeals for the District of Columbia Circuit. On petition of a party, the Circuit Court had discretion to accept cases for appellate review. *Saunders* was among the last cases heard under this court structure. As part of a gradual extension of partial home rule to residents of Washington during the late 1960s and early 1970s—a somewhat muted response to local claims of disenfranchisement and racial insensitivity[77]—Congress established a new court structure for the

---

[76] Three of the four tenant petitions were granted. Gladys Grant's motion was denied quickly on the ground of lack of jurisdiction. Her motion was denied on October 1, 1968, only one month after it was filed, in an order signed by Judges Danaher, Burger (later Chief Justice) and Tamm. Though I don't know for sure, it is possible a Motions Clerk (the same sort of employee as a judge's law clerk only working for the judges routinely rotating through motions' panels) spotted a jurisdictional problem with this case and recommended that it be pulled out and immediately dismissed. Since she had paid all of her rent after the HDC took over Clifton Terrace, the landlord-tenant court had no authority to entertain an eviction case against her. The motions in the other three cases were held for further consideration and, on January 16, 1969, granted. Gene Fleming and Florence Roisman filed a brief on Nov. 8, 1968 asking the court to hear these three cases. Herman Miller filed a response on behalf of First National Realty on Dec. 2, 1968. Chief Judge Bazelon and Judge McGowan signed the order granting review. Further briefs on the merits of the case were then filed during 1969.

[77] The jurisdictional changes were hardly motivated only by a desire to provide D.C. residents with more control over their city government. Opposition by many to the liberal

District and removed virtually all authority of the District of Columbia Circuit of Appeals to review local decisions.

Briefing in *Saunders* continued through much of 1969. Though longer and a bit more polished than the prior filings, the tenants' brief ploughed the same basic legal ground. After cataloguing the particular problems confronting black residents of inner city Washington seeking decent housing, Fleming argued that the housing code should be treated as a part of every residential lease and construed to invalidate the old rules imposing duties of repair on tenants. Tort cases like *Whetzel v. Jess Fisher Management Company*[78] imposing a duty of care based on the terms of housing codes, he argued, vitiated the idea that covenants in a lease were all independent from one another and supported the notion that diminution of rent was a perfectly acceptable form of relief. It was not an historical exegesis, but a well-crafted attempt to apply standard contract theory in landlord-tenant court.

Like the tenants, Herman Miller largely repeated—without many grammatical improvements—the same argument he made before the District of Columbia Court of Appeals. Enforcement of the housing regulations rests with the government, he contended. They "do not create any new contractual rights in the tenant."[79] But there also were two sets of new material. First, much of the first half of the brief was directed at convincing the court to ignore or discount the importance of the illegality holding in *Brown v. Southall Realty*.[80] Since that case came down after the briefs were filed before the District of Columbia Court of Appeals, this was the first opportunity Miller had to write about the result in the case. He claimed that the result of the case removed enforcement of the housing regulations from the appropriate authority and confused the granting of a license to operate an apartment with its regulation.

The other batch of new material—critiquing the impact of legal services attorneys and law students in clinical programs on the operation of landlord-tenant court—was much more interesting. While the case had been pending, the number of tenants represented by counsel in landlord-tenant court increased dramatically. In addition to the opening of legal services offices, law school clinical programs blossomed. The Prettyman Internship Program, funded by the Ford Foundation, began

---

decisions of the federal Court of Appeals led many conservatives to support a shift they might not otherwise have endorsed.

[78] *See supra* note 25.

[79] Brief for Appellee at 11, Javins v. First National Realty, 428 F.2d 1071, 138 U.S.App.D.C. 369 (D.C. Cir. 1970).

[80] 237 A.2d 834 (D.C.App. 1968).

at Georgetown in the mid–1960s. Graduate law students took classes, practiced in civil and criminal courts and obtained a Masters of Law in Trial Practice degree upon completion of the two year program. In addition, a consortium of law schools in Washington, including those at Georgetown, Catholic, George Washington, Howard, and American Universities, developed a proposal to allow third year students to practice in the local courts. These new programs were part of a concerted effort by universities in the Washington area to respond to racial unrest and to demands for action made by a variety of community groups during the late 1960s. A court rule was adopted in the fall of 1968 allowing students to appear under the supervision of a member of the District of Columbia Bar. Start up funding was obtained from the Council on Legal Education and Professional Responsibility (CLEPR), an organization that was involved in establishing law school clinical programs all across the country. A director was hired, offices were rented, and the program began operation in the fall of 1969, just after Miller's brief was filed with the federal Circuit Court in *Saunders*.[81] The program, one of the largest clinical program in the nation, is still running. Each participating law school contributes funds to operate the clinic.

As indicated by the fairly sophisticated pleadings filed by Gene Fleming in the *Saunders* case, poverty lawyers and law school clinical teachers began to develop a coherent strategy for litigating eviction cases during the late 1960s, some years before they were actually vindicated in the courts. By the time Miller prepared his brief in *Saunders*, the strategy was beginning to have an effect. In his brief, Miller complained about the impact of legal services attorneys and Prettyman Interns on the operation of the court. He also must have been worried about the changes that would occur when the Law Students in Court program began operating shortly after he filed his brief:

> Appellants complain that clogged dockets delay enforcement caused by many cases, appeal procedures and suspended sentences. But appellants fail to inform the court that these conditions militate also in favor the tenants, in that from many sources the tenants are encouraged not to pay and when action is brought in the Landlord and Tenant Court all of the judges sitting, zealously protect the tenants by referring the cases called to attorneys for the Neighborhood Legal Service (and by coincidence who, in every case, assert Housing Violations at the inception of the tenancy though no order had been issued regardless of the time when the tenancy commenced); or refer the case to the Georgetown Legal Intern Program, wherein third year law students under supervision of a member of

---

[81] *McCormick Picked to Head LSIC Program in District*, 3 Georgetown Law Weekly 1 (Mar. 14, 1969); *Students in Court Applications Set for 1969–1970 Year*, 3 Georgetown Law Weekly 1 (Mar. 27, 1969).

the bar takes over the case or reference is made to the Legal Aid Society. The familiar procedure then is to demand a jury trial during which no rent is collectable thus resulting in a very long delay before the matter is settled. * * * All of which results in favorable treatment for the tenants.[82]

The pace of the action in landlord-tenant court, of course, has been an issue for a very long time. As noted earlier, speedy eviction procedures were established during the nineteenth century to provide landlords with some relief from the technical and frequently slow proceedings in ejectment cases. Miller's brief inarticulately posed the very real concern that his clients would not receive rents during or after long eviction proceedings. Neither the tenants' main brief nor their reply made any efforts to deal with these issues. The court, as we will see, eventually did.

B. Another Wait and More Conflicts

While legal activity in the *Saunders* case quieted during the second half of 1969, it was an eventful year for Clifton Terrace and various people associated with its troubles. Though nothing could match the tumult of 1968, major controversies arose over the remodeling of the complex by HDC. In addition, Sidney Brown, refusing to leave the limelight, gained a reversal of the conviction underlying his 60–day jail sentence and initiated an ethics proceeding against Florence Roisman.

Reconstruction of Clifton Terrace proceeded apace during much of 1969. HDC hired the Winston A. Burnett Company, a black owned company based in Harlem, as the general contractor. The deal required minority sub-contractors to be used if at all possible. In addition, residents of Clifton Terrace and the surrounding Cardozo neighborhood were given a hiring preference to work on the project. The job was financed by a loan from the International Brotherhood of Electrical Workers guaranteed by the Federal Housing Agency. The union connection meant that everyone working on the site had to be union members. This resulted in a dramatic increase in the number of black construction workers from the neighborhood getting union cards. Over 250 black people worked on the project. One of the construction workers, Dickie Henderson, lived in Clifton Terrace and sat in the courtroom when Sidney Brown was sentenced to serve sixty days in jail. In reporting on the project for the Washington Post in February, Carl Bernstein quoted Henderson as saying, "No, I never thought then we'd be where we are now. * * * We've not only got heat all the time; but we're putting in the

---

[82] Brief for Appellee at 14, Javins v. First National Realty, 428 F.2d 1071, 138 U.S.App.D.C. 369 (D.C. Cir. 1970).

air conditioning ducts this week."[83] Henderson and other long time residents of Clifton Terrace finally moved into refurbished apartments in the fall of 1970, two years behind schedule.

Henderson must have been disappointed when, on April 25, a couple of months after he was interviewed by Carl Bernstein, the District of Columbia Court of Appeals reversed Brown's conviction and tossed out his sixty day jail term. "It was wrong," the court wrote, "to deny appellant a continuance in the circumstances of this case. While prompt trials and vigorous administration of the criminal laws are extremely desirable, a defendant is entitled to a reasonable opportunity to prepare his defense." Recall that the case was heard in haste amid efforts by the city to get heat turned back on at Clifton Terrace. Brown was summoned to court on one day's notice when his attorney was out of town. A request for a continuance of a couple of days, opposed by the government, was denied. Brown was then given a brief recess to call his attorney's office to see if another lawyer could come over to help him out. Someone did appear. But the attorney protested that he was unprepared for trial and showed up only because he was told there was an emergency.

Perhaps emboldened by his appellate victory, Brown filed ethics charges against Florence Roisman on July 14. He complained to the Committee on Admissions and Grievances at the United States Courthouse in Washington, D.C. that Roisman brought the federal action seeking to enjoin Brown from violating local housing codes without the knowledge of the parties named in the complaint as plaintiffs and that she urged the Office of Corporation Counsel in Washington, D.C. to continue pursuing criminal charges against Brown for housing code violations even after the District of Columbia Court of Appeals had reversed his conviction on such charges. He also claimed that without any foundation Roisman labeled him a "criminal" and accused him of taking "money from the poor at Clifton Terrace." Her interest in the matter, Brown wrote, went "far beyond that of a private citizen and far beyond that of any attorney practicing in this jurisdiction." Stating that "her attitude is engendered by pure malice, far beyond that of counsel for a litigant," he accused Roisman of "maintenance of litigation."[84]

---

[83] Carl Bernstein, *Black Builders Get a Big Job*, Washington Post (Feb. 27, 1969) at B1.

[84] "Maintenance" of litigation usually is defined vaguely as supporting or promoting litigation by one person against another. But that includes virtually every case in which a lawyer is involved. Charges of maintenance or "champerty"—the contribution of funds to support a lawsuit in return for a share of any proceeds produced by the litigation—were commonly brought against legal services lawyers in the early years of the program. The definitional difficulties associated with these rules has led most states to significantly

Brown wrote a similar letter to John Bodner, Chairman of the Board of the Neighborhood Legal Services Program, in an effort to have the board review the propriety of Roisman's conduct.[85]

The ethics complaint, which lacked any serious basis for disciplining Roisman, lingered unresolved for almost ten months. This was not the first time Brown made apparently spurious charges against attorneys. Just the year before, he lost a defamation case to Dennis Collins, who had filed a mechanics lien on a building owned by First National Realty Corporation. Brown called the lawyer who had brought Collins into the case and claimed that Collins was not concerned with settling the claim, filed the mechanic's lien "solely because of a personal grudge against Brown," was anti-Semitic and previously collected a fraudulent judgment against Brown for $14,000.[86] The Committee on Admissions and Grievances probably knew about the case; it was litigated in the D.C. federal courts and resolved by the Circuit Court of Appeals just a few months before Brown filed his charges against Roisman. In any case, the failure of the Committee to dismiss the ethics proceedings it initiated against Roisman, even after all procedural and evidentiary issues were resolved, led Roisman to file an action in federal district court on March 4, 1970 seeking to enjoin any further ethics proceedings. The Committee met nine days after the federal complaint was filed, dismissed the ethics proceeding against Roisman, and sent out a letter attempting to justify the Committee's slow response by blaming the parties for the delay.[87] The federal action was dismissed a short time later.

One more critical dispute enveloped Clifton Terrace before *Saunders* was finally resolved by the District of Columbia Court of Appeals. Though it had no impact on the litigation, it held up a number of rehabilitation projects in HDC's pipeline. A real estate entrepreneur

---

modify them to, at a minimum, require some sort of unsuitable motivation for supporting litigation of another.

[85] Letter from Sidney J. Brown to Mr. John Bodner (July 22, 1969). As far as I know nothing came of this letter. In at least one other setting, however, an attorney working with the tenants of Clifton Terrace was called before Legal Services authorities to personally justify his handling of their cases. Gene Fleming, who handled the landlord-tenant court cases, was told to appear before the board members after Brown mailed them a letter complaining of Fleming's activities. The board allowed Fleming to continue his work. Telephone Interview with Gene Fleming (May 29, 2002).

[86] Brown v. Collins, 402 F.2d 209 (D.C. Cir. 1968). Brown also previously lost a real estate fraud case in which a judgment for compensatory damages of $7,059.00 and punitive damages of $7,500.00 was affirmed on appeal by the same court. Brown v. Coates, 253 F.2d 36 (D.C. Cir. 1958).

[87] The federal litigation was filed several months after the last evidentiary issues in the ethics proceeding had been resolved. The Committee met on March 13 and dismissed Brown's complaint. Complaint, Roisman v. Jones, et al., Civil Action No. 638–70.

named George Kalavritinos filed suit in federal district court in early October claiming that the contractors rebuilding Clifton Terrace were cutting corners or that the Federal Housing Administration was failing to enforce various contract requirements. The suit led Senator Wallace Bennett (R–Utah) to request the Department of Housing and Urban Development to investigate whether HDC exerted undue pressure to win the federal contract to rebuild Clifton Terrace, whether costs were too high and whether work on the apartments by Winston A. Burnett Company met federal standards. In addition, Rep. Joel Broyhill (R–Va.) asked the General Accounting Office to audit the HUD report after its issuance and to review the expenditure of federal funds by HDC on other projects. Broyhill later asked George Romney, Secretary of the Department of Housing and Urban Development, to hold up any additional funding of HDC projects while the Kalavritinos charges were investigated. Romney took that step in mid-December, despite preliminary reports from the FHA finding that the rehabilitation work met federal standards.

The scope of Kalavritinos' labor in opposition to HDC was staggering. He gathered and turned over to Broyhill's staff "hundreds of pages of personal reports," including copies of "HDC's correspondence, contracts and other papers concerning Clifton Terrace."[88] The Washington Post described his motivations:

> Kalavritinos also sprinkles his observations liberally with references to "black power in action," "conspiracies," involving local and federal officials, and charges of "payoffs" and "conflicts of interest."

> His papers offer no proof of illegal acts.

> Kalavritinos makes clear in his booklet that he is opposed to the whole idea of nonprofit groups renovating slum housing.

> He ties these efforts to what he characterizes as pressures by activist tenants, poverty lawyers and city officials to force landlords out of property ownership in the inner city.

>   * * *

> A stocky, dark-haired man who smokes long cigars, Kalavritinos is described by Broyhill's staff as "a wealthy man who once owned slum property but sold it all, and has devoted himself to this crusade."

> Kalavritinos once owned several tracts of inner city property, including some on which he built large apartment buildings.

---

[88] Leonard Downie, Jr., *Complaint to Romney Halts Slum Projects*, Washington Post (Dec. 14, 1969) at A1.

But he lost most of his holdings through foreclosure during the collapse of Republic Savings and Loan Association, run by his brother, Pete Kalavritinos.[89]

Two days after these comments about Kalavritinos appeared in the paper, Rep. Henry Reuss (D.-Wis.), a member of the Subcommittee on Housing of the House Banking and Currency Committee, asked Romney to speedily complete his Clifton Terrace investigation and release the hold on other HDC projects. The next day HDC officials issued a blistering attack on HUD's willingness to pay so much attention to "irresponsible accusations."[90] In early February of 1970, shortly after the oral arguments in *Saunders*, HUD completed its investigation of Clifton Terrace, HDC and Winston A. Burnett Construction Company, concluding that there was no evidence of wrongdoing or misconduct and releasing its hold on all pending HDC project applications. Seven months later, the Government Accounting Office, Congress' investigative arm, reached the same conclusion.

C. Oral Arguments

As the Kalavritinos dispute began to wind down, *Saunders* was argued before the Circuit Court of Appeals. The case had been placed on the summary docket—a list of cases scheduled for brief hearings with each side limited to fifteen-minutes of oral argument. Fleming prepared a ten-minute presentation, planning to save five minutes for rebuttal.[91] He returned to Washington again to argue the case, this time from Massachusetts where he was Deputy Director of the Boston Legal Assistance Project. When he arrived and learned that Judges J. Skelly Wright, Carl McGowan and Roger Robb would hear the case, he thought, "Hey, we've got a chance here!" Though he assumed Robb might be a problem, Wright was an extraordinarily well-known liberal and McGowan often agreed with him.

As the argument began, Judge Wright informed Fleming that all the other cases on the calendar had been resolved and that he could have as much time as he wanted. Fleming was caught completely by surprise. Though he realized he had been presented with a golden opportunity, it required a spur of the moment reconstruction of his argument. After pausing for what seemed to Fleming a very long time, he began to speak. The argument went on for one hour and forty-five minutes. Fleming spent part of the time responding to unsympathetic inquiries from Judge

---

[89] *Id.*

[90] Leonard Downie, Jr., *HDC Scores Criticism of Slum Project*, Washington Post (Dec. 17, 1969) at B1.

[91] Appellants present their arguments first. They are generally allowed to reserve a small amount of time to rebut any contentions made by appellees during their argument.

Robb. But the questions from Wright and McGowan were thoughtful, probing and helpful. They allowed him a great deal of latitude to think through issues as they went along. It became an occasion to discuss rather than argue about the issues before them. Rick Cotton, Justice Wright's law clerk at the time *Saunders* was before the Circuit Court of Appeals, generally confirmed Fleming's recollections about the atmosphere of the arguments. Extending the length of oral presentations was not unusual for Wright. If he wanted some help, oral arguments became "thinking time." When Fleming sat down at the conclusion of his argument, he was hopeful that a reversal was in the offing. In contrast, Herman Miller's statement for the landlord lasted only about ten minutes and went largely uninterrupted by the court. Miller, Cotton opined, was "a caricature of a lawyer" who did not understand he was arguing an important case. To him "it was just another collection action."

D.   The Final Decision

At the first conference among the three judges after the oral argument, a vote was not taken. But there was general agreement among the judges that the law should be changed, that Wright should compose the opinion, and that the other two would sign on if he came up with a reasonable rationale for such a result. When all was said and done, Wright did get the votes of his two colleagues. But Judge Robb concurred only in the result and in the narrowest holding constructed by Wright's opinion—that housing codes construct a baseline for creating tenant remedies in eviction cases. Ironically, the argument accepted by Robb was very similar to those made by the tenants' attorneys. Wright, with significant help from his law clerk, attempted to reconstruct a broad swath of landlord-tenant law.

Judge Wright's opinion in *Saunders*[92] began by staking out a major role for itself—the reappraisal "of old doctrines in the light of facts and values of contemporary life."[93] Though the various briefs submitted on behalf of or as amici supporting the tenants certainly discussed the need to make some changes in the law, the language was not as bold as Wright's. Rather than calling for a reconstruction of basic rules, the brief authors argued that previously decided cases laid the groundwork for changing the operation of landlord-tenant court and that only small steps were required to provide tenants with the protections they needed. The housing codes, for example, had previously been used to establish baselines for tort duties of care. All that was needed now was to take the same step for eviction cases. This approach did not satisfy Rick Cotton, Judge Wright's law clerk. "Reliance on housing codes," he thought, "was

---

[92] Javins v. First National Realty Corp., 428 F.2d 1071 (D.C. Cir. 1970).

[93] *Id*. at 1074.

the least creative way" to deal with the issues. He urged Wright to change the structure of the underlying law. That, he thought would make the opinion "much more persuasive." The opinion evolved in that direction, though Wright was frustrated a bit at how long it took Cotton to put a draft together.

It took almost five months to compose and issue the opinion. Though Judge Wright's opinion in *Saunders* was the first to unequivocally hold that tenants could raise defenses based on implied warranties in eviction actions, it had only an eleven-day cushion. The New Jersey Supreme Court opinion in *Marini v. Ireland*[94] followed hard on the heels of *Saunders*. Indeed, *Marini* was a predictable result after *Reste Realty Corporation v. Cooper*[95] was decided on March 17, 1969. *Reste* was one of two important constructive eviction cases decided in other jurisdictions while *Saunders* was being briefed and argued. Both decisions made Wright's job a bit easier. *Reste* upended virtually all of the old common law rules, holding in a commercial case that lease covenants were dependent and that a common law implied warranty should be read into the lease. The court's willingness to imply landlord obligations in a commercial setting without reference to housing codes strongly suggested it would move in a similar direction if and when a residential case arose and that it would be favorably inclined to allow defenses in eviction actions. The suggestion became reality in *Marini*.

Though *Reste* was decided well before any of the briefs in *Saunders* were filed, neither the litigants nor the amici cited it. It is curious that *Reste* was ignored. Widespread knowledge of important new cases sometimes took months to spread around the country while lawyers and teachers waited for the arrival of printed advance sheets, but gossip networks often sped up the process. *Reste* was the subject of much discussion by poverty lawyers and clinical law teachers in New Jersey as soon as it came down. The fairly tight poverty law grapevine should have reached legal services lawyers in Washington, D.C. before *Saunders* was argued. It didn't, but Cotton found the case and relied upon it in drafting Wright's opinion.

The other important case that came down while *Saunders* was being prepared for argument was *Lemle v. Breeden*.[96] It was decided by the Hawaii Supreme Court on November 26, 1969, long after all the *Saunders* briefs were filed and about two months before it was argued. *Lemle* was also a constructive eviction case, this time residential. In a fashion

---

[94] 56 N.J. 130, 265 A.2d 526 (1970). The opinion was rendered by the New Jersey Supreme Court on May 18, 1970. The *Saunders* opinion was released on May 7.

[95] 53 N.J. 444, 251 A.2d 268 (1969).

[96] 51 Haw. 426, 462 P.2d 470 (1969).

similar to *Reste*, the court concluded that lease covenants were dependent, that an implied warranty of habitability was implied in residential leases and that the tenants, who had quickly departed after discovering the house was infested with rats, could recover their security deposit and prepaid rent. *Reste*, *Lemle* and *Saunders* were the first of a deluge of opinions on implied warranties rendered in the early 1970s. It was like a dam breaking.[97]

After Wright declared in his opinion that he wished to reappraise the "old doctrines," he structured the analysis as a contest between "the assumption of landlord-tenant law, derived from feudal property law, that a lease primarily conveyed to the tenant an interest in land" and the more modern view of the lease as a contract providing urban dwellers with a place to live.[98] Courts, he observed, "have been gradually introducing more modern precepts of contract law in interpreting leases. Proceeding piecemeal has, however, led to confusion * * *." The best approach, Wright declared, was simply to treat "leases of urban dwelling units * * * like any other contract."[99] The recognition of implied warranties in residential leases, like those in many other contracts for services and consumer products, ineluctably followed.

To modern readers, this must seem quite odd. The idea that "conveyances" were different from "contracts" and that the rules for conveyances of leases were dramatically different from those controlling transfers of interests in other things of value seems strange at best and inane at worst. But Wright's conveyance/contract dichotomy perfectly fit its historical moment. Though not yet reflected in law review literature, there was an ongoing debate in academic circles about the applicability of contract law to leases. As suggested by the terms of Wright's opinion, the discussion took the highly structured form of debating whether a lease represented a "property" conveyance or a "contractual" agreement. That form of debate emerged as a shorthand way of attempting to deal with the continuing vitality of the independent covenant rules in eviction law.[100] The exchange of rent for possession was said to be a

---

[97] See, e.g., Kline v. Burns, 111 N.H. 87, 276 A.2d 248 (1971); Mease v. Fox, 200 N.W.2d 791 (Iowa 1972); Jack Spring, Inc. v. Little, 50 Ill.2d 351, 280 N.E.2d 208 (1972); Boston Housing Authority v. Hemingway, 363 Mass. 184, 293 N.E.2d 831 (1973); Foisy v. Wyman, 83 Wash.2d 22, 515 P.2d 160 (1973); Steele v. Latimer, 214 Kan. 329, 521 P.2d 304 (1974); Green v. Superior Court, 10 Cal.3d 616, 111 Cal.Rptr. 704, 517 P.2d 1168 (1974). A number of states also adopted statutory versions of the implied warranty during the same time period.

[98] *Saunders*, *supra* note 92, at 1074.

[99] Id. at 1075.

[100] By the early twentieth century, the idea that a lease was different from a contract was pretty firmly established, despite the fact that the distinction had little to do with the

"property" transaction. The reformers discussing the issue lamented the use of old property rules and argued that a shift to contractual analysis would force courts to recognize the various terms of leases as dependent upon one another and to provide defenses in eviction actions.

In hindsight, the use of property versus contract terminology "conveyed" an erroneous description of the history. As already noted,[101] the combination of old contract rules, the limitations of early procedural systems, the desire to protect the budding rental housing business during the nineteenth century, the lack of lawyers to represent poor tenants, the biases of progressive reformers against tenement house residents and antipathy to the urban poor after World War II had more to do with the continued use of the independent covenant rules in eviction actions than any largely ephemeral distinction buried in the description of a lease as a contract or a conveyance. But, though historically misguided, the rhetoric of the legal debate did allow those seeking reform to use the consumer remedies—often based on tort, contract or implied contract theories—as a starting point for their analysis. Their eagerness to do so is certainly not surprising. Most of the new legal services attorneys who handled the vast bulk of the eviction litigation across the country during the late 1960s and early 1970s received their legal educations not too long after the consumer reforms were adopted. Not surprisingly, they used what they knew well as a baseline for structuring their reformist arguments.

Wright, with Cotton's help, took this debate and used it to turn residential leases into deals about consumer products. This move allowed him not only to accept housing codes as norms for landlords' maintenance duties, but also to embrace the use of implied warranty theory in leasehold settings. "In our judgment," Wright concluded, "the common law itself must recognize the landlord's obligation to keep his premises in a habitable condition."[102] Judge Robb was unwilling to agree to such a broadly worded rationale.[103] He ended up concurring in the result, but he

---

origins and maintenance of the independent covenant rules. Though the first two editions of Williston's treatise on contracts said nothing about this issue, the third edition, issued originally in 1920, laid it out in great detail. 6 Williston on Contracts § 890 (1936).

[101] *Supra* note 11 to 17 and accompanying text.

[102] *Saunders, supra* note 92, at 1077.

[103] There is more than mere rhetoric in the different approaches of Wright and Robb. Another area of landlord-tenant law that led to rely on the conveyance/contract dichotomy involved mitigation of damages. At common law, under a rule said to arise because a landlord simply conveyed possession to a tenant and had no further obligation until the lease ended, landlords did not have to mitigate damages when a tenant left before the lease expired. By the last third of the twentieth century that sort of rule had by and large disappeared in standard contract law, but it hung on longer in leaseholds. In any case, Wright's theory could be used to end the special landlord mitigation rule. Robb's would

aligned himself with only one substantive aspect of Wright's opinion—a narrower rationale that the local housing code "requires that a warranty of habitability be implied in the leases of all housing units it covers."[104] Gene Fleming's skepticism about getting Robb's vote turned out to be misplaced. Indeed, Robb basically adopted the argument made in the tenants' brief. But it was the undermining of the conveyance/contract dichotomy in Wright's opinion that caught the attention of academics and led them place to it in their first year property texts.

Wright's last task was to grapple with the landlord's claim that lengthy proceedings and tenant defenses endangered the ability of building owners to collect whatever rent was due. Though the briefs of the tenants did not discuss this problem directly, Judge Wright wrote that they had offered to pay rent into the registry of the court during the action.[105] "We think," he went on, "this is an excellent protective procedure."[106] Just two weeks before Wright released the opinion in *Saunders* containing this comment, he heard oral arguments in *Bell v. Tsintolas Realty Company*,[107] a case that directly raised questions about the propriety of requiring tenants to deposit money in court pending the outcome of eviction litigation. It was, therefore, predictable that Wright's opinion in *Tsintolas* would allow landlords to protect their interests by seeking pre-judgment rent deposits. Though he noted that use of protective orders was contrary to the general rule declining to guarantee plaintiffs the solvency of people they sue, Wright was also well aware of the impact of tenant demands for jury trials and defenses on the supposedly speedy eviction process. While declining to allow rent deposits in all cases, the court approved protective orders when tenants asked for jury trials or asserted a defense based on housing code violations, but only after notice and opportunity for oral argument was provided to both parties. The argument, Wright suggested, should focus on the likelihood of serious housing code violations existing in an apartment. The existence of such violations would be grounds for requiring a tenant to deposit only a portion of the contract rent with the court.[108]

---

not. For more on the mitigation debate, see Sarajane Love, *Landlord's Remedies When the Tenant Abandons: Property, Contract and Leases*, 30 U. Kan. L. Rev. 533 (1982).

[104] *Saunders, supra* note 92, at 1080.

[105] The answers of the tenants volunteered this action. *See supra* note 40. Fleming refused to hold money himself for fear of being accused of stealing it. That was a well-founded concern. Given the number of complaints about lawyers Brown scattered around the landscape, caution was appropriate. And, of course, Brown did accuse Fleming of stealing the rent money. *See supra* p. 22.

[106] *Saunders, supra* note 92, at 1083, fn. 67.

[107] 430 F.2d 474 (D.C. Cir. 1970).

[108] *Id.* at 484.

For many first year law students, reading the opinion in *Saunders* defines the extent of their knowledge of Judge Wright. But he is a major figure in twentieth century legal history. Shortly after he wrote the *Saunders* opinion, he was interviewed by CBS News about the case. Parts of his interview were broadcast in a 1971 program entitled "Some Are More Equal Than Others," the first of a three part series on Justice in America narrated by Eric Sevaraid. Wright said that law is systematically "biased against the poor." The courts implement a "vast body of law slanted against" a poor person who is "helpless as a child" without a lawyer. Indeed, Wright opined, "equal justice under law is a farce" without lawyers for the poor. Any lay person, he contended, would find "completely reasonable" the idea that a lease for an apartment has a warranty requiring that the place be "livable." If the landlord doesn't fulfill "all of his bargain, then why should the tenant have to fulfill all of his?"

These are bold statements from a sitting judge. They convey the sensibility of a man deeply conscious of the relationships between poverty and access to justice. His ruling in *Saunders* and the statements he made about it for CBS, certainly were not the first time Wright took strong positions on behalf of the poor. He authored the opinion in the famous unconscionability case, *Williams v. Walker–Thomas Furniture Co.*[109] And his actions ordering the desegregation of public schools in New Orleans during the 1960–1961 school year while sitting there as a federal district court judge are legendary indications of his courage and convictions. Indeed, President Kennedy is said to have promoted him to the federal circuit court in Washington rather than to a southern panel in order to satisfy the desires of Louisiana's senators to get him out of town. Wright ordered the desegregation of the city's schools effective the fall of 1960. When Governor Davis took over the New Orleans schools and ordered segregation to continue, Wright invalidated the state statute that gave the governor authority to take such steps. Governor Davis then asserted that the court had no authority over him and the state legislature enacted a series of segregation laws.

That led Wright to issue an injunction against the Governor, the Attorney General, the state police, the National Guard, the state superintendent of education, "and all those persons acting in concert with them," ordering them not to enforce the new laws. That was on November 10. On November 11, the state superintendent of education declared that November 14 was a state school holiday, which caused Wright to issue a decree against the holiday and to cite the superintendent for contempt. But the dragon of official segregation was not yet dead. The legislature declared November 14 to be a

---

[109] *Supra* note 21.

school holiday, whereupon Wright added all its members to the list of those ordered not to interfere with desegregation.

On November 14, four black children entered the first grade of two white schools. This caused the legislature to pass a resolution removing members of the New Orleans school board. Again Skelly Wright was up to the challenge to his, and the federal government's authority; he ordered that the resolution not be enforced. White anger exploded. Leander Perez addressed a mass rally in which he shouted, "Don't wait until the burr heads are forced into your schools. Do something about it now." Whites threatened to boycott the schools; the legislature threatened to cut off funding. But Skelly Wright prevailed. Jack Bass in his book, *Unlikely Heroes,* concludes: "With support by the full federal judiciary and ultimately the Justice Department and by his own personal resolve, Skelly Wright broke the back of the state's effort at massive resistance and prevented the closing of the New Orleans public schools. He upheld federal supremacy under the Constitution by facing down the full force and power of the entire state of Louisiana." Wright was alone, totally alone.[110]

After New Orleans, implying warranties in *Saunders* was a piece of cake.[111]

Judge Wright has candidly admitted that the civil rights movement had a significant impact on his decision in *Saunders*. In a letter to Professor Edward Rabin, he wrote:

I was indeed influenced by the fact that, during the nationwide racial turmoil of the sixties and the unrest caused by the injustice of racially selective service in Vietnam, most of the tenants in Washington, D.C. slums were poor and black and most of the landlords were rich and white. There is no doubt in my mind that these conditions played a subconscious role in influencing my landlord and tenant decisions.

* * * It was my first exposure to landlord and tenant cases, the U.S. Court of Appeals here being a writ court to the local court system at the time. I didn't like what I saw, and I did what I could to ameliorate, if not eliminate, the injustice involved in the way many of the poor were required to live in the nation's capital.

I offer no apology for not following more closely the legal precedents which had cooperated in creating the conditions that I

[110] Arthur Selwyn Miller, A "Capacity for Outrage": The Judicial Odyssey of J. Skelly Wright 81–82 (Greenwood Press 1984).

[111] Smuck v. Hobson, 408 F.2d 175 (D.C. Cir. 1969).

found unjust.[112]

V. Epilogue

A. The Apartment Buildings Today

And so the long, tortured journey of the *Saunders* litigation ended with the reversal of Judge Austin Fickling's refusal to allow the Clifton Terrace tenants to use mice feces, dead rodents and jars of bugs in defending against First National Realty Corporation's claim for possession of their apartments.[113] Though the *Saunders* saga ended, the story of Clifton Terrace was just beginning. Many thought the complex was headed to recovery in the early 1970s. At the end of the 1971 CBS News television special "Some Are More Equal than Others" in which Wright spoke about his experiences with landlord-tenant law in the *Saunders* litigation, scenes of an almost rehabilitated apartment complex flashed upon the screen. In the background, Eric Sevaraid described the project as a rare success in the reconstruction of inner city apartment housing. For a short time that was an accurate picture. Those living in Clifton Terrace after HDC finished remodeling the complex agreed.

But signs of trouble quickly appeared. The prime contractor, Winston A. Burnett Construction Company, was disbanded by its parent company, Boise Cascade. The parent had started up Burnett with $600,000 in seed money and claimed to have lost thirty-nine million dollars before giving up. Boise Cascade took over the Clifton Terrace job and completed it. By the end of 1972, HDC and Boise Cascade ended up in court feuding about how much the contractor was still owed for its work on the apartment complex. The dispute, according to the head of HDC, Reverend Channing Phillips, was likely to lead to foreclosure of the Clifton Terrace by the Electrical Workers' Benefit Association. Since the federal loan insurance and subsidy program used to rehabilitate the apartments required that rents be kept fixed and low, there was no way to raise funds to pay off the additional construction costs Boise Cascade claimed. Given the federal loan guarantee, the Department of Housing and Urban Development (HUD) was expected to end up owning the buildings. Problems similar to these had cropped up in projects all over the country. The underlying structure of the federal program—the provision of subsidies and loan insurance while requiring low rents—did not provide enough money for both the payment of construction debt

---

[112] The letter is reprinted in full in Edward Rabin, *The Revolution in Residential Landlord–Tenant Law: Causes and Consequences*, 69 Cornell. L. Rev. 517, 549 (1984).

[113] In August, 1970, First National Realty did seek review in the United States Supreme Court, but certiorari was denied. First National Realty Corp. v. Javins, 400 U.S. 925 (1970).

and daily operation of the buildings. Phillips' predictions of foreclosure came true early in 1973.

Problems emerged almost immediately after HUD took over the buildings. Maintenance declined and vandalism rose. HUD eventually agreed to change building managers and signed on Pride, Inc., the same group that had helped clean up Clifton Terrace after HDC took over the buildings. A short time later, P.I. Properties, the real estate arm of Pride, Inc., agreed to purchase the complex for $1,286,000. Initial impressions were quite good. The project seemed to right itself. Pride, Inc., was a well-known non-profit group devoted to working with youths with little education and criminal records. Pride seemed to be all business. Headed by Mary Treadwell Barry, it got lots of great publicity, including a visit full of praise from Mayor Walter Washington.

But tragedy has never seemed far from the halls of Clifton Terrace. Complaints about operation of the buildings grew fierce. Mortgage payments were not made. Hundreds of citations were issued for housing code violations. In 1978, HUD foreclosed again and took over the complex, though not without a fight from Pride. Things could hardly get worse, but they did. The real tragedy turned out to have very little to do with tenants not paying rent or vandalizing the buildings. In October, 1979, the Washington Post published the first of a series of stories on Mary Treadwell Barry and some of her colleagues at Pride, Inc. accusing them of stealing $600,000 from the government and tenants. Treadwell, it turned out, was not only playing a role as one of the most politically powerful women in Washington, but also living the high life on other people's money. By this time Marion Barry, who got his political start by working with Pride and was at one time the husband of Mary Treadwell Barry,[114] was mayor of Washington. He ordered a review of all city contracts with her organization. Treadwell and two of her colleagues, Joan Booth and Robert Lee were eventually indicted, tried and convicted in a highly publicized trial. She was sentenced to serve three years in prison.

Some time after Pride lost the building, HUD sold it to Phoenix Management Services. The same pattern repeated itself one more time. Initial hope was followed by another round of decay, with the additional burdens of rampant drug use, neighborhood disarray and lack of supervision over the funds dispersed in the heavily subsidized project. HUD finally foreclosed on the complex again in 1996. The government selected another new redevelopment team in 1999. Michaels Development Company of New Jersey and Community Preservation and Development Corporation of Bethesda, Maryland purchased the building for $1. They

---

[114] They separated in 1976. Barry was never accused of any wrongdoing in the affair, but his association with Treadwell led to the spilling of a great deal of newspaper ink.

also received a $9.2 million grant from HUD to help pay the $21 million dollar renovation cost, the third in a series of federal subsidy plans designed to help solve the "Clifton Terrace" problem. The plans included a reduction in the number of housing units from 289 to 232. Seventy-six of the apartments will be sold as condominiums; the rest will be rented at below market rates. With Mayor Anthony Williams and other dignitaries attending, groundbreaking ceremonies were held on October 17, 2001. Construction continues as this is written. Only time will tell whether the apartments, named Wardman Courts once again, will finally recover and maintain their original status as a worthy abode.

Sidney Brown died on November 26, 2000.

B. The Landlord–Tenant Court Today

And what about the landlord-tenant court? Has it changed very much since *Saunders* was decided? In some ways the answer is obviously "yes."[115] Defenses are available in eviction actions. Lawyers are available to help some tenants. The judges are not usually as hostile to tenant claims. Protective orders are routinely granted to landlords who move for them. The court often appears to operate fairly. But for a very large proportion of the tenants who are sued for possession for non-payment of rent, the process looks much as it did thirty-five years ago. Though it does not handle as many cases as in the 1970s,[116] the court's docket remains massive.[117] Poverty still is endemic in large sections of the city and the tenants appearing in the court are sill largely black. As Judge Wright noted in his comments to CBS News, many tenants don't show up in court. In 1997, default judgments against tenants were entered in thirty-four percent of the cases filed.[118] Anyone who watches the court operate will hear countless requests for default judgments from landlords' attorneys as the clerk calls the roll of cases each morning. Perhaps the no-shows have already moved and taken a "poor man's" eviction—

---

[115] And in some ways, the answer also is obviously "no." The court is still a forum of limited jurisdiction very much as it was in the nineteenth century. Procedures are rapid. Answers may be filed only upon motion of a tenant. Most actions are only about possession. Landlords suing for possession may serve process by door posting. Claims for back rent must be personally served. Counterclaims are still barred.

[116] Over 100,000 cases per year were filed in landlord-tenant court during the 1970s. See Joint Committee on Judicial Administration in the District of Columbia, 1978 Annual Report of the District of Columbia Courts 30 (1979).

[117] Though the population of the District has fallen between 1970 and 2000, new filings in landlord-tenant court still averaged of 55,977 each year from 1997–2001, with a high of 57,621 and a low of 53,970. That works out to about 225 cases per court day, all handled by a single judge. Joint Committee on Judicial Administration in the District of Columbia, 2001 Annual Report of the District of Columbia Courts 83 (2002); L–T Report at 25.

[118] 55,289 cases were filed and 18,717 ended up with defaults. L–T Report at 25.

not paying rent for a couple months and forfeiting a security deposit in order to have enough money to move into a different apartment. Or maybe they assume there is nothing they can do because they owe back rent. And, of course, some tenants never receive service of the court papers.[119]

After the clerk calls all the cases to see who is present and to enter default judgments against the non-appearing tenants, the tenants in attendance are encouraged to talk to their landlords' representative and work out a settlement. A formal court recess is called for that purpose. The various landlords or their attorneys sit behind tables set up by the court while their tenants line up to wait for a chat. The formulaic agreements reached during this period routinely require the tenants to pay each month's rent as it comes due in the future, along with a portion of their unpaid back rent. They also typically have clauses by which tenants waive their right to any further court proceedings if they fail to pay. In case of breach, the landlord need only apply to the clerk of the court to obtain authorization to evict the tenant. The settlement forms containing these terms are actually provided by the court![120] Tenants signing such agreements routinely do so without the advice of counsel. In 1997, a startling 99.3% of the tenant defendants lacked counsel while 86% of the landlords retained attorneys.[121] Each settlement agreement reached is reviewed in a brief proceeding by an Interview and Judgment Clerk to determine if the tenant understands its terms. The thoroughness of this review varies a bit, but the vast bulk of the agreements are approved. A judge only hears the cases left open after the completion of this process.

When the judge finally takes the bench after the recess, the remaining cases are called. At this point, tenants may be asked why they haven't paid rent. Some judges are more willing to inquire about the existence of potential defenses than others. If the court thinks it appropriate, tenants are asked if they would like to speak with a legal services

---

[119] Service of process is commonly made by posting papers on doors. Default judgments obtained after tenants fail to show up are particularly difficult to reopen. While the law is clear that failure to receive notice is grounds for vacating the default, proof of service failure must be gathered, motions must be filed and hearings scheduled. Legal assistance is crucial and often not obtained.

[120] The court provides a number of forms for use by landlords pursuing eviction actions, but none for tenants seeking to raise defenses. One of the forms for landlords, a Consent Judgment Praecipe, contains blanks for completing a tenant payment schedule and for repairs to be made by the landlord. The repair portion of the form is rarely used and largely ignored during the hallway "negotiations." The complete form is available for you to peruse online at http://www.dcbar.org/for_lawyers/courts/superior_court/pdf/dcsc107.pdf.

[121] L–T Report at 26.

lawyer or a third year law student. Given the timing of such requests so late in the day's proceedings, only a very small segment of tenants actually obtain legal assistance. Once a lawyer or a student speaks with a tenant, it is routine practice to ask for a continuance in order to have time to file an answer and demand a jury trial.[122] Only in these cases, together with a few more in which tenants seek out and obtain legal assistance before the date they are supposed to appear in court, do tenants have any chance of gaining the full benefits of the remedies provided by *Saunders*. One day, perhaps, judges and other persons of authority in Washington will recall Judge Wright's statement that "equal justice under law is a farce" without lawyers for the poor.[123] And if they do, perhaps they will reconstruct the operation of the landlord-tenant court so that more tenants have a shot at obtaining the legal assistance they need to properly use the remedies made available in *Saunders*.

Provision of legal services to tenants in eviction courts by itself, of course, will not fulfill Wright's desire to help all those most in need of housing assistance. In the absence of government subsidies, strong enforcement of housing codes—whether in eviction cases or administrative proceedings—is unlikely to dramatically improve the quality of the housing stock occupied by the poor or make it more financially accessible. This suggests that the desire of Judge Wright to provide lawyers to poor litigants must be significantly expanded beyond courtroom representation. In addition to providing assistance in eviction cases and other judicial disputes, lawyers are also needed to help tenants purchase, rehabilitate or build decent dwellings and to provide help developing a political constituency for a vast increase in public financial support for housing programs. The tenants' lawyers in *Saunders* were good role models for us all. Simultaneously working to change eviction law and to obtain subsidies for the reconstruction of Clifton Terrace, they understood well the limits of litigation and the importance of government assistance. We need many more like them if the true legacy of *Saunders* is to be fulfilled.

---

[122] These statements about the operation of the court result from my own observations and those of my first year property students. All of my students are required to visit the court at least once and write a brief memo on their impressions of its operations. Their observations are confirmed by all extant literature on the operation of the court.

[123] *Supra* p. 61.

7

Carol Rose

Property Stories: *Shelley v. Kraemer*

Introduction

In the middle of August 1945, J.D. Shelley and his wife Ethel, both African Americans, bought a house on Labadie Avenue in St. Louis. Their neighbors Louis and Fern Kraemer, with the very active support of a local "improvement association," sued to enjoin the Shelleys from taking possession.[1] The Kraemers based their claim on a restrictive covenant according to which the house was not to be used or occupied by "any person not of the Caucasian race."

Some months earlier, in November 1944, another African American couple, Orsel and Minnie McGhee, purchased and moved into a house in a Detroit neighborhood. Their neighbors Benjamin and Anna Sipes sued to remove them from possession, basing their claim on a similar restrictive covenant against use or occupancy by any person except "those of the Caucasian race."[2] These two lawsuits wound their way through their respective states' judicial systems, and in each case the state's highest court upheld the covenants. The two cases came together in 1948 as companion cases in the United States Supreme Court, where they were generally designated simply as *Shelley v. Kraemer*. In a major departure from previous law, the Supreme Court now overruled both state court decisions, holding that judicial enforcement of racially restrictive covenants was an exercise of "state action" for the purposes of the Four-

---

[1] Shelley v. Kraemer, 334 U.S. 1, 5 (1948) Clement E. Vose, Caucasians Only: The Supreme Court, the NAACP, and the Restrictive Covenant Cases 109–114 (1959). Vose gives the date of purchase and moving in as September 11, 1948, but describes the Kraemers' action as one to keep the Shelleys from taking possession. *Id.* at 109, 114.

[2] *Shelley*, at 7.

teenth Amendment. So understood, enforcement of these covenants violated that Amendment's requirement that no state deny its residents the equal protection of the laws.[3] Having decided this point, the Court immediately took up a pair of cases originating in Washington, D.C., where the Fourteenth Amendment did not apply since the District is not a state; here the Court held that it would violate public policy to permit Federal courts to enforce racial covenants in Washington when the same devices were not judicially enforceable in the states.[4]

Shelley mattered, and continues to matter, for several reasons. First and most obviously, the case abruptly terminated a half-century's efforts by developers, real estate professional organizations and neighborhoods to use deed restrictions and homeowner agreements as legal means to exclude racial and religious minorities. Prior to *Shelley*, these restrictions and agreements had been upheld by court after court, including federal courts and even the Supreme Court itself,[5] but *Shelley* departed sharply from these precedents. Second, the case gave some clues about Supreme Court's practical approach to racial questions in the late 1940's. Even though as a theoretical matter any racial group could have used restrictive covenants to exclude any other, in fact these restrictions had been deployed overwhelmingly to keep African Americans out of white neighborhoods. *Shelley* signaled strongly that the Court would pay attention to the actual patterns of discrimination resulting from such ostensibly neutral legal arrangements.[6] The culmination of this realism came several years later in the monumental invalidation of "separate but equal" educational facilities in *Brown v. Board of Education* (1954).[7] Third, and closely related, the case was one of the early links in a chain of victories by the National Association for the Advancement of Colored

---

[3] Shelley, at 20–21.

[4] Hurd v. Hodge, Urciolo v. Hodge, 334 U.S. 24, 34–35 (1948). An alternative ground was the Civil Rights Act of 1866, discussed as applicable in D.C. by analogy to the Shelley's construction of the Fourteenth Amendment with respect to the state courts; *Id.* at 33.

[5] Corrigan v. Buckley, 271 U.S. 323 (1926) (leaving covenants intact on jurisdictional ground that they presented no federal question); see also the citations to *Corrigan* in Mays v. Burgess, 147 F.2d 869, 870–71 (D.C. Cir. 1945), cert. denied 325 U.S. 868 (1945)(citing *Corrigan* and more recent cases); Kraemer v. Shelley, 355 Mo. 814, 198 S.W.2d 679, 683 (1946) (same) Sipes v. McGhee, 316 Mich. 614, 25 N.W.2d 638, 643–44 (1947) (citing *Corrigan* and noting the court knew of no court of last resort overturning private racial covenants on constitutional grounds);

[6] Shelley, at 22. Prior to *Shelley*, several courts had observed that residential deed restrictions entailed no inequality, since they could be used by any racial group. See, e.g. Parmalee v. Morris, 218 Mich. 625, 188 N.W. 330, 332 (1922); Torrey v. Wolfes, 6 F.2d 702 (D. C. Cir. 1925).

[7] Brown v. Board of Education of Topeka, 347 U.S. 483 (1954)

People (NAACP), in its systematic dismantling of legalized racial discrimination in the United States.[8]

But as a matter of constitutional law, *Shelley* mattered most of all because it left behind a lasting puzzle about the meaning "state action" under the Fourteenth Amendment. Racially restrictive covenants might reflect a deplorable prejudice that was clearly forbidden to public bodies and officials. But Fourteenth Amendment jurisprudence has generally countenanced *private* discrimination; we may find this morally repellant, but it is not necessarily illegal. However frail and contested the divide in between "public" and "private" in theory,[9] the distinction is thought to assure a space for personal decisions, so that people can do things in "private" that are off limits to public actors—for example, giving preference to friends and family, or contributing to particular religions or excluding unwanted solicitors from their property. Hence despite much trenchant criticism, our constitutional law has continued to distinguish "state action" that is subject to constitutional constraints from the "private actions" that are not, even though the cost of the distinction is that private individuals can behave in ways that would be grounds for lawsuits against official actors.

But *Shelley*'s location within "state action" doctrine is very ambiguous: no public legislature adopted a neighborhood's racially restrictive covenants; no local or state official took part in an official capacity in their creation or enforcement. The only thing that appeared to happen was that at some point in time developers reached deals with home purchasers, or home owners agreed with other home owners, and then they or their successors in interest used the courts to vindicate their private agreements—just as any person would go to court to vindicate any other private property or contractual right. Clearly courts are public bodies, and in that sense it is obvious that judicial enforcement entails the power of state. But insofar as there is anything at all that is considered "private law" between unofficial actors, be it contract or tort or simple trespass, then those actors of necessity must be able to resort to the courts to vindicate their private rights. Did *Shelley* leave no room for any such "private" legal rights? If the touchstone for "state action" was resort to the courts, would all private claims, when vindicated in

---

[8] The comprehensive work on the NAACP's role in invalidating racially restrictive covenants is Vose, supra note 1. For a briefer presentation, see Mark Tushnet, Making Civil Rights Law: Thurgood Marshall and the Supreme Court, 1936–1961, at 81–98 (1994) (restrictive covenants litigation in context of NAACP's overall efforts); Leland B. Ware, Invisible Walls: An Examination of the Legal Strategy of the Restrictive Covenant Cases, 67 Wash. U. L. Q. 737 (1989).

[9] Paul Brest, State Action and Liberal Theory: A Casenote on *Flagg Brothers v. Brooks,* 130 Penn L. Rev. 1296 (1982) (discussing state action and public-private distinction in Supreme Court jurisprudence).

court, henceforth be labeled "state action," subject to the same constraints that apply to official policies?[10]

Later decisions by the Supreme Court itself suggested very strongly
that the answer was "no," and that the bare potential for judicial
enforcement, taken alone, would *not* transform what we consider private
arrangements and preferences into state action, even when those private
relationships entailed racial discrimination.[11] But if that is the case, did
these later decisions mean that *Shelley* itself was a dead end, along with
its pronouncement that judicial enforcement of covenants was state
action? Should it be seen simply as an ad hoc expedient to get rid of one
type of private action that particularly embarrassed the United States in
its Cold War diplomacy[12]—another example of the old adage that hard
cases make bad law?

The argument of this chapter is that Shelley's "state action" enigma
can best be solved by inquiring into the character of racially restrictive
covenants specifically as *property*. This is an inquiry that is aided by
some new legal scholarship—in particular, new scholarly attention to the
differences between property and contract, and to the interrelations
between law and social norms.

I.   Opening Salvos in the Quest For Residential Segregation

Racially restrictive covenants (hereinafter RRCs) emerged at the
turn of the last century, at a time when many African Americans were
migrating from rural to urban areas. White Americans responded by
imposing racial segregation on a wide range of everyday fields of activity—transportation, employment, recreation, education. In that sense,
the housing segregation of RRCs was just one more instance, albeit an
important one, in the emerging patterns of early twentieth century racial
exclusion.[13]

Moreover, RRCs were only one of a range of *methods* for enforcing
residential segregation. Early in the century, white Americans also
attempted to deploy nuisance law and zoning to keep nonwhites out of

---

[10] See, e.g., Tushnet, supra note 8, at 86 (noting that judicial enforcement as state
action would collapse entire doctrine of state action).

[11] See, e.g. Peterson v. Greenville, 373 U.S. 244 (1963) (reversing trespass conviction in
antisegregation sit-in case in restaurant, but on the grounds that official state policy
supported segregation). The 1964 Civil Rights Act later banned racial discrimination in
such public accommodations.

[12] See Mary L. Dudziak, Desegregation as a Cold War Imperative, 41 Stan. L. Rev. 61
(1988) (describing postwar Federal desegregation efforts in context of international opinion).

[13] See, e.g., Jack Temple Kirby, Darkness at the Dawning: Race and Reform in the
Progressive South 23–25 (1972).

their neighborhoods. They used extralegal means as well, including both social norms and violence, and ranging from petty harassment to threats to arson, riot, and homicide. As it turned out, within two decades of the turn of the century, only RRCs remained standing as legal devices for racial exclusion, though the extralegal means lasted much longer.

Nuisance law was never very effective for purposes of racial exclusion, and it was largely abandoned quite early. Some very old cases from the Ante–Bellum south had treated liquor businesses as "common nuisances" because they attracted crowds of supposedly noisy and boisterous African–Americans; some other cases from the same era had described as "nuisances" the presence of newly-freed African Americans.[14] But these cases were closely linked with the law of slavery, and they had little authority after the Civil War. The most notorious later nineteenth century case in which an owner tried to use nuisance law for racial exclusion was *Falloon v. Schilling*, a case in which the plaintiff complained that a neighboring owner was harassing him and creating a nuisance by renting the adjacent property to "worthless negroes."[15] But the *Falloon* court categorically rejected this claim: no person could be a nuisance simply because of his or her race. Other courts took the same position,[16] and even the white complainants themselves generally raised additional factors such as potential noise and overcrowding. While some courts seemed sympathetic to nuisance cases with racial overtones, and while echoes of racial nuisance claims continued well into the twentieth century,[17] nuisance law never gained substantial traction as a basis for exclusion based on race alone.

Racial zoning had a somewhat more intense flurry, but zoning also soon evaporated as a legal basis for residential racial exclusion. Baltimore enacted the first racial zoning ordinance in 1910; several other

---

[14] See, e.g. U.S. v. Coulter, 25 F. Cas. 675 (D. C. Cir. 1805) (affirming fine against establishment as a common nuisance for selling liquor to "negroes and slaves, assembled in considerable numbers" on the Sabbath); Sanders v. Ward, 25 Ga. 109 (1858) (allowing will that emancipated slaves outside the state, describing freed slaves within the state as a "great nuisance").

[15] 29 Kan. 292 (1883).

[16] See, e.g. Boyd v. Board of Councilmen of Frankfort, 117 Ky. 199, 77 S.W. 669 (1903) (overturning city council's denial of building permit African American church, could not declare something a nuisance that was not); Diggs v. Morgan College, 133 Md. 264, 105 A. 157 (1918) (construction of residences for African Americans not "of itself" a public nuisance).

[17] See, e.g. Fox v. Corbitt, 137 Tenn. 466, 194 S.W. 88 (1917) (upholding nuisance claim against saloon after prominent discussion of African American patronage); Stratton v. Conway, 201 Tenn. 582, 301 S.W.2d 332 (1957) (rejecting neighbor's claim for damages due to sale of house to African Americans).

cities quickly followed, particularly in the south and lower Midwest.[18] The form of these ordinances was ostensibly race-neutral, presumably to satisfy the then-reigning doctrine of *Plessy v. Ferguson*, in which the Supreme Court had permitted state law to segregate the races in "equal but separate" railway facilities.[19] For example, the 1914 racial zoning ordinance of Louisville, Kentucky, provided that members of any given racial group could move only to those streets where their group constituted a majority; over time, presumably, every street would come to be occupied only by particular racial groups.[20]

A few years later, the newly-formed National Association for the Advancement of Colored People (NAACP) successfully challenged Louisville's ordinance in *Buchanan v. Warley* (1917),[21] one of the Court's few departures from "separate but equal" in the early twentieth century. In distinguishing the case from *Plessy*, the Court stressed that racial zoning impeded the ability to own and dispose of substantial tangible property.[22] Property ownership at the time was widely seen as a route to full civic participation by African Americans, and perhaps it was not so surprising that according to *Buchanan*, governments could not curtail racial minorities' access to property. But interestingly (and depressingly) enough, much contemporary legal commentary supported racial zoning. Some commentators described racial zoning as an element in maintaining property values, in ways reminiscent of the "City Beautiful" movement of which zoning was a part, but many others focused on the public interest in avoiding violence, a matter especially salient in the light of the then-recent race riots in American cities.[23] That the Supreme Court acknowledged but rejected these arguments, including that of preventing racial violence, is an interesting commentary on its belief in the importance of property ownership.[24] But then, the worst of the racial violence had not yet occurred—the horrific race riots in Chicago in the summer of 1919, in which at least thirty-seven persons were killed and enormous property losses incurred.[25] By the time these events shocked the nation,

---

[18] David E. Bernstein, Philip Sober Controlling Philip Drunk: *Buchanan v. Warley* in Historical Perspective, 51 Vand. L. Rev. 797, 834–36 (1998)

[19] Plessy v. Ferguson, 163 U.S. 537 (1896).

[20] Buchanan v. Warley, 245 U.S. 60 (1917).

[21] *Id.*

[22] *Id.* at 80–81.

[23] The arguments and outcome are extensively reviewed in Bernstein, supra note 18, at 836–60

[24] Buchanan, at 73–74, 80–81.

[25] See Thomas Lee Philpott, The Slum and the Ghetto: Neighborhood Deterioration and Middle–Class Reform, Chicago 1880–1930, at 170 (1978) (describing riot damage, death figures).

of course, *Buchanan* had narrowed the legal means for residential racial exclusion down to one: RRCs.

As David Bernstein has pointed out, *Buchanan* meant that municipalities and public officials could no longer participate in a formal way in enforcing residential segregation. Unlike zoning, RRCs required developers and homeowners themselves to bear the costs of creating and enforcing legal exclusion; this greater expense undoubtedly discouraged some level of racial exclusion and opened up a greater *total* amount of housing to minority members, even if minority residential areas remained segregated as they expanded.[26] But while RRCs may have been more costly for their proponents than racial zoning was, over the decades after *Buchanan*—and the Chicago race riots—RRCs took on much greater significance as the sole legal means for "holding the line" against minority residential expansion. And with that increased significance, RRCs began to generate a considerable amount of legal attention.

II. Legal Considerations About Early RRCS

Like the early zoning ordinances of the twentieth century, real estate covenants sprang from concerns to create and maintain the "City Beautiful"—to establish attractive and appealing neighborhoods that were free of nuisance-like activities and structures.[27] But sad to say, from a very early date, many private real estate plans included racial exclusion as one of their elements.[28] Indeed, decades later, in 1943, one homeowner asserted that such older well-to-do developments did not even have to make racial restrictions explicit. His subdivision's 1912 advertising had announced its "high class" character, and its deed restrictions had actually placed limits on buildings, and that was enough, this homeowner argued (unsuccessfully), to infer that the restrictions also implicitly prohibited future nonwhite occupancy.[29]

At the outset, however, there were some legal questions about whether racial segregation could be incorporated into these plans for newly-developed "high class" neighborhoods. Indeed, the very first major

---

[26] Bernstein, supra note 18, at 861–66. Bernstein notes, however, that municipal officials continued to evade *Buchanan*; *Id.*, at 862.

[27] Gerald Korngold, The Emergence of Private Land Use Controls in Large–Scale Subdivisions: The Companion Story to *Village of Euclid v. Ambler Realty Co.*, 51 Case Western L. Rev. 617–620 (2001); Evan McKenzie, *Privatopia: Homeowners Associations and the Rise of Private Government* 36–38 (1994).

[28] See Helen Monchow, The Use of Deed Restrictions in Subdivision Development 47–50 (1928) (describing racial deed restrictions in 40 of 84 planned subdivisions); Korngold, supra note 27, at 638–39 (noting possibility of indirect racial restraints in Shaker Heights subdivision).

[29] Kathan v. Stevenson, 307 Mich. 485, 12 N.W.2d 332, 334 (1943).

case about RRCs was at all not promising for exclusion. In Gandolfo v. Hartman (1891) a federal court in California had ruled against the legality of a one-lot residential deed restriction prohibiting occupancy by "Chinamen," observing that it would be an unduly narrow reading of the Fourteenth Amendment "to hold that, while state and municipal legislatures are forbidden to discriminate against the Chinese in their legislation, a citizen of the state may lawfully do so by contract, which the courts may enforce."[30] The court then went on to cite the United States' treaty with China as an alternative ground for its decision.

But it was *Gandolfo's* Fourteenth Amendment remarks, likening judicial enforcement of private contracts to official legislation, that became the mantra for the NAACP in its constitutional attacks on RRCs over the next decades. *Gandolfo* should have been especially relevant after *Buchanan* invalidated racial zoning: if municipalities could not enact racial zoning, how could developers and homeowners enact their own private racial zoning? But until *Shelley* itself, courts hearing these arguments either ignored *Gandolfo* or distinguished it, treating the case with only faintly-disguised disdain. Courts that mentioned the case at all said that it had simply been wrong in likening contractual relations to state action, since the former were private and not subject to Fourteenth Amendment constraints. Alternatively, it was said, *Gandolfo* rested on the Chinese–American treaty that specially protected persons of Chinese origin.[31] Hence *Gandolfo's* constitutional point was not much of an impediment to RRCs. Nor did *Buchanan* change this picture, even though NAACP lawyers later argued repeatedly that *Buchanan* invalidated RRCs along with municipal racial zoning. Michigan and Missouri, the future home states of *Sipes* and *Shelley*, each had an important early state supreme court case upholding RRCs, and both opinions all but ignored *Buchanan*, stating that restrictive covenants were private actions unaffected by any equal protection constraints on state action.[32]

---

[30] Gandolfo v. Hartman, 49 F. 181, 182 (S.D. Cal. 1892).

[31] See, e.g. Title Guarantee & Trust Co. v. Garrott, 42 Cal.App. 152, 183 P. 470, 471 (1919) (upholding constitutionality of RRC without mentioning *Gandolfo*); Parmalee v. Morris, 218 Mich. 625, 188 N.W. 330, 331 (1922) (distinguishing *Gandolfo*); Kraemer v. Shelley, 355 Mo. 814, 198 S.W.2d 679, 683 (1946) (describing *Gandolfo* as invalid) Hurd v. Hodge, 162 F.2d 233, 234, 240 (D.C.App. 1947) (majority not mentioning *Gandolfo* despite dissent's prominent citation). *Gandolfo* also reappeared in an influential 1945 article cited in Shelley v. Kraemer, for the proposition that state judicial enforcement of restrictive covenants would violate the equal protection of the law; see D. O. McGovney, Racial Residential Segregation by State Court Enforcement of Restrictive Agreements, Covenants or Conditions in Deeds is Unconstitutional, 33 Cal. L. Rev. 5, 7 (1945).

[32] The major case from Michigan was *Parmalee*, 188 N.W. 330; that from Missouri was Koehler v. Rowland, 275 Mo. 573, 205 S.W. 217 (1918). Other much cited early cases upholding RRCs were California's *Title Guarantee and Trust*, 183 P. 470, and Louisiana's Queensborough Land Co. v. Cazeaux, 136 La. 724, 67 So. 641 (1915), which predated

Most important of all, the same position was soon asserted by the United States Supreme Court in *Corrigan v.Buckley* (1926), a case originating with RRCs in the District of Columbia. Here the Court passed over the NAACP lawyers' citation of *Buchanan*, and instead asserted that none of the claimed Constitutional bases to strike down RRCs—the Fifth, Thirteenth or Fourteenth Amendments—"prohibited private individuals from entering into contracts respecting the control and disposition of their own property."[33] While *Corrigan*'s remarks on the Fourteenth Amendment were dicta, since that Amendment did not apply in the District of Columbia, the case seemed to put an imprimatur on the distinction between public racial zoning on the one hand, invalid after *Buchanan*, and the seemingly private arrangements of RRCs on the other. Indeed, in one sense, *Buchanan* worked against the NAACP's attacks on RRCs, because that case had displayed such great solicitude to insulate private property from governmental intrusion.

Nevertheless, other non-Constitutional legal concerns did cast some doubts on RRCs, doubts that affected the form of these covenants for several decades. As Gerald Korngold has pointed out, real estate covenants generally were a relatively new device for controlling private land developments in the early twentieth century. There were plenty of precedents for the view that such restrictions were disfavored by the law, that they were to be narrowly construed, or that they might violate rules that prevented current owners from extending their control too far into the future.[34] Even *Corrigan* itself was not so decisively pro-covenant as it seemed; it did not actually address the critical question whether RRCs would run with the land, since the parties to that suit were all original signatories to the covenants rather than subsequent purchasers—a distinction between contract and property that might have made a difference in subsequent RRC cases, as we shall see. None of these doubts or potential doubts stopped RRCs, however, or indeed other private subdivision deed restrictions that were not aimed at race. All the same, at least some of the skeptical legal precedents did appear to have some impact on the early forms that real estate developers used for RRCs.

III. The Impact of Older Common Law: Restraints on Alienation and the Rule Against Perpetuities

A. "Restraints on alienation."

One important question early in the century was whether RRCs were illegal "restraints on alienation." Alienability is widely thought to

---

Buchanan but was cited in later state cases that said nothing about *Buchanan*; see, e.g. *Title Guarantee* at 471; *Parmalee* at 331.

[33] Corrigan v. Buckley, 271 U.S. 323, 330 (1926).

[34] Korngold, supra note 27, at 618–23, 628–630.

be one of the "sticks" in the bundle that form property, and from the formalist viewpoint of the early twentieth century, restrictions on alienability could seem incompatible with the idea of property itself. A constraint on *who* can buy land, as opposed to what uses they can make of it, must have seemed peculiarly troublesome.

Even from our more modern pragmatic perspective—and quite aside from questions of racial equity—constraints that might reduce the set of potential bidders for a particular property could be a matter of some significance. After all, the smaller the class of people who will bid for an owner's property, all other things being equal, the lower the property's likely value on resale.

Modern law-and-economics scholars might suggest that this issue really should be left up to the contracting parties, since the prospect of a lower resale value should be capitalized into the purchase price and thus internalized by the same parties who originate any restraints on alienation. But another aspect of such restraints has a greater social impact: if an owner knows that she will face difficulties in finding a purchaser, she will have fewer incentives to make improvements or even maintain a property, and this fact can have deleterious effects on a others in the neighborhood. Indeed, as we shall see shortly, it is entirely plausible that an underinvestment problem resulted from RRCs themselves, especially in urban neighborhoods where occupancy was shifting from white to minority. Under those circumstances, white owners sometimes found themselves unable to rent or sell to the only persons—minority members—who would realistically bid on their properties, and their inability to rent or sell must have had some dampening effect on their willingness to keep up the properties. Deterioration of a few properties can set off a larger neighborhood deterioration; thus RRCs themselves suggested a more general pattern in which restraints on alienation can have a genuine social impact, external to the parties who adopt them.

Problems of underinvestment can be more than offset if the restraints themselves are valuable to a substantial class of bidders; for example, restraints to prevent noise or commercial uses might be valuable in a residential neighborhood, and they might make the properties *more* saleable as residences. These offsetting creations of value might justify what would otherwise seem damaging restraints. But once again, constraints on *who* can buy land, as opposed to what uses they can make of it, might seem peculiarly troublesome, as they did even to early twentieth-century courts.

As RRCs started to be litigated in large cities—particularly Detroit, St. Louis, Los Angeles, and Washington, D.C.—different jurisdictions' courts came to different conclusions on the restraint-on-alienation question. Some, notably Louisiana and Missouri, allowed these restraints on the grounds that they were only partial, leaving a large enough pool of buyers even after the exclusion of non-Caucasians; the implicit message was that any drop in value from disallowing one set of bidders would be offset by the other bidders' happiness at the exclusion of supposed undesirables.[35] Others, however, notably California and Michigan, took a more formalist approach, saying that it was impossible to draw a line of "reasonableness" once any set of bidders was excluded; hence RRCs could not bar ownership to any racial group. But having said this, the Supreme Courts in both states added still another formalism, holding that restraints on "occupancy"—as opposed to ownership—were not restraints on alienation after all.[36] Probably with this distinction in mind, many RRCs, including those later at issue in *Shelley* and the companion *Sipes* cases, were drafted to constrain "occupancy" instead of or in addition to ownership, leading to the odd conclusion that African Americans and other racial minority members might own property subject to RRCs even if they could not live there themselves.[37]

B.   The "Rule Against Perpetuities"

The Rule Against Perpetuities is a venerable constraint on the "dead hand" of the past, a formality that generally prevents landowners from extending their control over their property longer than, roughly speaking, a couple of generations into the future. The Rule was a live issue in the early part of the twentieth century, just as "restraints on alienation" were, and concerns about the Rule seem to have affected the initial forms that developers used for racial covenants as well as for other non-racial aspects of these new real estate control devices.

Covenants on real estate generally "run with the land" of everyone in a restricted neighborhood, which means that the mutual obligations incorporated in the covenants are binding on owners after the first who agree to them; through these "running" covenants, later owners can control other later owners' activities or buildings or other subjects of the covenants. That is in fact the legitimate value of real estate covenants and deed restrictions; they provide owners with the ability to maintain the character of the neighborhood over time, giving continuity to its land uses no matter how many times the neighborhood's individual properties change hands. But what this means is that the developer's initial vision

---

[35] *Cazeaux*, at 643; *Koehler* at 220; Kemp v. Rubin, 188 Misc. 310, 69 N.Y.S.2d 680, 685 (Sup. Ct. Spec. Term, 1947). Washington D.C. also permitted RRCs to restrict sales, though without discussing the specific issue of restraints on alienation; see, e.g., Torrey v. Wolfes, 6 F.2d 702 (D.C.App. 1925).

[36] Title Guarantee, at 471; Los Angeles Investment Co. v. Gary, 181 Cal. 680, 186 P. 596, 597 (1919); Porter v. Barrett, 233 Mich. 373, 206 N.W. 532, 534 (1925).

[37] See, e.g. Stratton v. Cornelius, 99 Cal.App. 8, 277 P. 893 (1929) (RRC restricting use and occupancy to Caucasians could not be used to halt sale to African Americans).

of the planned community potentially can go on indefinitely, even after the developer is long out of the picture. In the early part of the century, developers apparently feared that this aspect of covenants could violate the Rule Against Perpetuities.

One technique to avoid the Rule would have been to set a time limit on any covenants. Because of the technicalities of the Rule itself, a limit of twenty-one years or less was bound to be safe. But a time period this short might make the neighborhood plan seem unstable, and in fact, early developer restrictions of all kinds clustered around a duration of about thirty-three years.[38] A more widely-used technique was to avoid the covenant form—through which enforcement power would devolve to the subdivision homeowners themselves—and instead to structure the RRCs as "conditional fees" that would revert to the original seller if the condition were violated; such conditional fee arrangements were not subject to the Rule. Thus in a number of cases involving the early RRCs, one finds that the remedy for violation was reversion to the developer rather than injunction or damages by other subdivision owners.[39] This situation changed as courts became more accustomed to RRCs, but in California, for example, it was not until 1928 that it was clear that homeowners themselves could enforce RRCs against their neighbors directly, as opposed to a remedy that involved forfeiture to the development firm.[40]

IV. Unexplored Common Law Objections From Covenant Law: Horizontal Privity & "Touch & Concern"

Other aspects of covenant law probably gave developers pause about RRCs, or if they did not, they should have. Older covenant law had a number of specific limitations, especially where the remedy was for damages "at law" rather than for an injunction in equity. Two of these limitations should have been particularly salient to RRCs—doctrines with the rather odd names of "horizontal privity" and "touch and concern."

A. Horizontal Privity.

The doctrine of "horizontal privity" required that no promises or covenants could run with the land and bind future possessors unless the covenants were created in conjunction with a lease or sale of the property. Presumably the underlying reason was that these transactions would incorporate the covenants in a major document of transfer; subsequent owners would be likely to look into these documents or find

---

[38] Monchow, supra note 28, at 56.

[39] See, e.g. L.A. Investment Co.; Koehler (restrictions structured as defeasible fees).

[40] Wayt v. Patee, 205 Cal. 46, 269 P. 660 (1928).

them in the chain of title, and thus they would find out about the duties created by their predecessors in title.[41] This older doctrine, and the idea of notice behind it, could have been a useful analytic tool when a new form of RRC emerged, one instigated not by developers but by property owners themselves—that is, the neighborhood agreement, in which a group of homeowners agreed among themselves not to sell or rent to non-whites.

While there were early examples of such neighbor agreements for racial exclusion—*Shelley* itself involved such an agreement that dated back to 1911—this form of RRC became particularly prevalent during the 1920's. Perhaps, as the NAACP was to argue, this was because the neighbors wanted RRCs to take the place of the racial zoning that was outlawed in *Buchanan* in 1917. In any event, the cases suggest that these after-the-fact neighbor agreements occurred in areas that were less chic than those with developer-originated RRC, often in urban areas that seemed to lie in the direct path of minority expansion.[42] Moreover, whereas the developers' RRCs were generally just one element in a larger plan for an "exclusive" private community, the neighbor-driven RRCs had no other elements. They rather fixed all hope for gentility on promises of racial exclusion.

As a legal matter, these neighborhood RRCs were problematic from the perspective of "horizontal privity." When *developers* drew up RRCs, they generally incorporated the restrictions into all the initial deeds of sale, thus making the restrictions easily available to a title search, and also making them applicable uniformly to every purchaser and successor in interest. But the neighbor RRCs were considerably sloppier. Individual neighbors with a particular interest collected signatures door to door, with numerous irregularities and many ambiguities about proportions of signatories required to make the agreements valid through the neighborhood.[43] Moreover, while these RRCs were often recorded, they were not contained in actual deeds, and in that sense they lacked "horizontal privity" traditionally required for covenants to run with the land.[44]

---

[41] Another constraint was "vertical privity": covenant obligations would only apply to one who had the same type of interest as the promissor; such a successor also seems more likely to inquire about the predecessor's promises.

[42] See, e.g. Porter v. Johnson, 232 Mo.App. 1150, 115 S.W.2d 529 (1938) (upholding 1921 neighbor agreement adopted when African American purchased nearby) Wendy Plotkin, Deeds of Mistrust: Race, Housing and Restrictive Covenants in Chicago, 1900–1950, at 2–3 (working paper, 1997) (available at *http://tigger.uic.edu/?wplotk1/deeds/www/new.html*) (describing covenants pushed by Chicago real estate interests in neighborhoods adjacent to "black belt").

[43] See text at note 70, infra.

[44] Some neighbor-created RRCs required the signors to incorporate the restrictions in future deeds of sale, however; see, e.g. Wayt v. Patee, 205 Cal. 46, 269 P. 660 (1928).

The way around this problem had the ironic name of "equity." When neighbors went to court to enforce these RRCs, they sued to *enjoin* sales or occupancy rather than to collect damages—that is, they sued in equity rather than at law. And in equity, it was said, all that was required to enforce a covenant was that the purchaser knew of the prior promise. Technical horizontal privity, itself a kind of assurance that later occupants would find out about the restrictions, was not necessary if the purchaser or occupant actually knew about the restrictions, or had notice from the official records, even though those record documents were not major one like deeds.

Did subsequent owners and occupants know about the restrictions? On this issue of knowledge, it bears recalling that the entire history of RRCs was relatively short, and highly contentious at that. Under the circumstances, one might surmise that subsequent purchasers were likely to be aware of these restrictions, since few of the restrictions were very old, and since they were likely to be noisily publicized (although in fact, as we shall see, there was some question in *Shelley* itself). More-over, the litigated cases undoubtedly selected for instances in which everyone did know of the restrictions, since at least some people cared enough to try to enforce them. As one prominent NAACP lawyer observed at a 1945 conference, RRCs were usually only enforced if some self-selected "agitators" were especially active in stirring the pot; anoth-er lawyer at the same conference noted that litigating was expensive, and this fact dampened enthusiasm for doing so.[45] Given the patterns of neighborhood change in major cities, there doubtless were many RRCs that simply fell apart for lack of enforcement.[46] If RRCs had lasted for a longer period, the question of notice at the heart of "horizontal privity" might well have come to the fore more sharply.

B.   Touch and Concern.

The other older covenant doctrine that should have been relevant to RRCs was the requirement that a covenant had to "touch and concern" land if it were to run. This rather vague requirement, like horizontal privity, seems to have been aimed at in large part at notice—that is, a subsequent purchaser is more likely to be aware of an obligation that has something to do with land.

But the "touch and concern" doctrine goes beyond that simple guideline and goes on to another object as well: that is, it assures that real property not become too loaded down with idiosyncratic restrictions.

---

[45] Vose, supra note 1., at 58–59; the attorneys were, respectively, Spottswood Robinson III of Richmond (later a distinguished Federal judge), and Loren Miller of Los Angeles.

[46] See Arnold R. Hirsch, Making the Second Ghetto: Race and Housing in Chicago, 1940–1960, at 30 (2d ed. 1998) (describing collapse of many Chicago RRCs in mid-and later 1940's).

As several modern property scholars have pointed out, *contracts* can set out innumerable complicated obligations, because the parties do the negotiations themselves and presumably know all the intricate details of their bargains; normally, contractual obligations will not outlast the original parties to the deal. But property is different, because property— and especially landed property—goes on into the indefinite future to successive owners, who are increasingly remote from first-hand knowledge of the original transactions. Hence it is important that obligations attaching to landed property take relatively simple and standardized forms, so that distantly future buyers will not inadvertently get themselves into peculiar obligations, and so that buyers generally do not have to be on the lookout for such idiosyncratic arrangements.[47]

The "touch and concern" doctrine, generally speaking, served the function of limiting covenant obligations to those promises that most people would understand as enhancing the net value of the properties in question, taken in their entirety. For example, a promise to trim the hedges might be annoying for the front property owner, but her annoyance could well be less than back property owner's gain in maintaining a nice view. This is the kind of deal that neighboring owners might be expected to negotiate, and that they would want to have pass on to subsequent owners without requiring renegotiation, since such deals enhance the net *collective* value of the lots involved.

Value-enhancement of this sort was understood to be a part of covenant law in the early days of RRCs, including covenants enforced at equity.[48] But in what way does it "touch and concern land" that an owner is an African American or a Chinese or a Jew? What do those personal characteristics (supposing that they can be defined) have to do with the usual promises about building design, hedge trimming, lawn ornamentation, noise limits and so on? In a sense, the "touch and concern" doctrine echoes the legal problems with "restraints on alienation," which are generally only valid if they add offsetting benefits, and which are especially questionable where particular *persons*—rather than particular uses—limit the bidding pool. But sadly enough, American courts glided over the issues that lay behind "touch and concern," just as they did with respect to "horizontal privity."

---

[47] This thesis has been particularly developed in Thomas W. Merrill and Henry E. Smith, Optimal Standardization in the Law of Property: The *Numerus Clausus* Principle, 110 Yale L. J. 1 (2000). For a briefer account, see Carol M. Rose, What Government Can Do For Property (And Vice Versa), in The Fundamental Interrelationships Between Government and Property 209, 213–15 (1999).

[48] Monchow, supra note 28, at 17; see also *Cazeaux*, at 643 (remarking that conditions on land would be invalid "founded upon no substantial principle but merely in caprice.")

While it is true that courts of equity can dispense with technical common law doctrines, a more probing judicial exploration might have noticed the policies behind these seeming technicalities of covenant law, particularly the "touch and concern" requirement. The race of a purchaser or occupant seems particularly implausible as "touching and concerning" land, since a person's race has no obvious connection with the land *uses* normally associated with "touch and concern." Instead, as the African American defendant argued in Michigan's first major RRC case, the restriction treated him as if his very person constituted some kind of nuisance,[49] something not countenanced in nuisance law.

But in the context of covenant law in the 1920s and later, it apparently seemed entirely obvious that race was indeed relevant to property values, simply because white owners thought so. Real estate professionals found evidence that the presence of African Americans of other nonwhite minorities diminished the property values for whites,[50] and the courts seemed to take for granted that such market indicators lent legal support for RRCs, and that later white purchasers would naturally want the same racial restrictions that earlier owners had had.[51] In this easy assumption, the courts affirmed a whole set of customary practices—a point, as we shall see, that is critically significant in understanding *Shelley*'s ultimate outcome.

V. Patterns of Judicial Lenience

During the 1920s and later, the superficiality of the leading RRC cases is particularly remarkable in one respect: in a very important sense, these cases left untouched the question whether *any* RRCs should be binding on subsequent purchasers. The Supreme Court's *Corrigan* case was widely cited in cases that upheld RRCs, but *Corrigan* was a suit to prevent an *original* purchaser from selling to a nonwhite buyer, and the case discussed covenant obligations as if they were a matter of contract. Hence it was not clear at all that *Corrigan* meant that RRCs could pass on to *subsequent* purchasers, who were not parties to the original transactions creating the covenants.[52] In later cases, courts

---

[49] Parmalee v. Morris, 218 Mich. 625, 188 N.W. 330, 332 (1922).

[50] See, e.g. Stanley L. McMichael, McMichael's Appraisal Manual 51–54 (3rd ed. 1944).

[51] See, e.g. Schulte v. Starks, 238 Mich. 102, 213 N.W. 102 (1927) (excluding African American couple on basis of RRCs against "persons ... injurious to the locality," given evidence that this language had been stated to include African Americans, as well as evidence that their presence would diminish property values); see also Fairchild v. Raines, 24 Cal.2d 818, 151 P.2d 260, 263 (1944) (noting evidence that influx of African Americans caused drop in property values, and that the "damage" to the neighborhood in question had already occurred due the "influx of negroes" nearby.)

[52] The same was true of some important state cases, e.g. Wayt v. Patee, 205 Cal. 46, 269 P. 60 (1928) (upholding "covenants" where plaintiffs and some defendants were

repeatedly cited *Corrigan*'s language of "contractual" obligations to uphold RRCs, without pausing to consider whether subsequent purchasers really should have the same obligations as the original owners, who actually could be seen as contracting parties.[53]

In the period between *Corrigan* and *Shelley*, the courts generally displayed a growing certainty that RRCs were legal, even though this certainty was increasingly shadowed by discomfort and apology.[54] Even more than the developer-created restrictions, the neighborhood agreements gave the courts a particularly striking set of occasions to show just how willing they were to uphold RRCs, given the many irregularities in these post-hoc devices—and given, as one exceptional and astute dissenting opinion noted, the potential that neighborhood covenants could extend over much wider areas than developers' covenants had done previously.[55] The courts generally accepted the neighbors' RRCs with very little questioning, often using the arguments of "equity" to excuse the lack of horizontal privity, to explain away improprieties in signatures, and sometimes to uphold restrictions even in the face of widespread abandonment, while generally ignoring or putting to one side the impact of these restrictions on minority housing needs.[56] Nowhere, as we will see, was this lenience towards racial restrictions more evident than in the case history of *Shelley* itself.

Technicalities and doctrinal issues did doom a certain number of RRCs, as we shall see, but the general pattern of judicial approval suggested that the nineteenth century's skepticism of private land use

---

original signators); Queensborough Land Co. v. Cazeaux, 136 La. 724, 67 So. 641 (1915) (same).

[53] See, e.g. Sipes v. McGhee, 316 Mich. 614, 25 N.W.2d 638, 644 (1947) (describing rights as "contractual"); Torrey v. Wolfes, 6 F.2d 702, 703 (1925) (same); Letteau v. Ellis, 122 Cal.App. 584, 10 P.2d 496, 497 (1932). See also Mays v. Burgess, 147 F.2d 869, 875 (D.C. Cir. 1945) (also describing right as contractual); but see *Mays* at 875–76 (Edgerton, diss.) (one of the very few opinions to raising a distinction between contractual and covenant obligations)

[54] For the discomfort, see, e.g. *Mays*, 147 F.2d at 873 (noting social problem of racial discrimination); Sipes, 25 N.W.2d at 644–45 (same); Fairchild v. Raines, 151 P.2d at 267–269 (Traynor, conc.)

[55] Mays, 147 F.2d at 876 (Edgerton, diss.)

[56] See, e.g., *Sipes*, 25 N.W.2d at 641 (noting general policy of leniency with respect to signature formalities); Russell v. Wallace, 30 F.2d 981 (D.C. Cir. 1929) (upholding neighborhood RRC over one signator's objection hat he had withdrawn prior to recording); Porter v. Johnson, 232 Mo.App. 1150, 115 S.W.2d 529 (1938) (upholding restriction despite evidence of nonuse). For a neighbor RRC that was too sloppy for the courts, but that may suggest "improvement association" tactics, see Pickel v. McCawley, 329 Mo. 166, 44 S.W.2d 857 (1931) (overturning agreement where homeowner's signature had been recorded without her knowledge).

restrictions had turned into leniency in the twentieth. It is difficult to say whether RRCs were the beneficiaries of a generally more relaxed judicial attitude about covenants running with the land, as in the *Neponsit* case discussed elsewhere in this volume, or whether judicial sympathy with RRCs itself helped to create that more general relaxation. Perhaps both are the case.

In any event, judicial imprimaturs on RRCs were very much reinforced by contemporary social practices and beliefs, particularly the belief—something of a self-fulfilling prophecy—that racial mixing would cause neighborhood housing values to plummet. The National Association of Real Estate Boards (NAREB) began as early as 1913 to direct its members to avoid introducing racial minorities into neighborhoods of a different ethnicity, and from 1924 to 1950 the Association's "Code of Ethics" included a paragraph to this effect. Local real estate groups adopted the NAREB code, and they formally or informally punished brokers who refused to conform with its norm of racial "steering."[57] In some cities, notably St. Louis, these same local real estate boards helped neighborhoods to organize drives for RRCs and to enforce the restrictions after they were in place.[58] The Federal Housing Administration, created in the early 1930s to insure residential loans, specifically encouraged RRCs in its Underwriting Manual for the mortgages that it would insure, on the ground that "inharmonious racial groups" constituted an "adverse influence" on housing value.[59] The ostensible reasons behind these norms were given in the American Law Institute's Restatement of Property that appeared in 1944: racially exclusionary measures were acceptable and "reasonable" because they maintained property values, and because they alleviated social tensions.[60]

The latter point is especially significant, suggesting as it does that a threat of violence lay behind the norms of exclusion. Indeed, that threat—fueled by white residents fear of losing their housing investments—may have been the most powerful of all the incentives to maintaining residential segregation.

---

[57] Stephen Grant Meyer, As Long As They Don't Move Next Door: Segregation and Racial Conflict in American Neighborhoods 7 (1913); Luigi Laurenti, Property Values and Race: Studies in Seven Cities 16–18 (1960). The relevant section (the thirty-fourth of thirty-five) stated that "A realtor should never be instrumental in introducing into a neighborhood a character of property or occupancy, members of any race or nationality, or any individual whose presence will clearly be detrimental to property values in the neighborhood." Laurenti, supra, at 17; McMichael, supra note 50, at 368. Laurenti, supra at 17–18, argues that brokers continued to steer racially even after cosmetic changes were made in the NAREB code.

[58] Vose, supra note 1., at 100–109.

[59] Robert C. Weaver, The Negro Ghetto 72–73 (1948).

[60] 4 Restatement of Property, ch. 30, sec. 406, at 2411–12.

VI. Emerging Challenges

In spite of the great weight of legal authority behind RRCs, these devices had a few weaknesses that could be exploited successfully. Much of the best-known law on RRCs came from just a few jurisdictions, indeed just a few cities: Los Angeles in California, St. Louis and Kansas City in Missouri, Detroit and Pontiac in Michigan, and Washington, D.C. In these cities, local lawyers affiliated with the NAACP persistently challenged racial covenants, over the course of the organization's long and ever-more orchestrated assault on RRCs.[61] Until *Shelley*, NAACP lawyers lost again and again on their major constitutional claim—that judicial enforcement of RRCs constituted "state action"—but they succeeded in keeping the injustice of RRCs alive as a political issue while they forced white neighborhood organizations and real estate interests to bear the expense of litigating enforcement. They also managed to chip away at the legal margins of RRCs, attacking them on technical grounds such as signature problems and recording irregularities; indeed, shortly before the *Shelley* case, an NAACP lawyer in St. Louis was able to put together a small compendium of these potential technical challenges to racial covenants.[62]

From the perspective of modern legal scholarship, a particularly intriguing technique of NAACP lawyers in the 1940's was their challenge to the very concept of race itself. Willis Graves and Francis Dent made racial identity a central issue in *Sipes v. McGee,* the Detroit case that was to become the companion to *Shelley* in the Supreme Court. They flummoxed a white neighbor by asking how he knew that the couple moving in next door were "Negroes" (the answer: "I have seen Mr. McGhee and he appears to have colored features. They are more darker than mine ..."); and they brought in two members of the Wayne State University Department of Sociology and Anthropology to cast doubt on any lay abilities to recognize racial differences. The Michigan Supreme Court was unimpressed with this attack on what would now be called

---

[61] See generally Vose, supra note 1., at 55, 57–64. Chicago, though very much affected by RRCs and local anti-RRC activity, was notably absent as a generator of nationally-cited law. One challenge to RRCs from Chicago did reach the U.S. Supreme Court, but it was decided there, as in the Illinois Supreme Court, on the basis of technical jurisdictional questions: Hansberry v. Lee, 311 U.S. 32 (1940), reversing Lee v. Hansberry, 372 Ill. 369, 24 N.E.2d 37 (1939); see Plotkin, supra note42, at 3–6. Vose, supra note 1., at 57–64, also describes the NAACP's emerging strategy in 1945, one that excluded a lawsuit from Chicago on the ground that an adverse decision in the Illinois Supreme Court might be too damaging nationally. But see Tushnet, supra note 8, at 87–91 (presenting a somewhat more fractious relationship between local litigators and the national NAACP, also arguing that some in national group favored bringing a case from Chicago to the Supreme Court).

[62] Scovel Richardson, Notes and Comments: Some of the Defenses Available in Restrictive Covenant Suits Against Colored American Citizens in St. Louis, 3 Nat'l. B. J. 50 (1945).

the "social construction of race," but the Detroit lawyers were not alone in trying it out. Charles Houston of Washington urged that all the NAACP lawyers try to undermine racial definitions, describing the effort as an educational technique that might shake up white covenant enforcers.[63]

One pre-Shelley legal attack on RRCs did have some regular success: lawyers deployed a standard equitable principle in covenant law called "changed circumstances," according to which courts of equity would not enforce covenant restrictions that had outlasted their purpose or had lost their value.[64] "Changed circumstance" doctrine—like the general category of "restraints on alienation" and covenant law's more technical "touch and concern" requirement—thus refers to the concept of *value:* covenants will not be enforced unless they retain some reasonable value to landowners. Moreover, "changed circumstance" arguments were particularly revealing in the practical context of RRCs, because these "changed circumstances" cases hinted at the massive demographic changes that lay behind the litigation, as well as the curious practical alignments that developed to break down RRCs.

Continuing African–American urbanization—and increasingly, white suburbanization—set the stage for the "changed circumstance" attacks on RRCs.[65] As more minority members moved into ever more crowded urban "Negro" areas, especially in the war years, these areas grew in size, though by all contemporary reports nowhere nearly enough to satisfy minority housing needs.[66] For example, Detroit's African American prewar population of 160,000 grew by another 60,000 during WWII—60,000 persons with very few housing options.[67] As racial minorities sought to move into new locations, one white answer was violence; this occurred in a particularly dramatic way in Detroit in 1942, when a white mob—including the Ku Klux Klan—stoned and beat the African American war workers who attempted to move into a newly-available

---

[63] Sipes, 25 N.W.2d at 641; Vose, supra note 1., at 60–61, 84–85, 126–31. See also Vose, supra, at 86–87 (describing Houston in the *Hurd* case, his queries to the parties and experts on the meaning of race).

[64] "Changed circumstance" is one of the limited number of doctrines through which property rights can be altered without the consent of the rights-holder. Since covenants typically apply to large numbers of owners, with mutual rights over one another's property, owners can face transactions costs and strategic bargaining in renegotiating covenants, and hence more than other property interests, these restrictions need some way to impose post-hoc readjustments.

[65] See, e.g. Hirsch, supra note 46, at 28–29; Thomas J. Sugrue, The Origins of the Urban Crisis: Race and Inequality in Postwar Detroit 33–47 (1996).

[66] Id., at 17–25.

[67] Alfred M. Lee & Norman D. Humphrey, Race Riot (Detroit, 1942) 92 (1968).

housing project.[68] A second answer was white flight, particularly after the war concluded and the suburbs opened up; white departure, however, made racial transitions even more likely in the urban neighborhoods left behind. A third answer was to fall back on existing RRCs: when minority buyers attempted to acquire the homes vacated by departing white families, some of the neighbors, bolstered by city real estate interests, treated RRCs as a bulwark against change, and they did what they could to "hold the line" by enforcing the covenants.

When these racial transitions occurred, however, white owners of restricted properties sometimes found that they could attract very few white bidders, who made low offers; meanwhile, these owners were foreclosed by the RRCs from selling to the African Americans who would have bid more.[69] At least some of these white owners went ahead and sold to minority purchasers; indeed, in Chicago, some white owners and even real estate interests organized to *prevent* the enforcement of RRCs.[70] When such white sellers were challenged, they became defendants along with their minority buyers, and they claimed that "changed circumstances" had made the RRCs valueless. "Changed circumstances" thus became a way to knock down RRCs in the areas where they probably mattered most as a practical matter, that is, neighborhoods in transition; in so doing they created curious alignments between some white sellers of restricted properties and the minority members who moved into those properties.

These were not the only strange bedfellows. Some real estate brokers realized that there was arbitrage money to be made in racial succession. By encouraging minority entrance into white neighborhoods, or by simply spreading rumors of such moves, "block-busting" brokers could pounce on bargain sales and then resell the properties to hemmed-in minority buyers.[71] Such brokers were widely denounced for fomenting trouble in order to cash in. But on closer examination, the ethics of the practice actually seem considerably more ambiguous. The name of one of these brokers, Raphael Urciolo, floats through the annals of RRC controversies in the later 1940s in Washington D.C., where Urciolo became a defendant in one of the D.C. companion cases to *Shelley*. In the trial, Urciolo claimed to be interested only in making as much money as possible. But he also stated flatly, "I don't believe in covenants at all,"

---

[68] Id. at 93; see also Hirsch, supra note 46, at 36 (describing arson and violence with neighborhood transitions in Chicago in 1940's).

[69] See, e.g., Hundley v. Gorewitz, 132 F.2d 23, 24–25 (D.C.App. 1942) (describing the white seller's difficulty in finding a white purchaser, African American's higher bid). See also Weaver, supra note 59, at 266–68 (same).

[70] Hirsch, supra note 46, at 30; Plotkin, supra note 42, at 3–4

[71] Hirsch, supra note 46, at 34–36.

and he observed that if he were given a choice between selling to a "colored" or foreign purchaser, as opposed to a white purchaser, he would always sell to the minority or foreign person because that buyer had so much more difficulty in finding a house.[72] Needless to say, Urciolo was in bad odor with the Washington Real Estate Board, which had already expelled him.[73] But it is hard to see such a figure simply as the enemy of racial justice. The question of cooperating with blockbusting brokers came up at an NAACP conference on RRCs in 1945, and while some of those present thought that these middlemen were far too controversial, Charles Houston of Washington—perhaps thinking of Urciolo—argued that the brokers performed a very useful service in the long campaign against RRCs.[74]

The end of the Second World War created a critical juncture for RRCs. African American and other minority members had served their country and died for it during the war—a war that itself had raised profound questions about racism. The NAACP and sympathetic commentators—notably the Swedish economist Gunnar Myrdal in his influential book, *An American Dilemma* (1944)[75]—increasingly hammered on the sociological impact of segregation and discrimination on African Americans. Continuing patterns of segregation caused serious embarrassment to the United States in the newly unfolding Cold War. This point was noted when President Truman's new Committee on Civil Rights made its 1947 report, *To Secure These Rights*.[76] And among other matters, the report singled out racially restrictive covenants as a problem and called upon the Justice Department to intervene in challenges to their validity.[77] The Justice Department did indeed support the NAACP in the *Shelley* case—as did an impressive array of civil rights, labor, and religious organizations[78]—and its amicus brief specifically cited a letter of the Secretary of State, detailing the embarrassment that segregation caused for American diplomacy.[79]

---

[72] Vose, supra note 1, at 80.

[73] *Id.*

[74] *Id.* at 58–59.

[75] Gunnar Myrdal, An American Dilemma (20th Anniv. ed. 1962 [1944]).

[76] To Secure These Rights: The Report of the President's Committee on Civil Rights 100, 146–48 (1947); see also Dudziak, supra note 41, at 100–101 (describing State and Justice Department actions in connection with *Shelley*).

[77] To Secure These Rights, supra note 76, at 91, 169.

[78] See Vose, supra note 1, at 163–64, 169–70 (describing the amicus briefs and the NAACP's concern that too many might be filed; also describing Justice's decision to file immediately after Civil Rights report).

[79] Brief for the United States as Amicus Curiae at 19–20.

But another less publicly commented-upon factor may also have been played a role: the mad rush to suburbanization after the Second World War. It was clear that unless halted, RRCs were going to be an even larger part of the nation's new suburban demographics. In late 1947 and early 1948, the first several thousand homes went on sale in the huge and quintessentially middle-class new Levittown development on Long Island. By limiting ownership to Caucasians—following what was then the FHA's standard advice against racial mixing—Levittown's first sales forecast a future in which legal residential segregation would expand exponentially.[80] In this future, it seemed, RRCs would be the rule not just for some relatively small "high class" communities, as in the early developer restrictions, and also not just for the highly-motivated, diehard white urban dwellers, as in many of the neighbor restrictions; instead RRCs seemed poised to reach out into the whole new geography of a suburbanizing, white middle class America.

It was at this juncture that the Supreme Court decided *Shelley v. Kraemer* from St. Louis, and the companion case *Sipes v. McGee* from Detroit.

VII. *Shelley & Sipes*

However objectionable, however nationally embarrassing, however fundamentally unjust, as a *legal* matter in 1948, RRCs had been viewed for decades as private action—limitations created by *private* parties for the *private* governance of their *private* property. How could the mere judicial enforcement of these restrictions now turn into "state action"? That was the problem facing the *Shelley* and *Sipes* plaintiffs, as well as the NAACP attorneys and the numerous "friends of the court" that joined the case.

A.   State Action as Judicial Overreaching.

One possible answer to the state action puzzle—though not one actually given—emerges from the facts of *Shelley* itself: the case illustrated the way that a state supreme court could go out of its way to enforce racial restrictions. The house that J. D. Shelley bought was subject to an RRC in the form of a neighborhood agreement dating back to 1911. Unlike developer-created RRCs, neighbor agreements sometimes had gaps in coverage, since it was often difficult to get one hundred percent agreement ex post. And the Labadie Avenue agreement certainly did have gaps. The original agreement had been signed by only thirty owners out of thirty-nine in the designated area, covering forty-seven parcels out of fifty-seven. Moreover, five of the nonsigning owners were African Americans, and African Americans had lived continually in the

---

[80] Barbara M. Kelly: Expanding the American Dream: Building and Rebuilding Levittown 30–33, 60 (1993)

neighborhood in the intervening years. The Shelleys themselves claimed
not to have known of the restrictions at all. Indeed, how would they
know, unless they were actually told? The mixed character of the
neighborhood gave no notice that they should inquire about restrictions.
As Mrs. Shelley said at trial, "I see other people on the street, that's why
I bought it."[81] While the agreement was recorded, it was not in the
Shelley's deed and apparently not in any other major document of
transfer; older "horizontal privity" rules would have disallowed it, as
they would have disallowed the enforcement at law of any such post hoc
neighbor agreements. Finally, it is hard to see the value of these
restrictions to the white neighbors even on the racist assumption, since
African Americans had been a substantial part of the neighborhood all
along.

The Missouri Supreme Court, however, upheld the restrictions in
the face of all these weaknesses. As usual, the case was brought at
equity, which meant that a court could dispense with "horizontal privity" formalities and look only to notice to the purchasers. On that issue,
the Missouri Supreme Court was satisfied that because the RRCs did
appear somewhere in the records, they provided constructive notice to
the Shelleys, whatever the couple might or might not have known in
fact.[82] Moreover, the Court overturned the chancellor's ruling below that
these particular RRCs had been defective from the outset because they
had been intended to take effect only if all the parcels were signed on.
Nonsense, said the Supreme Court: the neighbors in 1911 could scarcely
have expected the African American owners to agree to RRCs that would
have prohibited their occupancy, and hence the signatories must have
expected some gaps all along.[83] Similarly, as to the question of value, the
Missouri court circumspectly hinted that simply holding the line against
further African American encroachment was enough.[84]

Thus the Missouri Supreme Court, in upholding these quite questionable property restrictions, rejected every objection, including a trial
court finding that was arguably a mixed question of law and fact.[85] In so
doing, this court seemed to go out of its way to enforce *racial* covenants
that in other contexts would have been unenforceable either at law

---

[81] Vose, supra note 1, at 111.

[82] Kraemer v. Shelley, 355 Mo. 814, 198 S.W.2d 679, 683 (1946).

[83] *Id.* at 681–82.

[84] *Id.* at 682.

[85] The California cases by this time were treating issues of this sort as questions of fact
and thus generally deferring to trial courts; see, e.g. Stone v. Jones, 66 Cal.App.2d 264, 152
P.2d 19, 22–23 (1944) (upholding trial court finding of fact that original covenant signators
had intended efficacy only if a certain number of owners signed).

(because of the failure of formalities) or at equity (because of the weakness of notice to the purchaser and value to the enforcing party).

It is in that sense that one might understand the U.S. Supreme Court's statement that judicial enforcement of RRCs was "state action": one could easily characterize the Missouri Court's upholding of the *Shelley* restrictions as a set of extraordinary steps that upheld *racial* restrictions that otherwise had little legal support.[86] But of course such an interpretation would confine the *Shelley* case to its facts—a legally weak set of covenants, taken together with a state supreme court that was altogether too eager to be lenient in the particular case. To be sure, the weakness of the *Shelley* covenants was not altogether idiosyncratic, given the widespread use of neighbor agreements with numerous irregularities. Even such a narrow understanding of Shelley—that state courts had to apply more and more rigorous legal standards of ordinary covenant law to RRCs—would have doomed quite a number of RRCs, especially those created by neighborhood petitions. But this path would have left intact the other kind of RRCs, the developer-driven restrictions that dotted the i's and crossed the t's of ordinary covenant law. With huge suburban communities like Levittown emerging in the postwar era, formally correct RRCs easily could have expanded into vast new areas of housing.

The *Shelley* case itself was pushed to the Supreme Court by George Vaughn, a somewhat maverick St. Louis lawyer;[87] other NAACP lawyers were cool to the case, perhaps because they thought that the rather doubtful Labadie Avenue neighborhood agreement could tempt the Supreme Court to decide simply on technical grounds, as it had in 1940 in a Chicago case, *Hansberry v. Lee*.[88] In order to increase the odds of making the Court face larger constitutional questions about RRCs, the Detroit NAACP also petitioned for certiorari on *Sipes v. McGee*.

Although all the Supreme Court's discussion was aimed at *Shelley*, *Sipes* too was decided in the same opinion. But the *Sipes* covenants were less irregular than *Shelley*'s, albeit not as good a test case as developer RRCs might have been.[89] *Sipes* too was based on a neighbor agreement, but unlike the *Shelley* agreement, it stated on its face that it would take effect upon the signature of eighty percent of the owners within the

---

[86] Cf. Corrigan v. Buckley, 271 U.S. 323, 331–32 (1926) (noting that a court decision could be a denial of due process if so arbitrary and contrary to law as to amount to "mere spoilation").

[87] Vose, supra note 1, at 157, 159–60; Tushnet, supra note 8, at 90–91.

[88] 311 U.S. 32 (1940).

[89] The McGhee's attorneys did argue the technical horizontal privity point—i.e. that the restricted properties, unlike developer restrictions, had never been in common ownership; see Vose, supra note 1, at 135.

affected area. Moreover, though the agreements were not part of a real estate transfer, they were recorded in 1935, and the McGhees' own 1944 deed referred to "restrictions of record." The question of actual notice was not at issue in the case, suggesting that the McGhees did know that the area was restricted. A few questions arose about technical problems with the signatures on the agreement, but these were decided in accordance with accepted state law precedent.

In *Sipes*, then, it was considerably harder to make the case that only judicial overreaching enforced the RRCs in question, thus turning an ordinary private law matter into judicial "state action" by virtue of a court's extraordinary effort. Why should judicial enforcement of *this* set of ostensibly private and relatively routine restrictions be "state action"? *Shelley* seemed simply to assert that judicial enforcement of covenants is "state action"; but this raises the familiar problem of constitutionalizing every private civil conflict that appears in court. Nevertheless, there are at least two other possible rationales for the "state action" designation as applied to judicial enforcement of RRCs. One of these was argued or at least strongly suggested by the NAACP lawyers, but the second was not.

B.   State Action as Private Takeover

Another possible answer to the state action puzzle came from other contemporary cases involving racial discrimination. *Shelley* was argued over against the recent background of one of the "white primary" cases, in which the Supreme Court had ruled that an ostensibly private political party's primary election could be "state action" because this group's choices were effectively a part of the state's own electoral process.[90] In planning for *Shelley*, the NAACP lawyers strategized to show a similar private take-over of state functions; they planned to draw on a burgeoning sociological literature to argue that RRCs were both widespread and damaging to minorities, and to analogize RRCs' pervasive character to the racial zoning invalidated thirty years earlier in *Buchanan*.[91] These linked arguments suggested that a pattern akin to the all-white primaries: in RRCs too, ostensibly private organizations—the neighborhood improvement associations, the real estate boards, the major developers—had effectively appropriated a governmental function and were using the courts to enforce what was in effect racial zoning.

---

[90] Smith v. Allwright, 321 U.S. 649 (1944); see also Terry v. Adams, 345 U.S. 461 (1953) (striking down segregated voting in "Jaybird Democratic Association" as effective delegation of state voting machinery to discriminating group). Both cases were decided under the Fifteenth Amendment.

[91] See Vose, supra note 1, at 151–52 (describing NAACP strategy for presenting case to Supreme Court).

This was by no means a far-fetched notion with respect to RRCs, as was amply illustrated in *Shelley*'s city of origin, St. Louis. The St. Louis Real Estate Exchange openly coordinated the city's numerous "neighborhood improvement associations" in a widespread pattern of covenanted segregation.[92] Indeed, widespreadness was exactly what made RRCs so pernicious. A handful of small-scale RRCs could have been insulting and annoying, but they could scarcely have had much impact in constricting of housing opportunities for African Americans. But widespread RRCs threatened to do just that, in a manner that was contrary to the ordinary American precepts of property law favoring free alienability of real estate. The 1944 Restatement of Property did indeed state that RRCs were legally acceptable, but the Restatement also conceded (with considerable circumlocution) that this view was contrary to the general policies disfavoring any alienability constraints that applied to large numbers of persons.[93] Widespreadness and inescapability—these were the aspects of RRCs that made them seem so much like a private takeover of governmental functions; it was a takeover in which ostensibly private persons used the courts seriously to disadvantage racial minorities.

C.   State Action as Enforcement of Custom

A final possible answer to *Shelley*'s "state action" puzzle has not been explored much, if at all, in the *Shelley* literature, but it goes most deeply of all into fundamental issues in property law. This answer would implicate judges in the enforcement of custom.

The route here begins with a reminder about the doctrinal background to *Shelley*: the Supreme Court in *Shelley* did not overrule *Corrigan v. Buckley*, its own prior case ostensibly upholding RRCs in Washington DC in 1926. The cases were distinguishable, as the Court in *Shelley* correctly noted, because *Corrigan* originated in the District and thus did not implicate "state action" under the Fourteenth Amendment.[94] But this distinction became quite implausible in light of *Hurd v. Hodge*, the consolidated D.C. case that accompanied *Shelley*; here the Court did overturn RRCs in Washington, but again without disavowing *Corrigan*.[95]

What, then, made *Shelley* and *Hurd* distinguishable from the earlier *Corrigan* case? In both *Shelley* and *Hurd*, the Court took pains to say that *Corrigan*'s restrictions were not illegal so long as they resulted from

---

[92] Vose, supra note 1, at 106–107. George Vaughn's brief for the Shelleys argued that the Exchange was part of a conspiracy to deprive his clients of their civil rights; Kraemer v. Shelley, 355 Mo. 814, 198 S.W.2d 679 (1946)

[93] Restatement of Property, supra note 60, at 2406–2408, 2410–2412.

[94] Shelley v. Kraemer, 334 U.S. 1, 8–9 (1948).

[95] Hurd v. Hodge, 334 U.S. 24, 29–30 (1948).

mere voluntarily compliance, without enforcement by the courts. But a much more plausible distinction was noted earlier in this chapter: *Corrigan* was in fact not about covenants running with the land at all. *Corrigan* involved only a promise between original signatories to the covenants, not an obligation of someone who had acquired the property later and whose duties, if any, derived merely from ownership of the land rather than from a personal agreement. *Corrigan*, in short, was a case about *contract*, whereas *Shelley*, *Sipes*, and *Hurd* were cases about *property*—even though the courts in these and most other RRC cases systematically overlooked the differences between these bodies of law.[96]

Why should it matter that the RRCs were property and not contract? The reasons take us back to the reasons why courts take into account land value and land-relatedness in various limiting doctrines, whether under the rubric of "restraints on alienation," "touch and concern," or the equitable doctrines of "changed circumstances." We know from modern scholarship that these limiting doctrines serve the real estate market in important ways. On the one hand, they do permit valuable private land use arrangements to "stick" with the land, free from future purchasers' threat of evasion or strategic bargaining. But on the other hand, the limiting doctrines also corral these arrangements in order to reduce the chances that future purchasers will be taken by surprise by unexpected covenant obligations; they cut back on buyers' and sellers' negotiation costs by voiding covenants that reflect only the idiosyncratic wishes of earlier owners; and in the same way, they lower the search costs for third parties in real estate markets, since these parties are freed from the obligation to track down odd restrictions that are outside the range of the things that landowners normally might negotiate.[97]

Notice the difference that these land-value considerations make between *contract* law on the one hand, and *property* law on the other— here, property law in the form of covenant rights and obligations that pass to subsequent purchasers of land. When a court simply enforces a contract between the contracting parties, the court need not consider whether other people in the world at large would like to have such an arrangement; the contracting parties have said for themselves what they

---

[96] See, Kraemer v. Shelley, 198 S.W.2d at 683 (describing parties rights under covenants as matter of "contract"); Sipes v. McGhee, 25 N.W.2d at 643 (same); Hurd v. Hodge, 162 F.2d at 234 (same); see also, e.g., Mays v. Burgess, 147 F.2d 869, 871 (D.C.Cir. 1945) (same); Burkhardt v. Lofton, 63 Cal.App.2d 230, 146 P.2d 720, 724 (1944) (same); but see *Mays*, at 875–76 (Edgerton, diss) (noting difference between contract and covenants)

[97] Merrill & Smith, supra note 47, at 3–4, 25–27, 33–34 (describing the limited forms of property law and the special relevance to third party search costs); Rose, supra note 47, at 213–15 (describing reasons for limiting doctrines in covenant law and elsewhere in property law).

want. But when a court holds that a covenant "runs" to subsequent purchasers as a part of the property, the court implicitly makes assumptions about what landowners *in general* would be likely to expect and to value in owning the land in question.[98] These subsequent parties have not explicitly stated what they want; the question rather is whether they are bound by things that *prior* owners wanted. According to the limiting doctrines of covenant law, when a court imposes such an earlier-arranged covenant on subsequent landholders, the court must explicitly or implicitly suppose that some substantial number of persons in their situation would find the covenant restrictions valuable.

Consider this interpretive fact in the context of racially restrictive covenants. Would a court have been correct in assuming that, as a general matter, the subsequent purchasers of property were likely to value such restrictions and to expect that they might find them on any given property? In fact, the probable answer is "yes," this would indeed have been correct with respect to many white purchasers. But to make such an assumption even about white purchasers (while ignoring everyone else), a court would have to acknowledge and give force to a widespread customary norm of racial disparagement. As noted earlier, in Michigan's first major RRC case, the African American home purchaser argued that a court upholding such a covenant would be equating him with a nuisance, simply because of his race.[99] However much white landowners may have disliked their minority neighbors—or however much they merely thought that *other* white owners would dislike minority neighbors—these customary norms of disparagement had never been recognized in the law of nuisance, and they need never have been recognized in the law of covenants either.

In enforcing RRCs, then, courts were not simply enforcing "private contracts," even though that language appeared so often in the cases. Instead, courts were enforcing *covenants*, as lasting *property* obligations, and in doing so, they perforce endorsed well-established and widely-known customary norms of discrimination against racial minorities.[100]

---

[98] This was recognized even in the first major RRC case in a state court: Queensborough Land Co. v. Cazeaux, 136 La. 724, 67 So. 641, 643 (1915) (noting that a condition on alienability was only valid if based on a "substantial reason" and not merely "caprice"); Monchow, supra note 28, at 17; Merrill & Smith, supra note 47, at 17.

[99] Parmalee v. Morris, 218 Mich. 625, 188 N.W. 330, 332 (1922).

[100] Cf. Barrows v. Jackson, 346 U.S. 249 (1953) where the Supreme Court invalidated judicial enforcement of an RRC in an action for damages against a white seller. At first blush *Barrows* looks simply like a contracts case, since the defendant was an original signatory to the neighborhood agreement; but here the "property" aspect of the case was on the plaintiffs's side: one of those seeking enforcement was a successor purchaser of a "benefited" property; 346 U.S. at 252, n. 1. Indeed, Vose points out that securing enforcement rights to successor owners was a matter of great concern to owners' associa-

And it is well known from other Fourteenth Amendment jurisprudence that the enforcement of a custom is "state action." *Shelley* cited this point in passing, and it was not controversial at the time.[101]

But an even deeper question is why custom itself should count as "state action." No official actors enact custom; why should custom count as if they did? Here again modern scholarship is useful. We know from the recent scholarly exploration of social norms that norms and customs may be so widespread and so powerful that they have the practical force of law, or indeed they may even override the formal law.[102] When nudged along by judicial recognition, norms *become* law, in the formal as well as the informal sense.[103]

Given the interactions between covenant law, land value, and customary practice, then, we could easily interpret *Shelley*'s watchword of "judicial enforcement as state action" as something that is intimately connected to the law of property, and to property law's insistence that ownership rights and obligations fall into easily anticipated patterns—patterns that are relatively simple and limited, and that a court can justifiably regard as having some more than idiosyncratic value for landowners. RRCs purported to bind future owners to obligations that had nothing to do with the usual land use practices covered by such covenants—setbacks or yard maintenance or signage control or indeed any other features that buyers might normally expect and value in a planned neighborhood. They concerned not the occupants' land uses, but rather the occupants themselves, and their value rested critically on the culture and customs of prejudice against those occupants. After *Shelley*, American courts could not be used to fortify that culture and those prejudices.

VIII. Aftermath

When one looks to its practical impact, *Shelley* was no doubt one of a number of factors that opened up many urban neighborhoods to minority purchasers and residents over the next decades, though white suburbanization may well have been more fundamental.[104] Much more

---

tions, apparently because they understood that RRCs could not last long unless successors in interest, as well as the original contracting parties, could enforce them. See Vose, supra note 1, at 233, 243.

[101] *Shelley*, at 14 (citing Civil Rights Cases, 109 U.S. 3, 11, 17 (1883)).

[102] Robert C. Ellickson, Order Without Law: How Neighbors Settle Disputes 52–62 (1991).

[103] See, e.g. Ghen v. Rich, 8 F. 159 (D.C. Mass. 1881) (adopting whalers' norms on ownership of animals despite deviance from common law rule).

[104] See Douglas S. Massey & Nancy A. Denton, American Apartheid: Segregation and the Making of the Underclass 45–46 (1993) (describing increase in minority residents in

resistant to change was the pattern of *segregation* as between different racial groups. Here *Shelley* appeared to change very little. The case certainly did not change the opinion of real estate appraisers, who continued to believe that racial mixing was detrimental to housing value, or of real estate brokers, who continued to "steer" customers according to race.[105] Indeed, Richard Brooks points out that RRCs played a role in segregation even after *Shelley*; although they could no longer be enforced in court, they continued to signal neighborhood preferences to brokers and lenders.[106] Residential segregation has even outlived the Fair Housing Act of 1968, which finally outlawed the realtors' "ethic" of racial steering. Despite the law, there is considerable evidence that this and other illegal discriminatory real estate practices persist.[107]

What appears to drive more recent racial segregation is a continuing norm of discrimination, albeit a relatively thin one by comparison to the segregationist norms of the earlier part of the twentieth century. In a famous argument, Thomas Schelling pointed out that even a relatively mild preference for living with one's own racial group can lead to total segregation. If everyone says, "I'd like to live in an integrated neighborhood, as long as the majority is my race," there will be no integrated neighborhoods.[108]

A set of attitudes like this may not be easily challenged by what academics call "norm entrepreneurs," in this case the courageous people who try something new.[109] Violence, the residual enforcer of segregation, may be just around the corner, a terrible deterrent to change. And behind people's willingness to use violence may lie once again another weak norm of segregation, but a weak norm that has powerful effects in

---

urban areas, along with white suburbanization); Hirsch, supra note 46, at 28–30 (same in Chicago, discounting RRCs as major factor).

[105] Davis McEntire, Residence and Race: Final and Comprehensive Report to the Commission on Race and Housing 238–48 (1960); Rose Helper, Racial Policies and Practices of Real Estate Brokers 42–46, 117–23, 195–217 (1969). For continued segregation, see Massey & Denton, supra note 104, at 47.

[106] Richard R. W. Brooks, Covenants and Conventions 12 (draft on file with the author, 2002)

[107] See Sheryll D. Cashin, Middle-Class Black Suburbs and the State of Integration: a Post-Integrationist Vision for Metropolitan America, 86 Cornell L. Rev. 729, 744 (2001), and sources cited therein (noting continuation of discrimination in housing markets).

[108] Thomas C. Schelling, Micromotives and Macrobehavior 140–55 (1978); see also Cashin, supra note 107, at 737, 768 (noting preference for majority status especially among whites but increasingly also among African Americans).

[109] See Cass R. Sunstein On the Expressive Function of Law, 144 U.Pa.L.Rev. 2021, 2030–2031, 2043 (1996) (noting role of "norm entrepreneurs" in changing gender and race norms, but also stressing importance of support of law).

preventing neighborhood change. A majority homeowner may fear minority entrance not only because of her own prejudices but also because
of her assessment of the prejudices of others. If she believes that many
others will refuse to share a neighborhood with minorities, she will resist
the first step toward integration, because she thinks that this first step
sets off the devaluation of her most important economic asset, her home.
That belief about the preferences of others can be a critical factor in her
opposition to change—in the worst case including her willingness to
acquiesce in violence to "save" the neighborhood.[110]

In spite of this dismal and ongoing saga, the half-century beyond
Shelley gives some modest reason for hope. Studies suggest that with
respect to this most difficult of hurdles for integration—that is, residential integration—there has been some slow progress since the 1990s.
This progress is due in part to the movement of racial minorities to the
suburbs, where it once appeared that RRCs would help to bar the
gates.[111] If nothing else, *Shelley* prevented those bars at a critical
moment after the Second World War, and in that sense helped to further
a halting but, one hopes, ongoing progress toward racial justice.

When looked at through the lens of property law, one sees in RRCs
some of the nastiest and most mean-spirited aspects of property—the
ways that even thinly-held prejudices, widespread through communities
or simply *believed* to be widespread, can exclude, insult and grievously
injure those who are considered outsiders. And one sees in the *Shelley*
case itself, cryptic though it was, some of the best instincts in property
law: the idea that you can own property, use it, and can dispose of it
pretty much the way you want, including placing lasting conditions on
it—so long as those conditions do something to make all the land in
question collectively more valuable. What your conditions cannot do is to
is to make it impossible for *other people* to own property too, and to use
it and dispose of it the way they want as well, just because of who they
are.

---

[110] See, e.g. Charles Abrams, Forbidden Neighbors: A Study of Prejudice in Housing
108 (1955) (citing fear of loss of property values as one of contributing factors in Cook
County violence); see also Laurenti, supra note 57, at 5 (noting that fear of loss of property
value as most-cited reason for opposition to integration).

[111] See Cashin, supra note 107, at 738–39 (noting modest decline in urban segregation
though describing it as "unimpressive").

8

Peter Salsich

A Short Course in Land Transactions: Protecting Title to Land
Brown v. Lober, 389 N.E.2d 1188 (Ill. 1979)

Introduction

People buy and sell land for a variety of reasons: to acquire a family home, to develop a shopping center, to raise cattle or grow wheat on a farm, to extract coal or oil from the ground, to build a nest egg for retirement. The list is almost endless, but most situations involve long-term commitments. Because of the permanent nature of land and the potentially infinite duration of the fee simple estate, the history of the title to a particular tract of land and any restrictions on the use, enjoyment or transfer of that title are extremely important to land owners and prospective purchasers.

The American legal system employs three techniques for identifying and protecting the owner of the title: 1) the common law covenants of title that are implied in contracts of sale of land and are expressed in warranty deeds, 2) the public land recording acts and 3) title insurance. These techniques evolved seriatim. Title covenants were recognized in the English Common Law. Recording acts were enacted by the states in the 19th century. Title insurance developed in the 20th century. All are important elements in the process by which people buy and sell land in the United States. The common law covenants of title are included both in the contract for the sale of land and in the deed that the seller gives to the buyer as evidence of the transfer of title. Deeds are recorded in the public land records to provide notice to all the world of the title transfer. Buyers and lenders purchase title insurance as a protection against mistakes that people who carry out title searches in the public records may make.

As with any human institution, the commercial land transaction system is not perfect. Mistakes happen. Buyers don't record their deeds to land when they receive them, or they fail to discover adverse interests because they did not have the records searched carefully before paying for and accepting a deed. Owners sell the same or competing interests to several buyers, through negligence or through fraud. Purchasers decline or forget to purchase title insurance. Title insurance companies fail to discover adverse interests in the public records. Injured parties may seek redress from the courts, and may obtain damages or specific performance in some cases because of the common law notion that each parcel of land is unique.[1]

A case decided by the Supreme Court of Illinois in 1979, *Brown v. Lober*,[2] offers a short course on title covenants and the public land records system. It also illustrates the long-term nature of real estate investment and the responsibilities owners and purchasers have for protecting their interests in land. Finally, it provides a vehicle for examining transactional dispute resolution processes and the responsibilities undertaken by professionals such as attorneys, title examiners, and real estate brokers who provide services to buyers and sellers of land.

A Short History of Title Protection

Professor Ronald Volkmer, in his discussion of transfers of land by deed,[3] notes that the medieval predecessor to the modern covenants of title was the clause of warranty. In this clause, "the grantor doth, for himself and his heirs, warrant and secure to the grantee the estate so granted."[4] The modern covenants of title found in the warranty deed are

---

[1] For example, specific performance often is available for breach of a contract to transfer land because of the notion that land is unique. 5A Corbin on Contracts § 1143 (1964).

[2] 75 Ill.2d 547, 27 Ill.Dec. 780, 389 N.E.2d 1188 (1979).

[3] Ronald R. Volkmer, *Transfers by Deed*, in 9 Thompson on Real Property, Thomas Edition, §§ 82.07(b) & 82.10(a) (Thomas ed.1994), citing 2 Edward Coke, Institutes of the Law of England; or a Commentary Upon Littleton, chapter 13 (1st Am. Ed., from the 19th London ed., Charles Butler ed. 1853); 2 William Blackstone, Commentaries on the Law of England *300–03 (1765); IV James Kent, Commentaries on American Law Part VI— Lecture LXVI at 458 (1830). *See also* William B. Stoebuck & Dale A. Whitman, The Law of Property, 3d, §§ 11.1 & 11.13 (2000).

[4] Volkmer, *supra* n. 3, at 316, quoting Blackstone, *supra* n. 3, at *242.

express promises by the grantor. Traditionally, the covenants number six: (1) seisin; (2) right to convey; (3) against encumbrances; (4) quiet enjoyment; (5) further assurances; and (6) warranty.[5] A number of states have enacted statutes that specify particular covenants being implied in deeds by use of specific terms such as "grant." For example, the Illinois statute provides that the word "grant," "bargain," or "sell" in a conveyance of a fee simple "acts as an express covenant" to the grantee, the grantee's heirs and other legal representatives that the grantor was the owner of an indefeasible estate in fee simple; that the estate was free from encumbrances made by the grantor, except those rents and services reserved in the document; and that the grantee will enjoy "quiet enjoyment" from the grantor, and the grantor's heirs and assigns unless expressly limited in the document. This statutory provision permits these covenants to be enforced as if they were expressly in the document.[6]

The practice of recording documents of title in public land records can be traced to the Statute of Uses (1536) and its promotion of written documents rather than feoffments as the evidence of land transfer. Recording became the substitute for the public ceremony of enfeoffment.[7] As Professor John McCormack notes, by the mid–1600s, the Massachusetts Bay Colony had in place a recording system that contained all five elements of the modern American system: 1) recording affects the legal priority of named transferees, 2) but not the operative effect of the conveyance; 3) entire texts are recorded, not just summaries or memoranda; 4) the recording governmental agency does not evaluate or warrant the legality of documents that are recorded, and 5) documents must be signed and notarized by public officials before they can be recorded.[8] This system spread across the United States in the Nineteenth Century, receiving impetus from law reform efforts in England, particularly the second of four reports by the Real Property Commissioners recommending a public land registration system.[9] The policy of the

---

[5] Volkmer, *supra* n. 3, at 353.

[6] Ill. Comp. Stat. 765 § 518 (2000).

[7] Francis S. Philbrick, *Limits of Record Search and Therefore of Notice*, 93 U. PA. L. REV. 125, 137–38 (1944).

[8] John L. McCormack, *Recording, Registration, and Search of Title*, in 11 Thompson on Real Property § 92.02 (1994), citing George L. Haskins, *The Beginnings of the Recording System in Massachusetts*, 21 B.U. L. Rev. 1 (1948). *See also* A.W.B. Simpson, A History of the Land Law, 2d 280 (1986) ("The idea of recording in official, national, or local registers all transactions transferring or creating property interests has a long history.").

[9] Simpson, *supra* n. 8, at 280. The term, "registration," used in this context meant recording. An alternative system of land registration in which transfer of title actually is accomplished by a governmental entity accepting and publicly registering a deed or other

recording acts is to protect those who protect themselves: 1) land owners who record their property interests, and 2) purchasers for value who check the public records before accepting title. Three types of statutes are in effect, *race, notice,* and *race-notice* statutes. Under a *race* statute, the first person to record will prevail in any dispute about title. Only two states, North Carolina and Louisiana, have general race statutes.[10] Under a *notice* statute, a person who has paid value and who has no notice of a prior interest will prevail over that prior interest. About half the states have such acts.[11] Under *race-notice* statutes in effect in the remaining states, persons who qualify under a notice statute (value paid and no notice of prior unrecorded interest) also must record before the prior unrecorded interest is recorded in order to prevail in any dispute with the owner of the prior interest.[12]

Title insurance has become the predominant method of protecting title today.[13] Title insurance companies provide a service and a promise. The service is examination of the public land records to ascertain and describe the state of title to a particular tract of land. The promise is to be responsible for any errors made by the title examiner. The examina-

---

title document was developed by Sir Robert Richard Torrens in South Australia in 1857. *Id.* at 281–82. The Torrens system is in effect in nine states, Colorado, Georgia, Hawaii, Massachusetts, Minnesota, North Carolina, Ohio, Virginia, and Washington, as well as Guam and Puerto Rico. Stoebuck & Whitman, *supra* n. 3, at 923. Ironically, the Real Property Commissioners' recommendation for a recording system was not accepted. Years of debate took place before a system of title registration similar to the Torrens System was accepted in England in the Land Transfer Act of 1897. A.W.B. Simpson attributes some of the opposition to the reform recommendations to "solicitors and their Law Societies." He opines that "[l]aw reform promoted by professional lawyers is unlikely to express a radical stance; indeed the concept of a radical lawyer is scarcely intelligible." Simpson, supra n. 8, at 283. The plot in George Eliot's famous novel, Middlemarch, revolved around the Real Property Commissioner's work.

[10] N.C. Gen. Stat. § 47–18; La. Reve. Stat. Ann. § 272. *See also* Stoebuck & Whitman, *supra* n. 3, at 873 (identifying North Carolina as a race jurisdiction); Department of Transp. v. Humphries, 496 S.E.2d 563 (N.C.1998).

[11] McCormack, *supra* n. 8, at § 92.13(b), noting that many of the notice statutes were enacted in response to judicial decisions refusing to accept the claims of persons who recorded first under race statutes if they had notice of prior unrecorded claims.

[12] *Id.* at § 92.13(c), citing statutes in twenty-five states including California, Colorado, Georgia, Illinois, Michigan, New Jersey, New York and Pennsylvania. Stoebuck & Whitman, *supra* n. 3, at 873, n. 13, comment that classification of statutes can be difficult. The Colorado statute was the subject of considerable confusion until it was amended in 1984 to state "this is a race-notice recording statute." *Id.*

[13] *See generally* D. Barlow Burke, Jr., Law of Title Insurance (1986), with annual supplements; John L. McCormack, *Title Insurance*, 11 Thompson on Real Property, ch. 93 (1994); Joyce D. Palomar, *Bank Control of Title Insurance Companies: Perils to the Public that Bank Regulators Have Ignored,* 44 SW. L.J. 905 (1990); Quintin Johnstone, *Title Insurance,* 66 Yale L.J. 492 (1957).

tion can take place in two ways: 1) physically reviewing the public land records in the county courthouse, or 2) reviewing a summary of the records, called an abstract, which has been prepared by a commercial enterprise. Today, most title companies maintain their own title records, called "title plants," that are organized by tract indexes, which list all property interests attached to a particular tract of land. Title insurance is not the same as conventional automobile or fire insurance. It does not protect one from title defects. Rather, it protects one from the failure of the title examiner to find a title defect.

The public land recording system and title insurance process are not perfect. Mistakes happen. There are holes in both systems. For that reason the common law covenants of title are useful "band-aids for patching over imperfections in the record system."[14]

Brown v. Lober: the Parties and the Issues

A case that illustrates the role and limits of title covenants in the modern land transactions system is *Brown v. Lober*[15], decided by the Illinois Supreme Court in 1979. *Brown* involved a lawsuit by the owners, James and Dolly Brown, of an eighty-acre tract of land in southern Illinois against the executor, Maureen Lober, of the estate of one of the persons who sold the land to the Browns twenty years earlier. When the Browns acquired the property in 1957 they received from the sellers, William and Faith Bost, who held title as joint tenants, a statutory warranty deed that contained no exceptions. The Illinois statute in effect at that time[16] provided that every deed following the format of the statute and executed in accordance with the statutory requirements conveyed fee simple title, along with three specific covenants. Under the statute, a grantor conveying fee simple title promised:

> 1) that at the time of the making and delivery of [the] deed he was lawfully seized of an indefeasible estate in fee simple, in and to the premises therein described, and had good right and full power to convey the same;
>
> 2) that the same was then free from all incumbrances; and
>
> 3) that he warrants to the grantee, his heirs and assigns, the quiet and peaceful possession of such premises, and will defend the title thereto against all persons who may lawfully claim the same.

---

[14] Gerald Korngold & Paul Goldstein, Real Estate Transactions 60 (Teacher's Guide, 4th ed. 2002).

[15] 75 Ill.2d 547, 27 Ill.Dec. 780, 389 N.E.2d 1188 (1979).

[16] Ill. Rev. Stat. 30 § 8. The statutory warranties remain in effect. 765 Ill. Comp. Stat. 5/9 (2000).

The covenants in subsection 1 of the statute are the equivalent of the common law covenants of seisin and of good right to convey. Subsection 2 expresses the common law covenant against encumbrances, while subsection 3 states the common law covenant of quiet enjoyment.

While the deed stated that the grantors were conveying the described land in fee simple, a prior grantor in the chain of title had reserved a two-thirds interest in the mineral rights in 1947.[17] The Browns were not aware of this prior reservation when they obtained title to the property on December 21, 1957. The statement from the case indicates that the purchasers (the Browns) had their abstract of title examined in 1958 and then again in 1968 for the purposes of a loan. There is no indication whether they examined the title prior to actually accepting the deed in 1957.

The defendant of record, Maureen Lober, was the successor executor for the estate of Faith Bost, one of the sellers who had died on December 21, 1974. In an interview in May 2002, Ms. Lober indicated that she did not know why this problem occurred but she speculated that an attorney had failed to uncover the reservation of mineral rights when the title was examined. Ms. Lober explained that at the time of these transactions (the 1950s through the 1970s) the standard way of checking real estate titles in southern Illinois, and many other parts of the country, particularly rural areas, was for an individual, often an attorney retained by the buyer, to review the land records and prepare an outline and subsequent summary (abstract) of the items affecting the title that are located in the public land records. The buyer's attorney would then issue an opinion letter concerning the quality of the title, as evidenced by the findings in the outline and abstract of title.

The record in *Brown* did not indicate whether the normal title search process had been filed prior to the Brown's purchase of the property. Whatever record search took place, the Browns accepted a deed containing no evidence that title to the mineral rights was not being transferred along with the title to the land. The problem came to light in 1976 when the Browns learned that a coal option that they had granted in 1974 to a coal company was, in fact, only an option for one-third of the coal. When the coal company exercised the option in 1976 the coal company tendered only $2000, instead of the contract price of $6000 that the Browns expected to receive. The Browns accepted the $2000, then filed a lawsuit against the estate of William and Faith Bost seeking as damages the $4000 balance under the coal option contract. Ms. Lober, as the executor of the estate of Faith Bost, was the named defendant.

In her interview, Ms. Lober stated that the lawyer, now deceased, who filed the original lawsuit was someone that she had known since

---

[17] Brown v. Lober, 63 Ill.App.3d 727, 20 Ill.Dec. 286, 379 N.E.2d 1354, 1356 (1978).

they were children. She stated that he brought the suit without talking to her beforehand. Her tone suggested that she was surprised by his failure to contact her first. Ms. Lober's law firm is in Litchfield, Illinois, which is the county seat of Montgomery County, a rural county with a population of slightly more than 30,000 in 2000.[18]

The farm at the center of this dispute is located in a area of small farms in rural Illinois about forty five miles northeast of St. Louis, Missouri. The property is on Shoal Creek road, just east of the community of Walshville in Grisham Township, Montgomery County, Illinois. Ms. Lober told me that Mr. Bost had been a dairy farmer who later dabbled in real estate. She stated that she believes he drew up the deed when the property was sold in 1957 to James and Dolly Brown.[19] That deed describes the property as being in the Township of Walshville but the Montgomery County plat books for 1966 and 1997 locate the property in Grisham Township.[20] Faith Bost, for whose estate Ms Lober was serving as trustee, had been Ms. Lober's junior high school math teacher.

Defendant, Lober, Prevails at Trial

Ms. Lober argued successfully to the trial court that the Illinois 10 year statute of limitations for written contracts[21] barred the action. The plaintiffs' complaint did not state specifically which covenants they believed were breached, but the trial court found that only the present covenants of seizin and right to convey had been broken.[22] As present covenants, they were breached, if at all, upon the effective date of the conveyance, December 21, 1957. The limitation period thus expired on December 21, 1967, well before suit was filed on May 25, 1976.

An interesting aspect of the case is the interplay of the statute of limitations, the adverse possession concept, and the legal theory on which the case was brought. Illinois has several statutes of limitations that affect real estate, with three different limitation periods. While the limitation period for breach of written contract actions is ten years, actions for the recovery of lands have a twenty year period of limitations.[23] But actions for the recovery of lands because of a breach of a

---

[18] U. S. Bureau of the Census, Table DP–1, *Profile of General Demographic Characteristic:2000 (Montgomery County, ILL., CENSUS 2000).*

[19] Interview with Maureen Lober at her office in Litchfield, Ill. (May 14, 2002).

[20] Rockford Map Publishers, *Tri-Annual Atlas & Plat Book: Montgomery County, Ill.* (Rockford, Ill., 1966 & 1997).

[21] Ill. Rev. Stat. 83 § 17 (1975) (now at 735 Ill. Comp. Stat. 5/13–206 (2000)).

[22] Brown, 379 N.E.2d at 1356.

[23] Ill. Rev. Stat. 83, § 1 (1975) (now at 735 Ill Comp. Stat. 5/13–101 (2000)).

condition subsequent or termination of an estate upon limitation must be brought within seven years of accrual.[24] Presumably, the Illinois legislature has made a policy decision that persons who have been ousted from possession and enjoyment of land should have twice as long to discover the ouster and bring an action for recovery of the land than persons who have suffered some loss as a result of breach of a written contract respecting that land. The applicability of the ten year statute of limitations becomes doubly important in a case like Brown. The Statute of Frauds requires all contracts for the sale of lands to be in writing and signed by the party to be charged.[25] The common law doctrine of merger applies to commercial real estate transactions. Promises in a contract for the sale of land respecting the quality of the title to be transferred upon payment of the sale price are merged into a warranty deed when it is delivered, absent evidence that the parties intend contract promises to survive the real estate closing.[26] As a result, the covenants in a warranty deed become the controlling covenants.

Reversal on Appeal

On appeal, the plaintiffs focused on the covenant against encumbrances and the covenant of quiet enjoyment. While the covenant against encumbrances is a "present" covenant, the covenant of quiet enjoyment is called a "future" covenant because, although it becomes legally binding when it is created, it does not "accrue" (create a cause of action) until some "eviction occurs or disturbance of the possession is caused by one having a paramount title." Actual eviction is no longer necessary to prove a breach, only "something equivalent" to an actual eviction is required. The statute of limitations clock is not activated until a cause of action for breach of one of the covenants "accrues." [27]

---

[24] Ill. Rev. Stat. 83, § 1a & 1b (now 735 Ill. Comp. Stat. 5/13–102 & –103 (2000)).

[25] *See, e.g.,* 740 Ill. Comp. Stat. 80/2 (2000), (formerly Ill. Rev. Stat. 59 § 2 (1975)).

[26] The doctrine of merger is a Common Law concept that presumes that the last writing in a transaction is intended to include all the promises and undertakings made by the parties. Commercial real estate transactions traditionally involve two stages: 1) negotiation of a contract for the sale of land, and 2) transfer of title through a deed in return for payment of the sale consideration. Deeds are recorded in the public land records, but contracts of sale typically are not. The doctrine of merger operates to set limits on the expectations of successors and potential successors to the parties in the transaction. *See generally* 6A Powell on Real Property 81–297 (1996). *See also* Paul Teich, *A Second Call for Abolition of the Rule of Merger by Deed,* 71 U. Det. Mercy L. Rev. 543 (1994).

[27] Brown, 379 N.E.2d at 1357.

Well-Settled Legal Rules

The legal rules involved in this case are well settled. The covenants of seisin and right to convey land are broken, if at all, at the time title is conveyed. The statute of limitations clock would start at the time. On the other hand, the covenant of quiet enjoyment operates prospectively. It is broken, if at all, by an actual or constructive eviction some time after conveyance of title. The earliest that could have occurred in *Brown* was 1976, when, in the words of the appellate court "the [Browns] were compelled to yield up two-thirds of the consideration which was the *quid pro quo* for the subject of the warranty—the underlying coal interest."[28]

The court of appeals was persuaded that the covenant of quiet enjoyment was the controlling covenant.[29] The covenant "constitutes an obligation that the covenantor shall be barred, as well as his heirs, as well as personal representatives, from ever claiming the estate and that they shall undertake to defend it against a claim of paramount title."[30] The covenant applied to the fee interest in the entire eighty acres, not just the mineral interest, the court noted. The covenant was breached because the entire mineral estate was not conveyed, but the statute of limitations did not begin to run until the breach was discovered, which was shortly before the suit was filed.

The appellate court also discussed the covenant against encumbrances which, the court stated, "extends to cases where, by reason of the burden, claim or right, the owner does not acquire complete dominion over the land conveyed by his conveyance or deed."[31] The covenant against encumbrances is a present covenant and so a breach would cause the statute of limitations clock to start at the time of conveyance. But if breach of that covenant results in a breach of the covenant against quiet enjoyment, an action could be maintained under the covenant of quiet enjoyment even though the statute of limitations had run on the covenant against encumbrances, the court asserted.[32]

A Dissenting View

A strong dissent provided encouragement to Ms. Lober in deciding whether to appeal to the Illinois Supreme Court. Reviewing Illinois case law, much of it from the Nineteenth Century, the dissenting judge stressed the difference between covenants that operate *in prasenti* (cove-

---

[28] *Id.* at 1360.

[29] The court also discussed the covenant of warranty, noting that the two "are treated as synonymous in Illinois." *Id.*

[30] *Id.*

[31] *Id.* at 1362.

[32] *Id.*

nant of seisin and right to convey) and covenants that operate prospectively (covenant of quiet enjoyment). The dissent emphasized that Illinois case law requires "an actual or threatened disturbance, plus an
assertion of a paramount title" in order to establish a constructive
eviction necessary for breach of the covenant of quiet enjoyment.[33]

In arguing for an affirmance of the trial court, the dissenting judge
stressed that "[n]either of these events transpired here."[34] No effort had
been made to oust plaintiffs from the mineral interest, nor did the coal
company assert paramount title to the coal. All they did was refuse to
pay for what they concluded plaintiffs did not own.[35] The dissent emphasized that under Illinois law, the mineral estate may be severed from the
surface estate and, when that occurs, "possession of the surface does not
carry possession of the minerals." Possession of the mineral estate is
accomplished by undertaking to remove the minerals from the ground or
performing "such other act as will apprise the community that such
interest is in the exclusive use and enjoyment of the claiming party."[36]
Stressing that neither party was in possession of the severed mineral
interest and that the plaintiffs had not been deprived of anything, the
dissent posed a hypothetical question to the majority: "Suppose no
person or persons ever attempt to mine or remove coal from the land in
question?" Answering its question, and observing in an aside that such
"is a decided possibility," the dissent observed that "[i]n that event . . .
the plaintiffs will never have been evicted from the two-thirds interest in
the coal and they will still have defendant's $4000 received in the
judgment granted."[37]

The dissent's aside that his hypothetical was realistic most likely
was based on developments in the Illinois coal industry. Despite its
location in the mid-western farm belt and its reputation as part of the
"bread basket" of the world, Illinois for years has been an important
coal producing state. Extremely rich seams of coal throughout southern
Illinois first attracted coal-mining companies in the period immediately
after the Civil War[38] because of the coal's "high BTU (British Thermal

---

[33] Brown, 379 N.E.2d at 1363.

[34] *Id.*

[35] *Id..*

[36] *Id.* The dissent quoted at length from Scott v. Kirkendall, 88 Ill. 465, 466–469 (1878)
and Barry v. Guild, 126 Ill. 439, 446, 18 N.E. 759, 761 (1888), emphasizing from *Barry* that
*"there must be a union of acts of disturbance and lawful title to constitute a breach of this
covenant for quiet enjoyment." Id.* (Emphasis in original.)

[37] *Brown, supra* n. 15, at 1365.

[38] For example, the Litchfield Mining Company was organized in 1887 by local citizens
and the first load of coal was taken from the mine, located immediately southeast of the

Unit) rating (producing more heat per pound).''[39] For close to a century, coal production flourished in southern Illinois. During the 1950s, the period when the transactions that led to the *Brown* litigation took place, Illinois was a major producer of coal. I grew up, and still live, in the inner-ring suburbs immediately southwest of St. Louis, Missouri. As a child and young adult, I recall mile-long trains containing 100 or more cars filled with Illinois coal chugging west through our neighborhood. I used to wonder where the coal was going.

However, Illinois coal also has a high sulfur content that produces more damaging emissions when the coal is burned. Passage of the Clean Air Act of 1970[40] signaled the beginning of what became a long decline of the Illinois coal industry. While Illinois mines had become safer and more efficient because of advances in mining technology, the high sulfur content caused increasing problems for Illinois coal users as emissions standards became stricter. Coal from western states became more desirable, despite its lower BTU rating, because its low sulfur content enabled users to meet Clean Air Act standards in more economical ways. Because of the high cost of meeting environmental standards, many Illinois mines were not able to compete with western mines. Between 1978 and 1996, an estimated 50 of the 71 mines operating in Illinois closed. Jobs in the industry declined from 18,000 to 5000 during that period.[41] I now regularly see 100–car coal trains heading east through my neighborhood.

The Supreme Court Reverses

When asked why she decided to appeal the appellate court's decision, Maureen Lober gave two reasons, the strong dissent and her belief that she was right. "I guess I was stubborn," she said.[42] Ms. Lober enlisted the help of another lawyer, Gerald Huber of Raymond, Illinois, and filed a petition for leave to appeal, which the Illinois Supreme Court accepted. The case was submitted on briefs and the trial court transcript. No oral argument was held.[43] In a concise, three-and-one-half page, unanimous opinion, the Illinois Supreme Court reversed the appellate

---

Litchfield city limits, in March of 1869. *See* http://www.litchfield.il.us/ (last modified July 18, 2002).

[39] Mike Vessell and C. Dennis Hoffman, *Coal Mining in Illinois: Seeing Light at the End of the Tunnel*, 2(3) Ill. Labor Market Rev. (1996), http://lmi.ides.state.il.us/lmr/article8.htm, (last updated May 1, 2002).

[40] 42 U.S.C. § 7401 *et seq.* (2000).

[41] Vessell & Hoffman, *supra*, n. 39.

[42] Interview with Maureen Lober, *supra*, note 19.

[43] *Id.*

court and affirmed the trial court.[44] Emphasizing the same Nineteenth
Century precedents as were used by the dissenting appellate court judge,
the Court "decline[d] to expand the historical scope of [the] covenant [of
quiet enjoyment] to provide a remedy where another of the covenants of
title is so clearly applicable."[45] The Court expressed little support for the
plaintiff's plight. Acknowledging that the covenant of seisin was broken
when the Browns received the deed from the Bosts and that the
reservation of the interest in the mineral rights was a matter of public
record, the Court noted that the plaintiffs had failed to bring an action
within the ten-year statutory period.

> The likely explanation is that plaintiffs had not secured a title
> opinion at the time they purchased the property, and the subsequent
> examiners for the lenders were not concerned with the mineral
> rights. Plaintiffs' oversight, however, does not justify us in overrul-
> ing earlier decisions in order to recognize an otherwise premature
> cause of action.[46]

The Court concluded that the "mere fact" that the Brown's contract
with the coal company had to be modified because of the discovery that
the Browns did not have paramount title to the entire mineral estate did
not constitute the requisite constructive eviction for breach of the
covenant of quiet enjoyment.[47]

A Short Course on Land Transactions

i) The Two–Step Transfer Process

The two opinions in *Brown v. Lober* can serve as a short course on
commercial real estate transactions. Both contractual and conveyance
elements of such transactions are featured, as well as the two-step
transfer process. In *Brown*, as in the typical commercial real estate
transaction, the parties negotiated a contract to buy and sell a particular
parcel of property. The contract was in writing, as required by the
Statute of Frauds.[48] In most cases, the purchaser plans to borrow money
to pay the agreed-upon price and needs time to negotiate a loan. The
loan will be secured by a lien on the property being purchased. If the
buyer-borrower defaults on the loan, the bank or other lender can order
the property to be sold at auction and the proceeds used to pay off the

---

[44] Brown v. Lober, 75 Ill.2d 547, 27 Ill.Dec. 780, 389 N.E.2d 1188 (1979).

[45] *Id.* at 1193.

[46] *Id.*

[47] *Id.*

[48] 740 Ill. Comp. Stat. Ann. 80/2 (West 2002).

loan. Even if the buyer and lender have agreed upon the basic terms of the loan before a purchase contract is negotiated by the buyer and seller, as is happening with greater frequency in the purchase of single-family homes and condominium units, the buyer and lender both need time to arrange for any necessary inspections of the property, such as for termites, radon gas, or mold, to name a few of the current popular ones. In addition, buyer and lender also have an interest in examining the public land records to determine the state of the title that will be transferred, but for different reasons. The buyer wants to be certain that the title being transferred conforms to the title that the purchaser promised to transfer in the contract the parties signed. The lender, on the other hand, is interested in ascertaining that whatever title is being transferred is sufficiently valuable to be effective security for the investment the lender is making through the loan it has promised to make to the buyer. Both property inspection and title review take time, so even if a loan commitment is made before the contract, the actual exchange of money for possession and title does not take place until several weeks or months after the contract is signed.

ii) Public Record Review: The Differing Interests of Buyer and Lender

While property inspections were not at issue in *Brown*, title was. The nature of the dispute is a graphic illustration of the differing interests buyer and lender may bring to the tasks of record review and title examination. Both courts noted that the Browns had the title examined twice, in 1958 and 1968 for loan purposes. Thus the interests of the lender were paramount in both inspections. Apparently, no mention was made of the previous mineral rights reservation, even though it was recorded. This is not surprising because the value of the land and the quality of the title being transferred, even without the two-thirds mineral interest, presumably was high enough to support the loans being sought. Thus the lender probably did not care whether or not the mineral rights were part of the loan security. It's likely that the lender ordered the record search and title examination, at the borrower's expense. Once the lender decided to approve the loan sought by the borrower, there would be no reason for the lender to report the lack of full mineral rights to the borrower, unless the lender had been requested to do so. The lender was willing to provide what the buyer had sought, and what had triggered the title search, a loan. The borrower probably would not even think to ask for the title report because, again, the lender's decision to approve the loan satisfied the buyer's needs.

iii) The Long–Term Nature of Real Estate Investment

Brown also illustrates the long-term nature of real estate investment. The prior reservation of mineral rights occurred in 1947. The

Browns purchased the property from the Bosts in 1957, and granted a coal option to Consolidated Coal Company in 1974. The reservation came to light in 1976, twenty-nine years after it was recorded. As dramatized by the issuance of an opinion by the highest court of the state of Illinois thirty-two years after the prior owner reserved the mineral right interest, decisions with respect to land titles can have long-term consequences.

iv) Responsibilities of Owners and Purchasers of Land

The case also is useful for examining the responsibilities owners and purchasers have for protecting their interests in land. As noted earlier, the public land records were established in the Nineteenth Century to provide a means for land-owners to notify the public of their interests. While the recording acts did not change the common law principle of first-in-time, first-in-right,[49] they provided a mechanism for resolving disputes between two innocent parties who had become ensnared in a triangular dispute caused by a "wrongdoer." The classic scenario has O conveying land to A on Monday and the same land to B on Tuesday.[50] Prior to enactment of the recording statutes, if A had not taken immediate possession of the land, B might well be able to claim that she had no idea that O was not the rightful owner of the property and prevail in a dispute with A, particularly if she took possession of the property before A did. With the recording acts in place, A can protect his interest by recording evidence of his title immediately upon receipt. Likewise, B can protect her interest by inspecting the public records prior to paying O and accepting a deed from him. Thus, the recording acts created a "standard operating procedure"[51] for both owner-seller and buyer-owner: inspect the land records before closing a purchase of land and record your interests as soon as you complete the transaction.

In *Brown*, the source of the problem was the apparent failure of the purchasers to inspect the land records effectively before accepting the deed from the Bosts on December 21, 1957. They failed to follow the standard operating procedure. As a result, they were not aware of their claim against the Bosts for breach of the deed covenant of seisin, the ten-

---

[49] *See, e.g.,* Durand State Bank v. Earlywine, 286 Ill.App.3d 210, 221 Ill.Dec. 604, 675 N.E.2d 1028 (1997); *see also* Lawrence Berger, *An Analysis of the Doctrine that "First in Time is First in Right,"* 64 Neb. L. Rev. 349 (1985).

[50] The original grantee from the United States of all the land on which the city of Cincinnati, Ohio was erected allegedly attempted to finance an expedition through the center of the earth to China by selling deeds to the same piece of vacant property to hundreds of unsuspecting "investors." *Cf.* Ewing v. Burnet, 36 U.S. (11 Pet.) 41, 48–51 (1837) (adverse possession doctrine used to resolve dispute between two grantees of same tract).

[51] *See* Korngold & Goldstein, Real Estate Transactions 269 (4th ed. 2002).

year statute of limitations began to run, and by the time Consolidated Coal Company discovered the problem almost twenty years later, it was too late to bring an action under that deed covenant. Their only hope, then, was to persuade the courts that the grantor's conveyance of an imperfect title, by itself, constituted the requisite constructive eviction when the grantee discovered the imperfection. Neither the trial court nor the Illinois Supreme Court was willing to overturn century-old precedent to reach that result.[52]

v) The Interplay of Title Covenants, Public Land Records, and Title Insurance

Brown can illustrate how the three elements of the American title protection system—title covenants, public land records, and title insurance—are used (and should be used) in a commercial real estate transaction. The most important promises a seller makes to a buyer—that the seller has the title claimed and the right to transfer that title, and that no one claiming from the seller will disturb the buyer's enjoyment of the property in the future—were contained in the deed the Bosts gave the Browns. The public land records were examined at least twice in conjunction with loan transactions by the Browns. The outstanding coal interest reservation was recorded and should have been discovered but was not. When the reservation later was discovered by Consolidated Coal Company, the statute of limitations had run on the present covenants of seisin and good right to convey, and a cause of action had not yet accrued from breach of the future covenant against encumbrances. Thus, the Browns had no remedy against the Bosts for the $4000 loss they incurred because of their inability to convey the full coal rights to the coal company. They might have had a cause of action against the person who conducted the title searches and failed to note the mineral reservation, if they had hired that person. But because the title searches were in connection with loan applications, the bank considering the loans likely ordered the searches. The Browns already had taken title when those searches were made, so it would be difficult for them to argue that they were relying on the bank to protect their interests in the quality of the title.

Title insurance was created to respond to weaknesses in the public land records systems, including failures to index records properly and failures to discover recorded interests, as occurred in *Brown*. Judicial decisions that real estate professionals were liable only when purchasers could prove that they were negligent in their record reviews helped spur the growth of title insurance. While the Real Estate Title Insurance Company became the first title insurance company in the United States

---

[52] Brown v. Lober, 389 N.E.2d at 1193.

in 1876, the real growth in the industry did not take place until the rise of the secondary mortgage markets and expanded the development of the western part of the country, both of which occurred after World War II.[53] Title insurance was a relative newcomer to southern Illinois in the late 1940s and 1950s when the disputed transactions in *Brown* took place. Ms. Lober noted that the custom at the time was for a lawyer to examine an abstract, or summary, of the entries in the public land records in the grantor's chain of title.[54] Today, employees of a title insurance company perform this task, using a "title plant" (duplicate set of records) maintained in their offices that is organized around a tract index. Errors are minimized with a tract index because all transactions affecting a particular tract are indexed together, rather than under the names of individual grantors and grantees.

Had title insurance been available and had the Browns purchased a policy, they likely would have had a claim. Purchasers of title insurance buy a service,—accurate record review and analysis,—as well as insurance against loss if any of the following occurs: 1) the title turns out to be different from what the title company reports it to be, 2) the title contains a defect, lien, or encumbrance not included in the title company's report, 3) the title is unmarketable, or 4) there is no right of access to the land.[55] In *Brown,* title was different from what the Browns thought it to be and an unreported encumbrance, the mineral interest, was present. However, more likely the title company would have reported the reservation as part of the title, and the Browns would not have had a claim against the insurance policy. Title insurance protects against errors in the title search process. It does not guarantee a perfect title.

A Lesson in Dispute Resolution and Professional Responsibility

Finally, *Brown v. Lober* offers important lessons about dispute resolution and the responsibilities of attorneys and other professionals participating in commercial real estate transactions.

---

[53] Michael Braunstein, *Structural Change and Inter-professional Competitive Advantage: An Example Drawn from Residential Real Estate Conveyancing*, 62 Mo. L. Rev. 241, 248–49 (1997).

[54] Interview with Maureen Lober, *supra* n. 19. The chain of title is based on a chronological review of the transfers of ownership of the tract in question, through use of grantor-grantee indexes maintained by county recorders of deeds. *Cf.* Fairfax Leary, Jr. & David G. Blake, *Twentieth Century Real Estate Business and Eighteenth Century Recording*, 22 Am. U. L. Rev. 275, 283–286 (1973).

[55] *See e.g.*, American Land Title Association ("ALTA") Owner's Policy 1992 in James L. Gosdin, Title Insurance: A Comprehensive Overview, 552 (2nd ed. 2000). Gosdin notes and describes common exclusions from coverage as well as coverages of additional risks that may be purchased.

i) Dispute Resolution

The parties in *Brown* litigated to the highest level of the state court system in Illinois. The Supreme Court's opinion was handed down almost three years to the day the Browns filed their lawsuit. Was litigation necessary to resolve this dispute? The parties and their attorneys lived in a small rural community. They were not strangers. Several had gone to school together. Ms. Lober expressed surprise that the Brown's attorney filed suit without first talking to her, even though they had grown up in the same neighborhood.[56]

Might a less adversarial approach have saved considerable time and money, not to mention the emotional wear and tear the suit must have engendered? Maureen Lober, the defendant, was the successor executor of the estate of Faith Bost. William and Faith Bost, the couple who sold the farm to the Browns *sans* two-thirds of the mineral rights, had promised the Browns that they had fee simple title. But, apparently unknown to them at the time, their title, while fee simple in duration, lacked the full mineral rights. Because of an incomplete or mistaken title search, nobody discovered the discrepancy until years later when it was too late to pursue redress under the broken promises of seisin and right to convey the same.

The litigation that ensued was between innocent parties. The wrongdoers, or at least the persons responsible for the wrongdoing, were deceased. The Browns, who brought the suit, had not been ousted from the farm nor had they lost any of their money. Their loss, which triggered the litigation, was of an expectation, an expectation to make a profit from the sale of coal that they were not using. Under the circumstances, might the phone call that never came to Ms. Lober have produced a different result? Might the parties, with a little help from perceptive advisors, have been able to work out some accommodation that recognized the Browns' expectation loss while acknowledging their failure to secure a complete and accurate search of the land records? We cannot answer these questions, but the case cries out for more sensitive dispute resolution techniques than simply filing a lawsuit.

ii) Professional Responsibility

While the Bosts may have triggered the problem by preparing the deed without professional advice,[57] whoever examined the Browns' abstract of title in 1958 and 1968[58] either missed the mineral rights reservation in their searches or failed to notify the Browns that the

---

[56] Interview with Maureen Lober, *supra* n. 19.

[57] *Id.*

[58] Brown v. Lober, 75 Ill.2d 547, 27 Ill.Dec. 780, 389 N.E.2d 1188, 1190 (1979).

reservation had been made. Such examinations were a staple of property law practice at the time, particularly in rural communities. Assuming the examiner, attorney or otherwise, had been hired by the lender, did the Browns have a claim against the examiner and/or the lender for the failure to notify them of the mineral rights reservation? The question raises another question: does the bank make any kind of promise, express or implied, to a borrower that it will look after the borrower's interests when examining the title of property that will be security for a loan that the borrower is seeking from the bank? Courts have been reluctant to hold lenders liable to purchaser/borrowers for defects in title absent evidence that the lender has in fact promised to do so. Without strong evidence, courts have refused to imply a promise because of the belief that the parties' interests are sufficiently different as to negate the presence of an implied promise or fiduciary duty by the lender to the purchaser/borrower.[59]

Taking the question one step further, the Supreme Court of New Hampshire concluded, in a case of first impression, that attorneys are not vicariously liable for mistakes of others who conduct title searches. Attorneys can be held liable for their own negligence in selecting and supervising title examiner or in giving opinions based upon reports from such examiners. But holding them responsible for an independent contractor's error in failing to disclose an encumbrance "might require attorneys to guarantee the results obtained by any number of specialists hired as independent contractors, even when the attorneys did not agree to assume this responsibility," the court asserted.[60]

The American land title system places a heavy premium on careful and accurate review of the public land records. *Brown v. Lober* is an example of what can go wrong when mistakes are made or the standard operating system is not followed. Buyers and sellers rely heavily on professionals, including attorneys, in the land transfer process. Professionals have a special responsibility to be accurate and complete in the review and analysis of the land records. When mistakes are made, as *Brown* illustrates, years can pass before they come to light and can be rectified.

Conclusion

The public land records are at the heart of the American land transfer system. Title covenants provide a means for allocating responsi-

---

[59] *See, e.g.*, Page v. Frazier, 388 Mass. 55, 445 N.E.2d 148 (1983); Craig R. Thorstenson: *Mortgage Lender Liability to the Purchasers of New or Existing Homes*, 1988 U. Ill. L. Rev. 191.

[60] Lawyers Title Insurance Corp. v. Groff, 148 N.H. 333, 808 A.2d 44, 48 (2002); *see also* 18 ABA/BNA Lawyers' Manual on Professional Conduct 601 (2002).

bility for the quality of title being transferred. Title insurance offers purchasers protection against mistakes that may be made in land record review. The permanence of land, the long-term nature of the estate concept, and the large investment required for most real estate transactions place heavy premiums on an accurate and efficient system of land record review and analysis. As computers are brought into the process through Geographic Information Systems (GIS)[61] and other automated records systems, the role of the professional will change, but not diminish. *Brown v. Lober* emphasizes the importance of competent professionals, and the disruption that can occur when parties or their professional advisors make mistakes.

---

[61] *Cf.* George B. Korte, The GIS Book, 5th ed. (2001). *See also*, http://www.usgs.gov./research/gis/title.html (last modified Aug. 19, 2002) (GIS homepage explaining that "[g]eographic information systems technology can be used for scientific investigations, resource management, and development planning").

*

9

Vicki Been*

Lucas v. The Green Machine: Using the Takings Clause to Promote More Efficient Regulation?

In the early 1980's, burly, full-bearded David Lucas was well on his way from rags to riches. Born into a hard-working, Methodist family, Lucas had escaped "the cotton fields and tobacco barns" of Turkey Creek, South Carolina by "grasp[ing] a rung on the [economic] ladder." But his climb up that ladder was threatened by "his own government ... through unnecessary and oppressive regulation." Or, at least that's how Lucas tells the tale of his David and Goliath victory over "The Green Machine"[1] of environmentalism in *Lucas v. South Carolina Coastal Council.*[2]

Lucas is one of the Supreme Court's latest attempts to define when the "takings" clause of the Fifth Amendment of the United States Constitution requires the government to compensate property owners for reductions in the value of their property caused by government regulations. Both scholars and judges have bemoaned the difficulty the

* Professor Been would like to thank Professor Peter Byrne and participants in his Georgetown Law School Environmental Research Workshop Series, along with Dana Beach, William Blackwood, Sarah Chassis, Eileen Connor, Bill Eiser, William Fischel, Matthew Hand, Daryl Levinson, Richard Revesz, Michael Schill, Qiong Sun, and Katrina Wyman for their suggestions for improving this chapter. She gratefully acknowledges the research assistance of Ashley Miller NYU '04, William Blackwood, NYU '06, and Amy Widman, NYU '02, and the support of the Filomen D'Agostino and Max E. Greenberg Research Fund at New York University School of Law.

[1] David Lucas, Lucas vs. The Green Machine 6–7 (1995).

[2] 505 U.S. 1003 (1992).

Court has had in articulating the exact contours of the compensation requirement. Justice Stevens has complained, for example, that "[e]ven the wisest lawyers would have to acknowledge great uncertainty about the scope of this Court's takings jurisprudence."[3]

Many scholars and legal practitioners have echoed Stevens' exasperation, defining takings jurisprudence, for example, as the "leading candidate for the 'doctrine-in-most-desperate-need-of-a-principle prize.' "[4] Such despair results, in part, because the complexity and messiness of real-world dramas like the one in which David Lucas starred make it exceptionally difficult for either courts or commentators to agree upon the justification for the compensation requirement.

The takings debate typically identifies four reasons for a compensation mandate. Two view the compensation requirement as necessary to promote efficiency; the other two believe the requirement promotes fairness. First, some argue that compensation is necessary to ensure that governments take only those regulatory actions that will maximize aggregate social welfare. This *cost-internalization* theory posits that governments will not pay sufficient attention to the costs their regulations impose unless they are forced to compensate those whose property values are diminished by the regulation for their losses. If a government must pay those costs, the theory continues, regulators will be much more likely to adopt only those measures that produce greater benefits than costs.[5] Second, other theorists suggest that unless compensation is mandatory, investors' decisions will be so distorted by their fear that government regulation might destroy the fruits of their labor that they will not put resources to their most efficient use. This *insurance* rationale argues that the way to counter investors' aversion to the risk of regulatory losses is to insure property owners against such losses by mandating

---

[3] Nollan v. California Coastal Comm'n, 483 U.S. 825, 866 (1987) (Stevens, J., dissenting).

[4] Abraham Bell and Gideon Parchomovsky, *Givings*, 111 Yale L.J. 547, 558–59 (2002), *quoting* Jed Rubenfeld, *Usings*, 102 Yale L.J. 1077, 1081 (1993).

[5] The cost-internalization justification for a compensation requirement is usually traced to Frank I. Michelman, *Property, Utility, and Fairness: Comments on the Ethical Foundations of "Just Compensation" Law*, 80 Harv. L. Rev. 1165, 1173–83 (1967), although he actually argued only that a utilitarian argument for compensation would require compensation whenever the "demoralization" costs of a measure, such as the losses suffered by victims of the regulation, exceed the "settlement" costs of a measure, such as the cost of determining who suffered from the measure and arranging payments to those victims. Michelman did not explicitly argue that compensation was necessary to force governments to internalize the costs of regulatory measures. That argument derives from scholars such as Richard A. Posner, Economic Analysis of Law 64 (5th ed. 1998). For judicial endorsement of the theory, *see, e.g.*, Pennell v. City of San Jose, 485 U.S. 1, 22 (1988) (Scalia J., concurring in part and dissenting in part).

compensation.[6] Third, the most common, albeit least precise, theory posits that mandating compensation will prevent the government from forcing a small group of property owners to bear the burdens of regulation that *fairness* requires to be spread more broadly.[7] A fourth theory asserts that the political process is systematically unlikely to protect certain kinds of property owners from exploitation. In the event of such a *political process failure,* the argument contends, compensation should be paid to ensure fairness.[8]

The story of David Lucas has been hailed as "exquisitely illustrat[ing]" the wisdom of the first, cost-internalization, justification.[9] A close look at the twists and turns of the saga of the colorful Lucas and his two beachfront lots, however, reveals instead several very serious problems with the cost-internalization justification for a compensation requirement. First, the story of South Carolina's decision to relax its restrictions on beachfront development after Lucas won a compensation award suggests that the award may have played much less of a role in that decision than adherents of the cost-internalization justification claim. Second, the difficulty of assessing what effect, if any, the compensation award actually had on the legislators and regulators involved in *Lucas* reveals that we have so little understanding of how governmental actors make decisions that we cannot be sure whether forcing government regulators to compensate those affected by regulations will lead to more efficient or to less efficient regulation (or have no effect at all). Third, to the extent that a compensation requirement may discipline government decision-makers, the *Lucas* story reveals several reasons to believe that such a requirement is likely to result in too *little* regulation of coastal development. History suggests that the political power of beachfront property owners has caused state and local governments to be much too reluctant to prevent inefficient land development in areas

---

[6] *See, e.g.,* Lawrence Blume & Daniel L. Rubinfeld, *Compensation for Takings: An Economic Analysis,* 72 Cal. L. Rev. 569 (1984).

[7] *See, e.g.,* Andrea Peterson, *The Takings Clause: In Search of Underlying Principles Part II—Takings as Intentional Deprivations of Property Without Moral Justification,* 78 Cal. L. Rev. 53, 60 (1990).

[8] *See, e.g.,* William Michael Treanor, *The Original Understanding of the Takings Clause and the Political Process,* 95 Colum. L. Rev. 782, 860 (1995). For the argument that political process failures may sometimes require compensation not to protect property owners, but to protect the public from the superior political power of property owners, *see* Glynn S. Lunney, Jr. *A Critical Reexamination of the Takings Jurisprudence,* 90 Mich. L. Rev. 1892, 1963–64 (1992); Hanoch Dagan, *Takings and Distributive Justice,* 85 Va. L. Rev. 741, 743–47 (1999); Glynn S. Lunney, Jr., *Takings, Efficiency, and Distributive Justice: a Response to Professor Dagan,* 99 Mich. L. Rev. 157, 158–59 (2000).

[9] William A. Fischel, *Takings and Public Choice: The Persuasion of Price, in* The Encyclopedia of Public Choice 549 (Charles Kershaw Rowley, ed., 2003).

subject to natural hazards such as erosion and coastal storms. Adding a compensation requirement to the political tool-kit of those owners may lead to even less efficient levels of land use regulation. Further, if a compensation mandate disciplines governments at all, forcing government regulators to internalize the costs of the regulations they adopt and enforce, but not allowing them to internalize the benefits of those regulations, again is likely to encourage governments to adopt a lower level of regulation than is efficient. For all those reasons, *Lucas* shows not that cost-internalization occasioned by a compensation mandate will promote efficiency, but that the cost-internalization theory, at least in its current blunt form, is too seriously flawed to justify requiring government agencies to compensate property owners for losses caused by government regulation.

David Lucas and His Beachfront Lots

David Lucas: From Picker to Partner to Plaintiff

In the late 1970s, Lucas was a "young, struggling, single family homebuilder," who picked country and bluegrass guitar on the side.[10] In one of those "in the right place at the right time" coincidences, Lucas was invited to play a few tunes at a party held by Governor Jim Edwards, South Carolina's first Republican governor since Reconstruction.[11] Trying to quell his nerves before going on stage, Lucas struck up a friendship with Anne Finch, who had been invited to show off her talents at the piano for the guests. Anne happened to be the wife of one of the Governor's top political advisors, Raymon Finch.[12]

When Raymon Finch decided to run for Governor himself in 1978, Lucas offered Anne his band's entertainment services for Raymon's campaign.[13] Despite the good music, Finch lost the primary election. With his political career on hold, he turned instead to a partnership with his brothers to develop the Wild Dunes Beach and Racquet Club on the Isle of Palms, a barrier island just outside Charleston. Lucas then let Finch know that he "was interested in participating in more than just his political campaigning" and Finch soon hired Lucas to "head[] up a custom home building company" for the Club.[14]

---

[10] Green Machine, *supra* note 1 , at 29.

[11] Lucas' attorney had been instrumental in Governor Edwards' campaign, and the attorney's wife was then appointed manager of the Governor's mansion. She invited Lucas to play at the party. *Id*. at 14–15, 19.

[12] *Id*. at 21–23.

[13] *Id*. at 25–26.

[14] *Id*. at 30.

Working for Finch exposed Lucas not just to the "good life," but
also to the special cadre of businessmen involved in the Beach and
Racquet Club, including J.C. Long, "reputed to be one of the most
successful real estate developers in the entire Southeast."[15] Finch also
drew Lucas, who had for many years been involved in Republican
campaigns, further into politics: when Finch became Ronald Reagan's
campaign financial director for South Carolina, Lucas joined in to help.
In that role, Lucas rekindled a friendship with Lee Atwater, with whom
he had worked briefly during the 1968 Nixon campaign. Finch, Atwater,
Lucas and their fellow "dedicated Reaganites" sold "Doctor Ronald
Reagan's True Government Limiting Elixir"[16] to South Carolina voters,
and helped Reagan reap his first primary victory in the South. The band
of true believers was rewarded by then-Governor Edwards' appointment
as Reagan's Secretary of Energy, Finch's appointment to Edwards'
transition team, and Atwater's meteoric rise to Chair of the Republican
National Committee.[17]

The "Reagan revolution" disappointed Edwards and Finch, however, and they returned to South Carolina convinced that President Reagan's budget deficits meant the country was in for rough times. Finch
believed "that by 1986 or 1987 the real-estate values of the country
would be in a tail spin." He also was worried that "green politics, no
growth policies, and the drawbridge mentality" had "taken over the
local government." Finch decided it was time to sell the Beach and
Racquet Club, and he "convinced his other partners that they should get
out of the resort business while the getting was good."[18] They offered the
resort to "rich Arabs, wealthy Latinos, sophisticated Europeans, and
even some very famous American businessmen."[19] When those investors
failed to show sufficient interest, Finch sold the resort in March 1984 for
$25 million in cash to the home-town boy, David Lucas, and a team of
partners Lucas had assembled.[20]

The partnership Lucas created, known as Wild Dune Associates,
developed Wild Dunes, a 1500 acre project involving 2500 condominiums
and single family homes built around two "world famous" golf courses
and one of the southeast's largest boat marinas.[21] The partnership was

---

15 *Id.* at 32–33.

16 *Id.* at 36, 38.

17 *Id.* at 38.

18 Green Machine, *supra* note 1, at 42–43.

19 *Id.* at 43.

20 *Id.* at 51–59. The buyers also assumed an undisclosed amount of existing debt. *Id.* at
51.

21 Carl Babcock, *Wild Dunes Building Large "Resort Marina,"* The News and Courier
(Charleston, S.C.), Feb. 5, 1984, at 1–C; Michael Trouche, *Wild Dunes Club Owners to*

very successful, bringing in total sales of $64 million in its first year, and more than $100 million in its second. Soon, however, tensions arose between the partners. Lucas favored limiting the number of units sold each year, in order to prevent "too much product" from "flood[ing] the market," while his partners were "interested in as many sales, as quickly as possible, for as much money as possible."[22] Further, Lucas failed in his efforts to lobby Congress to reject the proposed Tax Reform Act of 1986 (which limited tax deductions for vacation homes), and his friend Lee Atwater told him the bill was bound to pass. The differences between him and his partners, along with his fear about the tax-reform legislation would dampen enthusiasm for second homes, convinced Lucas that he too should "get out ... while there was still time."[23] By July, 1986, Lucas came out of the deal "wealthy," and began such pursuits as collecting Egyptian Arabian horses.[24]

According to Lucas, he then made the fateful decision that would eventually land him in the Supreme Court of the United States. Lucas contends that after he cashed out of the partnership, he was offered the chance to buy some of the last of the undeveloped beachfront lots in the resort. Lucas claims that he "bit hard" at the offer and bought the two lots, numbers 22 and 24, at 11 and 13 Beachwood East, in 1986.[25] The lots were approximately 90 feet wide and 160 feet deep, and located about 310 and 340 feet (roughly the length of a football field) from the mean high water line of the ocean.[26] A "substantial" house built in the early 1980's separated the two lots.[27] Lucas intended to build his own family home on lot 24, and to build another house on lot 22 as a speculative investment. Lucas paid $475,000 and $500,000 for the lots—four times what the lots had sold for when they were first put on the market in 1979.[28] But because Wild Dunes was built out, with only a few beachfront lots left, Lucas anticipated that "within a year or two ...

Build 240–Condo Complex, The News and Courier (Charleston, S.C.), Apr. 10, 1984, at 1–B; Patricia McCarthy, *Second Wild Dunes Golf Course Should Rank Among the World's Best*, The News & Courier, (Charleston, S.C.), May 25, 1984, at 2–C.

[22] Green Machine, *supra* note 1, at 61, 64.

[23] *Id.* at 63.

[24] *Id.* at 64, 70–71.

[25] *Id.* at 72.

[26] Trial Transcript at 17 (Testimony of David Stevens), Lucas v. South Carolina Coastal Council (S.C. Ct. C.P. 1989) (No. 89–CP–10–66).

[27] Lucas v. South Carolina Coastal Council, No. 89–CP–10–66, slip op. at 4 (S.C. Ct. C.P. Aug. 10, 1989).

[28] Trial Transcript at 44–45 (Testimony of Donald Pardue), *Lucas* (No. 89–CP–10–66).

these lots could be perhaps worth as much as a million dollars apiece.''[29]

Some experts in land development have questioned Lucas' assertions about how he acquired the properties.[30] It does seem strange that Lucas would spend almost $500,000 to buy a lot for investment purposes just months after deciding to cash out of the partnership because of fears that the political and economic climate for real estate development had soured. Lucas reports that he was "smart enough to get out of the speculative real estate development business at the right time, while business was still good and prices were high."[31] Why then, would he purchase a new lot for speculation a few months later?

It also seems odd that a partner—indeed, the father of the partnership itself, as he tells it—waited to pay full market price after leaving the partnership to secure a lot for his family residence. Newspaper accounts of the *Lucas* controversy report that when Lucas first began developing the project in the early 1980's, he "picked out two choice oceanfront lots for himself."[32] It would have been logical for Lucas to take ownership of those lots as part of his initial partnership share, or as a portion of his buy-out.

Although it is hard to understand why Lucas would have acquired the lots at the high end of fair market value after he had cashed out of the partnership, it's much easier to understand why he might want to describe his acquisition that way if attention were ever focused on the transaction. Taxes on capital gains if Lucas were to sell the properties, for example, would be lower if the acquisition price could be described as the properties' fair market value in 1986, rather than as an earlier, lower value. Or, if one were trying to "position" the transaction for purposes of a subsequent takings lawsuit, it undoubtedly would be preferable to be seen as a "little guy" with just two lots whose value was destroyed than to be cast as a wealthy developer of more than 2500 homes, prevented from building on just two lots.[33]

---

[29] *Id.* at 32 (Testimony of David Lucas). Lucas testified at trial about his intimate familiarity with the island and real estate sales on the island. Because he owned Wild Dunes Real Estate, he "was the last word in setting the prices" for between 1000 and 1500 of the properties on the island. *Id.* at 34.

[30] *See* Dwight Merriam, *Rules for the Relevant Parcel*, 25 U. Haw. L. Rev. 353, 373 (2003).

[31] Green Machine, *supra* note 1, at 71.

[32] *See* Lyn Riddle, *Court Sinks a Choice Lot*, N.Y. Times, Mar. 31, 1991, § 8, at 1.

[33] For an introduction to the problems of how to define which portions of a takings claimant's holdings should be considered in determining the extent of the owner's losses, *see, e.g.*, William W. Fisher III, *The Trouble with Lucas*, 45 Stan. L. Rev. 1393, 1401–05 (1993).

In any event, Lucas retained architects and engineers to design homes for both lots. The plans for the house Lucas intended to build for resale were completed first. As a gated community, Wild Dunes sported an extensive array of restrictive covenants and other rules to protect its residents. Under those rules, the Wild Dunes Homeowners' Association had to approve Lucas' plans before he could seek permits from the local government. The Homeowners' Association rebuffed Lucas' plans for the house he planned to resell because the proposed structure would extend ten feet seaward of the neighbor's house. Not wanting to "rock the boat, or get off on the wrong foot with [the] neighbor," Lucas agreed to redraw the plans.[34] But Lucas came to realize that because "the lot was just too narrow to allow for everything that the market dictated we build," there was no satisfactory way to accommodate the neighbor.[35]

In the late fall of 1987, Lucas heard that legislation regarding beachfront property was pending in the South Carolina General Assembly. He "immediately asked if the legislation contained a grandfather clause" exempting existing projects. When told that it would, he "relaxed [his] guard."[36] He made no effort to obtain a building permit from the City of Isle of Palms, or from the South Carolina Coastal Council.

The South Carolina Beachfront Management Act of 1988:

In 1977, six years before Lucas sought to develop the lots, the South Carolina legislature adopted the Coastal Zone Act.[37] Responding both to growing concerns about the erosion of the state's beaches and to the incentives the Federal Coastal Zone Management Act of 1972[38] gave states to plan for coastal development, South Carolina's Coastal Zone Act established the South Carolina Coastal Council ("the Council"), and directed it to develop a comprehensive coastal management program. The legislation empowered the Council to designate areas of "critical state concern" within the coastal zone and to regulate both development and the use of erosion control devices within those zones.

The Coastal Zone Act did not, however, give the Council jurisdiction landward of the "primary front row dune." Many property owners took

---

[34] The Green Machine, *supra* note 1, at 77.

[35] *Id.*

[36] *Id.* at 78–79.

[37] 1977 S.C. Acts 123 (codified as amended at S.C. Code Ann. §§ 48–39–10—48–39–220 (2003)). For descriptions of the history of South Carolina's coastal protection program, *see, e.g.,* Newman Jackson Smith, *Analysis of the Regulation of Beachfront Development in South Carolina*, 42 S.C. L. Rev. 717 (1990–91); James G. Titus, *Rising Seas, Coastal Erosion, and the Takings Clause: How to Save Wetlands and Beaches Without Hurting Property Owners*, 57 Md. L. Rev. 1279, 1333–39 (1998).

[38] 16 U.S.C. §§ 1451–1465 (2003).

advantage of that crucial limitation by building structures just a foot or two back from the high tide line.[39] Further, the Council routinely granted permits for erosion control structures, and those structures proliferated even as evidence mounted that they actually caused, rather than prevented, significant erosion.[40]

Several events in the mid–1980s convinced the Council that a different strategy was needed to protect the state's beaches. In 1984, the U.S. Environmental Protection Agency and the South Carolina Sea Grant Program sponsored a conference that drew public attention to the dangers that the rising sea levels projected to result from global warming (among other factors) would pose for South Carolina's shoreline and barrier islands. In addition, storms in the winter of 1986–87 resulted in significant damage to sea walls, buildings, and pools close to the beach.[41] The Council responded both by tightening its permitting practices and by commissioning a Blue Ribbon Committee to study erosion control and recommend reforms to the Coastal Zone Act.[42] The Committee recommended an expansion of the Council's jurisdiction over erosion areas behind the dunes. It also advocated a "retreat" program to move new development, as well as the rebuilding of damaged structures, back from the beach.[43] After considerable public debate, the South Carolina General Assembly enacted the Beachfront Management Act of 1988 ("the BMA") to implement the Committee's recommendations.[44]

The BMA's preamble notes that the Coastal Zone Act did not enable the Coastal Council "to effectively protect the integrity of the beach/dune system" and that "consequently, ... development unwisely has been sited too close to the [beach/dune] system ... [and] has jeopardized the stability of the beach/dune system, accelerated erosion, and endangered adjacent property."[45] After finding that "it is in both the public and private interests to protect the system from this unwise development," the BMA sought "a gradual retreat from the [beach/dune] system

---

[39] Smith, *supra* note 37, at 720; Fred Rigsbee, *New Deputy Director of Coastal Council Highly Critical of Beach Development Trend*, The News and Courier/The Evening Post (Charleston, S.C.), Sept. 15, 1984, at 1–B.

[40] Smith, *supra note* 37, at 718–19.

[41] *Id.* at 719. *See also* Carol Farrington, *Out with the Tide, S.C. Beaches in Danger*, The State (Columbia, S.C.), May 22, 1988, at 1A (storm on Jan. 1, 1987 caused $20 million in damages.)

[42] Smith, *supra* note 37, at 720.

[43] Report of South Carolina Blue Ribbon Committee on Beachfront Management (1987).

[44] 1988 S.C. Acts 634 (codified as amended at S.C. Code §§ 48–39–250—48–39–360 (2003)).

[45] S.C. Code § 48–39–259(4) (2003).

over a forty-year period."[46] The BMA accordingly required the Council to establish "a baseline" for inlet erosion zones at "the most landward point of erosion at any time during the past forty years."[47] The BMA then required the Council to establish "setback lines" landward of the baseline at a distance equaling 40 times the annual erosion rate, or a minimum of twenty feet.[48] The BMA therefore allowed the Council to regulate not just the existing beachfront, but the area in which the beach and dunes were projected to move over the next forty years given the natural forces of erosion.[49]

The BMA prohibited the construction of any new structures in a "dead zone" twenty feet landward of the baseline, except for "grandfathered" projects for which the property owner had already obtained a building permit or planned development approval and had begun construction prior to March 1988.[50] The BMA then limited construction in the area between the dead zone and the forty-year setback line to homes no larger than 5000 square feet, placed as far landward on the lot as possible. The BMA also prohibited owners of structures damaged or destroyed by fire or natural causes from rebuilding in the dead zone, and limited rebuilding between that zone and the setback line to the size of the original structure.[51]

Pursuant to the BMA, the Council established an interim baseline and setback line. Within months after the BMA was passed in 1988, Lucas discovered that the "vast majority" of both his Wild Dune lots was seaward of the lines the Council had drawn.[52] The lots therefore could not be developed under the BMA.[53]

Standing Up For the Right to Build:

Faced with the roadblock the BMA imposed upon his plans, Lucas decided he had to fight: he "owed it to the people of the country and of

---

[46] S.C. Code §§ 48–39–250—48–39–260 (2003).

[47] S.C. Code § 48–39–280(A)(2) (2003).

[48] § 48–39–280(B).

[49] The technique of establishing "floating setbacks" based on the annual erosion rate has been used as well by such coastal states as New York, Florida, New Jersey, and North Carolina. For a description of the various states' coastal zone policies, *see* Dennis J. Hwang, *Shoreline Setback Regulations and the Takings Analysis*, 13 U.Haw. L. Rev. 1 (1991).

[50] S.C. Code Ann. §§ 48–39–290—48–39–300 (Supp. 1988) (amended 1990, current version at S.C. Code Ann. §§ 48–39–290—300 (2003)).

[51] S.C. Code Ann. § 48–39–290 (Supp. 1988) (amended 1990, current version at S.C. Code Ann. § 48–39–290 (2003)).

[52] Complaint at ¶ 5, *Lucas* (No. 89–CP–10–66).

[53] *Id.* at ¶ 6.

[the] state" who had made his "good fortune possible" by allowing him "the freedom to live the American dream."[54] Further, his "father and mother, Big John Wayne, Charles Starrett, Randolf Scott, Gene Autry, and all [his] other boyhood heros had taught [him] to fight for the principles in which [he] believed."[55]

Taking stock of the situation, Lucas decided to forego the opportunity the BMA provided for property owners to challenge the way in which the baseline and setback lines had been drawn. That route could become a "quagmire," Lucas reasoned. He knew the engineers who had drawn the lines personally—they had once worked for Wild Dunes. But Lucas feared that such a personal connection was "no guarantee" that they would redraw the line to suit him.[56]

Perhaps inspired by the Duke's example, Lucas decided instead to come out with all guns blazing by filing suit. His complaint alleged that the Act would "prohibit any kind of development, building or construction" on his property, thereby denying him "all reasonable use of property," squashing all "reasonable investment-backed expectations" he had for the property, and rendering the property "valueless."[57] Prior to the passage of the BMA, Lucas claimed, the Isle of Palms property had a market value of more than $2 million. After the BMA, he complained, the property was bereft of all "market or other economic value."[58] The complaint alleged that the BMA accordingly violated both the Fifth Amendment and the Takings Clause of the South Carolina Constitution, as well as both constitutions' Equal Protection guarantees.

In response, the Council denied that the BMA had effected a taking of Lucas' property.[59] The Council also argued that if the court should

---

[54] Green Machine, *supra* note 1, at 81.

[55] *Id.*

[56] *Id.* at 80–81. The Council had redrawn the lines in several instances, including elsewhere in the Palm Beach Isles development. *See, e.g.,* Prentiss Findlay, *Number of "Endangered" Folly Home Reduced*, News and Courier (Charleston, S.C.), Feb. 17, 1989, at 1–B, 2–B. Indeed, another developer on the Isle of Palms challenged the lines with the assistance of the engineer who had helped draw them for the Council, and succeeded. Telephone Interview with Dana Beach, Executive Director, South Carolina Coastal Conservation Council (Dec. 5, 2003).

[57] Complaint at ¶ 6, *Lucas* (No. 89–CP–10–66).

[58] *Id.* at ¶ 8.

[59] The answer also asserted that the court lacked jurisdiction because the controversy was not yet ripe, in that Lucas had not sought authorization from the Council to use the property, nor challenged the location of the baseline or setback line, so that there had been no final agency decision concerning the use of his property or the location of the lines. That argument had force under Williamson County Regional Planning Commission v. Hamilton Bank, 473 U.S. 172 (1985), but seems to have been abandoned by the Council.

find that a taking had occurred, it should "remand" the matter back to the Council to allow it to choose whether to issue a building permit or pay compensation.[60]

Lucas and the Council both stipulated that the BMA would prevent "construction of any habitable structures or recreational amenities on the lots,"[61] but would allow Lucas to build a "walkway to the beach" and a "small deck."[62] They also stipulated that although the beach generally was growing, "erosion does occur."[63]

Judge Larry R. Patterson of the Court of Common Pleas held a one-day trial in August, 1989. Just a few days after the trial, he issued an opinion finding that the building restrictions "deprived Lucas of any reasonable economic use of the lots."[64] Indeed, he noted, the enforcement of the Act "deprived Lucas of all the essential elements of ownership."[65] The Court further emphasized that the setback line rendered "property which was otherwise perfectly suitable for single-family residential development valueless. The damage to the two lots by virtue of the restrictions prohibiting any form of development is total."[66]

Judge Patterson ordered payment of $1,232,387 plus interest—$1.17 million in fair market value of the property on the effective date of the BMA plus the real property taxes and mortgage interest Lucas had paid on the property after that date.[67] Upon receipt of that sum, Lucas was to transfer title to the land to the state.

Because Judge Patterson found that the imposition of the setback lines had resulted in a "total taking" of Lucas' property, and because Lucas had specifically declined to challenge the legitimacy of the BMA, Judge Patterson regarded as irrelevant the state's evidence about its justifications for prohibiting Lucas from building.

The Shifting Sands of the Lucas Lots

At trial, the expert in coastal processes and shoreline management who had helped the Council establish the baseline and setback lines explained why the lines had been drawn so far inland. The Lucas lots are

---

[60] Amended Answer at ¶ 13, *Lucas* (No. 89–CP–10–66).

[61] Trial Transcript at 13 (Stipulation of Parties, ¶ 11), *Lucas* (No. 89–CP–10–66).

[62] *Id.* (Stipulation of Parties, ¶ 10)

[63] *Id.* (Stipulation of Parties, ¶ 12).

[64] *Lucas*, No. 89–CP–10–66, slip. op. at 5.

[65] *Id.* at 7.

[66] *Id.* at 6.

[67] *Id.* at 8.

on the Isle of Palms, a barrier island. Barrier islands are long, narrow bars of sand found just offshore that serve as buffers to protect the mainland against storm-driven waves. The Isle of Palms, as a whole, is accretionary—over the long term it is adding more sand than it is losing. But the Lucas lots are located on an "inlet erosion zone" of the island that is affected by what is called "shoal attachment phenomena."

The beach on which the Lucas lots are located is built up by sand migrating from the shoals or sandbars of the inlet that separates the Isle of Palms from an adjacent barrier island. The process by which sand detaches from the shoal in the inlet, is pushed to shore by waves, and finally attaches to the Isle of Palms, makes the area very "dynamic." As the shoal migrates towards the island, the areas of the island to the north and south of the migrating shoal suffer severe erosion, while the area in front of the shoal bulges and rapidly accretes. Once the sandbar attaches to the island, the sand spreads out and generally fills in the eroded areas at either end. Under these conditions, within just a few years a beach can be subject to substantial erosion of the areas on either side of a migrating sandbar, then benefit from substantial re-building once the sandbar finally attaches.[68] There is no way to predict when a shoal will begin to come ashore, where the bulge will form, and where the erosion will occur.[69] In the last fifty years, this "shoal attachment phenomena" has occurred on the Isle of Palms at least fifteen times.[70]

At trial, the state's expert presented evidence that the shore line of the Lucas property had been peripatetic over the past few decades. In 1949, the shoreline was entirely landward of the Lucas lots. By the 1950s, it had shifted as much as 200 feet back towards the ocean . In 1963, the shoreline was back to the landward side of the lots. In 1973, it had plunged even further inland than the landward boundary of the Lucas lots, and a pond formed over portions of the two lots. By the late 1970's, the shoreline was back to the seaward side of the lots.[71]

---

[68] Trial Transcript at 72–77 (Testimony of Christopher Jones), *Lucas* (No. 89–CP–10–66).

[69] *See* Summer House Horizontal Property Regime v. South Carolina Department of Health and Environmental Control, No. 97–ALJ–07–0403–CC, 1998 WL 268396 (S.C. Admin. Law. Judge Div. Apr. 28, 1998), for an especially clear explanation of the shoal attachment phenomenon. *See also* Bob Deans, *Fighting Erosion: Some Ways Working Better than Others,* The News and Courier (Charleston, S.C.), Apr. 8, 1984, at 1–A, 2–A (reporting a description of the phenomenon by Timothy Kana, director of Coastal Science Engineering Inc., who helped engineer erosion control efforts for the Wild Dunes Development).

[70] *Summer House*, 1998 WL 268396, at *3.

[71] Lucas and his witnesses focused on the island's overall accretion, although on cross-examination an engineer who had been involved in the development of the Island admitted that, in 1983, areas to the south of Lucas lots had suffered major erosion. The engineer also

The expert testified that the "shore line could be expected to move landward again and might move back to the 1963 line [inland of the lot lines] or even further."[72] During the erosion episode captured in the 1963 and 1973 photos he presented, Lucas' lots were "on the active beach ... [and] were probably wet at all stages of the tide."[73] The state's expert concluded by noting that the area was accreting "at the rate of two or two and a half feet per year over the long term, but it does so in a cyclic fashion and in the process it may accrete or erode ... three hundred feet or so."[74] Further, he emphasized that over the past 40 years, the "beach has occupied part or all of the Lucas property" fifty percent of the time.[75]

The Council also introduced evidence demonstrating that in the early 1980s, the portion of the Wild Dunes development containing the Lucas lots had been subject to exactly the kind of erosion episode the state's expert had described as typical of shoal attachment phenomena.[76] Then, Wild Dunes had sought emergency orders to allow property owners to move sand and place sandbags to protect their structures. After Wild Dunes had shown an imminent threat to homes within the development, the Council allowed the Wild Dunes Development to place an unusually long 1300–foot long granite wall, or "revetment" to protect the beach.[77] Wild Dunes also piped 350,000 cubic yards of sand in front

---

acknowledged that at some time the high water mark had been landward of the Lucas lots. Trial Transcript at 21–22 (Testimony of David Stevens), *Lucas* (No. 89–CP–10–66).

[72] *Id.* at 74–81 (Testimony of Christopher Jones).

[73] *Id.* at 82.

[74] *Id.* at 83.

[75] *Id.* at 84. Cross-examination of the expert focused on his agreement that the island was generally accreting. *Id.* at 94–95.

[76] *Id.* at 99–103 (Testimony of Steven Moore). *See also* Deans, *supra* note 69, at 1A—2A, noting that:

> Bankers ... deal in months, not centuries. And while scientists say the Isle of Palms is continuing to build up overall, the short-term effects of sporadic beach erosion have worried investors at Wild Dunes.... More than a million dollars worth of property was imperiled last year at Wild Dunes, when the Atlantic Ocean gouged deep into two sections of beach, threatening to take with it two sets of luxury condominiums....

Lucas testified that "every study that we had, and every study that I'm aware of, said that the beach was an accretion area—an accreting beach; that over the past fifteen hundred years that the ocean has built oceanward, but that there would be sometimes intermittent and temporary erosion during that period of time." Trial Transcript at 26 (Testimony of David Lucas), *Lucas* (No. 89–CP–10–66). He admitted that, in 1983, the "scarp line" was at the face of some of the buildings in the Wild Dunes development, meaning that the ocean came up to that point. *Id.* at 37.

[77] *Id.* at 99–104 (Testimony of Steven Moore).

of, and on top of, the revetment.[78] The revetment runs in front of a portion of the lot Lucas planned to develop for sale. It does not, however, protect the entire lot. Nor does it cover any of the lot Lucas planned to develop for his own home.

Back and Forth in the Higher Courts

The trial judge did not reject any of the Council's evidence of the dangers posed by development of such a "dynamic" beach. Lucas had conceded the validity of the BMA, so Judge Patterson focused instead on Lucas' argument that regardless of the state's reasons for prohibiting development, the state should compensate Lucas because the BMA had destroyed the entire value of his property. Judge Patterson held:

> It is manifest that the imposition of the setback lines by the Coastal Council have resulted in a total taking of Lucas's two beachfront lots. Accordingly, Lucas is entitled under both the State and Federal Constitutions to the payment of just compensation.[79]

The Council appealed. Before the case was argued, Hurricane Hugo struck the Isle of Palms with 135 mile-per hour winds, leaving awesome destruction in its wake. The Isle was in "shambles physically and economically."[80] As many as twenty percent of the homes on the island were destroyed, some even ripped from their foundations and dumped on their neighbors' grounds. The hurricane's storm surge unleashed rampant flooding, inundating almost all the houses on the island with mud and sewage. More than eighty homes on the Isle eventually were condemned. The Wild Dunes resort was closed for many months for reconstruction, and all beach-front businesses on the island also were shuttered for several months.[81]

The tremendous devastation wrought by Hurricane Hugo did little to dampen South Carolinians' enthusiasm for "the folly of building on the beach."[82] Instead, the calamity united beachfront owners, who insisted loud and clear that they wanted to rebuild, despite the provisions of the BMA. The Council, along with the state legislature, heard the message. Soon after the hurricane, the Council interpreted the BMA in a way that allowed owners of more than ninety percent of the seriously

---

[78] Deans, *supra* note 69, at 1A.

[79] *Lucas,* slip op. at 8.

[80] Rudolph A. Pyatt, *Two Months Later, Hugo Still Packs a Punch: Despite Rebound in Tourism, Boom in Construction, Many Industries Face Long, Uncertain Return to Stability,* Wash. Post., Nov. 19, 1989, at H01.

[81] *Id.*

[82] Mary T. Schmich, *After Hugo, Residents Rebuild,* Chi. Trib. , Apr. 15, 1990, at 12.

damaged beachfront houses to rebuild.[83] The legislature went further, amending the BMA to eliminate the no-construction zone and to allow new structures to be built, or damaged structures to be rebuilt, between the baseline and the setback line.[84] The 1990 amendments also established a special permitting procedure by which the agency could allow building even seaward of the baseline, as long as it was not on a primary oceanfront sand dune or on an active beach and would not be detrimental to the public health, safety or welfare. In order to obtain a special permit for a structure, however, the amendments required the property owner to agree to remove the structure should the Council order its removal because of erosion.[85] The BMA prohibited the construction of any new erosion control devices, and limited the repair or replacement of already installed devices, so the effect of the 1990 Amendments was to allow property owners to develop their properties, but to bear the risk that uninhibited erosion could either damage a structure or force the owner to move it back from the shifting beach.[86]

After the 1990 amendments went into effect, the State Supreme Court reversed Judge Patterson's decision in a 3–2 opinion.[87] The majority opinion reasoned that Lucas had failed to attack the legislature's findings that new construction on the beach would cause serious public harm and had therefore conceded that the "nuisance-like exception" to the compensation requirement articulated in *Mugler v. Kansas*[88] applied. The court noted that Lucas' argument that he was entitled to compensation "regardless of how the proposed use of his property harms the public ... because all economically viable use of his land has been extinguished" tracked Justice Rehnquist's dissent in *Keystone Bituminous Coal Ass'n v. DeBenedictis*.[89] The South Carolina Supreme Court declined to follow that dissent.

Lucas' trial attorneys, who also had argued the appeal to the South Carolina Supreme Court, had worked on a contingency fee basis. When the trial attorneys declined to continue on that basis, Lucas persuaded two Columbia, South Carolina lawyers, along with David Bederman, a law professor at Emory University, to take the case on contingency.[90]

---

[83] *Id.*

[84] 1990 S.C. Acts 607, § 3.

[85] S.C. Stat. Ann. § 48–39–290 (2003).

[86] *Id.*

[87] Lucas v. South Carolina Coastal Council, 304 S.C. 376, 404 S.E.2d 895 (1991).

[88] 123 U.S. 623 (1887).

[89] 480 U.S. 470 (1987).

[90] Lucas also turned to the Pacific Legal Foundation (PLF), a conservative organization devoted to the protection of private property. PLF agreed to take the case to the United

Lucas had become convinced that the case was "possibly the last stand of private property in America," and that if he gave up or lost, "private property could face annihilation."[91]

The United States Supreme Court reversed the South Carolina Supreme Court, holding that "[w]here the State seeks to sustain regulation that deprives land of all economically beneficial use, . . . it may resist compensation only if the logically antecedent inquiry into the nature of the owner's estate shows that the proscribed use interests were not part of his title to begin with."[92] The Court accordingly remanded the matter back to the South Carolina Supreme Court so that it could determine whether Lucas' expectation to develop the property was part of his title.

The South Carolina Supreme Court was quick to close the door the United States Supreme Court had left open to the State. It found that no "common law principle" would allow the Council to prevent the development of the land.[93] The Court assumed that the Council would grant Lucas a permit to build, and that the taking of his land therefore was only temporary. It directed the trial judge to determine the damages appropriate to compensate Lucas for the temporary taking, which typically would be measured either by the rental value of the property for the time the challenged restriction was in effect, for the lost income caused by the delay, or for the rate of return the property owner would have received had the owner invested the value of the property in the stock market or other investments.[94] The Court noted that if the Council refused to grant a permit, Lucas then would have the right "to litigate any subsequent deprivations which may arise. . . ."[95]

States Supreme Court if Lucas would pay expenses. Lucas reports that, because his real estate investments had taken a beating from the downturn, he couldn't afford even the expenses of the appeal. He therefore convinced his South Carolina lawyers both to take the appeal on contingency and to advance the out-of-pocket costs of the appeal. Green Machine, *supra* note 1, at 165. PLF filed an amicus brief in the case.

[91] Green Machine, *supra* note 1, at 182.

[92] 505 U.S. at 1027.

[93] Lucas v. South Carolina Coastal Council, 309 S.C. 424, 424 S.E.2d 484 (1992).

[94] *See* Robert Meltz et al., The Takings Issue 483–510 (1999); Richard J. Roddewig & Christopher J. Duerksen, *Measuring Damages in Takings Cases: the Next Frontier, in* 1993 Zoning & Planning Law Handbook 273 (Kenneth H. Young ed.); Joseph LaRusso, *"Paying for the Change":* First English Evangelical Lutheran Church of Glendale v. County of Los Angeles *and the Calculation of Interim Damages for Regulatory Takings,* 17 B.C. Envtl. Aff. L. Rev. 551 (1990).

[95] 424 S.E.2d at 486.

The Aftermath of the U.S. Supreme Court's Decision:

Back in the trial court, Lucas filed an amended complaint alleging, among other things, that he was entitled to a permit under the 1990 amendments. The Council's answer denied that particular allegation, and asked that Lucas be required to prove his eligibility for the permit. Lucas reacted by filing a new lawsuit, naming the members of the Council as defendants both in their official and in their personal capacities. In the new challenge, Lucas alleged that the Council had discriminated against him by denying him a permit even though it had granted such permits to other similarly situated property owners.[96]

The parties then began settlement negotiations. Lucas claimed that he was owed three million dollars for the properties, his carrying costs, and his legal fees. He settled for $1,575,000 and building permits for the lots, which he transferred to the Council along with title to the lots. After he paid off the mortgage and gave the lawyers their fees and expenses, Lucas was left with "less than $100,000."[97]

Lucas went on to develop low-cost housing in Poland and Mexico.[98] He continued to reside on the Isle of Palms, although he claims that his house lies farther from the beach than the house owned by Cotton Harness, the attorney for the Council.[99] In the fall of 1993, Lucas helped form the Council of Property Rights.[100] He has become a spokesperson for the property rights movement—or, as he puts it, the "Ralph Nader of private property rights."[101] His speeches and appearances contributed to the enactment of the Bert Harris Jr. Private Property Rights Protection Act in Florida.[102] His efforts to secure legislation establishing stricter compensation rules in South Carolina, however, resulted only in a measure that changed the procedures by which property owners can contest land use regulations to allow pre-litigation mediation of the dispute.[103]

---

[96] Green Machine, *supra* note 1, at 247–48.

[97] H. Jane Lehman, *Case Closed, Settlement Ends Property Rights Lawsuit*, Chi. Trib. July 25, 1993, at 3G.

[98] Green Machine, *supra* note 1, at 237–240; Lehman, *supra* note 97.

[99] Green Machine, *supra* note 1, at 286.

[100] *Id.* at 279–80.

[101] Robert Aalberts, *Whatever Happened to David Lucas?*, 25Real Est. L. J., 211, 213 (1997).

[102] Fla. Stat. Ann. § 70.001 (West 2003).

[103] The Land Use Dispute Resolution Act, 2003 S.C. Acts 39. *See generally* Jennifer Dick and Andrew Chandler, *Shifting Sands: the Implementation of Lucas on the Evolution of Takings Law and South Carolina's Application of the Lucas Rule*, 37 Real Prop. Prob. & Tr. J. 637 (2003).

Meanwhile, the Coastal Council made a remarkable about-face. Noting that the *Lucas* lots were located in a gated community and therefore could not be opened to the public, and that the adjacent lots were already developed, the Council pronounced the lots unsuitable for a public park. The Council declared that the lots therefore would have to be sold for development. It sold both lots and special permits for $730,000. A five bedroom house was built on the lot Lucas had planned to use for his own home; the lot he had hoped to develop for investment now sports a four bedroom house.[104]

But time may still prove the wisdom of the Council's setback lines. The beach on which the lots sit suffered a "temporary erosion episode" shortly after the lots were developed. "About 200 feet of shoreline disappeared in two years"[105] and high tides swept within ten to fifteen feet of some of the houses.[106] To protect their houses, the new owner of one of the *Lucas* lots, along with neighboring property owners, applied for a permit to control erosion by building either a rock wall, a six-foot high wall of "sand bags" weighing approximately 2.5 tons each, or a six-foot high sand-filled tube.[107] The Office of Ocean and Coastal Resource Management (OCRM) (the Council's successor agency) denied the application. Some of the property owners then sued, claiming that the OCRM's denial of permission for erosion control barriers constituted a taking.[108] Judge Patterson, the trial judge in *Lucas*, denied the property owners' motion for a temporary injunction, finding that the BMA's prohibition on erosion control barriers constituted an inherent limitation on the owner's title and accordingly was not a taking.[109] The property

---

[104] *See* Charleston County Property Information System, *at* http://gisweb.charleston-county.org/ccpa/ccpa.htm (for parcels No. 604–10–00–043 and No. 604–10–00–041); *see also* Dana Beach and Kim Diana Connolly, *A Retrospective on* Lucas v. South Carolina Coastal Council: *Implications for Public Policy for the 21*st *Century*,—Southeastern L. Rev.— (forthcoming, 2004).

[105] *See* Christina Binkley, *Coalition Plans to Push "Takings Law,"* Wall St. J., Dec. 18, 1996, at S1.

[106] Lynne Langley, *Sandbar, Season Erode Wild Dunes*, Post and Courier (Charleston, S.C.), at 1–B.

[107] *See* Lynne Langley, *Palms Board Oks Giant Sandbags*, Post and Courier (Charleston, S.C.), Oct. 21, 1995, at 17–A.

[108] *See* Lynne Langley, *Six Landowners Sue State Over Erosion*, Post and Courier (Charleston, S.C.), July 19, 1996, at 1–B.

[109] Jerozal v. South Carolina Dep't of Health & Envtl. Control, No. 95–CP–10–4365 (S.C. Ct. C.P. 1996) (denying temporary restraining order). *See also* Lynne Langley, *Judge Hears Wild Dunes Arguments*, Post and Courier (Charleston, S.C.), July 30, 1996, at 1–B; Lynne Langley, *Wild Dunes Sandbag Injunction Denied*, Post and Courier (Charleston, S.C.), Aug. 21, 1996, at 1–B; Lynne Langley, *Sandbag Proposal Beached*, Post and Courier (Charleston, S.C.), Oct. 12, 1996, at 1–B.

owners dropped the matter when the erosion shifted north, according to Mary Shahid, former counsel for the OCRM.[110]

Lucas and the "Persuasion of Price"

The standard law and economics model of contract, tort and property law posits that rational economic actors in a market environment will produce the efficient quantity of a particular good or service—the quantity that maximizes overall social welfare—only if the actor is forced to bear, or internalize, the full costs of its activity. If the developer of beachfront resort facilities were to build in such a way that nearby property owners suffered erosion, for example, and the developer were allowed to ignore the costs that erosion imposed upon its neighbors, the developer would build more than the socially optimal amount of resort facilities. But if the developer were forced to internalize those costs by paying a damages remedy to the neighbors, or by paying neighbors not to assert any rights they might have to prevent the building, for example, the developer would continue to build facilities that generate erosion only as long as the total benefits of the development outweigh its total costs. Cost-internalization accordingly is essential to the efficiency of the free market.

The cost-internalization theory that underlies the takings arguments at issue in *Lucas* follows the same form: only if the government is forced to pay the full costs of its regulations will it choose the efficient level of regulation—the level at which the benefits from the regulation outweigh its costs. The theory asserts that government policymakers will suffer from "fiscal illusion" if they aren't forced to pay the costs regulations impose on property owners: they will underestimate costs they do not actually bear, and thus act under an illusion about the value of their policies.[111]

Given the Council's decision to sell the lots, *Lucas* is now routinely cited as "Exhibit A" for the role that compensation, or "the persuasion of price," can and should play in ensuring that governments act efficiently.[112] Economics Professor Bill Fischel, for example, has written

---

[110] Robert C. Ellickson and Vicki L. Been, Land Use Controls 209–210 (2000) (reporting the interview with Ms. Shahid). In 1998, however, other Isle of Palms owners sought permission to protect their property against erosion, and again were rebuffed. *See* Lynne Langley, *Panel Sacks Sandbag Request*, Post and Courier (Charleston, S.C.), Sep. 12, 1998, at 1–B.

[111] *See, e.g.*, Louis Kaplow, *An Economic Analysis of Legal Transitions*, 99 Harv. L. Rev. 509, 567 (1986).

[112] Fischel, *supra* note 9, at 552.

extensively about the Fifth Amendment's compensation requirement, and argues:

> ... Prior to the *Lucas* decision, South Carolina perceived the price of Lucas's lot (and others like it) as being low, since it did not expect to have to pay for them. At that price—zero dollars and zero cents—even the least environmentally sensitive legislator would have to concede that environmental values should prevail. No highways or hospitals or airports—that is, alternative uses for the state's money—needed to be given up to preserve the coast. The legislature did not have to risk the wrath of voters by raising taxes to pay for the lots. All it had to do was pass a regulation, whose burden fell upon a small number of landowners.
>
> Once the state came into possession of the land, however, it had reason to pay attention to its market price relative to its environmental value.... The state's agents then surely noticed that developers were willing to pay nearly half a million dollars for each of the lots, and the state's agents did what rational and faithful public servants should do: they sold the lots to developers.
>
> The state ... simply responded to the higher price of preserving this tiny (less than one acre) stretch of the beach and did the sensible thing. ... Having to pay money out of scarce budgetary resources makes officials calculate whether it is worthwhile to undertake a particular project....[113]

Law and economics scholars like Fischel, then, view the story of the *Lucas* lots as a rather embarrassing object lesson that governments will over-regulate unless they are forced to pay compensation to property owners affected by regulations. But a closer look at the story both casts doubt on the role that the compensation award in *Lucas* played in South Carolina's softening of its beachfront management policies, and reveals that the cost-internalization theory for requiring compensation itself is an embarrassingly inadequate justification for the Fifth Amendment's Takings Clause.

Money or Votes?

The Council, in its treatment of the property owners seeking to rebuild structures damaged by Hurricane Hugo, and the General Assembly, in its 1990 amendments to the BMA, both backed away from the dead zone retreat policy reflected in the BMA. Under the cost-internalization theory, the prospect of having to compensate those injured by the retreat policy must have been crucial to that turnabout.[114] Other disci-

---

[113] *Id.* 552. *See also* William A. Fischel, Regulatory Takings (1995).

[114] Fischel's arguments about *Lucas,* quoted *supra* text accompanying note 112, focus on the Council's decision to sell the lots to a developer, rather than on the Council's and

plinary constraints—the wrath of voters affected by the policy, for example—would have been insufficient, by themselves, to make South Carolina's regulators and legislators pay attention to both the costs and the benefits of the retreat policy. Only when the Council and the General Assembly faced the threat of the compensation requirement, the theory would assert, did they realize that the costs of the retreat were not worth its benefits.

The history of the General Assembly's turnabout from the retreat policy, however, raises serious questions about the argument that the threat of compensation played a crucial role in the decision to amend the BMA. First, the legislative history of the 1988 Act indicates that the legislature was well aware when it passed the BMA that the dead zone retreat policy might be ruled a taking and therefore require compensation.[115] Concerns about property rights and the state's liability for takings judgments led supporters of the proposed legislation to compromise on various aspects of the bill during the legislative debate.[116] Further, the Conference Committee specifically revised the legislation to give a property owner the right to challenge the BMA when an owner believed the law's application to a particular piece of property effected a taking.[117] That procedure, modeled after one North Carolina had used in its coastal protection scheme, gave the Council the option of either allowing property owners who proved a taking to build or paying them for their land. But at least one member of the Conference Committee reported that he expected money to change hands more often than

General Assembly's turnabout on the dead zone retreat policy. But once that turnabout took place, it made little sense for the Council to treat the *Lucas* lots under the terms of the BMA when all other lots were subject to the more favorable terms of the 1990 Amendments. In order for the Council's treatment of the lots to illustrate the role that a compensation mandate plays in promoting cost-internalization, then, the turnabout reflected in the 1990 Amendments must have been motivated by the compensation mandate.

[115] *See, e.g.,* Cindi Ross, *Major Provisions of the Beachfront Protection Legislation Bill is [sic] Approved as Tide Rises in Favor of Beach Protection,* The State (Columbia, S.C.), June 2, 1988, at 1A. *Compare also "Dead Zone" Elimination Sought,* News and Courier (Charleston, S.C.), Feb. 10, 1989, at 1–B (reporting that the Senator James Waddell, the past chairman of the Council, had become concerned about the potential liability the Council might bear for the dead zone provisions of the BMA and hoped to amend the BMA); *with Waddell's Proposal on Beach Act Blasted ,* News and Courier/Evening Post (Charleston, S.C.), Feb. 18, 1989, at 1–B (quoting several legislators as rejecting Waddell's attempt to "gut" the BMA and noting that they "knew what we were doing" when they passed the BMA).

[116] *See,* Bruce Smith, *Coastal Council "Stretched,"* The State (Columbia, S.C.), Mar. 19, 1988, at 3D; Ross, *supra* note 115.

[117] S.C. Code Ann. § 48–39–290 (Supp. 1988) (amended 1990, current version at S.C. Code Ann. § 48–39–290 (2003)).

building permits, and declared: "If that's the price we have to pay, that's the price we have to pay for our policy of retreating."[118]

The fact that the General Assembly considered the possibility that compensation would be required before enacting the BMA does not, without more, disprove that the actual court order of compensation was a motivating factor behind the General Assembly's retreat from the BMA. The General Assembly could have understood that compensation might be required, and even have been prepared to pay the price of that compensation, but nonetheless decided to pass the legislation without offering compensation on the chance that the courts would refuse to order compensation.[119] Because states are not subject to punitive damages, legislatures will suffer no financial penalty for waiting to pay compensation until ordered to do so by a court (other than attorneys' fees, and any dishonor that attaches to those whose legislation is found to constitute a taking).[120] Proponents of the cost-internalization theory accordingly would argue that even explicit consideration during the legislative process of the costs the state theoretically faces from compensation awards is no substitute for the disciplinary effect of a real compensation mandate.

But the argument that Judge Patterson's mandate motivated the General Assembly's pull back from the BMA is further belied by the fact that the pull back began even before Judge Patterson issued his mandate. Proposals to eliminate the dead zone from the BMA were introduced in the General Assembly early in 1989, just months after the BMA was enacted.[121] Charleston newspapers began to decry the undoing of the

---

[118] Ross, *supra* note 115.

[119] The General Assembly might have assessed the risk that the South Carolina Supreme Court would find the legislation to effect a taking as low, because the justices all had served in the legislature before being appointed to the bench. Cindi Ross Scoppe, *High-Level Reformers Want to Change Way S.C. Selects Judges*, The State (Columbia, S.C.), Feb. 16, 1994, at B5 (in 1991 all Supreme Court justices had served in General Assembly). *See* generally, Martin Scott Driggers, Jr., *South Carolina's Experiment: Legislative Control of Judicial Merit Selection*, 49 S.C. L. Rev. 1217, 1235 (1998). Indeed, Justice Toal, who eventually wrote the state Supreme Court's opinion finding that the BMA did not effect a taking, had been a member of the legislature until just a month before the BMA was introduced. The assertions of legislators who were property rights supporters that the General Assembly's decision to provide an expedited procedure by which property owners could bring takings challenges, and its decision to place the burden of proof in those challenges on the state, was a victory for property owners, however, would be inconsistent with a belief that the courts were likely to reject takings claims. *See* Ross, *supra* note 115.

[120] If the legislature passes legislation without budgeting for the possibility that the courts will require compensation, a compensation award could wreak serious havoc on the state's budget. Fear of such turmoil might reduce a legislature's incentive to gamble on the chance that the courts will not find a taking.

[121] *See "Dead Zone" Elimination Sought*, News and Courier (Charleston, S.C.), Feb. 10, 1989, at 1–B; *see also Waddell's Proposal on Beach Act Blasted*, News and Courier/Evening Post (Charleston, S.C.), Feb. 18, 1989, at 1–B.

BMA by the real estate and banking industries as early as February of 1989.[122] Further, the media reported that a "deal" to revise the BMA had been struck in May, 1989, and the state Senate passed the bill that would eventually become the 1990 Amendments before adjourning in June, 1989, well before Judge Patterson's August, 1989 ruling.[123]

While the General Assembly did not finally adopt the amendments to the BMA until 1990, after Judge Patterson issued his decision, it passed the amendments while that decision was still on appeal to the South Carolina Supreme Court. If the General Assembly's primary concern were the threat of compensation, given the difficulty of passing any legislation and given the controversy that had surrounded the passage of the BMA just two years before, it would have been odd for legislators to rush to address that concern *before* waiting to see whether the trial court's decision would even be upheld[124] Something more had to be behind the State's quick turnabout.

That something more most likely was Hurricane Hugo. The strategy reflected in the BMA was one of gradual retreat from the beach as existing structures that were damaged or destroyed were rebuilt further inland. Absent a catastrophe greater than South Carolina had seen in the several decades before it passed the BMA, that strategy would affect relatively few property owners in any given year. But Hurricane Hugo caused a significant number of property owners unexpectedly to be constrained by the BMA . That sudden critical mass of angry voters, coupled with the political and public relations difficulties of denying people who had just suffered a disaster the right to rebuild, likely proved too much for the members of the General Assembly.

The history of the General Assembly's backtracking on the BMA thus doesn't square neatly with the argument that it was the cost-

---

[122] *Takings Sides With the Beachfront*, News and Courier (Charleston, S.C.), Feb. 24, 1989, at 8–A; *see also* John Burbage, *Focusing in On Our Environment,* News and Courier (Charleston, S.C.), at 8–A; *Those Who Will Not See the Beach*, News and Courier (Charleston, S.C.), May 12, 1989, at 8–A.

[123] *Tentative Deal Struck on Beach Bill Revisions*, News and Courier (Charleston, S.C.), May 31, 1989, at 4–B; Cindi Ross Scoppe, *S.C. Lawmakers Wind Up Session of Compromise*, The State (Columbia, S.C.), June 4, 1989, at 1–A .

[124] The media stressed the possibility that the state might be ordered to pay compensation in reporting on the General Assembly's 1990 deliberations about whether to soften its coastal protection rules. *See, e.g.,* Russell C. Munn, *Beachfront Management Act Revised as Session Ends*, S.C. Bus. J., July 1, 1990, at 13 ("The changes to the act were proposed to prevent what could have become a financial nightmare for the state."). Critics of the amendments, however, faulted not the court's compensation mandate, but "the political power of a very small number of people who live on these islands." *See, e.g.,* Schmich, *supra* note 82, quoting Orrin Pilkey, a "prominent Duke University beach management expert."

internalization effected by the *Lucas* compensation award that disciplined the state legislature. An examination of the Council's dealings with Lucas also gives reason to doubt that cost-internalization was responsible for the Council's turnabout.

Principles, The Posture of Litigation, and Emotions

The Council did an about-face not just on the dead zone retreat policy, but on whether to allow development on the particular lots at issue in *Lucas*. Adherents of the cost-internalization justification for a compensation requirement argue that the Council's behavior in initially denying Lucas the right to build, but then allowing houses to be built on the lots, shows that the Council took the value of the land for development into account only when forced to actually bear the cost of destroying that value.[125]

Again, the argument doesn't account for a host of other factors that might have explained the Council's turnabout. First, a legislator or regulator writing rules intended to be generally applicable usually cannot anticipate the specific costs or benefits a rule will impose on each and every property it will govern. Both land use and environmental regulations typically provide an individual variance or special permit procedure that gives property owners an opportunity to ask regulators to conduct a more fine-tuned analysis of the costs and benefits of applying the general rule to a particular piece of property. The BMA did not contain such a special permitting procedure, at least in the usual form. As noted earlier, in a concession to property owners, the bill that became the BMA was revised by the House and Senate Conference Committee to include both an administrative mechanism by which landowners could challenge the baseline and setback line and a judicial procedure by which landowners could contest the reasonableness of the application of the law to their property and receive either a building permit or compensation, at the state's option.[126] The General Assembly may have believed that those provisions took the place of a special permit procedure. But Lucas chose not to use either of those mechanisms, and the Council did not insist that he do so.[127] The procedural posture of Lucas' takings claim therefore forced the Council (and the trial court) to treat Lucas' claim as

---

[125] *See* Fischel, *supra* note 9.

[126] *See supra* text accompanying note 117; *see also* Ross, *supra* note 22 (describing the provision as a compromise to protect property rights).

[127] The Supreme Court of the United States earlier had held that takings claims should not be litigated until a property owner has invoked such administrative processes, unless to do so would be futile. Williamson County Reg'l Planning Comm'n v. Hamilton Bank, 473 U.S. 172 (1985). The Council's amended answer to "clarify" the remedies available if the trial court found a taking may have been a clumsy attempt to raise a *Williamson County* objection. *See supra* text accompanying note 60.

a test of the general principle whether the Council should pay compensation for the costs imposed by the BMA, rather than to focus on the particular costs or benefits of prohibiting development on the *Lucas* lots in particular.

After the trial, the 1990 amendments introduced what was clearly a special permit procedure. There were only twelve lots in South Carolina—the two Lucas lots and ten others—that were undeveloped and completely barred from development by the BMA. The owners of the other ten lots used the 1990 amendments to seek special permits, and each received a permit.[128] Only Lucas declined to seek the permit. Typically, courts refuse to allow takings litigation to proceed until the property owner has availed himself of the available variance or special permit procedures. Those "ripeness" rules ensure that a regulator has had an opportunity to consider the characteristics of a particular piece of land and determine the appropriateness of standing firm on a policy under the circumstances.[129] While the courts could have interrupted Lucas' lawsuit once the special permit procedures were adopted in 1990, both the South Carolina Supreme Court[130] and the U.S. Supreme Court declined to do so.[131] Accordingly, in the South Carolina and United States Supreme Courts, the Council had to defend the general principle that it should not have to compensate property owners for diminutions in value caused by the Beachfront Management Act, rather than deciding whether the value of preventing construction on Lucas' lot was cost-efficient.[132]

The net costs or benefits of prohibiting new development—and the rebuilding of destroyed structures that was the state's primary concern—undoubtedly are quite different than the net cost or benefit of prohibiting Lucas alone from building. The Council therefore might rationally have taken a different position on the efficiency of building on the two Lucas lots once the litigation was concluded than it took during

---

[128] Dwight Merriam, *Reengineering Regulation to Avoid Takings*, 33 Urb. Law. 1, 17–18 (2001).

[129] *See* Vicki Been, *The Finality Requirement in Takings Litigation after* Palazzolo, *in* Taking Sides on Takings Issues (Thomas E. Roberts ed. 2002).

[130] *See* Respondent's Brief on the Merits at 5, Lucas, 505 U.S. 1003.

[131] 505 U.S., at 1011.

[132] Lucas' litigation strategy contributed to the inattention to the specifics of his particular lots. Lucas claimed at trial (and before the South Carolina Supreme Court) that regardless of the costs his development imposed upon the public, because the regulations "destroyed all value" in his lots, he was entitled to compensation for the lots. At trial, he objected to the introduction of any evidence about the particular harms that would be caused if he developed the property. The trial court allowed the Council to introduce some such evidence, on the condition that it "won't take too long." In his order, the trial court ignored all such evidence.

litigation testing the broader principle of its right to regulate coastal development without paying compensation to those affected by the regulation.

Second, the cost/benefit calculation had changed since the Council first began litigating with Lucas. Under the 1990 Amendments, Lucas' neighbors, and beachfront owners in general, are able to build, or rebuild, under a much broader range of circumstances than they could under the BMA. The benefits of prohibiting development on just the two Lucas lots therefore had decreased markedly. Once Lucas' neighbors were given the right to rebuild in the event of destruction like that occasioned by Hurricane Hugo, it made much less sense to insist that Lucas never build. The Council's "about-face" on Lucas' lots accordingly may have been a rational response to the State's change in policy from the BMA's absolute prohibition on building or rebuilding in the dead zone to the 1990 Amendments' strategy of allowing property owners to build but preventing them from interfering with the natural forces of erosion.

Third, the Council's decision to buy the lots from Lucas, then resell them for development, may have resulted from Lucas' unwillingness to accept the special permit on the terms specified by the 1990 Amendments, or from his demands for compensation in addition to the special permits. Lucas regarded the special permits as a "real landmine," and objected to the fact that the permit would limit the square footage of the house that could be built and would require him to agree to remove the structure if the Council ordered it removed. He viewed the latter requirement as a "set[] up," complaining that "if they [the 'bureaucrats at the . . . Council'] found in their vast expert wisdom, that you were in the way of reverse progress (erosion or mother nature, as the case may be), then off with your home."[133] Rather than litigate their right to insist upon those provisions, the Council rationally may have decided to save the litigation costs by buying Lucas out and selling to someone who wasn't intent on fighting over whether the permits could be conditioned. Similarly, if the Council considered Lucas' demands for compensation for the "temporary taking" before the permits were granted to be too high, it might rationally have concluded that it was cheaper to buy the lots and resell them than to give Lucas the special permits as well as compensation for the temporary taking.

Finally, the Council's behavior may reflect the irrationality sometimes exhibited by survivors of litigation battles. Studies show that the litigants in nuisance actions sometimes act in such counter-productive ways, refusing to trade the entitlement the court awarded to the victor, even where such a trade would promote a more efficient result, for

---

[133] Green Machine, *supra* note 1, at 148–49.

example, because of hostility fostered by the litigation.[134] Similarly, personal animosities and other "economically irrational" preferences may have influenced the Council's judgment about what to do with the lots in the aftermath of the U.S. Supreme Court's decision.[135]

Disciplining Government Decision–Makers

The reasons just given to doubt the role that cost-internalization played in the General Assembly's and Council's decisions to back away from the dead zone retreat policy and to allow development on the *Lucas* lots do not disprove the broader argument that a compensation mandate may discipline government decision-makers. But the difficulty of establishing precisely what role the compensation mandate played in the General Assembly's or Council's deliberations illustrate the central problem with that broader argument: our understanding of how political actors respond to different incentives or disincentives in determining whether to enact legislation or regulation currently is simply too inadequate to support the cost-internalization justification for a compensation mandate.

The argument that governments will enact more efficient regulation if they are faced with a compensation mandate implicitly assumes that government decision-makers act like the rational profit-maximizing firms envisioned in property, tort and contract law.[136] But that assumption is unlikely to be accurate in the context of government. Various political scientists and economists offer differing accounts of what governments (or the politicians and bureaucrats that people the government) do seek to maximize, but those scholars do not view governments as directly motivated by a desire to make "profits."[137] A government decision-maker accordingly may pay little attention to a compensation award unless having to pay compensation to property owners makes it harder for the decision-maker to achieve whatever he or she is trying to maximize.

---

[134] *See* Ward Farnsworth, *Do Parties in Nuisance Cases Bargain After Judgment? A Glimpse Inside the Cathedral*, 66 U. Chi. L. Rev. 373 (1999).

[135] *See, e.g.,* Peter H. Huang, *Reasons within Passions: Emotions and Intentions in Property Rights Bargaining*, 79 Or. L. Rev. 435 (2000).

[136] Several important legal theories in corporate law, such as the theory of state competition for corporate charters, also have assumed that governments act like firms. There too, the assumption is coming under sharp challenge. *See, e.g.,* Marcel Kahan & Ehud Kamar, *The Myth of State Competition in Corporate Law*, 55 Stan. L. Rev. 679 (2002).

[137] *See, e.g.,* Ian Ayres & John Braithwaite, Responsive Regulation (1992); Daniel A. Farber & Philip P. Frickey, Law and Public Choice (1992); Sam Peltzman, *Towards a More General Theory of Regulation,* 19 J.L. & Econ. 211, 213–14 (1976).

For those elected members of a state legislature who are most interested in trying to maximize their chances of reelection, for example, the threat of having to pay compensation may matter only if that threat makes a significant number of voters decide to oppose the legislator's re-election. But voters, who would each bear only a few dollars of the cost of the award, may pay no attention to the award, or may blame it on the courts, rather than on the legislator who voted for the program held to be a taking. Or, voters concerned about the compensation award may be outnumbered by voters concerned about the costs building too close to the beach may impose upon them as taxpayers.[138]

Predicting the effect compensation requirements will have on governments deciding whether to regulate in situations such as that posed in *Lucas* accordingly requires "a model of government decisionmaking that explains how the social costs and benefits of government activity are systematically translated into private, political costs and benefits for government decisionmakers, and what role, if any mandating ... [compensation] plays in this process."[139] Absent a consensus about such a model—which does not exist—we can not be certain whether a compensation requirement will result in too little, too much, or just the right (efficient) level of regulation. A compensation requirement might produce better government decision-making and more efficient regulation, but it just as well might lead governments to be too timid to adopt measures that will maximize social welfare.

Indeed, at least two special features of the economics and politics of beachfront development suggest that if a compensation requirement disciplines government decision-makers at all, it is likely to result in too little, rather than too much, regulation of beachfront development.[140]

---

[138] Just as it is difficult to evaluate the effect that the compensation requirement had on the General Assembly because of uncertainty about what legislators seek to maximize, and how a compensation requirement influences their ability to reach those goals, to fully understand the role that the compensation requirement played in the Council's decisions would require agreement upon what motivates the Council (and its employees). It might be, for example, that the political appointees and career civil servants at the Council would be concerned about having to pay compensation to property owners like Lucas only if they thought that doing so would threaten their prospects for career advancement, or leave them with fewer resources for the programs they care most about. But neither of those concerns would necessarily be realized: losing the litigation in *Lucas* might not be "blamed" upon the Council or its individual members or staff; and some or all of the compensation required by *Lucas* might come (as it eventually did) from a special appropriation of the General Assembly, rather than from the Council's budget.

[139] Daryl J. Levinson, *Making Government Pay: Markets, Politics, and the Allocation of Constitutional Costs,* 67 U. Chi. L. Rev. 345, 357 (2000).

[140] The controversy over the 1988 Act produced "one of the hottest and longest debates of the [legislative] session." Bobby Bryant, *Some of Year's Legislation Flared While Other Bills Fizzled,* The State (Columbia, S.C.), June 5, 1988, at 12A. *See also,* Farrington, *supra*

The Political Power of Beachfront Property Owners

Public choice theory—the application of economic theory to the study of politics—suggests that groups that are relatively small in number, homogenous in their interests, with high stakes in the outcome, and with pre-existing networks or other organizational advantages, are better able to influence legislators or other decision-makers than are diffuse, heterogenous, difficult-to organize groups of people who have relatively little at stake individually.[141] Beachfront owners in South Carolina (and elsewhere) are a relatively small group—only a few thousand at most, for example, were impacted by the BMA's retreat policy.[142] They all have an interest in being able to develop their lots so as to maximize their property values at the lowest possible personal risk. They each have hundreds of thousands of dollars at stake in the battle. They are thus likely to have, and exercise, more political power than the average taxpayer,[143] whose share of the benefits that might be realized by preventing unwise coastal development would be relatively small.

The history of both beachfront development and disaster relief policies confirms what political theory predicts: beachfront owners repeatedly score considerable victories in federal, state and local political battles over the regulation of development on the coast.[144] The result has

note 41 (describing how "heated" public hearings over the legislation became as some beachfront property owners lamented the prospect of the forced retreat from the beach and others decried the "New Jerseyization" of the South Carolina coast).

[141] *See, e.g.,* Anthony Downs, An Economic Theory of Democracy (1957); Daniel A. Farber & Philip P. Frickey, Law and Public Choice: A Critical Introduction 1 (1991); Russell Hardin, Collective Action (1982); Mancur Olsen, The Logic of Collective Action (2d ed. 1971).

[142] Before Hurricane Hugo hit, the Coastal Council estimated that 2059 structures stood seaward of the setback line, including 1239 that stood within the 20 foot dead zone. It is not clear how many of those property owners suffered damage by Hugo and therefore would have been part of the group demanding the 1990 Amendments. Bruce Smith, *2059 Beach Structures Defy Setback,* The State (Columbia, S.C.), Sept. 29, 1988, at 1C.

[143] Indeed, Lucas' description of himself, while perhaps self-aggrandizing, certainly doesn't portray a hapless victim of South Carolina politics. His connections to the political and business elite of South Carolina, his considerable success in beachfront development on a very large scale, and his conscious decision to move out of real estate development when the risks of successes by anti-development forces were increasing beyond his comfort level, all evidence considerable political savvy and access to the political process. His description of his efforts to lobby Congress about the federal 1986 Tax Reform Act, including his conversations about the bill with his congressmen and his old friend Lee Atwater, one of the most important political strategists of the 1980s, make it hard to imagine that he would have had much trouble bringing his concerns about the BMA to the attention of the South Carolina General Assembly, had he chosen to do so.

[144] *See, e.g.,* Rutherford H. Platt, Disasters and Democracy 165–286 (1999); David Salvesen and David R. Godschalk, Development on Coastal Barriers: Does the Coastal

been a "hesitation at all levels of government to enforce effective land use controls" on new development or redevelopment on eroding coasts.[145]

Forcing Internalization of Costs Alone?

The cost-internalization justification for a compensation requirement posits that government regulators will be prone to "excessive enthusiasm" about the benefits of the regulations they are considering, and must have the costs of the regulation brought forcefully to their attention so that they will accurately calculate whether the regulation is worthwhile. Yet the regulators at issue in *Lucas* (and the South Carolina voters that choose whether to re-elect them) do not stand to realize all, or even many, of the benefits of preventing coastal erosion. A compensation mandate to force the internalization of costs, when no mechanism is required—or available—for such decision-makers to internalize the benefits, is unlikely to cause legislators or regulators to accurately assess the net social benefits or costs of beachfront management.

Preventing development that exacerbates coastal erosion, or increases the damage caused by hurricanes or other coastal hazards, results in many benefits. Coastal wetlands act to buffer storms. They provide habitat and serve as breeding grounds for thousands of species of fish and birds. They improve water quality by filtering pollutants.[146] Such benefits, however, are extraordinarily difficult to quantify.[147] Further, the value of those benefits is not limited to South Carolina's voters, but accrue to the nation as a whole (and perhaps to other nations as well). To the extent that a compensation mandate influences government decision-making at all, then, forcing South Carolina to bear all the costs of preserving its coast, when the benefits of preservation are so hard to measure and are distributed so broadly, is unlikely to result in the efficient regulation. If anything, it is likely to cause South Carolina to under-regulate, to allow *more* beachfront development than would maximize social welfare.

Barrier Resources Act Make a Difference? 6–7 (2002), *available at* www.coastalli-ance.org/cbra/cbrarep2.pdf (reviewing battles over the designation of areas in which the federal government is forbidden from subsidizing development on coastal barrier islands); Marc R. Poirier, Takings and Natural Hazards Policy: Public Choice on the Beachfront, 46 Rutgers L. Rev. 243, 271–84 (1993) (reviewing the outcome of controversy over proposals to rebuild following damage from a December 1992 nor'easter in New Jersey and New York).

[145] Platt, *supra* note 144, at 99, 102. *See also* David Godschalk, et al., Natural Hazard Mitigation (1999); Dennis S. Mileti, Disasters by Design (1999) for critiques of the regulation of beachfront development.

[146] *See* Salvesen and Godschalk, *supra* note 144; Ross B. Plyler, Note, *Protecting South Carolina's Isolated Wetlands in the Wake of* Solid Waste Agency, 53 S.C. L. Rev. 757 (2002).

[147] *See, e.g.,* Oliver A. Houck, *Land Loss in Coastal Louisiana: Causes, Consequences, and Remedies*, 58 Tul. L. Rev. 3, 92 (1983).

The savings realized by ending subsidies to coastal property owners are perhaps the easiest benefits to measure, so they serve as a vivid illustration of the effects the inability to internalize the benefits of a measure could have on state regulators. Federal, state, and local governments allow coastal property owners to impose a significant part of the risk of erosion and storm damage on others by making taxpayers and less risky properties in the insurance pool subsidize such losses.[148] The subsidies take four main forms. First, federal, state, and local governments invest heavily in infrastructure such as roads, drinking water supply and wastewater treatment facilities that make it possible for developers to build in coastal areas. Studies of the impact of the Coastal Barriers Resources Act (CBRA) provide the best estimates of how much those subsidies are worth. The CBRA, passed by Congress in 1982, prohibits the federal government from subsidizing the development of some 1,326,000 acres of designated coastal barrier islands.[149] As then-President Reagan noted in signing the bill into law, the CBRA "simply adopts the sensible approach that risk associated with new private development in these sensitive areas should be borne by the private sector, not underwritten by the American taxpayer."[150]

In reauthorizing the CBRA in 2000, Congress directed the U.S. Fish and Wildlife Service (FWS) to evaluate how much money the CBRA has saved taxpayers by restricting Federal spending for roads, wastewater systems, potable water supply, and disaster relief. The FWS study revealed that a conservative estimate of the costs the federal government incurs for development on barrier islands includes $6,022 per acre for roads, $17,189 per acre for wastewater treatment facilities, and $6,270 per acre for water supply.[151] Using the FWS estimates, federal subsidies

---

[148] U.S. Fish and Wildlife Service, The Coastal Barrier Resources Act: Harnessing the Power of Market Forces to Conserve America's Coasts and Save Taxpayers' Money 2 (2002), available at http://www.fws.gov/cep/TaxpayerSavingsFromCBRA.pdf.

[149] Pub. L. No. 97–348, 96 Stat. 1653 (1982), as amended by Coastal Barrier Improvement Act of 1990, Pub. L. No. 101–591, 104 Stat. 2931. For discussions of the CBRA, *see* Elise Jones, *The Coastal Barrier Resources Act: A Common Sense Approach to Coastal Management*, 21 Envtl. L. 1015 (1991); Robert R. Kuehn, *The Coastal Barrier Resources Act and the Expenditures Limitation Approach to Natural Resources Conservation: Wave of the Future or Island Unto Itself*, 11 Ecology L. Q. 583 (1984).

[150] 18 Weekly Comp. Of Pres. Doc. 1340, 1341 (Oct. 18, 1982).

[151] U.S. Fish and Wildlife Service, *supra* note 148 at 12. The estimates are in 1996 dollars. The FWS cautions that its estimates are conservative because it did not consider the geology of coastal barriers, which may increase infrastructure costs; it considered only on-site construction costs; it did not include the costs of connecting new infrastructure to existing infrastructure; and it did not include the costs for maintaining infrastructure. *Id.* at 25. It also does not include many forms of infrastructure, such as bridges and beach stabilization. *Id.* at 3, 27.

for the 1500 acre Isle of Palms Wild Dunes Development alone may have totaled some $45 million dollars.

Second, the federal, state and local governments spend billions to shore up eroding shorelines to protect homes and businesses that have been built in coastal areas. After Hurricane Hugo, for example, the government spent $65 million to rebuild the sand dunes that had been destroyed in South Carolina, in order to protect property owners from future flooding during high tides.[152]

Third, the federal government's National Flood Insurance Program (NFIP) insures private property owners against losses. NFIP provides insurance that private insurers generally would not offer, at least at the premiums NFIP charges, and accordingly allows development in flood prone areas that would otherwise be too risky to finance.[153] NFIP rates are thought to be only ten to forty percent of the rates private insurers would charge.[154] Although NFIP rates are required by law to be actuarily

---

Other estimates of the federal subsidies for infrastructure provided to barrier islands are even higher. A 1981 study, for example, found that the federal government was spending an average of $53,000 in 1980 dollars per developed acre to supply infrastructure to coastal barrier islands. *See* Jones, *supra* note 149 (citing Barrier Islands: Hearings Before Subcomms. On Fisheries and Wildlife Conservation and the Environment and on Oceanography of the House Comm. on Merchant Marine and Fisheries, 97th Cong., 1st & 2nd Sess., 54,139 (1981 and 1982) and Scheagger & Roland, Inc., Barrier Island Development Near Four National Seashores (April 1981), reprinted in Barrier Islands: Hearings, at 55–125).

[152] Robert Dvorchak, *Storm Brews Over Beachfront Building; Environmentalists Say Overdevelopment Threatens Shores, Public Access*, Wash. Post,., Oct. 14, 1989 at F31.

[153] For discussions of the NFIP, *see, e.g.,*Platt, *supra* note 144, at 28–33; Jones, *supra* note149, at 1028–30; Oliver Houck, *Rising Water: The National Flood Insurance Program and Louisiana*, 65 Tul. L. Rev. 61 (1985); Rutherford H. Platt, *Congress and the Coast*, Env't, July-Aug. 1985, at 12; Poirier, *supra* note 144, at 299; Saul J. Singer, *Flooding the Fifth Amendment: The National Flood Insurance Program and the "Takings" Clause*, 17 B.C. Envtl. Aff. L. Rev. 337 (1990). *See also* National Flood Insurance Program: Hearings Before the Subcomm. On Policy Research and Insurance of the House Comm. On Banking, Finance and Urban Affairs, 101st Cong., 1st Sess. (1989).

[154] *See, e.g.,* FWS, *supra* note 148, at 28 ("Through NFIP, an owner with a single family home in ... [the highest risk zone] can acquire $250,000 worth of structural coverage, and another $100,000 worth of coverage for furniture and other belongings, for about $1,000 to $1,500 per year. Private-market premiums dwarf NFIP.s rates; anecdotal evidence suggests yearly premiums through a bank such as Lloyd's of London range anywhere from $2,500 to $7,500. Moreover, unlike NFIP, private-market insurance is often encumbered by high deductibles and can be canceled with little warning. Private market flood insurance is far more costly and insecure, and some coastal barriers are so risky that insurance companies will not offer flood insurance for any price."); Salvesen and Godschalk, *supra* note 144, at 41 (private flood insurance "for a $200,000 beachfront home would cost from $2,500 to $10,000 per year, depending on factors such as the amount of the deductible and flood risk. Insuring the same house through the National Flood Insurance Program would cost approximately $500 per year.").

sound, the program "does not charge a premium sufficient to cover its multiyear risk exposure" and has incurred net losses over its history of more than $500 million.[155]

Some of that shortfall is due to "repetitive loss" properties—those that have received payments of $1000 or more on more than one occasion. Although repetitive loss properties represent only two percent of all properties insured by the NFIP, they claimed 40 percent of all payments.[156] The Isle of Palms is one of the worst offenders—even though its permanent population is less than 5000 people, it is one of the "Top 200 Repetitive Loss Communities Ranked By Payments."[157] The problem of repetitive loss properties has prompted calls for reform such as the frankly titled "Two Floods and You Are out of the Taxpayers Pocket Act,"[158] but residents of the Isle of Palms and other barrier islands continue to be covered,[159] and to file repeated claims for damage made almost inevitable by their location.

David Lucas himself highlighted the role that the NFIP played in enabling development on the Isle of Palm Beach. After an interview with Lucas, a Barron's editorial noted:

> Lucas believes it's safe and sensible to build on his section of the Isle of Palms. In Hurricane Hugo, houses on either side of his lots sustained only "superficial" damage. They were newer houses built to hurricane code; only older houses on the island suffered anything close to total destruction, he claims.
>
> But don't take away his federal flood insurance, or this champion of property rights and liberty will get upset—not merely because he collected $35,000–$40,000 from Uncle Sugar for Hurricane Hugo's damage to his current house on the Isle of Palms. Lucas also says flood insurance brought prosperity to his once-impoverished region. "The flood insurance program was the keystone," he asserts. "You have to look at what the program has accomplished: jobs, economic development. Because of the federal flood insurance program, we now have tourism and a healthy economy."[160]

---

[155] General Accounting Office, Flood Insurance: Challenges Facing the National Flood Insurance Program, Testimony Before the Subcomm. on Housing and Community Opportunity, Comm. on Financial Services, House of Representatives at 5 (2003).

[156] National Wildlife Federation, Higher Ground: Voluntary Property Buyouts in the Nation's Floodplains, A Common Ground Solution Serving People at Risk, Taxpayers and the Environment (1997).

[157] *Id.* at Table 3.II.

[158] H.R. 253, 108th Cong., 1st Session (2003).

[159] *See* GAO, *supra* note 155 , at p.11.

[160] Thomas G. Donlan, *Editorial Commentary: Liberty and Property——The Rights of Owners Don't Include a Federal Subsidy*, Barron's, June 1, 1992, at 10.

Finally, the government steps in after disasters to cleanup and rebuild and to provide relief for its victims. The cost to the federal government just of cleaning up after Hurricane Hugo in South Carolina alone was estimated to be $215 million. Although South Carolina was obligated to pay twenty five percent of the costs the federal government incurred in the clean-up, President George Bush waived that $50 million charge, thus requiring taxpayers across the country to further subsidize those people who had chosen to settle along South Carolina's hurricane-prone coast[161]. The cost to the federal government of rebuilding infrastructure destroyed by Hugo along the East Coast, as well as in the Virgin Islands and Puerto Rico, was almost $500 million.[162] Another $540 million in federal assistance was given to individuals to help them rebuild after Hugo; in South Carolina alone, 42,650 storm victims applied to FEMA for disaster assistance.[163]

Indeed, noting that both the hotel industry and the construction industry were quickly rebounding from Hurricane Hugo, one reporter pointed out that "in one of the disaster's ironies, many of [Charleston, South Carolina's] hotel rooms are occupied by an army of insurance claims adjusters, federal disaster assistance workers and clean-up volunteers, the agents of huge transfusions of insurance payments, federal aid and other outside assistance that is feeding a construction boom."[164] So great was the influx of money to rebuild that the South Carolina economy was predicted to have higher personal income growth in 1990 than the rest of the nation.[165] That local "boom" represents the savings that could accrue to the federal government, its taxpayers, and insured owners of properties developed in less risky areas if South Carolina were to limit storm damage by controlling high-risk oceanfront development.[166]

---

[161] Bill McAllister, *Bush Waives Hurricane Cleanup Costs; Tax Burden in Islands, South Carolina Eased*, Wash. Post, Nov. 23, 1989 at A13.

[162] Federal Emergency Management Agency, Hugo: Recollections of a Storm, *available at* http://www.fema.gov/regions/iv/1999/r4_44.shtm.

[163] *Id.*

[164] Rudolph A. Pyatt Jr., *Two Months Later, Hugo Still Packs a Punch; Despite Rebound in Tourism, Boom in Construction, Many Industries Face Long, Uncertain Return to Stability*, Wash. Post, Nov. 19, 1989 at H1.

[165] *Id.*

[166] The influx of federal funds to rebuild South Carolina also vividly illustrates the unfairness of a compensation requirement that requires South Carolina's taxpayers to pay for property value that their (and others') federal tax dollars created. While it is difficult to quantify exact amounts, at least some of the benefits of the infrastructure governments provide and the beach nourishment and rebuilding programs governments undertake, as well as the reductions in risk that disaster aid and government sponsored flood insurance

Of course, there is no way of knowing how much of the costs just enumerated would have been avoided had South Carolina's adopted its retreat policies earlier. Nor is it possible to predict with any accuracy how much damage from future storms, sea-level rise, and other natural forces might have been avoided had South Carolina held firm on the BMA's retreat policy and prevented Lucas from building, and his neighbors from rebuilding. But the savings undoubtedly would be far from trivial. As more and more people have moved to the coast, and as development on the coast has changed from modest summer cottages to developments like Wild Dunes, the economic impact of hurricanes and other natural disasters has risen dramatically over the past two decades.[167] At least some of that increase represents the costs of land use policies that fail to deter coastal development.

The problem, however, is that the benefits of avoiding those costs will accrue to taxpayers and others across the nation who have no vote in South Carolina. Asking South Carolina's taxpayers to bear all the costs of protecting against the risks and harms of coastal development, while so many of the benefits of that protection accrue elsewhere is at least as likely to result in inefficiently low levels of coastal protection than it is to force efficient decision-making. *Lucas* accordingly persuasively illustrates the conservative one-sidedness of a compensation-to-force-*cost*-internalization rule.

Conclusion

Despite the claims of adherents of the cost-internalization justification for a compensation mandate, *Lucas* and its aftermath do not prove that a compensation requirement will encourage more efficient regulation. In the case of Lucas himself, it is far from clear that the compensa-

---

offer, are capitalized into the value of beachfront properties. The value government actions create in private property is normally thought of as a "giving," and although governments may recoup some of the value of givings through tax policies, no effort is made to systematically recoup givings. Accordingly, when governments are required to compensate property owners for the decrease in value that coastal protections may cause, they may in effect have to buy back value that the government (or other levels of government) itself created. The classic argument that government should be able to seek recompense for its "givings," if it must pay compensation for "takings," is Windfalls for Wipeouts (Donald Hagman & Dean Misczynski eds., 1978). For more recent explorations of the general argument, *see generally* Bell and Parchomovsky, *supra* note 4; Eric Kades, *Windfalls*, 108 Yale L.J. 1489 (1999); Levinson, *supra* note 139 , at 418. For an insightful examination of the problem of givings in the context of coastal land, *see* Daniel D. Barnhizer, *Givings Recapture: Funding Public Acquisition of Private Property Interests on the Coasts*, 27 Harv. Envtl. L. Rev. 295 (2003).

[167] *See, e.g.,,* Platt, *supra* note 144, at 11–46, chronicling the rise in various federal disaster relief payments.

tion mandate was responsible for the State's decision to allow more development on the *Lucas* lots in particular or on the South Carolina coast in general. Nor is it clear that the state's decision to allow more coastal development was more efficient—produced greater social welfare—than its earlier strict retreat policy. More generally, the real story of "Lucas v. The Green Machine" shows the difficulty of predicting how, if at all, a compensation mandate will influence government decision-makers, given our lack of understanding about how elected and appointed officials make decisions. To the extent that a compensation mandate does discipline government decision-makers, the *Lucas* saga reveals that a blunt cost-internalization rule that ignores the political power of certain property owners and focuses only on the costs and not on the benefits of government regulation is more likely to lead governments to allow more development than is socially optimal than to encourage efficiency.

*

10

Andrew P. Morriss

Cattle vs. Retirees: Sun City and the Battle of *Spur Industries v. Del E. Webb Development Co.*

The Arizona Supreme Court's March 1972 decision in *Spur Industries v. Del E. Webb Development Co*,[1] surprised many. *Spur Industries* seemed to be a routine nuisance case over claims that a cattle feedlot[2] created a nuisance for surrounding residential property owners. No one

---

[1] 108 Ariz. 178, 494 P.2d 700 (Ariz. 1972).

[2] For readers unfamiliar with feedlots, and if you've encountered one you'd know it, here is the official definition (from the U.S. Environmental Protection Agency). A feedlot is "one of the following:

"1. A high concentration of animals held in a small area for periods of time in conjunction with one of the following purposes:

    a.   production of meat

    b.   production of milk

    c.   production of eggs

    d.   production of breeding stock

    e.   stabling of horses

2.   The transportation of feeds to the animals for consumption.

3.   By virtue of the confinement of animals or poultry, the land or area will neither sustain vegetation nor be available for crop or forage production."

Environmental Protection Agency, Office of Air and Water Programs, Effluent Guidelines Division, Development Document for Effluent Limitations Guidelines and New Source Performance Standards for the Feedlots Point Source Category (1974) at 8.

As this is not a law review article, I have reduced the usual practice of citing sources for every sentence and substituted a footnote for each section listing the sources used therein. Direct quotes and statistics are cited individually.

would have been surprised if the court had upheld the trial court and held that the feedlot was a public nuisance and ordered it to close, as the 20,000 to 30,000 cattle on the lot were producing over a million pounds of wet manure per day, attracting flies and producing unpleasant odors.[3] The court could have also, using the time-honored doctrine of "coming to the nuisance,"[4] held for the feedlot on the ground that it predated the residential development whose residents were offended by the flies and odors. The court might even have declined to enjoin the feedlot's operations but ordered it to pay damages to the property owners, consistent with the landmark case of *Boomer v. Atlantic Cement Co.*,[5] without doing anything too unusual. What the court did instead, however, was to find that there was a public nuisance, enjoin the feedlot from continuing operations, and shift the cost of relocating the feedlot's operations to the real estate developer who had sold the complaining homeowners their properties.

With this clever remedy, a state court not known for its innovative jurisprudence created a landmark and somewhat unique nuisance case that is still featured in many property casebooks over thirty years later.[6] Perhaps most astonishingly, as Professors Jesse Dukeminier and James Krier later observed, the court invented this new, fourth approach to nuisances at the same time as Yale Law School Professor Guido Calabresi and attorney A. Douglas Melamed worked out a similar rule as part of their landmark article *Property Rules, Liability Rules, and Inalienability: One View of the Cathedral.*[7] Considering that that article is still recognized as one of the most important contributions of law and economics scholarship,[8] the Arizona court did well to invent the rule on its own. As

---

[3] *Spur*, 108 Ariz. at 183, 494 P.2d at 705.

[4] "Coming to the nuisance" is a defense available where the complaining property owner has moved near the offending property. Thus urban residents who move close to a farm could be barred by the "coming to the nuisance" defense from complaining about the neighboring farm's crowing roosters.

[5] 26 N.Y.2d 219, 309 N.Y.S.2d 312, 257 N.E. 870 (1970).

[6] *See, e.g.,* James A. Casner, et al., Cases and Texts on Property (4th ed. 2000) at 910–917 (reprinting opinion); Jesse Dukeminier & James E. Krier, Property (4th ed. 1998) at 765–776, 1146–1147 (reprinting opinion); John E. Cribbet, et al., Property: Cases and Materials (8th ed. 2002) at 621–623 (reprinting opinion); Edward H. Rabin, et al., Fundamentals of Modern Property Law (4th ed. 2000) at 566–579 (reprinting opinion).

[7] Guido Calabresi & A. Douglas Melamed, Property Rules, Liability Rules, and Inalienability: One View of the Cathedral, 85 Harv. L. Rev. 1089 (1972). *See* Dukeminier & Krier, *supra* note 6, at 774–775 (discussing similarities between *Spur* and Calabresi and Melamed's analysis).

[8] Andrew P. Morriss, John C. Moorhouse and Robert Whaples, *Law & Economics and Tort Law: A Survey of Scholarly Opinion* 62 Albany Law Review 667 (1998) (noting that

Dukeminier and Krier noted, the court invented the rule "out of the logic of necessity" while Calabresi and Melamed created it "as the logical product of a modeling exercise."[9] Not bad work for an obscure state supreme court.

This chapter describes the background to this landmark decision. The story illustrates how the common law process worked to create a remedy suited to the facts without the theorizing Calabresi and Melamed brought to the same topic later that year. Necessity managed to produce from an undistinguished[10] court a rule that shortly thereafter acquired an impressive academic pedigree. Common law reasoning, often scorned as less worthy than comprehensive statutory "reforms," adapted the law to produce an outcome that not only makes economic sense but strikes many as a just result. Reading *Spur* is a good way to learn how common law reasoning works, and how it differs from theoretical approaches such as Calabresi and Melamed's even when it reaches similar results.

Reading *Spur* together with the history of the cattle feeding industry and suburban development also illustrates an important aspect of nuisance law. The dispute between the feedlot and the housing developer was a classic case of a conflict created by changes in land use. The question of whose land use had to accommodate whose—the same question in some respects as in *Sturgis v. Bridgman* as discussed in Chapter 1—is at the heart of all the means of resolving such conflicts. Zoning, private agreements such as real covenants, and nuisance law all allocate property rights among competing uses. Zoning does so by granting to governmental bodies the power to control development; covenants settle the matter by contract; and nuisance relies on the courts.

By looking at how the conflict arose, one can evaluate how well the courts did in resolving the dispute. This in turn could be useful in determining when nuisance law is a reasonable means of handling such conflicts. The dispute between Spur Industries and the Del E. Webb Development Co. was a clash between two changing sectors of Arizona's economy. On the one hand was Arizona's post-World War II boom in

---

Calabresi and Melamed's article is one of the top two articles law and economics scholars think law students should read.).

[9] Dukeminier & Krier, *supra* note 6, at 774.

[10] The court was "undistinguished" in that its members were neither nationally recognized leaders in the law (such as California Justice Roger Traynor) nor marked by careers that resulted in attention outside the Arizona bar. For example, then-Vice Chief Justice (and later Chief) James Cameron's main accomplishment, as given in his obituary on the court's web page, was his contribution to judicial administration. See *Retired Arizona Supreme Court Chief Justice James D. Cameron Dies*, May 28, 2003, http://www.supreme.state.az.us/media/archive/CameronObit.htm (last viewed 10/17/2003).

housing. Fueled by federal defense spending and New Deal financing, Arizona underwent a rapid transformation from an extractive, resource based economy to a high tech, intensely urban economy following the war, with the "new" Arizona growing outward from the booming urban centers of Phoenix and Tucson. Riding high on the boom was Delbert "Del" E. Webb, a Horatio Alger-style success story who built himself from a virtually penniless typhoid sufferer to a construction magnate, largely through federally funded projects and casino construction in Las Vegas. On the other side was the cattle feeding industry, part of the traditional resource-based economy of the state but also transformed in the post-war era from small scale feedlots into enormous operations processing tens of thousands of cattle to satisfy the prosperous nation's growing demand for beef. How the Arizona courts resolved the problems created by the intersection of these social and economic changes is a good example of the advantages and disadvantages of relying on courts to resolve such disputes.

Arizona's growth[11]

The popular image of Arizona is of the Grand Canyon and saguaro cactus. The reality is that since World War II it has become an intensely urban state. Arizona's transformation was rapid, with the state's rate of growth rapid relative to the country as a whole throughout the twentieth century. Population expanded by more than four times between 1900 and 1940, to more than half a million.[12] Despite its cowboy image and reputation as a bastion of western individualism and conservative politics, Arizona's growth was largely the product of federal spending programs. Those programs also made Del Webb a success by providing the contracts that helped his firm grow and by transforming the building industry.

Promoters have long touted Arizona's climate. For example, Patrick Hamilton's *Resources of Arizona*, published in San Francisco in 1883, proclaimed: "Here the climate is almost perpetual spring, and even in the dryest [sic] season the feed never fails, and the owner can sit under the shade of his comfortable hacienda and see his herds thrive and increase winter and summer." As a later author noted, "Suddenly desolate, cactus-ridden Arizona was being touted in the same Biblical

---

[11] This section draws from William Stuart Collins, *The New Deal in Arizona* (unpublished Ph.D. dissertation, Arizona State University, May 1999); Timothy D. Hogan, *Arizona Population Trends*, in Arizona's Changing Economy: Trends and Prospects (Bernard Ronan ed.1986); Bradford Luckingham, Phoenix: The History of A Southwestern Metropolis (1989); Thomas E. Sheridan, Arizona: A History (1995); and Charles Ynfante, The Transformation of Arizona into a Modern State (2002).

[12] Hogan, *supra* note 11, at 1.

terms of abundance formerly reserved for California."[13] The promotions worked, at least in attracting cattle. By 1917, over 1,434,000 head of cattle roamed Arizona.[14] Two bars to human population growth remained: too little water and too much heat. Both were solved in the twentieth century.

Water was the most immediate problem. During the nineteenth century there had been enough available surface water to satisfy the Phoenix area's (the Salt River Valley's) needs in only one out of every three years.[15] The lack of water led an early government report to label the area valueless, concluding that "[a]fter entering it, there is nothing to do but leave."[16] Water projects changed that and a boom followed, funded with the new federal reclamation funds flowing out of Washington, DC. The Salt River Project, the first federal water project under the reclamation act of 1902, and the Roosevelt Dam, completed in 1911, made the massive twentieth century population growth possible by stabilizing and increasing the water supply. Since the water projects limited the amount of water an individual landowner could receive, rather than the total amount of water available to a particular acreage, the water projects also created an incentive to subdivide, which would produce increased water allotments by expanding the number of landowners. Citrus and cotton also became important crops, now that water was available. The availability of water allowed Arizona to diversify its economy but, as the state entered World War II its economy was still primarily a resource-based, extractive one.

Solving the water problem cleared the way for new forms of economic development. One of the first was an expansion of the tourist industry in the 1920s. Even before the water projects had been completed, "[f]ollowing the arrival of the railroad, doctors around the country started sending patients to the urban Southwest for the winter. Phoenix became an 'ideal spot' for the health seeker and the seasonal visitor."[17] As a result, "Phoenix became a haven for health seekers as well as a prime location for tourist resorts; it became known for its hospitals as

---

13 Sheridan, *supra* note 11, at 131–132.

14 Collins, *supra* note 11, at 209.

15 Metro Arizona (Charles Sargent, ed., 1988). at 56. People immediately began building canals to bring water to the area, and one, "the English scholar-adventurer-inebriate, 'Lord' Darrel Duppa, gave Phoenix its name. "Commenting upon the ancient ruins and canals in the Salt River Valley, he said, 'A city will rise phoenix-like, new and more beautiful, from these ashes of the past.' " Silver Anniversary Jubilee: A History of Sun City, Arizona (1984) at 1.

16 Silver Anniversary, *supra* note 15, at 3.

17 Luckingham, *supra* note 11, at 3.

well as its hotels.''[18] Although the summer climate remained undesirably hot, winter visits grew and brought with them more permanent residents to service the visitors' needs. With the water problems addressed, Phoenix and Arizona grew rapidly, with Phoenix becoming the leading city in Arizona and the second largest urban center in the Southwest by 1930.[19]

Arizona was primed for a boom by the 1930s; the New Deal and war spending ignited the fuse and transformed the state from an extractive resource and agricultural economy into a high tech industrial economy. In part, Arizona was simply in the right place at the right time. Cheap land, plentiful transportation links, and good weather helped draw the high tech aviation industry to the state. Moreover, as war loomed, a change in military policy in the late 1930s and 1940s dispersed military facilities and industry into interior locations, a policy that benefited the interior West generally and Arizona in particular. To take but one example, the Goodyear aviation facility outside Phoenix in rural Maricopa County employed 7,500 people at its peak, making it the largest employer in Salt River Valley.[20] The boom was also fueled by the active support and subsidies Arizona business and political leaders provided for federal facilities. During the war, for example, Phoenix purchased a 1,440 acre tract for $40,000 and then leased it for $1 per year to the military for Luke Air Base.[21] The deal was a good one for the city: "Local boosters celebrated for good reason; one of them noted 'Base development will bring to the Valley an estimated income of $3,500,000 per year, in addition to the $1,500,000 initial cost of establishing the field. This seems good business in anybody's language.' ''[22] It was good business for Del Webb as well, as his firm built the base.

The war boom brought new residents and the state's population soared, growing by more than fifty percent from 1940 to 1950, outpacing the region (40.9%) and country as a whole (14.5%).[23] The newcomers concentrated in Phoenix and Tucson, producing "an urban explosion that rearranged the political and economic landscape of the state. In 1940, about half of Arizona's population lived in Phoenix and Tucson. Ten years later, two-thirds did, a direct consequence of federal military

---

[18] Luckingham, *supra* note 11, at 3.

[19] Luckingham, *supra* note 11, at 8.

[20] Sheridan, *supra* note 11, at 272.

[21] Ynfante, *supra* note 11, at 66.

[22] Luckingham, *supra* note 11, at 137. *See also* Sheridan, *supra* note 11, at 272 (base "generated an estimated $3.5 million a year for local businesses.").

[23] Hogan, *supra* note 11, at Table 2, at 14.

policy."[24] As a result of war-induced growth, Phoenix and Tucson grew "[f]rom small southwestern cities with populations of 64,000 and 36,000 respectively in 1940, ... to rank among the major urban areas in the United States."[25]

The changes were not limited to increased population, however. The New Deal in particular changed the way housing in Arizona was built.

> Until the 1940's, residential plans were marketed in the traditional manner—as individual lots on which the buyer had a custom-built house constructed, usually by a local carpenter. Most of the house plans came from published 'pattern books' in which there was a fairly wide range of architectural styles, as the inner districts of Phoenix and the larger outlying towns bear witness. A few came from the Sears catalog of homes.[26]

The New Deal brought a new means of financing construction, which in turn brought changes in how construction was done. Federal Housing Administration (FHA)

> standards encouraged the vertical integration of subdivision developers, architects, and builders into a single firm. Increasingly, the developer retained ownership of the lots until sold as finished homes. The developer then offered the buyer a choice from a limited selection of models, which he then constructed. These methods encouraged larger scale production which brought down the per-unit cost of housing.[27]

---

[24] Sheridan, *supra* note 11, at 273.

[25] Hogan, *supra* note 11, at 3. Arizona's growth was primarily through in-migration from other states, rather than international immigration or internal growth. Hogan, *supra* note 11, at 1 ("more than one-half of Arizona's population growth has resulted from net inmigration."). Even for the West generally, Arizona led the pack in migration. *Id.* ("net migration has played a more important role in the growth of Arizona than has been the case for the Western region as a whole.") Migration into Arizona has fueled its growth throughout the century and the state has consistently been a national leader in internal migration. The state ranked third in net migrations from 1935–40 and second for 1955–60 and 1965–1970. Metro Arizona, supra note 15, at 64. The pattern of migration to Arizona changed after the war. Previously, immigrants had been primarily Southerners; post-war they began to come primarily from other states in west, especially California, and the Midwest. Hogan, *supra* note 12, at 9.

[26] Metro Arizona, supra note 15, at 107. *See also* Collins, *supra* note 11, at 442–443 ("FHA used its subdivision standards to encourage more efficient production of housing to bring down price. Through the 1920s, the standard practice of subdivision development in Phoenix was for a developer to subdivide his land, perhaps providing a transportation incentive such as an expansion of the streetcar line, and to sell lots individually or in small groups. An individual might then hire a contractor to construct a house. Alternatively, a builder might buy a small number of lots and build houses on speculation.")

[27] Collins, *supra* note 11, at 442–443.

FHA rules influenced the character of development, creating incentives to use simplified mass construction methods, reducing the cost of housing. The FHA's influence was particularly pronounced in Arizona, where Valley National Bank (VNB) in Phoenix enthusiastically embraced FHA financing. By March 1936 VNB ranked fifth in the country in FHA loans and continued to lead aggressive lending based on federal financing into the 1940s: "Due to increasing prosperity and the FHA, the value of loans and discounts in Arizona banks had doubled to $30 million. It would double again by 1945 and again by 1947. A boom was begun that would transform the state."[28] Indeed, one analysis concluded that "[n]o organization played a more critical role [in transformation of Arizona into "suburbia triumphant"] than Walter Bimson's Valley National Bank (VNB), the largest financial institution in the state."[29] VNB also led in other financing innovations, being the first bank in the state to offer loans with only twenty percent down and twenty year terms. As a director of VNB, Del Webb saw first hand the success of the bank's strategy; as a builder he reaped the rewards of the construction boom.

The rapid growth of the war years required new business methods to satisfy the ever-growing demand for housing. As thousands of defense workers poured into Phoenix during wartime, entire new communities such as Goodyear were built to house workers. The massive federal construction projects of the war years created the firms that could provide those new methods. Del Webb, for example, employed 2,500 men to build Mesa Military Airport, a training base that was the second major air facility built in the state. Webb also built the Phoenix Military Airport, which included 126 buildings and was capable of accommodating 2,500 men.

The growth sparked by federal spending and the new financing methods during the war led to a new form of city. The changes in construction prompted by the FHA standards meant that large tracts were being developed rather than single lots, converting rural land into new communities rather than a gradual, linear expansion out from the city boundary. Development "jumped the canals and leapfrogged out into farm lands and cactus-strewn desert, devouring everything in its path."[30] "To some, rapidly growing Phoenix appeared to be on the cutting edge of a new urban America. Modern Americans, declared an observer, 'desired not a unified metropolis but a fragmented one,' thus they 'opted for the dissolution of the city and, with the aid of the automobile, created the dispersed and fragmented metropolitan world of the late twentieth

---

[28] Collins, *supra* note 11, at 440.

[29] Sheridan, *supra* note 11, at 281.

[30] Marshall Trimble, Arizona: A Cavalcade of History (1989) at 297.

century."[31] Part of this was a general regional phenomenon, with the west enthusiastically embracing a motor vehicle culture starting in 1920s. But part was also unique to Arizona, where urban leaders in Phoenix embraced dispersed development, and the suburban way of life "joined the amenities that provided the good life promoted by Phoenix boosters."[32]

This new form of city needed a new form of government to thrive, as well. Through the 1940s, Phoenix's government was a traditional urban political machine. The outbreak of racially-tinged riots which threatened the city's prosperity in 1942 brought home to the business community the need to control local government if they were to sustain the economic boom. Dissatisfied with the political leadership's response to the riots, the business community forced through changes in personnel and structure in city government.[33] The nonpartisan Charter Government Committee (CGC) put forward a model of government that "was undoubtedly influenced by the corporate approach to military buildup that characterized World War II." The CGC "wanted a clean, efficient city run by a clean, efficient government, and they wanted that government to continue to attract new businesses, particularly aeronautics and electronics firms with strong ties to the Pentagon." This led to a crack down on "embarrassing old-style graft and nepotism because military contractors and corporate site-selection teams frowned on such bottlenecks and the image of a corrupt, sluggish past they conveyed."[34] The business commu-

---

[31] Luckingham, *supra* note 11, at 9.

[32] Luckingham, *supra* note 11, at 5.

[33] Luckingham, *supra* note 11, at 150 ("the CGC became the force that truly changed the direction of Phoenix city government."). The episode that sparked the Charter Government Committee's formation was an altercation between African–American federal troops on leave in late 1942 and military police attempting to arrest a particular soldier. After the resulting riots had ended, the local troop commander declared Phoenix off-limits to troops on leave until the city cleaned up problems with prostitution and gambling.

> The city's aggressive young business community soon answered [Col.] Hoyt's call. Recognizing that, as one merchant put it, 'The army's payrolls constitute one of the community's largest sources of revenue,' more than seventy-five business leaders grilled Mayor Newell Stewart and his city commissioners in the card room of the Adams Hotel. After hours of such pressure, most of the exhausted commissioners finally agreed to fire the city manager, clerk, magistrate, and chief of police. Payoffs from pimps, madams, gamblers, and drug dealers were no longer acceptable. Three days later Col. Hoyt lifted his ban. Lawyer Frank Snell later said, 'It was kind of like a coup, and we called it 'The Cardroom Putsch.'

Sheridan, *supra* note 11, at 274. *See also* Luckingham, *supra* note 11, at 145. This was also the beginning of the revolution in Arizona politics that brought a conservative, white business elite to control the state's politics. Sheridan, *supra* note 11, at 274–275. *See also* Luckingham, *supra* note 11, at 6 ("Phoenix from its founding was run by Anglos for Anglos."), 150.

[34] Sheridan, *supra* note 11, at 275.

nity first pushed through a new city charter in a referendum campaign in 1948, under the theme of the need to "take politics out of city hall," winning a 3–1 vote in favor of a new, nonpartisan, professional structure. This still left the old guard in office, however, and so business leaders next led a campaign that brought a business-sanctioned leadership to power in 1949 election under leadership of CGC. The business community continued to dominate local elections through the committee into the 1970s.[35] With local government firmly under control, the business community was able to maintain its pro-growth policies, extending the war boom into the 1950s and 1960s.

Both Arizona and Phoenix were different places at the end of the war. The "changes triggered by World War II were sea changes, even in the desert. Arizona no longer was an isolated Southwestern state with an extractive colonial order. On the contrary, it was a rising star of the Sunbelt, that new regional constellation reshaping the demography and political character of the nation."[36] This new Arizona was limited to the Phoenix and Tucson areas, however, and the rest of the private land in the state[37] remained in the old extractive industries. Sheridan concluded that "Arizona became two states" after the war, one urban and forward looking and one rural and more traditional.[38]

---

[35] Luckingham, *supra* note 11, at 180. The rise of the CGC had many consequences. Some were predictable. For example, the business elite also fought organized labor to make the area more attractive to new businesses, obtaining an open shop law in 1946 through a constitutional initiative despite the overwhelming Democratic leanings of the electorate. Luckingham, *supra* note 11, at 158; Sheridan, *supra* note 11, at 277. Similarly, "[i]nfluential Phoenicians helped to get changes in state tax laws that made the business climate of the Phoenix area even more attractive" including the repeal in December 1955 of a state sales tax on products manufactured for sale to federal agencies. Luckingham, *supra* note 11, at 157. Others were unintended: the CGC (and the right to work campaign) helped Barry Goldwater get his start, Luckingham, *supra* note 11, at 151, Sheridan, *supra* note 11, at 277, laying the groundwork for the Goldwater campaign of 1964 and, in the long run, the election of Ronald Reagan in 1980. It also represented a means by which a conservative, primarily Republican business elite could control politics in an overwhelmingly Democratic state and region. Control by the business elite did encourage smoother social transitions to avoid disrupting the business climate. For example, in 1953 Superior Court Judge Frederic C. Struckmeyer, Jr. ordered the end of segregation in high schools and Judge Charles E. Bernstein ruled elementary school segregation unconstitutional. School boards accepted rulings without engaging in the type of resistance seen elsewhere. Luckingham, *supra* note 11, at 174. Struckmeyer's ruling was the first legal opinion against school segregation in the United States. Sheridan, *supra* note 11, at 283.

[36] Sheridan, *supra* note 11, at 288.

[37] Much of Arizona was (and is) federal land and Indian Reservations, which until the recent rise of Indian gambling were not economically significant.

[38] Sheridan, *supra* note 11, at 278 ("In a sense, during the postwar years Arizona became two states, or a state with two very different sectors. Phoenix and Tucson devoured their flat desert valleys, splattering the maps of the planners with Rorshach blots of urban

These "two states" produced by the war boom coexisted in the 1940s and early 1950s in part because they remained mostly physically separated. Urban Arizona was concentrated around Phoenix and Tucson, while the rural, agricultural and mineral economies existed in the remainder of the state. More importantly, however, conflict was minimized because where urban expansion took place, the gains were so large that all parties could profit. Wartime expansion, for example, created enormous wealth for everyone from the landowners who sold out to the federal government to the workers who secured employment in the new factories, and the service industries that expanded to meet the increased demand caused by growth. War industries and the increased population demanded Arizona agricultural and mineral products as well, from cotton to cattle to copper. Best of all, everything was paid for with the money flowing into the state through the FHA and defense spending. Not surprisingly, dividing a rapidly increasing pie produced few conflicts.

Peacetime did not end the boom. After the war "[t]he future was bright for Arizona. The war had brought aviation to the forefront of Arizona's development. The state's climate attracted thousands of veterans and industrial workers after the war. Hope for opportunities and wealth was widespread. These positive sentiments were expressed even as the war was being fought."[39] The experience with FHA financing of Valley National Bank during the 1930s readied it to finance continued growth. Rapid as population growth had been before 1940, after that date Arizona's population increased even faster, expanding by more than five times over the next forty years.[40] Population in the 1950s grew over 73%, outpacing both the region (38.9%) and country (18.5%).[41] As a result, "[t]he second and more sustained wave [of growth] swept across the state during the 1950s, the most explosive decade of growth in Arizona history."[42] Manufacturing continued to boom, becoming Phoenix's primary source of income by 1955, with farming and tourism in second and third places respectively.[43] The manufacturing drawn to Arizona was primarily "clean," particularly electronics firms for whom Arizona's climate was an advantage and for whom the state's relatively

---

sprawl. The countryside, in contrast, remained wedded to the old extractive order or locked up in bombing ranges, Indian reservations, and national forests. Miners, ranchers, and farmers continued to wield a disproportionate amount of power in the legislature, but their contributions to Arizona's economy dwindled.").

[39] Ynfante, *supra* note 11, at 128.

[40] Hogan, *supra* note 12, at 1.

[41] Hogan, *supra* note 12, at Table 2, at 14.

[42] Sheridan, *supra* note 11, at 279.

[43] Luckingham, *supra* note 11, at 9.

isolated location was unimportant. Among the major firms in the Phoenix area by the 1950s were Motorola, General Electric, Kaiser Aircraft and Electronics, Goodyear Aircraft, AiResearch, and Sperry Rand—firms that "represented the kind of industry local promoters wanted to attract: clean and employing thousands of trained workers."[44] The increase in manufacturing thus continued to draw new residents. "Surpassing El Paso in the 1950s, the Arizona capital was well established at the top of the regional urban hierarchy by 1960."[45]

The post war years also brought increasing in-migration by older Americans, seeking to escape cold weather and higher living costs elsewhere. A net increase of more than 20,000 in residents over 60 occurred between 1955 and 1960, making Arizona third among all states in elderly immigration.[46] "Already by 1960, when there were 100,000 residents over 65, the 'threshold population' was in place that could bring onto the townscape the affluent retiree districts and the more modest and numerous retirement villages and mobile home parks that became increasingly visible on the urban fringe."[47]

In particular, Phoenix continued to boom in the 1950s. "Between 1948 and 1960 nearly three hundred manufacturing enterprises opened their doors and manufacturing employment in the metropolitan area tripled."[48] The value of construction in 1950s went from $22 million in 1955 to $94 million in 1960 and "there was more construction in Phoenix in 1959 than in all of the years from 1914 to 1946 combined."[49] An *Arizona Republic* story asked "what was built?" in 1959 and answered with a "total of 5,000 new dwellings, 429 swimming pools, 115 office buildings, 94 new stores, 25 new churches and religious structures, 13 motels, 55 service stations, 10 government buildings, and 25 educational facilities."[50] Boosters continued to work hard to attract new businesses.

Technology played an important role in solving the remaining climatic obstacle, the summer heat, as first "swamp coolers" and then refrigeration cooling transformed Phoenix.[51] As one Motorola executive exclaimed, "Refrigeration cooling has transformed Phoenix into a year-

---

[44] Luckingham, *supra* note 11, at 156.

[45] Luckingham, *supra* note 11, at 136.

[46] Metro Arizona, supra note 15, at 65.

[47] Metro Arizona, supra note 15, at 68.

[48] Luckingham, *supra* note 11, at 156.

[49] Luckingham, *supra* note 11, at 160.

[50] *1959 Construction Sets Phoenix Mark,* Arizona Republic (January 2, 1960) at 11.

[51] Sheridan, *supra* note 11, at 279.

round city of delightful living."[52] By end of the 1950s, Phoenix was "the most thoroughly air-conditioned town on earth."[53] The result was enormous population growth. "During the 1950s the population increased a remarkable 311 percent, the highest rate of growth among the nation's fifty largest cities during the decade. By 1960 Phoenix was the largest city in the Southwest, with a population of 439,170, up from 106,818 in 1950 and from 65,414 in 1940."[54] Although growth rates slowed in the 1960s, Arizona's population nonetheless still grew by over 36% in that decade, and continued to outpace the region (24.1%) and nation (13.2%).[55] As the urban center continued to expand previously rural areas, however, it was bound to come into conflict with rural interests. Even in Maricopa County, which had the fast-growing Phoenix, agriculture remained an important industry in the 1950s.

Moreover, the costs of expansion began to appear more significant in the 1950s. Despite the generally clean nature of the new industry, Phoenix and Maricopa County's growth was not without environmental impact. Air pollution increased in 1950s—particularly a mixture of dust and smoke residents termed "smust."[56] Combined with temperature inversions, air pollution meant that on some days residents could not see the nearby mountains, leading the *Wall Street Journal* to call Phoenix the city with dirtiest air in nation in 1960. This is not surprising. The first manufacturing operations in the area had a relatively small marginal impact on regional environmental quality because there were so few of them. After two decades of a manufacturing-led boom, however, this was no longer true.

By the time *Spur Industries v. Del E. Webb Development Co.* arose therefore, urban Arizona was an almost entirely different state than it had been forty years earlier, populated by immigrants, built around high tech manufacturing, and with a booming residential construction sector that had grown by adopting new methods and financial innovations. Rural Arizona, outside the two main urban areas of Phoenix and Tucson was also changing. In particular, throughout the 1950s and 1960s the cattle feeding industry was undergoing a transformation every bit as thorough as urban Arizona's. That transformation made cattle feedlots much less pleasant neighbors just as the transformation of urban Arizona brought large numbers of urban dwellers into rural areas where they would encounter the feedlots.

---

[52] Quoted in Sheridan, *supra* note 11, at 279.

[53] Luckingham, *supra* note 11, at 160.

[54] Luckingham, *supra* note 11, at 153.

[55] Hogan, *supra* note 12, at Table 2, at 14.

[56] Trimble, *supra* note 30, at 302.

Cattle Feeding[57]

Although talking about cattle in Arizona brings to mind the mythology of the American West, with cowboys herding cattle through the set of a John Ford western, the modern cattle industry is organized quite differently from romantic Hollywood images. Cattle still start on the range, but they are now brought to feedlots when they weigh roughly 350–600 pounds. The feedlots "finish" them off to 1000–1200 pounds, before shipping the cattle off for slaughter and processing.[58] This finishing process takes approximately 130–180 days.[59]

In the feedlot, the cattle are confined in groups, which allows customization of feed mixes and helps with disease prevention.[60] The cattle are fed high-energy foods which add 400–700 pounds of weight to each animal, bringing it to market weight.[61] In addition to adding weight, the grain feeding also alters the taste of the beef by adding the marbled fat present in high-grade beef. Purely grass-fed beef, as produced in Argentina for example, has less fat and a different taste than the grain-fed beef most common in the United States.[62]

The purpose of the feedlot is thus to add weight to the cattle as

---

[57] This section draws on Council for Agricultural Science and Technology (CAST), Waste Management and Utilization in Food Production and Processing (Task Force Report No. 124) (1995); Development, *supra* note 1; W.C. Fairbank, *Manure Management,* in The Feedlot (G.B. Thompson & Clayton C. O'Mary, eds. 1983); Joseph P. Harner III & James P. Murphy, *Planning Cattle Feedlots,* Kansas State University Agricultural Experiment Station and Cooperative Extension Service, MF–2316 Livestock Systems; Samuel A. Hart, *Manure Management,* in The Feedlot (Irwin A. Dyer & C.C. O'Mary, eds. 1972); Kenneth R. Krause, Cattle Feeding, 1962–89: Location and Feedlot Size (Agricultural Economic Report No. 642, USDA Economic Research Service, Commodity Economics Division); V.E. Mendel & W.J. Clawson, *Location,* in The Feedlot (Irwin A. Dyer & C.C. O'Mary, eds. 1972); Elmer L. Menzie, William J. Hanekamp, & George W. Phillips, *The Economics of the Cattle Feeding Industry in Arizona* (Arizona Experiment Station Technical Bulletin 207, 1973); Donn A. Reimund, J. Rod Martin, and Charles V. Moore, Structural Change in Agriculture: The Experience for Broilers, Fed Cattle, and Processing Vegetables, USDA Technical Bulletin No. 1648 (1981), and Edward Uvacek, Jr., *Economics of Feedlots and Financing,* in The Feedlot (Irwin A. Dyer & C.C. O'Mary, eds. 1972).

[58] Development, *supra* note 1, at 12.

[59] Development, *supra* note 1, at 11.

[60] Krause, *supra* note 57, at 12 ("The words feedlots, yards and pens are used to describe the physical facilities associated with the feeding of cattle in a small confined space per head.")

[61] Krause, *supra* note 57, at 1.

[62] *See* Corby Kummer, *Back to Grass,* 291 The Atlantic Monthly 138 (May 2003) (ruminating on the differences in taste between grass-fed and grain-fed beef.)

efficiently as possible, while minimizing the risk of illness.[63] Feedlot design focuses on reducing costs by facilitating efficient delivery and consumption of feed and removal of wastes (more on this below), and encouraging the cattle to eat. For example, many feedlots provide twenty-four hour lighting, which both calms cattle and spurs more eating. Since many of the major costs of the feedlot are fixed (e.g. the land and structures),[64] feedlots prefer to operate as close to capacity at all times as possible, to spread the fixed costs over the largest number of cattle. As a result, a well-run, well-designed feedlot will have a large number of cattle, more or less continuously eating and eliminating waste in a relatively small space. The crucial characteristics of a feedlot from its neighbors' points of view are that "[t]he beef animal in a feedlot is confined to a pen; he eats, sleeps, and defecates there."[65] Obviously, this creates a number of potential problems with respect to cattle waste products.

Cattle feeding flourished in Arizona for several reasons. The state has a number of advantages as a location for feedlots. It is easier to manage cattle in hot weather than cold, for example, and locations near major highways and railroads, both of which Arizona has, are important for reducing transportation costs. Other features of Arizona also make it an attractive place to build feedlots: flat areas are better for feedlots since they are cheaper to build on, a low water table helps prevent ground water pollution, a lack of rainfall and streams reduces surface water pollution problems from runoff of manure. As the state is a major hay producer, Arizona feedlots have access to an important input. Arizona does have some disadvantages as a feeding location. However it has a major feed grain deficit (mitigated by the closeness of feed grain production areas in eastern New Mexico, western Texas, Oklahoma, Kansas, Nebraska, and Colorado) and is relatively far from some of the major sources of cattle on the Great Plains, although Arizona herds provide a large source of cattle to be fed.

Although cattle are raised all around Arizona, cattle feeding is geographically concentrated. Until 1964, most of the feeding occurred in Maricopa County around Phoenix. After 1964, however, growth in the industry there shifted primarily to Pinal County to the southeast,

[63] The close quarters in a feedlot mean that one sick cow or steer can quickly infect many others. To avoid illnesses, some feedlots administer antibiotics to their cattle, an issue that has raised concerns about long term impacts on drug resistance. *See* KeepAntibioticsWorking.com, http://www.keepantibioticsworking.com/pages/basics/overuse.cfm (last visited October 26, 2003).

[64] Uvacek, *supra* note 57, at 21 (10,000 head lot requires investment of $375,000 and annual expenditures of over $2 million).

[65] Hart, *supra* note 57, at 169.

cutting Maricopa's share of the industry almost in half by 1972 even though the existing industry remained.[66]

Feedlots on the scale of the Spur Industries lot involved in this case are a comparatively recent phenomenon. Prior to the 1960s, feedlots were relatively small operations. Cattle feeding began as a means for "traditional farmer-feeders" who produced cash crops like corn to gain an alternative means of marketing their corn.

Looking back, one industry observer described the process of building a feedlot in earlier times as "[f]amily-size farmers or large lot investors ... [deciding] that they want to locate a lot of a certain size in a certain location, pour[ing] a little 'feed bunk concrete,' fenc[ing] the lot, obtain[ing] a water supply, and start[ing] feeding cattle in a month or less."[67]

New, much larger feedlots began to appear in the 1950s, not just in Arizona but all across the nation although Arizona was an early leader in the increased size of feedlots. Shortly thereafter small feedlots began to decline and disappear. For example, in 1962 there were 189 feedlot firms in Arizona, a number which declined to only 53 by 1972, with the reduction due to "the exodus of small feeding operations."[68] Other statistics tell the same story: The number of feedlot firms with a capacity of 8,000 head or less fell from 171 in 1962 to 27 in 1972[69] and the share of cattle marketed by lots with capacity under 1,000 fell from 6.3% in 1962 to less than one percent in 1970.[70]

As the small lots vanished, large lots were increasing. Feedlots with a capacity of 16,000 head or more went from seven in 1967 to eighteen in 1972; lots with a capacity of 32,000 head or more went from none in 1967 to nine in 1972.[71] (These trends have continued: By 1970 lots over 16,000 head were supplying over seventy percent of cattle marketed in Arizona, up from thirty-seven percent in 1962.)[72] The feedlot operations

---

[66] Menzie, et al., *supra* note 57, at 4 ("The heaviest concentration of cattle feeding in Arizona traditionally has been in Maricopa County. In 1964, over 70 percent of the cattle on feed were in this county with 8.9 percent in Pinal and the remainder in other counties. However, the major part of the increase in feeding capacity since 1964 has been in Pinal County. Total numbers on feed in Maricopa have not changed significantly but the percent of the total for the state had declined to 35.3 by 1972.")

[67] Krause, *supra* note 57, at 38.

[68] Menzie, et al., *supra* note 57, at 3.

[69] Menzie, et al., *supra* note 57, at 3.

[70] Krause, *supra* note 57, at 21.

[71] Menzie, et al., *supra* note 57, at 3.

[72] Krause, *supra* note 57, at 21.

at issue in this case grew as well, with Spur Industries "on occasion" feeding "in excess of 30,000 head of cattle."[73]

The rise of larger feedlots was caused in part by changes in the market for beef. Demand for beef was growing, due to the increase in population after the war and the post-war economic boom's rise in per capita income. For example, beef consumption rose from 64.2 lbs. per person to 83.9 lbs. per person from 1960 to 1970.[74] Retail sales of beef were also shifting to supermarkets. These stores demanded the consistency, quality control, and volume provided more easily by the larger lots. Federal meat inspection standards also played a role, hastening the demise of small, local meat packers and giving larger operations an advantage.

Supply side changes also were important, as changes in feedlot technology lowered the cost of larger units. The development in the 1950s of "feed additives, growth stimulants, and liquid protein feeds" together with "[o]ther developments in pest control and medicine [which] also came on stream during this period" had the effect of making "it feasible to confine cattle in much larger concentrations than the existing feeding methods allowed."[75] These new feeding techniques gave an advantage to the larger lots that were faster adopters of innovations.[76] Technology that allowed substitution of capital for labor "opened the way for major increases in the size of cattle feeding operations;" larger operations in turn allowed a greater division of labor, producing additional efficiencies. The result was the transformation of cattle feeding into "an industrialized process."[77] As part of the transition from family farm lots to larger commercial lots, feedlots went from seasonal to year-round operations.

Large numbers of cattle concentrated into a small area produce some definite externalities. Cattle, and particularly cattle manure, smell.

---

[73] Answer, at 20.

[74] Richard J. Crom, Economics of the U.S. Meat Industry, Agricultural Information Bulletin 545 (1988) at 7.

[75] Reimund, et al., *supra* note 57, at 16.

[76] Consider, for example, the adoption of the use of Rumensin, an antibiotic-like feed additive that boosted food efficiency by "aiding microbial digestion in the rumen" of cattle. "Many of the physical efficiencies in cattle feeding may have been attained in earlier years when there was considerable improvement in average daily gain and in feed required per hundred pounds of gain. For 1980, 57 percent of farm feedlots used Rumensin ... and 40 percent used hormone materials to improve feed efficiency. In feedlots of more than 500 head, almost 90 percent used Rumensin. Daily gains have improved because of rations, crossbreeding, and the weight and type of cattle placed on feed." Crom, *supra* note 74, at 80.

[77] Reimund, et al., *supra* note 57, at 19–20.

Cattle and cattle manure in quantity attract flies. Cattle walking around in dirt pens produce substantial dust. None of these things makes cattle desirable neighbors. As a USDA study concluded, in an understatement, "[p]eople and confined livestock operations do not mix well."[78]

As noted earlier, feedlots exist to feed cattle up to slaughter-weight. Cattle that eat also excrete, which means disposing of the waste produced. Given that "[a] feedlot animal discharges at least two tons of manure, consisting of approximately equal volumes of urine and feces, while in the feedlot,"[79] this is not a trivial problem. There are various estimates of the amount of waste produced by cattle each day, ranging from 50[80] to 58 pounds[81] per day wet weight (approximately 0.8 cubic feet or six gallons)[82] per 1,000 pound beef animal. Worsening the situation in *Spur Industries* is that warmer weather, available in abundance in Arizona, increases odor problems.

Manure is more than a source of annoying odors: a study using 1974 numbers found that the total annual manure production of the United States feed lot industry was 112 million dry tons and that the manure contained 4.1 million tons of nitrogen, 1.1 million tons of phosphorus, and 0.4 million tons of potassium,[83] making it a significant potential water pollution problem.[84] "In practical terms, one day's manure from a 1,000–lb steer will pollute and consume all the oxygen in 24,000 gallons of water"[85] Moreover, "because not all of the constituents and available energy of the feed are assimilated or removed in its passage through the animal's digestive tract ... manure has sufficient nutrient and energy content to support fly larvae [and] culture organisms that generate foul odors...."[86] Although incidence of disease in human neighbors to feed-

---

[78] Mendel & Clawson, *supra* note 57, at 9.

[79] Hart, *supra* note 57, at 162.

[80] Fairbank, *supra* note 57, at 197.

[81] CAST, *supra* note 57, at 56.

[82] Fairbank, *supra* note 57, at 197.

[83] CAST, *supra* note 57, at 56.

[84] "The problem of nitrogen in animal waste originates with the large quantities of nitrogen that comes from the atmosphere and is fixed naturally or fixed artificially to form fertilizers. This nitrogen is accumulated in crops and harvested. The harvested crops are fed to livestock but a large portion of the accumulated nitrogen is left as waste in the feedlot. This nitrogenous waste is difficult to handle because of its bulk and often cannot economically compete with commercial fertilizer in crop production." A.E. Erickson, et al., *Soil Modification for Denitrification and Phosphate Reduction of Feedlot Waste*, EPA–660/2–74–057 (1974) at 4–5

[85] Hart, *supra* note 57, at 165.

[86] Hart, *supra* note 57, at 164.

lots is small, the risk of "Q-fever, leptospirosis, and tuberculous diseases," which the industry admitted "have been caused from animals and perhaps from their manure" would be likely to alarm neighbors even if the incidence could be shown to be "infinitesimally small."[87] Manure "can contain pathogens (including fecal coliform and other forms of coliform bacteria) that can, for example, contaminate drinking water and cause gastrointestinal illnesses."[88] Large-scale confinement operations also emit "hydrogen sulfide, ammonia, and methane."[89] These problems may or may not be minor in reality, but they certainly do not sound like conditions the neighbors are likely to welcome. Being told that the feedlot next door is emitting hydrogen sulfide, ammonia, and methane is a potential source of pathogens in the drinking water, and produces smells that even the ordinary person can detect, will not increase neighbors' tolerance for the feedlot.

Industry suggestions for minimizing problems focus on keeping people who might object to the odor and flies away from the feedlot. For example, design experts recommend measures such as surrounding feedlots by cropland as a buffer from people to reduce problems with neighbors. The cropland serves the additional purpose of providing an area where the manure can be used. Choosing locations where prevailing wind conditions are away from neighbors who might object to odors is another. Once the feedlot is built, however, "[p]rimary odor-control approaches are to keep manure dry and inventory minimal."[90] Unfortunately, feedlot owners prefer "to clean out as infrequently as possible" since doing so reduces total volume of manure due to compaction—so "it is to the feedlot operator's advantage to minimize costs by infrequent clean-out."[91]

To summarize, just as Arizona's housing industry and population underwent major changes in the post-war period, so too did its cattle industry. As housing developments grew in size and new developments sprang up on previously undeveloped land outside Phoenix, so too the cattle feeding industry began building ever bigger feedlots, creating more potential problems for neighboring landowners. The new residents were not rural Arizonans moving to the city but immigrants from the midwest and other urban areas in the West. The romance of the cowboy might have provided them with a theme for decorating their new homes

---

[87] Hart, *supra* note 57, at 166.

[88] Natural Resources Defense Council, *America's Animal Factories: How States Fail to Prevent Pollution from Livestock Waste* (http://www.nrdc.org/water/pollution/factor/) at *3.

[89] *Id*. at *4.

[90] CAST, *supra* note 57, at 61.

[91] Hart, *supra* note 57, at 163.

in Arizona, but the new residents were generally not used to being around livestock. As a center for both the growth in housing and the expansion of feedlots, the collision of these two trends in Maricopa County was inevitable.

Del Webb[92]

Delbert Eugene Webb's life was a classic Horatio Alger story. Born in Fresno, California on May 17, 1899, Webb started out to become a professional baseball player. He dropped out of high school to play semi-pro ball at age sixteen, working construction jobs on the side. "[H]e often pitched baseball under an assumed name rather than offend his aunts who were 'so religious they squeaked' and who thought playing baseball was 'trafficking with the devil.' "[93] In 1926 a collision with another player at home plate produced torn ligaments and cracked ribs, followed by "a violent bout with typhoid fever" that cut his weight from 204 to 99 pounds.[94] At the urging of friends, Webb went to Arizona to recuperate in the dry climate in 1927. Reminiscing about those days, Webb later told a Rotary audience that "[p]eople thought of Phoenix (in those days) as a primitive, under-developed desert and hot as hell. There were few paved roads and no air-conditioning. Lots of Indians around and I don't know how they stood it, except I suppose they were used to the desert's furnace-like heat. Electric fans were scarce. We slept either on the roof or in the yard, soaking bedsheets with cold water, to get our breath."[95]

Once in Arizona, Webb took a job on a hotel construction site. When that job ended, the contractor gave Webb work erecting cabinets and shelves for a local merchant. When the contractor skipped town during the job, Webb took over the job with the merchant's backing and started the Del E. Webb Construction Company. The company prospered, building hotels in Las Vegas, including the Flamingo Hotel, which was backed by notorious mobster Bugsy Siegel.[96]

---

[92] This section and the next two draw on Margaret Finnerty, Del Webb: A Man, A Company (1991); Sheridan, *supra* note 11, Silver Anniversary, *supra* note 15; Calvin Trillin, *A Reporter At Large: Wake Up and Live,* The New Yorker (April 4, 1964); and Jack M. Tucker, Sun City: 60–plus and Hanging Tough (1985).

[93] Silver Anniversary, *supra* note 15, at 8.

[94] Silver Anniversary, *supra* note 15, at 8; Sheridan, *supra* note 11, at 269.

[95] Tucker, *supra* note 92, at 373–374.

[96] Silver Anniversary, *supra* note 15, at 9. Webb later claimed that he had tried to get out of the job when he learned of Siegel's involvement. *Id.* Interestingly, Webb may have been doing business with Siegel the night Siegel was gunned down in his mistress's apartment. Sheridan, *supra* note 11, at 270.

Webb was extraordinarily successful in business, with his personal wealth estimated at more than $100 million in 1969.[97] In part, Webb succeeded by thorough organization of his business dealings, reducing most aspects of the construction business to a set of standard procedures.[98] Webb's business success may have been also partially related to his knack for political connections. Silver's flattering biography terms him "[a] friend of every president since Franklin D. Roosevelt" and says Webb was "often called to Washington as an advisor."[99] Webb was also a friend of Howard Hughes, a connection that one associate later claimed brought Webb "over a billion dollars of business."[100] Webb maintained his interest in baseball as well, becoming co-owner of New York Yankees in 1945.[101] Webb died on July 4, 1974 of lung cancer after asking to have his ashes scattered in Arizona.

At the start of World War II, Del E. Webb & Company was the largest construction firm in Arizona, positioning the firm to profit handsomely from the federal-spending boom the war brought. The firm "built every major military installation in Arizona except [one]."[102] It also built a concentration camp for interned Japanese–Americans in Parker, Arizona in under three weeks.[103] After the war ended, "Webb's close ties with the federal government brought more contracts for

---

[97] Silver Anniversary, *supra* note 15, at 11.

[98] Finnerty, *supra* note 92, at 38–39 (quoting associates on Webb's high degree of standardization and organization.)

[99] Silver Anniversary, *supra* note 15, at 11.

[100] Finnerty, *supra* note 92, at 63.

[101] Silver Anniversary, *supra* note 15, at 11. Webb's co-owners were Topping, described as a "playboy sportsman," and Leland Stanford McPhail, who initially played the most active role of the three in the club. Robinson & Jennison, at 83–84. McPhail sold his interest to the others thirty-three months later. Robinson & Jennison, at 92. One history of the NY Yankees describes Webb as "an Arizona construction magnate who had a very sincere interest in making money" and notes that he left baseball decisions to his co-owners. Robinson & Jennison, at 84. The mentions of Webb in the book are only of occasional memorable quips Webb made to the press, suggesting that Webb played no real role in devising Yankees strategy, as later owners like George Steinbrenner d*I*d. Other works on the Yankees concur. Harvey Frommer, The New York Yankee Encyclopedia (1997) at 253. ("Webb was into owning the Yankees more for the fun of it than the money. But he and [Dan] Topping made plenty of money as Yankee owners. They also let the baseball people like [George] Weiss run the show and take the heat.") Webb's ownership was a good business decision: the three initial partners bought the club for $2.8 million in 1945 and sold it to CBS in 1962 for $11.2 million. Robinson & Jennison, at 83, 163. A Webb company-commissioned biography suggests that Webb helped bring business sense to baseball. Finnerty, *supra* note 92, at 48–49.

[102] Sheridan, *supra* note 11, at 269.

[103] Finnerty, *supra* note 92, at 41.

veterans' hospitals, air bases, and missile silos."[104]

Webb did more than build on federal contracts. After the war, he built manufacturing plants in twenty states "and acquired enormous acreage to build shopping centers, motels and housing complexes."[105] He pioneered the building of entire communities with his Pueblo Village project outside Tucson in 1948, creating one which included stores using frame construction rather than the traditional adobe techniques and with FHA assistance with financing. That project also began the firm's use of equity financing to enable it to take on larger projects.[106] He built a town in San Manuel near Tucson in 1953 for Magma Copper Co. and the Clairemont Estates development near San Diego. These projects "taught the company new lessons about building communities where none had been before."[107] By 1960 Webb had built Luke Air Force Base, Williams Field, Fort Huachuca, multiple Veterans Administration hospitals, the Union Oil Center in Los Angeles, office buildings in Salt Lake, Phoenix, and Albuquerque, the Beverly Hilton Hotel, the Phoenix Towers, the Kansas City Stadium, and the World's Fair Building in New York and projects in twenty-six states.[108] Despite the company's size, the company's publicity materials assured readers that Webb was personally involved in all his firm's projects, and was able to do so because he "travels exclusively by air."[109]

Some of Webb's success was due to the federally funded building boom in Phoenix but Webb was more than lucky in being in a position to take advantage of the boom: "No one recognized a growth industry faster than Webb, and no one did more to build the boom, transforming Arizona from an extractive colony into a military and recreational one."[110] Webb also recognized the need for a hedge against the cyclical nature of the construction business, with the firm expanding its equity participation in projects in the post-war years to ensure steady work and develop revenue streams to finance future operations. One area of

---

[104] Sheridan, *supra* note 11, at 270. Webb used his ties well, often winning contracts without bidding. Finnerty, *supra* note 92, at 107.

[105] Tucker, *supra* note 92, at 376.

[106] Finnerty, *supra* note 92, at 112. In "equity financing," the developer participates in the funding of the construction in exchange for a share of the equity in the completed development.

[107] Finnerty, *supra* note 92, at 71.

[108] *Del E. Webb: American Success Story*, Advertising supplement, Arizona Republic (January 1, 1960).

[109] *Del E. Webb: American Success Story*, Advertising supplement, Arizona Republic (January 1, 1960).

[110] Sheridan, *supra* note 11, at 270.

diversification was the casino industry, with Webb building and operating multiple casinos in Nevada over the next decades. Webb later said that he got into the business after consulting with J. Edgar Hoover and being encouraged to enter the gambling business to help clean it up. The company was also a different entity than it had been before the war. Despite its size, the pre-war Webb company was a "very personal company;" by 1960 it had been transformed into a "diversified developer, moving with the times, even ahead of the times, responding to social and economic change."[111] The company went public in December 1960 and was listed on the New York Stock Exchange within three years.

Webb's talent for spotting opportunities led to Sun City when a new development for retired people caught his attention. A Russian immigrant named Ben Schliefer moved from New York to Arizona to escape the cold, and began selling real estate in the 1950s. Schliefer had the idea of a retirement community and, in 1954, created the first in the country[112] west of Phoenix where land was relatively cheap.[113] Schliefer named his development "Youngtown" and it was a modest success, suggesting that the conventional wisdom that retirees would not want to live in a community without younger people was wrong.[114]

The Webb company was intrigued by the idea and began to research the possibilities. The company commissioned a study by the Urban Land Institute in Washington, D.C. The Institute held a three day meeting of top developers at a resort and produced a negative report. Webb also spent $10,000 on a report from a Phoenix consulting firm and again received a negative report. As a *New Yorker* story on Sun City later summed it up, the experts "were almost unanimously opposed to communities restricted to old people, on the ground that the old needed to remain part of the fabric of normal society and could only depress each other by living in a group."[115] As a Webb executive noted, "when we started this there wasn't one builder I talked to who didn't say I was out of my goddam mind."[116] The company persevered, however, convinced that there was a market for a retirement community that emphasized an active retirement. From interviews with retirees in Florida, the company

---

[111] Finnerty, *supra* note 92, at 74.

[112] Metro Arizona, supra note 15, at 68 ("Youngtown ... was in 1954 the first community designed to tap the retired cohort of the population.").

[113] Tucker, *supra* note 92, at 364 (when Schliefer moved to Arizona, real estate in Sun City area selling for $400 acre).

[114] A California developer also pioneered the idea of restricting residence to those over sixty before Sun City. Silver Anniversary, *supra* note 15, at 15.

[115] Trillin, *supra* note 92, at 120.

[116] Trillin, *supra* note 92, at 175.

learned that one of the main complaints was broken promises and so made its keeping promises a central selling point. A concept paper listed the core of the project as "Activity, Economy, and Individuality."[117]

Although some have concluded that Youngtown was "copied in concept and location" by Webb's Sun City,[118] Sun City was more than a copy. When Webb began investigating the possibilities, Youngtown was "still only a cluster of houses and a store."[119] Webb took the idea of a subdivision designed for older Americans and constructed a way of life. Webb used numerous innovations in designing and marketing Sun City that made it much more than a larger version of Schliefer's development. As a company official told Calvin Trillin of the *New Yorker* in 1964, "We've always sold a Way of Life. The homes are secondary."[120] Sun City's emphasis on providing golf courses and other recreational opportunities, as well as the extensive shopping opportunities, set it apart from Youngtown, as did Webb's marketing of the concept.

The site

The area that eventually became Sun City was originally settled by R.P. Davie, a "business adventurer" from Marinette, Wisconsin. He named the settlement he founded after his hometown and developed a deep well irrigation system to irrigate thousands of acres. The town grew enough that a post office in Marinette opened in 1912. Unfortunately Davie gambled on developing sugar beets as a crop and failed when the Arizona soil did not produce a sweet enough beet. He sold the area to the Southwest Cotton Co., a subsidiary of Goodyear Tire and Rubber in 1920 for $1,000,000 and the town of Marinette became a Goodyear company compound.[121]

Goodyear first tried cultivating "Yuli," a type of sagebrush whose roots produce "a white sticky substance resembling the base of synthetic rubber." That proved no more successful than sugar beets, however, and the company switched to cotton production. Marinette became a "town of labor and sweat" of largely Hispanic cotton workers.[122] Goodyear in turn sold the property in 1936 to the J.G. Boswell Co., a cotton farming company and cotton production grew. Boswell's operations on the future

---

[117] Finnerty, *supra* note 92, at 84.

[118] Metro Arizona, supra note 15, at 68.

[119] Finnerty, *supra* note 92, at 83.

[120] Trillin, *supra* note 92, at 134.

[121] Silver Anniversary, *supra* note 15, at 3.

[122] Silver Anniversary, *supra* note 15, at 3.

Sun City site became "one of the nation's most prosperous [cotton] plantations."[123] The Boswell family accumulated more land in the area, buying more property from Goodyear and from the Santa Fe Railroad, ultimately amassing 20,000 acres that stretched from Peoria, Arizona to Luke Air Force Base.[124] By the end of the 1950s, however, the Boswells were ready to get out of the cotton business.

At the same time, feedlots were beginning to appear on the property around the Boswells'. Two feedlots were built in 1956 on the land that would become Spur's feedlot and by 1959 there were twenty-five feedlots and dairy operations within seven miles of what became the Spur property. On the land owned by the then-owners of Spur's original thirty-five acres, between 7,500 and 8,500 head of cattle were being fed in 1959.[125] In 1960 Spur bought the thirty-five acres and over the next two years bought an additional seventy-nine acres, bringing its total property to 114 acres.[126]

Sun City

By 1959, the three things necessary for Sun City's birth had come together. First, Webb had formed an interest in developing a retirement community and was on the lookout for sufficient land that would allow him to build the project. Second, Webb had the size and resources to try something new, despite the scholarly and industry consensus that such a project would fail. Third, the Boswells had amassed a tract of land big enough to accommodate the project and were ready to think about selling. Thus when James G. Boswell II, the son of one of three original brothers who had formed the company, heard that the Webb company was looking for land, he stopped by the Webb company offices to offer them the cotton farm.

James told L.C. Jacobson, a Webb executive, that his firm had 10,000 acres west of Phoenix. The two men went to look at the property and on the drive back, James mentioned that the company also had a second 10,000 acres across the road. After hearing this "Jacobson's interest erupted into an enthusiastic suggestion that they return immediately to work out the deal. By two o'clock the next morning the men had hammered out the essentials of an agreement on a piece of yellow legal-size scratch paper."[127] Both agreed to a phased transfer of the land,

---

[123] Silver Anniversary, *supra* note 15, at 4.

[124] Silver Anniversary, *supra* note 15, at 20.

[125] Spur at 182, 704.

[126] Spur at 182, 704.

[127] Silver Anniversary, *supra* note 15, at 21.

which allowed the Webb Company to buy the land it needed without immediately tying up its capital in land and let the Boswells gradually exit from their agricultural operations.

Together with the Boswells, Webb formed the Del E. Webb Development Company to build Sun City. The firm was capitalized at $100,000, made up by equal contributions from Webb and the Boswells.[128] The Boswells also loaned the new firm $600,000 and Webb made a $600,000 in kind contribution, putting the total at risk at $1.3 million.[129] The plan was to create something more than a subdivision—the plan was to market to retirees a community where they could experience, as Webb's advertisements put it, "An Active Way of Life!"[130] The goal was to create a community for middle income retirees. The Sun City radio jingle, later made into a record for those residents who loved it as well as played on the development's bell tower, summarized the "active way of life":

> Wake up and live in Sun City
> For an Active New Way of Life,
> Wake up and live in Sun City,
> Mr. Senior Citizen and wife.
> Don't let retirement get you down.
> Be happy in Sun City; it's a paradise town.
> Wake up and live in Sun City,
> Mr. Senior Citizen, the rest of your life,
> Mr. Senior Citizen and wife.[131]

To create this new lifestyle, and offset the relatively remote location of the land, Webb planned an extensive set of amenities to be built before the houses were sold. These included a shopping center, a nine hole golf course (ultimately to expand to eighteen holes) and other recreational facilities, all of which were to be completed before houses were sold. The shopping center was to include a supermarket, a variety store, a laundromat, a barber shop, a drug store, and a filling station. After five months of hectic construction, the company had completed five model homes, nine holes of the golf course, the swimming pool and recreation center, and part of shopping center in time for the January 1, 1960 opening. Webb hired a nationally known landscape architect to design the development, who provided each buyer with a variety of individual home landscaping layouts at no additional charge. The prices

---

[128] Silver Anniversary, *supra* note 15, at 22. Boswell later reduced its stake to 49% for tax reasons. *Id.*

[129] Silver Anniversary, *supra* note 15, at 23.

[130] Silver Anniversary, *supra* note 15, at 25. This was the theme of a two page ad spread in the Arizona Republic in December 1959.

[131] Quoted in Trillin, *supra* note 92, at 120.

were reasonable, $8,500 to $11,300 for the first phase, ranging from 500 to 1200 square feet.[132] Nonetheless, Sun City was relatively remote. Calvin Trillin described the drive out from Phoenix in 1964

> The thirty-minute drive from Phoenix to Sun City begins with a dreary line of motels, most of them built before motels were called motor inns, and some of them before cabins and tourist courts were called motels. A few miles past Glendale, a suburb of Phoenix, the motels begin to give way to fields of alfalfa and cotton, and the fields are almost uninterrupted after Peoria, a drab farming town that calls itself, for reasons nowhere in evidence, the Rose Center of the World. Then, two or three miles up the highway, the visitor gets his first view of Sun City across the cotton fields—a view of palm trees tilting up unexpectedly in all directions.[133]

The weekend before the opening, Webb ran a special multipage supplement in the Arizona Republic touting the "Completely Planned, Completely Different" plans "for an Active 'New Way of Life.' " The community was "designed exclusively for those who wish to actively enjoy the best years of their lives."[134] The supplement featured "Master Builder" Webb's life story[135] and his call to "together . . . realize a way-of-life unprecedented in America." Sun City was no mere development. It was, the copywriters assured readers, "an unprecedented achievement," a "miniature metropolis," that had everything that "years of extensive research indicated you wanted most . . . for luxurious but economical living, for endless creative and recreational activity." Residents would "enjoy complete individuality, privacy, and the freedom to live exactly as you wish for the best years of your life." This community, Webb promised, was "created to be shared with those who have taken part in the years of America's greatest growth and development." Ironically the same Sunday paper also contained a section on the 12th Annual Arizona National Livestock Show, in town for the coming week.[136]

Selling Sun City was more than a matter of local advertising. Webb ran two page ads in *Time* and *Newsweek*, and a concerted publicity

---

[132] *Del Webb's Retirement Sun City of 1600 Homes Will Open Today,* Arizona Republic (January 1, 1960) at 2.

[133] Trillin, *supra* note 92, at 123.

[134] Advertising supplement, Arizona Republic (January 1, 1960). Except where otherwise noted, the quotes in this paragraph are taken from this document.

[135] *Del E. Webb: American Success Story,* Advertising supplement, Arizona Republic (January 1, 1960).

[136] Blake Brophy, *Livestock Lives it Up in Phoenix,* Arizona Days and Ways, The Republic Magazine (January 3, 1960) at 2.

campaign brought in nationally syndicated columnists to tout the project. Once the development opened, "[v]irtually every major magazine and television network in America plus hundreds of newspapers made household words out of 'Sun City,' Del E. Webb's 'Active Retirement Community.' They called it by other names too: 'most famous,' 'first planned community,' and 'Webb's Resort Retirement Community.' "[137] The publicity continued even after the first year of the project.

Opening day, January 1, 1960, looked like the Oklahoma land rush:

> When the models finally opened at 8:00 a.m. on Thursday, New Year's Day, 1960, the rush was on. Sales were brisk that first day but nothing like the stampede on the following Friday, Saturday and Sunday. Since the required down payment was a mere $500, the risk of buying was small. Many people bought within an hour after arriving. A long line of people waited for hours to sign contracts with salesmen sitting on the floor of a tiny office. Owen Childress, in charge of contracts, had to put in frantic calls to Webb secretaries to come help with the line of people waiting to buy.
>
> The salespeople ran out of official contracts and had to resort to printed receipts hastily purchased from a store. Not surprising, since more than 100,000 inquisitive people jammed the area, eager to see the new homes ... A line of cars that first Sunday afternoon extended for two miles along U.S. 60–70–89, the main Phoenix–Los Angeles highway.[138]

"Special guests" at the opening dedication included the governor and mayors of Phoenix, Peoria, and Glendale. During the first 72 hours of sales 237 homes sold for a total of $2,500,000.[139] Deposits on 126 were received even before the official opening.[140] Clearly Webb had hit on something big. While most of the opening weekend sales were to Arizonans, people from California, New Jersey, Oregon, Colorado, Minnesota, Michigan, Texas, Iowa, and New Mexico also bought that weekend.

The Webb company excelled at marketing Sun City. In one innovation, it ran vacation specials in rental apartments, where it was not unusual to have 8,000 visitors a year.[141] The marketing pitch was impressive: "Many Sun Citians who toured the model home remember seeing a film written and directed by Harvey Shahan, 'The Story of

---

[137] Silver Anniversary, *supra* note 15, at 32.

[138] Silver Anniversary, *supra* note 15, at 29–30.

[139] Tucker, *supra* note 92, at 13.

[140] *Retirement Village to Open Today*, Arizona Republic (January 3, 1960) at 17.

[141] Silver Anniversary, *supra* note 15, at 76.

Arizona and Sun City,' narrated by Senator Barry Goldwater."[142] A 1962 state contest to find the town with most flags led to the company giving every buyer a flag when the buyer moved in. The company also organized a garden club, plowing, irrigating, planting a large garden and then inviting the residents to take produce.

Webb's personal involvement in the development was not as great as the publicity materials suggested, but the new residents "began to associate him personally with the construction of their homes. One of the big selling points to prospective buyers was the testimony of Sun Citians that, 'If anything goes wrong with your house, Del Webb will fix it.' "[143] The firm's, and Webb's, reputation for fixing problems were an important part of the success of the development.

The early success led to rapid expansion. "The original forecast called for the sale of 1,680 homes in seven years; 1,250 were sold that first year."[144] In Arizona, Webb doubled the size of shopping center in 1961, making it largest in Arizona outside of Phoenix. A second unit of homes, representing a $25 million investment, opened in January 1961, bringing more than 40,000 people to the first weekend.[145]

The Sun City model quickly spread across the country. By 1964, Webb had opened three more "Active Retirement" developments, two in California and one in Florida.[146] Ultimately the company developed a total of nine.[147] Others cashed in too: More than 250 retirement communities had opened nationally by 1964.[148] While the expansion was not trouble free for Webb, the company profited immensely from its innovation.[149] The rapid growth, the theme of an "active" life, and the sense of participating in something new produced a tightly knit community.

---

[142] Silver Anniversary, *supra* note 15, at 76.

[143] Silver Anniversary, *supra* note 15, at 13. ("Webb's personal involvement in all decisions affecting Sun City was also part of the legend.")

[144] Silver Anniversary, *supra* note 15, at 71.

[145] Silver Anniversary, *supra* note 15, at 61.

[146] Silver Anniversary, *supra* note 15, at 48.

[147] Kenneth E. Bloom, Come to the Sun: The Economic and Fiscal Effects of Sun City and Sun City West on Maricopa County, Arizona (Masters Thesis, University of Cincinnati, School of Planning 1997) at 5.

[148] Trillin, *supra* note 92, at 120.

[149] Its new status as a public company led to accounting issues in 1965, the write-down of half the company's net worth, and the company's first reported loss. Finnerty, *supra* note 92, at 123. H. Allen Winter, a company financial analyst, later recalled "Webb had to take action, traveling around the country reassuring the investors; he was fighting for his life." *Id.*

Despite the occasional glitch,[150] in general Webb succeeded in creating a new community quickly.

Sun City was quickly important for Arizona. The retirees had an economic impact by bringing an inflow of transfer payments (pensions, social security, and savings) into the state. By population, Sun City would have been the eighth largest city in the state by 1970 if it had been incorporated.[151] Sun City, whose density of development was much higher than the rest of the county, contributed more than twice the property taxes as the average community in the county.[152] Of course, with those tax revenues came a group of voters generally uninterested in schools, leading to conflicts with other areas of the county.[153]

Webb's success, however, brought thousands of people, largely from urban areas, into the rural portion of Maricopa County. These new residents expected an "active lifestyle," including barbeques on their patios, golf, swimming, and other outdoor sports. They expected any problems they had to be fixed by Del Webb—perhaps not personally, but certainly quickly. Those whose corners of paradise included the stink of cattle manure and battles with swarming flies did not hesitate to voice their frustration.

The case

Conflict between homeowners and feed lots was nothing new in the country as a whole or Arizona in particular. A 1951 *American Law Reports 2d* annotation on "Stockyard as a Nuisance" collected over forty-seven opinions from across the country on the topic and concluded that "Generally, where a stockyard is situated in such a place or maintained in such a manner as to result in a material annoyance, inconvenience, or discomfort to an adjacent property owner, the latter

---

[150] Silver Anniversary, *supra* note 15, at 217 (one problem was that the first unit properties did not have covenants in their deeds requiring the payment of association dues. These were added to the deeds for the second unit, which led to disputes between the two groups of residents over unpaid dues from the first group.).

[151] Metro Arizona, supra note 15, at 68. Sun City residents vigorously resisted incorporation, making Maricopa County the closest unit of government. Silver Anniversary, *supra* note 15, at 163.

[152] Bloom, *supra* note 147, at 44.

[153] Sun City was initially in the Peoria school district, whose schools were overcrowded. Sun City residents quickly became a majority in the district and voted down bond issues repeatedly (17 times between 1962 and 1974). The only exception was a bond issue in 1963 for $218,000. No more passed until 1974, when another passed by 387 votes. Silver Anniversary, *supra* note 15, at 218. The problem was ultimately solved by splitting Sun City off from the Peoria district into an unincorporated area, with school taxes going into a state pool. Silver Anniversary, *supra* note 15, at 219.

has been awarded an injunction against the continued maintenance of the stockyard, or damages for past maintenance, on the ground that it constitutes a private nuisance."[154] As the annotation made clear, the issues in such cases were straightforward. The main issues were evidentiary (did the stockyard actually produce offensive odors or insects that affected the plaintiff's property?), whether municipal laws could prohibit stockyards, and whether state regulations authorizing a facility overrode nuisance law. The only real defense was the doctrine of coming to the nuisance, for which the annotation cited two cases applying the defense.[155] The feedlots discussed in the annotation, however, were not the large, modern operations that existed by the 1960s. Modern feedlots, which began to appear in the 1950s and 1960s, operated on a much larger scale.

Webb began to experience what it termed "sales resistance" to the lots nearest Spur's property in 1963[156] but the problem did not become acute until approximately 1967. People whose lots were closest to the Spur feedlots began complaining to Webb and to the homeowners association. The residents' options were limited. As residents of the unincorporated section of Maricopa County, there were minimal zoning rules governing Spur's property and the rules that did exist favored Spur.[157] A contractual solution was possible (Webb could simply buy Spur's facilities) but, as later events made clear, Webb and Spur had quite different ideas about who owned the legal rights at issue, which would affect who was going to have to compensate the other. Until that issue could be resolved, bargaining between Webb and Spur could not resolve the dispute. That left a nuisance suit as the residents' primary remedy. Feedlots in Arizona were obviously worried about the outcome of nuisance suits, since several feedlots moved when threatened with nuisance actions during the 1960s.[158]

---

[154] R.B. Kaman, *Stockyard as a Nuisance,* 18 A.L.R.2d 1033, § 3[a] (1951).

[155] *Id.* at § 5[c] citing Ashbrook v. Commonwealth, 1 Bush 139, 89 Am.Dec. 616 (Ky. 1866) and Ballentine v. Webb, 84 Mich. 38, 47 N.W. 485 (1890) (allowing defense). A later edition added Curry v. Farmers Livestock Market, 343 S.W.2d 134 (Ky. 1961) and Spencer Creek Pollution Control Ass'n v. Organic Fertilizer Co., 264 Or. 557, 505 P.2d 919 (1973) (rejecting the defense.)

[156] Spur, at 182–183, 704–705 (quoting testimony by Webb officials).

[157] Indeed, much of Webb's initial legal response was to attack the validity of the county zoning ordinances. *See* below.

[158] "In 1963, one of the first major lawsuits was threatened by property owners in Tempe against a feedlot operation adjacent to their community. Fearful of the nuisance suit coming to court, the 30,000 head operation moved to Yuma at the expense of the feedlot corporation. Similar legal action threats were responsible for the relocation of at least four additional feeding operations in recent years." Menzie, et al., *supra* note 57, at 38.

The homeowners association encouraged Sun City residents to file nuisance suits against Spur, and donated $1,000 to assist with the legal actions. By the end of 1967, suits seeking over $450,000 in total damages, with individual claims of between $1,000 and $8,500, had been filed against Spur.[159] The residents alleged "[m]anure is daily accumulated on the property, odors are not kept under control, and the operation has emitted into the air vile, stinking, nauseating and obnoxious odors which are frequently carried by air currents over the nearby residences."[160]

Both the association and Webb tried to resolve the matter through negotiation. The association proposed that Spur use chemical methods to control the odors and Webb offered to buy the feedlot. Both efforts failed—not surprising since Webb and Spur held such dramatically different views of the legal rights at stake. Residents continued to file lawsuits, and by June 1968 seventy-five residents were suing Spur, seeking over $2.1 million in damages. Hot weather that month brought forty-eight more suits and more than $2.6 million additional damage claims.[161] Webb then brought suit as well, alleging Spur's feedlot was a public nuisance.[162] By this time, Spur had between 20,000 and 30,000 head of cattle on its lots.[163] Although the individual actions were filed first, the suit by Webb was heard first.

Nuisance law is one of the common law's primary responses to pollution. One of the criticisms of nuisance as a remedy for pollution is that it presents a classic "free-rider" problem, where individuals with relatively small claims will be reluctant to bring actions to vindicate their rights although it would be socially beneficial for them to do so. Each resident will be tempted to hang back, allowing neighbors to bring suit, since a resident who does not sue gets the benefits of the lawsuit without paying for lawyers or court costs. As a result, too few nuisance actions will be brought against polluters, particularly where the harm is spread over a large number of individuals. The existence of free-rider problems is one of the primary justifications often posited for shifting pollution-control to the government, which can use tax dollars to fund regulation and litigation against polluters.

---

[159] Silver Anniversary, *supra* note 15, at 220.

[160] Silver Anniversary, *supra* note 15, at 221.

[161] Silver Anniversary, *supra* note 15, at 221.

[162] One of the reasons the case often appears in casebooks is its distinction between public and private nuisance. The distinction lies in whether the harm caused by the nuisance affects only particular property owners or whether it affects the public generally. Your dog barking in your yard at 3 a.m. every night could be a private nuisance to your neighbors; your dog running out and biting anyone who walks on the sidewalk in front of your house could be a public nuisance.

[163] Spur, at 183, 705.

In this case, there seems to have been less of a free-rider problem, as Sun City's residents were filing suit against Spur at an impressive rate. Three factors reduced the free rider problem for the Sun City residents. First, the residents were already organized into a homeowners association. The costs of cooperating against Spur were thus reduced—residents could exchange information and share the common costs of the litigation. Second, the residents were accustomed to having their complaints taken care of quickly and so felt entitled to an environment that permitted the promised "Active Way of Life." As economic research has shown, people who feel entitled to something place a higher value on the item than those who do not. The Sun City residents had come to Sun City to be active, particularly out-of-doors. This, combined with their expectations from the Del Webb reputation for resolving problems promptly, led them to view fixing the problem as protecting something to which they were entitled. Given their high valuation, residents were less likely to try to "free ride" on the efforts of others. Third, Webb had enormous reputational capital resting on the success of Sun City—the *New Yorker* described it as "a new version of the company town—a town in which a single company has a financial interest in keeping the residents happy in order to attract more residents."[164] The recommendations of current residents were important selling points, particularly since the company had scaled back national media campaigns and was relying more on word of mouth. Webb needed to solve the problem to protect its investment, giving the company a reason to join the litigation.

Nothing about the case suggested it was anything but a straightforward nuisance case. Webb's complaint noted the "vile, stinking, obnoxious, nauseating, and noisome odors" caused by the feedlot.[165] The only participants found in the research for this chapter, one of Spur's attorneys and the trial judge, both indicated that they did not view the case as unusual at the time. Spur expected to win because it was there first and was located in a traditionally rural area, making a "coming to the nuisance" defense available. Webb apparently expected to escape that doctrine and prevail on public nuisance grounds because of the health issues posed by the flies and odor and, most likely, because it had a large number of registered Maricopa County voters on its side. Thus the only real question was whether Spur was there sufficiently long enough before Webb to justify a verdict for Spur, as the feedlot was clearly an unpleasant neighbor for the "active" retirees in Sun City, although the parties certainly also litigated over how unpleasant a neighbor Spur was. Spur also insisted from the start that Webb was liable for any costs it

---

[164] Trillin, *supra* note 92, at 135.

[165] Complaint, at 8.

might incur to eliminate the nuisance.[166] There was little sense of urgency to the proceedings below, with motions often pending before the trial court for months at a time.[167]

The two sides developed internally consistent, but mutually contradictory stories of the case, which they stuck to throughout. For Spur the case was simple: it was there first, in a rural area, where it was conducting an agricultural business, licensed by the state in a non-negligent manner. Webb caused the problem by trying to get land more cheaply than it would have been able to in a more urban part of the county, vastly increasing Webb's profit from the deal by an estimated seventeen million dollars.[168] If anything, Webb had created the problem by misrepresenting to the residents of Sun City that their property was suitable for an active outdoor lifestyle. Webb's role in the creation of the problem meant that Webb, not Spur, should bear any financial burden caused by the conflicting land uses. As Spur phrased it in its opening brief on appeal, the question was

"(1) Which of two actors is primarily responsible for loss, damage, and expense incurred or to be incurred where:

(a) An activity is carried on in an area by one actor which is a lawful activity licensed by the State of Arizona and compatible with the other uses then and theretofore made of the area so that no loss, damage or injury was then being occasioned to any third person under the existing conditions which passive condition but for the conduct of the second actor would obtain for many years;

(b) The second actor, with knowledge of the conditions existing as above stated, for financial gain misrepresents the area through active advertising and promotion as one suitable and available for a use plainly not compatible with the existing uses and conditions; . . ."[169]

Spur elaborated on this theory at great length in its pleadings but its arguments can be summarized as focusing on Webb's conduct in luring the homeowners to the area, when Webb knew full well that the area was primarily agricultural.

---

[166] Spur asked for indemnification in its initial answer and counterclaim and stuck to that throughout the litigation.

[167] Petition, Ex Parte, at 7–9 (describing pace of litigation).

[168] *See, e.g.,* Petition, Ex Parte, at 2 ("It was admitted that the cost of the land to WEBB Corporation as agricultural land was in the order of magnitude of $3,000,000, whereas its resale value, on a lot basis and giving no effect to any profit on the residences constructed and sold, would exceed $20,000,000.")

[169] Opening Brief of Appellant and Cross–Appellee, at 20–21.

For legal support, Spur relied primarily on two cases, *MacDonald v. Perry*[170] and *Dill v. Excel Packing Co.*[171] In *MacDonald* the Arizona Supreme Court had overturned a verdict against an individual who maintained an irrigation ditch which carried foul smelling water away from a City of Phoenix septic tank. The trial court had erroneously instructed the jury that the plaintiff had an "absolute right" to be free of odor interfering with the use and enjoyment of his land. Spur's interpretation of *MacDonald* was "that anyone moving into an agricultural area is bound to accept the agricultural pursuits carried on in the area or which under reasonable circumstances might be expected to be carried on in that area."[172] In *Dill* the Kansas Supreme Court overturned a permanent injunction against a feedlot, and Spur quoted the holding that "Plaintiffs chose to live in an area uncontrolled by zoning laws or restrictive covenants and remote from urban development. In such an area plaintiffs cannot complain that legitimate agricultural pursuits are being carried on in the vicinity, nor can plaintiffs, having chosen to build in an agricultural area, complain that the agricultural pursuits carried on in the area depreciate the value of their homes."[173]

Applying these cases to the dispute at hand, Spur concluded

"In the instant case the evidence is uncontroverted that Webb possessed actual knowledge of the existence of the agricultural character of the community which it selected for conducting its business venture. Webb possessed actual knowledge of the fact that the area was devoted to the growing of crops for many miles in all directions, and knew of the existence of substantial cattle feeding facilities, including those owned by Spur's predecessors, which were located in close proximity to the point it selected to commence development of an urban area.

Had it not been for the active conduct of Webb in inducing thousands of person to purchase homes from Webb by the use of deceptive and misleading advertising, thereby creating an island of urban use in the midst of a vast sea of agriculture, Spur would have continued to coexist with its neighbors in peaceful harmony for many years to come. In accordance with well settled authority cited above, Webb cannot now call upon a court of equity to make that place suitable for its profit-making venture which was not so when it was selected."[174]

---

[170] 32 Ariz. 39, 255 P. 494 (1927).

[171] 183 Kan. 513, 331 P.2d 539 (1958).

[172] Opening Brief of Appellant and Cross–Appellee, at 29.

[173] Quoted in Opening Brief of Appellant and Cross–Appellee, at 32.

[174] Opening Brief of Appellant and Cross–Appellee, at 35–36.

Spur used other legal arguments to reinforce the point, but this was its essential argument throughout: Webb created the conflict by bringing urban conditions into the midst of agricultural land.

Webb's response to Spur's framing of the issues was twofold. First, Webb argued that its use of agricultural land was as legitimate as Spur's use of its land because residential development in Youngtown began before Spur's operations.[175] Moreover, Spur increased the size of its operations, expanding toward Webb's property. Second, Webb argued that the issue was the public nuisance character of Spur's operations, not priority of use.[176] Public nuisances should be abated by the party creating them, Webb argued. To hold otherwise would grant Spur a "vested right" to maintain the agricultural character of the property.[177] *MacDonald*, Webb argued, was inapplicable on the point for which Spur cited it because it "does not deal with an area which was changing in its general character or which had been changed in its general character."[178] *Dill* was distinguishable because it dealt with a "sparsely populated agricultural area" while this case concerned high density housing.[179]

The trial court empanelled an advisory jury,[180] which was later discharged by agreement for reasons that are unclear today, and the case continued before the judge alone. The trial was vigorously litigated, with testimony over thirteen days and an additional day of oral argument, plus various intermediate appeals. In September 1970 Superior Court Judge Kenneth Chatwin found the feedlot a nuisance and ordered it closed by December 31, 1970. Chatwin granted a stay of his order until February 1971, however, in response to numerous motions filed by Spur, entering a final order in favor of Webb on February 19, ordering Spur to close its operations by February 28, 1971. Spur immediately appealed to the state supreme court for a stay, arguing that it could not move the more than 10,000 cattle currently on the feedlot without suffering great

---

[175] *See, e.g,* Appellee's Answering Brief at 7 ("approximately nine months and twenty-two days before any cattle were fed in any feed pens located on the parcels presently belonging to Spur").

[176] *See, e.g,* Appellee's Answering Brief at 15 ("restating" the issue as "If a housing developer sells a residence in an area where there is a public nuisance....")

[177] *See, e.g,* Appellee's Answering Brief at 23.

[178] Appellee's Answering Brief at 37.

[179] Webb's opening brief on its appeal focused on an issue the court paid little attention to in its opinion: whether or not Spur's operations complied with Maricopa County zoning ordinances. The issue, fought out in both parties' briefs, concerned whether Maricopa County had authority under Arizona law to restrict agricultural operations.

[180] A suit for injunctive relief is normally tried before a judge, but courts can empanel advisory juries to hear evidence and give the court the benefit of the jury's views on factual issues.

harm.[181] The high court agreed, and, granting a temporary stay to allow further argument, also took jurisdiction of the appeal.[182] In the course of these intermediate appeals, Spur eventually agreed to close the yard down, pending resolution of the legal questions and without prejudice to its rights. While the appeal was pending, "feeling that the long delays were proving too expensive and that the final decision would be adverse, [Spur] agreed to move if Webb would pay the bill."[183] Webb was not willing to pay enough to satisfy Spur, however, and so the appeal continued. The parties' arguments on appeal continued the same themes from the lower court.

When the state supreme court issued its opinion in April 1972, the decision surprised everyone. The feedlot was undoubtedly a public nuisance, something the court distinguished from a private nuisance as "generally one of degree" relating to the number of people affected.[184] If the harm from the nuisance was "slight," then damages were the appropriate remedy. The residents of Youngtown, who also experienced the odors and flies but to a much lesser extent than the southern Sun City residents, would therefore, "at most ... be entitled to damages rather than injunctive relief."[185] The court found that it had "no difficulty" in agreeing with the lower court that the southern Sun City residents would be entitled to an injunction.[186] Moreover the facts met the requirements of a state statute on public nuisances, defining as a public nuisance "any condition or place in populous areas which constitutes a breeding place for flies, rodents, mosquitos and other insects which are capable of carrying and transmitting disease-causing organisms to any person or persons."[187] The residents of Sun City could therefore bring an action to enjoin Spur's operations.

The case before the court did not involve the residents of Sun City but the Webb company as plaintiff. Webb had standing, since it was losing sales in the southern portion, and so could stand in place of the residents. But this led to the next question: "Must Del Webb Indemnify Spur?"[188] The court began its analysis of this question by noting that "In addition to protecting the public interest, however, courts of equity are

---

[181] Petition, Ex Parte, at 6.

[182] Order, 2–24–71.

[183] Silver Anniversary, *supra* note 15, at 221.

[184] Spur, at 183, 705.

[185] Spur, at 184, 706.

[186] Spur, at 184, 706.

[187] Ariz. Rev. Stat. § 36–601(A)(1).

[188] Spur, at 184, 706.

concerned with protecting the operator of a lawfully, albeit noxious, business from the result of a knowing and willful encroachment by others near his business."[189] Quoting at length from *Dill*, the Kansas Supreme Court coming to the nuisance case relied on by Spur,[190] the court concluded that as to Webb, the doctrine would have resulted in a victory for Spur in this case and no relief for Webb. If the facts had been different and Spur had built its feedlot on the outskirts of a city, which then grew toward the feedlot, the court noted, Spur would have had to bear the costs of abating the nuisance.[191]

Neither precedent fit exactly in this case. Webb was not alone in suffering the consequences of the nuisance. Neither was Spur responsible for the unexpected event that a "new city" had "[sprung] up, full-blown."[192] Spur had to move, not because it was at fault but because of "a proper and legitimate regard of the courts for the rights and interests of the public."[193] Webb got its injunction, "not because Webb is blameless, but because of the damage to the people who have been encouraged to purchase homes in Sun City." As a result, the court reasoned, "It does not seem harsh to require a developer, who has taken advantage of the lesser land values in a rural area as well as the availability of large tracts of land on which to build and develop a new town or city in the area, to indemnify those who are forced to leave as a result."[194] Therefore the court found that "Having brought people to the nuisance to the foreseeable detriment of Spur, Webb must indemnify Spur for a reasonable amount of the cost of moving or shutting down."[195] The court limited this holding to "a case wherein a developer has, with foreseeability, brought into a previously agricultural or industrial area the population which makes necessary the granting of an injunction against a lawful business and for which the business has no adequate relief."[196] It then remanded the case for the determination of damages.

The cattle moved out the same month the state supreme court ordered Webb to pay for the costs of the move.[197] The case was ultimately remanded for the lower court to determine the cost of the move. "The

---

[189] Spur, at 184, 706.

[190] Dill v. Excel Packing Company, 183 Kan. 513, 331 P.2d 539 (Kan. 1958).

[191] Spur, at 185, 707.

[192] Spur, at 185, 707.

[193] Spur, at 186, 708.

[194] Spur, at 186, 708.

[195] Spur, at 186, 708.

[196] Spur, at 186, 708.

[197] Silver Anniversary, *supra* note 15, at 222.

suits finally ended in June 1974 when a mutual agreement was reached out of court by Spur and DEVCO. What recompense was agreed upon is unknown but, definitely, dollars prevailed over 'scents.' "[198] Spur and Webb continued to litigate over Webb's responsibility to indemnify Spur in the residents' nuisance suits, however.[199]

Settling the legal rights thus seems to have made possible the private bargain that eluded Spur and Del Webb at the outset. (This is not an unusual role for courts and a preliminary decision on a contested issue of law or fact is often enough to produce a settlement.) When willing buyers and sellers meet in the marketplace, the terms of a sale are influenced by the presence of other buyers and sellers. If one landowner tries to charge too much for a tract of land, a lower price from another landowner will draw business from the high priced seller. Out of the interaction of many buyers and sellers, the price of the land will emerge. The problem here was that there was only one buyer, Webb, and only one seller, Spur. Without a competitive market, they had no way to resolve their difference of opinion over how much Webb should pay Spur to move its facilities to enhance Webb's land's value. It seems clear today that Spur was willing to sell and Webb was willing to buy, but that there was no market for the rights in question because of the ambiguous legal status of those rights. Once the court clarified them, the deal became possible.

Aftermath

Who won and who lost? In Arizona *Spur* was seen as a win for the cattle industry, with one observer noting that "The future stability of the state's feeding industry appears to be greatly enhanced by the Del E. Webb vs. Spur Industries, Inc. judgment." The case meant, the study concluded, that "construction and development companies must plan their ventures more prudently in the future. Since development firms are now liable for indemnification for the forceable relocation of industrial or agricultural businesses, the responsibility should limit future development projects in cattle feeding areas."[200] The case did not stop the change in land use, however. Feedlots continued to migrate away from Phoenix: "In 1963, 14 to 16 firms with feeding capacities exceeding 3,500 head operated in the area. Due to relocation, the number of lots in the

---

[198] Silver Anniversary, *supra* note 15, at 222. Cattle manure just brings out the worst in many writers and produces horrible puns like this one.

[199] Spur Feeding Co. v. Superior Court of Maricopa County, Arizona, 109 Az. 105, 505 P.2d 1377 (1973).

[200] Menzie, et al., *supra* note 57, at 39.

Phoenix area dropped to eight in 1971."[201] Favorable zoning regulations in Pinal County to the southeast drew some feedlots, while others shifted their operations onto Indian lands, where "the absence of zoning boards and ordinances have attracted a number of firms" to reservation lands.[202]

Some observers critical of nuisance law have feared that nuisance law could lock in existing patterns of land use, preventing the migration of uses to higher (i.e. more valuable) uses. *Spur* suggests common law courts, from the "logic of necessity," are capable of finding ways to prevent nuisance law from short-circuiting change. Ultimately *Spur* was a case about the pace of change. Webb's innovations in constructing Sun City—logical as it may seem in retrospect—induced more rapid demographic change that imposed significant costs on Spur. The decision in *Spur* balanced the gains made possible by the conversion of Arizona's past into Arizona's future with the transition costs of that conversion. The past could not block the future, but the future had to pay its way.

Spur's subsequent history is also a lesson on how courts handle changes in the common law. If we ask how important *Spur* has been in the law of nuisance by examining its importance to courts' written opinions, the answer is that *Spur* has not had much direct influence. Only one subsequent Arizona case has relied on it to explicate nuisance law, although a few more have cited it in passing. In *Armory Park Neighborhood Association v. Episcopal Community Services*[203] the court looked to *Spur* as authority for the statements that a lawful business could be a public nuisance and that an activity could simultaneously be a public and private nuisance. A food for the homeless program run by a church in a residential area could, therefore, be enjoined. In *Salt River Valley Water Users' Association v. Giglio*[204] the court rejected a *Spur*-like claim, noting simply that the holding in *Spur* was "to a large extent confined to the particular facts presented by those cases and they are not applicable to the facts in this case." In the intermediate appellate court, *Spur's* fate has been the same, with courts generally rejecting claims brought under it as not fitting within the narrow confines of the decision in *Spur*.[205] The only reported decision from outside Arizona to consider in detail the doctrinal developments in *Spur* came in an Ohio Common Pleas Court decision rejecting *Spur* as inapplicable because of the greater

---

[201] Menzie, et al., *supra* note 57, at 37.

[202] Menzie, et al., *supra* note 57, at 37.

[203] 148 Ariz. 1, 712 P.2d 914 (1985).

[204] 13 Ariz. 190, 549 P.2d 162 (1976).

[205] *See,* Brenteson Wholesale, Inc. v. Arizona Public Service Company, 166 Ariz. 519, 803 P.2d 930 (App. 1990); Salt River Project Agricultural Improvement and Power District v. The City of Scottsdale, 24 Ariz.App. 254, 537 P.2d 982 (Ariz. Ct. App. 1975).

amount of open space in Arizona.[206] Although Arizona (and other states) have kept *Spur's* innovation carefully within narrow bounds, settling property rights proved critical to allowing the developers and feedlots to negotiate solutions to conflicts. But legal decisions' importance is best measured by more than frequency of subsequent citation. By settling legal rights, private parties learn where they stand and are able to arrange their affairs without public intervention. The absence of citations to *Spur* in Arizona and elsewhere may reflect the opinion's success at enabling private ordering rather than the lack of importance of the holding.

Conclusion

This chapter began by asking two questions: how does the Arizona Supreme Court's common law reasoning compare to Calabresi and Melamed's simultaneous formulation of the same rule in their article? and how well did the courts in the *Spur* case handle the collision of feedlot and housing development?

In their 1972 article, Calabresi and Melamed noted that the *Spur* rule[207] was not "part of the cases legal scholars read when they study nuisance law," but still "may well be the most frequent device employed."[208] Their examples of its use, however, were the compensation of developers when their property development was restricted to solve environmental problems. Without the *Spur* rule, they argued, "traditional doctrine" would lead to an award of nuisance damages as "the only way we thought we could test out the value of the pollution was by the only liability rule we thought we had.... At least this would be the position of a court concerned with economic efficiency which believed itself limited to" an injunction, nuisance damages, or no damages.[209] Having the *Spur* rule in addition to the traditional range of outcomes in nuisance cases gave courts more options to maximize efficiency or bring about desired distributional goals.[210]

The Arizona Supreme Court does not appear to have been maximizing efficiency or aiming for a desired distributional goal. At the least, if it was, it did not say anything about those goals in its opinion. What it did do was solve a quite specific problem: how to value Spur's property

---

[206] Prijatel v. Sifco Industries, Inc., 47 Ohio Misc. 31, 353 N.E.2d 923 (Ohio C.P. 1974).

[207] Since they were writing their article simultaneously with *Spur*, they didn't call it the "*Spur* rule" but "rule four."

[208] Calabresi and Melamed, *supra* note 7, at 1117.

[209] Calabresi and Melamed, *supra* note 7, at 1120.

[210] Calabresi and Melamed, *supra* note 7, at 1121.

rights in the situation where the growth of Sun City required Spur to move. The court created a property rights allocation that allowed Spur and Webb to negotiate the distribution of costs associated with the move and which allowed future developers and feedlot owners to predict the rights allocation sufficiently well enough that no further litigation over the subject of feedlots and developments appeared in Arizona. The common law may not have been as theoretically elegant as the law review article, but it got the job done. Once the property rights were allocated, the parties were able to negotiate their way to a solution—a good illustration of the Coase Theorem at work.[211]

How well did the courts handle the social conflict caused by the collision of the new type of feedlot and the new type of city represented by Sun City? It did pretty well by most accounts. The problems (flies and odors) caused by the feedlot's location were solved, the developer who created the conflicting use bore the costs, and the rules were clarified for everyone else in such a way that no further disputes of this type appeared. How might a legislature or regulatory agency have handled the same problem? Neither solution could have directly forced Webb to pay Spur to move; more likely outcomes would have been operating standards for Spur to reduce the harm inflicted on the home owners by its operations or restrictions on Webb's ability to develop its property near the Spur lots. Given the large number of voters in Sun City, Webb's economic clout, and the Phoenix area's CGC-dominated "business-friendly" government, could Spur have gotten a fair deal in the political arena? Even if it could have, the innovative nature of both Spur and Webb's operations would have made it unlikely that either a legislature or regulator would have anticipated the problem far enough in advance to prevent it from arising. This case demonstrates that nuisance law can do a reasonable job of handling fairly rapid and dramatic changes in land use, including ones unanticipated even a short time before, even where regulatory solutions cannot.

---

[211] See Chapter 1 for an in depth, somewhat skeptical discussion of the Coase Theorem.

11

Stewart E. Sterk*

Neponsit Property Owners' Association v. Emigrant Industrial Savings Bank

Turn of the century New York City. The Rockaway peninsula, fronting on the Atlantic Ocean. Beaches and amusements rivaling Coney Island, New York's top summer destination.[1] Once an exclusive resort for the very wealthy, now made more accessible by rail connections built in the 1870s and 1880s.[2] Hotels and boarding houses, joined more recently by summer cottages and bungalows.

A large parcel of land, however, remained undeveloped, occupied principally by squatters in their tents. That parcel was plagued by a title dispute. In 1872, the United States government had begun operating a life saving station on the parcel.[3] Five years later, the New York state legislature passed an act quit-claiming title to a predecessor of the Neponsit Realty Company.[4] By 1910, the parcel was valued at $12,000,000, but the cloud on title cast by the federal government's occupation had prevented substantial development.[5] Indeed, the federal government had promised the land to the City of New York, which

---

* Mack Professor of Law, Benjamin N. Cardozo School of Law. The author thanks Elliot Gardner for helpful research assistance.

[1] Rhoda Amon, The Rockaways, A Paradise for Everyman, at http://www.lihistory.com/spectown/hist0012.htm.

[2] Peter Reinharz, Rockaway Riviera? City Journal, Summer 1999 (volume 9, number 3).

[3] U.S. Loses Its Fight, Rockaway Wave, August 13, 1910.

[4] *Id.*

[5] *Id.*

planned to incorporate the parcel into a great ocean park. To facilitate transfer to the city, the federal government brought an action to resolve the title dispute, but investigation by a title company raised serious doubts about the government's claim.[6] As a result, the federal government settled. In return for a 15–acre strip of beachfront land, valued at $100,000, the government relinquished its claim to the remainder of the parcel.[7] The federal judge who approved the settlement found, as a matter of law, that the United States government had never held title to the disputed tract.[8] Neponsit Realty Company—controlled by Realty Associates, one of the largest real estate corporations operating in the New York area[9]—was now free to develop the property.

Against that background, Neponsit Realty developed a novel idea: why not build a community of upper-class, year round homes with beach rights? Each home would be distinctive; the same plans could be used for no more than four houses in the development.[10] The homes would be built in light colors to suggest a vacation resort, but with materials that would suggest solidity and permanence.[11] The houses featured tile roofs to resist the spread of fire,[12] and were also designed to resist the salty air.[13] Many of the streets would be lined with parks.[14] In pursuance of this exclusive community, the Realty Company, in January, 1911, filed a map subdividing its land into thirty-four city blocks, comprising 1600 residential lots intersected by a grid of streets.[15] The development's name—Neponsit—was alternatively said to be an Indian word for "place between the waters" or the name of a local Indian sachem.[16] Not

---

[6] U.S. Secures Land Valued at $100,000 and Withdraws its Court Action, New York World, August 11, 1910.

[7] U.S. Loses Its Fight, Rockaway Wave, August 13, 1910.

[8] *Id.*

[9] A $1,500,000 Improvement, Rockaway Wave, September 13, 1910.

[10] Vincent Seyfried and William Asadorian, Old Rockaway, New York (Dover Publications, 2000) at 93.

[11] *Id.*

[12] *Id.*

[13] Http://www.thequeensscene.org/Rockaway.html.

[14] *Id.*

[15] Matter of City of New York (Public Beach), 269 N.Y. 64, 68, 199 N.E. 5,6 (1935).

[16] Seyfried and Asadorian, supra at 93. A local historian, however, failed to identify any chief with the name Neponsit, and the area was not known as Neponsit before the development (Letter from Davis Erhardt, Head of Long Island Division, Queens Borough Public Library, dated July 6, 1971, quoting former Queens Borough Historian Herbert F. Ricard, on file at Queensborough Public Library).

subdivided into lots was a large beachfront parcel designated "Ocean Park."[17] Neponsit's plan was to give purchasers of the residential lots an exclusive right of access to use the adjacent private beach.

The new development required Neponsit to confront some practical legal problems. First, how would the realty company guarantee homeowners an exclusive right to use the beach? That problem was easily solved by retaining ownership of the beach, and conveying each individual lot with an easement to use the beach.

Assuring adequate maintenance of the beach, roads, and other common areas presented a more difficult legal problem. Because Neponsit wanted to preserve exclusive beach access for residents of the new community, the company did not want to convey the beach or the roads to the City of New York. Nor did the company want to undertake long-term maintenance at its own expense. Leaving maintenance to resident-homeowners, on a voluntary basis, would have created what have now come to be known as freerider problems: because each resident would benefit from improvements or maintenance by any other resident, each resident has an incentive to wait for his neighbors to do the work—resulting both in too little maintenance, and in unequal sharing in the burdens of maintenance. Neponsit was aware that in other developments, this problem had resulted in neglect or ruin of common areas.[18]

The Neponsit Realty Company's objective was to obligate each of the homeowners to contribute toward maintenance. Ordinary contract, however, would not have created the necessary obligations. Only the original purchasers of the homes would have been in privity of contract with the developer. As a result, if Neponsit Realty Company obtained a contractual commitment from each home purchaser to contribute toward maintenance, Neponsit would have no basis for enforcing those commitments once the original purchasers died or sold their homes.

What Neponsit Realty did instead was to insert in each deed the following language:

> "[t]he party of the second part [the purchaser] for the party of the second part and the heirs, successors and assigns of the party of the second part further covenants that the property conveyed by this deed shall be subject to an annual charge in such an amount as will be fixed by the party of the first part [Neponsit Realty Company], its successors and assigns, not, however, exceeding in any year the sum of four ($4.00) Dollars per 20 x 100 feet."[19]

---

[17] *Id.*

[18] A $1,500,000 Improvement, Rockaway Wave, September 3, 1910.

[19] Neponsit Property Owners' Association v. Emigrant Industrial Savings Bank, 278 N.Y. 248, 253–54, 15 N.E.2d 793, 794 (1938).

By this language, Neponsit Realty Company sought to bind not only the original purchaser, but also successors and assigns, to a covenant that would "run with the land;." a property right rather than a mere in personam contract right.

At roughly the same time, a number of other prominent developers of upperclass communities across the country were following a similar strategy. Roland Park, Maryland was among the earliest to include deed covenants binding homeowners to pay assessments for maintenance.[20] In 1910, J.C. Nichols, the leading figure in popularizing the homeowner association concept, began to develop Kansas City's much-imitated Country Club District.[21] St. Francis Wood in San Francisco, Kensington on Long Island, and Forest Hills Gardens in New York's Queens County were among other early communities to make use of covenants imposing assessments on homeowners.[22] In these communities, assessments were part of a broader strategy of using deed restrictions—limiting parcels to residential use, imposing architectural restrictions—to ensure that attractive communities would retain their character over time.

Nevertheless, when Neponsit Realty created its development, the legal status of privately-imposed assessments was far from certain. English common law courts had recognized real covenants "running with the land," but only in limited circumstances: when "privity of estate" existed between the covenanting parties, and where the covenant "touched or concerned" the land.[23] Under English law, privity of estate existed only when the covenanting parties were landlord and tenant.[24] In Tulk v. Moxhay[25], however, the English Court of Chancery held that privity was unnecessary when a landowner sought to enforce a restrictive covenant in equity—so long as the burdened landowner knew of the restrictions when he acquired the land. The New York Court of Appeals, in Trustees of Columbia College v. Lynch[26], embraced Tulk, holding that

---

[20] See Wehr v. Roland Park Co., 143 Md. 384, 388, 122 A. 363, 365 (1923) [describing maintenance covenants in 1898 deed issued by Roland Park Co.]; Roland Park Civic League, http://archives.ubalt.edu/rpcl/intro.htm (discussing origins of Roland Park development); Oak Park Homes Association, http://207.228.227.194/opha/associat.htm (attributing groundwork for homeowners association to Roland Park development in 1891).

[21] See Evan McKenzie, Privatopia (Yale University Press 1994) at 38–43.

[22] See Roland Park Civic League, http://archives.ubalt.edu/rpcl/intro.htm (discussing origins of Roland Park development); Oak Park Homes Association, http://207.228.227.194/opha/associat.htm (attributing groundwork for homeowners association to Roland Park development in 1891).

[23] These doctrinal rules were derived from Spencer's Case, 77 Eng. Rep. 72 (1583).

[24] Keppell v. Bailey, 39 Eng. Rep. 1042 (1834).

[25] 41 Eng. Rep. 1143 (1848).

[26] 70 N.Y. 440 (1877).

Columbia could enforce a deed restriction prohibiting business use of a neighboring parcel. The court wrote:

> "Whoever purchases lands upon which the owner has imposed an easement of any kind, or created a charge which would be enforced inequity against him, takes the title subject to all easements, equities and charges however created, of which he has notice."[27]

This dictum, however, did not mean that the New York courts would routinely enforce real covenants. In 1909, for instance, just a few years before Neponsit was developed, the Court of Appeals refused to enforce a recorded deed covenant obligating a landowner to pay a neighbor $500 toward the cost of a party wall built at the neighbor's expense.[28] The Court of Appeals never cited Trustees of Columbia College v. Lynch, and concluded that the original agreement—despite express language purporting to bind "assigns"—did not create any privity of estate between the contracting parties.[29] As a result, the covenant was not enforceable against successors-in-interest. Enough, however, about the niceties of legal doctrine (at least for now). Suffice it to say that when Neponsit began to insert covenants in the deeds to individual parcels, the legal status of those covenants remained uncertain. Of course, the covenants were binding, as contracts, on the original purchasers of the lots, and even assigns would have found it advisable to pay their assessments, if only to avoid, at relatively low cost, a significant cloud on title (Remember that the maximum assessment permitted was only $4.00 per year for each 20 foot lot).

During the process of marketing and developing the Neponsit subdivision, Neponsit Realty had a clear financial interest in assuring that the beaches and roads were attractive and well-maintained. But Neponsit Realty undoubtedly had no interest in maintaining roads and beaches on a permanent basis. As a result, Neponsit provided in each deed that its right to enforce the annual charge could be assigned to a "Property Owners' Association which may hereafter be organized .. And in case such association is organized the sums in this paragraph provided for shall be payable to such association."[30] In addition, the Realty Company included an end date for the covenants—January 31st 1940—limiting the total financial liability any landowner would incur as a result of the deed covenants.[31]

---

[27] Id. at 450.

[28] Crawford v. Krollpfeiffer, 195 N.Y. 185, 88 N.E. 29 (1909).

[29] Id.

[30] Neponsit Property Owners' Association v. Emigrant Industrial Savings Bank, 278 N.Y. 248, 253, 15 N.E.2d 793, 794 (1938).

[31] Id. at 253, 15 N.E.2d at 795.

Creation of the Association and Condemnation of the Beach

As contemplated by the deed covenants, the Neponsit Realty Company did organize an association—the Neponsit Property Owners' Association (the Association). The Association's certificate of incorporation described its objects. First among those objects was "to preserve the settlement known as Neponsit on Rockaway Beach ... as a highly restricted, well kept and properly maintained suburban home community."[32] In addition, the Association was designed "to acquire title to and hold such portions of said property, including the beach front, as may be granted to it by deed or otherwise, for the benefit of all property owners in said Neponsit, and to make such use of such property ... as shall be for the best interests of the property holders at said Neponsit."[33] The Association's bylaws conferred membership status on "all record holders of lots at Neponsit."[34]

On January 13, 1920, the Neponsit Realty Company conveyed to The Association its beachfront land—Ocean Park—subject to an easement in favor of all Neponsit lot owners, who retained the right to "make use of such beach for bathing and other recreations and sports but not for commercial uses and purposes."[35] The scheme envisioned by Neponsit Realty Company was close to fruition. Indeed, on August 16, 1919, Neponsit Realty Company auctioned off the last of its Neponsit lots.[36]

Enter the City of New York. Attempting to expand the public beachfront in Queens County, the city brought a condemnation proceeding to acquire Ocean Park. In that proceeding, however, the city sought to acquire the beachfront land for a nominal sum. The city argued that the Association, as fee owner of the land, had suffered no substantial damage as owner of a fee interest in the beach, because the beach was "so incumbered by easements that it cannot be put to any beneficial use by the owner of the fee."[37] And the city's argument persuaded New York's intermediate appellate court, which awarded "unknown owners" of the beachfront land a total of six cents![38]

---

[32] Matter of City of New York (Public Beach), 269 N.Y. 64, 72, 199 N.E. 5, 8 (1935).

[33] *Id.*

[34] *Id.*

[35] *Id.* at 67–68, 199 N.E. at 5.

[36] Seyfried and Asadorian, supra at 94.

[37] *Id.* at 71, 199 N.E. at 7.

[38] *Id.* at 67, 199 N.E. at 5.

The Association appealed to the Court of Appeals. The state's high court reversed, rejecting the city's argument and holding instead that the Association essentially acted on behalf of the individual easement holders. As a result, the court concluded, "[The damage to the corporation by the taking of the land is the value of the use of that land by the corporation for the benefit of those accorded membership rights therein."[39] As a result, the city ultimately had to pay $88,162.80 to the Association.[40]

The condemnation played a critical role in the development of the Neponsit case. First, when the city condemned Ocean Park, the Association had less to do. The city had already assumed responsibility for maintenance of streets in the subdivision. With the city's assumption of maintenance obligations for the beach, some residents began to wonder how the association was spending the assessments it was collecting.[41]

Second, the condemnation award filled the Association's coffers, raising questions about how the money should be distributed. The Association was now in an unexpected position: rather than collecting money from its members, the association would soon have to pay those members a share of the condemnation award. This, too, created uncertainty: would members who had not kept up their payments be entitled to an equal share of the condemnation award?[42]

Third, condemnation of the beachfront property deprived the Association of ownership of any property in the development, creating (as we shall see) a doctrinal obstacle to enforcement of the covenant.

The Litigation Unfolds

The genesis of the Neponsit litigation was a deed dated June 25th, 1917 conveying five 20 x 100 foot lots in Neponsit from Neponsit Realty

---

[39] *Id.* at 75m 199 N.E. at 9.

[40] Matter of City of New York (Public Beach), 288 App.Div. 455, 17 N.Y.S.2d 2 (1940).

[41] See, e.g. Appellant's Brief to the Court of Appeals, Neponsit Property Owners' Association v. Emigrant Industrial Savings Bank (278 N.Y. 248, 15 N.E.2d 793) [hereinafter Appellant's Brief] at 13:

"The assignee, the Neponsit Property Owners' Association, is merely a scheme by which several individuals in Neponsit seek to levy tribute upon all the property holders at Neponsit Beach. Although a membership corporation in name, these individuals pay themselves salaries when in truth and in fact the New York City Department of Sanitation and the Park Department maintain all streets, paths, parks, roads, beach and sewers, etc."

[42] See Matter of City of New York (Public Beach), 258 App.Div. 455, 458, 17 N.Y.S.2d 2, 4 (1940) [noting and affirming trial court order that Association should pay unpaid lot charges to itself before distributing balance of condemnation award].

Company to Robert Oldner Deyer and Charlotte Ingram Deyer, a married couple.[43] The deed included the covenant requiring payment of the annual assessment, the provision permitting assignment to a property owners' association, and a clause providing that on the first day of May of each year, the assessment charge "shall become a lien on the land and shall continue to be such lien until fully paid."[44] The Deyers paid the annual assessment to Neponsit Realty Company for each year through 1920. In that year—1920—Neponsit Realty Company assigned its rights to the Association, and Deyer stopped paying the annual assessment.[45] The Association, however, took no action to enforce the annual assessment.

In February 1935, the Emigrant Industrial Savings Bank acquired title to the Deyer parcel at a foreclosure sale.[46] The referee's deed—like all of the other intervening deeds in the bank's chain of title—recited that it was subject to covenants and restrictions of former deeds of record. Emigrant, however, did not pay the current assessment or any past due assessments, despite a demand by the Association.[47] Then, in July 1937, the Association brought an action seeking an adjudication that it held a valid lien on the property for $340 plus interest (17 years of unpaid assessments), and an order that the property be sold and the sale proceeds be used to satisfy the association's lien.[48]

Emigrant's answer set forth a number of defenses. First, Emigrant alleged that the Association had not provided any maintenance services during the period 1920–1937.[49] Second, Emigrant alleged that Association was not, and had not been since at least 1926, the fee owner of any of the roads paths, parks, beach, streets, and sewers located in Neponsit.[50] Third, Emigrant alleged that the City of New York owned the public areas, and had levied and collected taxes for the purpose of

---

[43] Neponsit Property Owners' Association v. Emigrant Industrial Savings Bank, 278 N.Y. 248, 253, 15 N.E.2d 793, 794 (1938).

[44] *Id.*

[45] Respondent's Brief to the Court of Appeals, Neponsit Property Owners' Association v. Emigrant Industrial Savings Bank (278 N.Y. 248, 15 N.E.2d 793)[hereinafter Respondent's Brief], at 5.

[46] Complaint, Neponsit Property Owners' Association v. Emigrant Industrial Savings Bank, (Point "Sixth").

[47] *Id.* (Point "Eighth").

[48] *Id.* (Complaint Verified July 8, 1937).

[49] Answer, Neponsit Property Owners' Association v. Emigrant Industrial Savings Bank, (Point "Fourth").

[50] *Id.* (Point "Fifth").

maintaining those areas.[51] Emigrant's fourth defense alleged waiver and abandonment by failing to foreclose on the lien for seventeen years.[52] Emigrant also sought cancellation of the covenant based on a change in neighborhood conditions,[53] argued that the covenants were against public policy because Association had not obtained authorization from the City to maintain public facilities,[54] and finally, that the statute of frauds barred enforcement of the covenant because neither Emigrant nor any of Emigrant's predecessors had signed the deed creating the covenant[55] (Typically, only the seller, not the buyer, signs a deed). As a result, Emigrant sought judgment dismissing the complaint.

In 1937, justice was swift. Thirty-six days after Emigrant's answer was verified, the New York Law Journal reported that Emigrant's motion to dismiss the complaint had been denied.[56] Denial of Emigrant's motion could not have been a surprise; the Appellate Division had, just six months earlier, denied judgment on the pleadings to another defaulting property owner in a nearly identical action by Association.[57] Nor should it have been a surprise, in light of its own prior decision, that the Appellate Division affirmed without opinion[58] (although, by modern standards, it is astounding that the case was decided by the Appellate Division less than five months after the complaint was filed!)

Neponsit in the Court of Appeals

Emigrant appealed the Appellate Division's affirmance to the Court of Appeals, New York's highest court. At the Court of Appeals, the issue was one of first impression: the court had never dealt with the power of a homeowner's association to enforce assessments against individual landowners.

A. Emigrant's Brief

In seeking to enforce the assessments, the Association secured help from an unexpected source: the lawyers for Emigrant Industrial Savings

---

[51] *Id.* (Point "Eighth").

[52] *Id.* (Point "Tenth").

[53] *Id.* (Point "Seventeenth").

[54] *Id.* (Point "Twenty–Second").

[55] *Id.* (Point "Twenty-third").

[56] New York Law Journal, August 26, 1937.

[57] Neponsit Property Owners' Association v. Mayer, 250 App.Div. 738, 294 N.Y.S. 735 (1937).

[58] Neponsit Property Owners' Association v. Emigrant Industrial Savings Bank, 252 App.Div. 876, 300 N.Y.Supp. 1341 (1937).

Bank. Emigrant's brief on appeal discussed the law in eight short pages.[59] Most of those pages were devoted to out-of-context quotations from prior opinions.[60] The brief raised only one significant point, and never made an affirmative case for Emigrant's position.

The one argument Emigrant did make was that because the Association did not own land for the benefit of which the covenant was created, the Association had no foundation for enforcement of the covenant.[61] Emigrant cast this issue as one of "privity of estate." Some property teachers today would cast the issue differently: can the burden of a covenant bind successors-in-interest to the burdened land when the benefit of the covenant is held "in gross?"[62] Of course, the Association *did* succeed to the interest in land originally held by Neponsit Realty Company; in particular, the Association succeeded to a fee interest in the beachfront land. It was the city's condemnation proceeding, and not any action by Neponsit Realty Company or by the Association itself, that deprived the Association of title to benefitted land.

Why have a rule limiting enforcement of covenants to parties who own estates in land? On that issue, Emigrant's brief was completely silent. In general, however, there are reasons to prevent non-landowners from enforcing covenants. As time passes, one or both parties to a covenant might find the need to modify the covenant, or to terminate it altogether. So long as the benefitted and burdened parties are neighboring landowners, parties seeking to renegotiate should be able to find each other whenever modification seems appropriate. By contrast, if the original beneficiary of a covenant could assign the benefit to an entity with no ownership interest in the land, that entity might become difficult to locate over time. Indeed, the entity might cease operations altogether. Consequently, removal or modification would become problematic.[63] Even if the burdened landowner knew that the covenant would not be enforced, the covenant would remain as a cloud on title, perhaps discouraging prospective purchasers interested in the burdened land.

This reason for limiting enforcement of covenants to those who own benefitted land, however, had little force on the facts of Neponsit. First, membership in the Association was limited to owners of land with the subdivision. As a result, there was little danger that the association

---

[59] Appellant's Brief at 6–13.

[60] *Id.*

[61] *Id.* at 6–11.

[62] See, e.g. Joseph William Singer, Introduction to Property 250–51 (2001); Roger A. Cunningham, William B. Stoebuck, and Dale A. Whitman, The Law of Property 494 (2000).

[63] See Susan F. French, Servitudes Reform and the New Restatement of Property: Creation Doctrines and Structural Simplification, 73 Cornell L Rev 928, 945–46 (1988).

would lose touch with the burdened landowners; the landowners collectively were the association. The Association made much of this in its brief, starting with the premise that "there could be no question" that the individual landowners who had paid their own assessments would be entitled to enforce the covenant against Emigrant.[64] The Association then noted that the action had been brought "at the instance of the lot owners in Neponsit, any one of whom would have had the right to maintain the same in his own name."[65]

Second, the assessment covenant in Neponsit was time-limited. By its terms, the covenant would expire in 1940. As a result, the danger that the covenant would become an obsolete clog on title was significantly reduced; within two years after the decision in Neponsit, the landowners would no longer be bound to pay assessments.

B. The Association's Brief

Two other potential obstacles to enforcement of the covenant were raised not in Emigrant's brief, but in the brief written by the Association's lawyers. Perhaps concerned that the Court of Appeals would raise these issues on its own, the Association's lawyers followed a practice of disclosing doctrines unfavorable to their client, and then demonstrating how those doctrines did not prevent enforcement of the covenant. In particular, the Association's brief included the words "touch and concern"[66]—words found nowhere in Emigrant's brief. In addition, the Association acknowledged that New York courts had refused to enforce "positive or affirmative covenants."[67]

1. Touch and Concern

The touch and concern requirement for enforcing real covenants was first articulated in England in Spencer's Case[68], decided in 1583. Spencer's case involved a covenant by a lessee for himself and his executors that the lessee, his executors, administrators, or assigns, would build a brick wall on the leased premises. At the time Spencer's case was decided, enforcement against assigns of a covenant made between neighbors would have been unthinkable; the prevailing conception of privity of estate permitted enforcement against successors only when the original covenanting parties were landlord and tenant. But the court in Spencer's case concluded that mere privity of estate was not enough to permit

---

[64] Respondent's Brief at 10.

[65] *Id.* at 10–11.

[66] *Id.* at 6.

[67] *Id.*

[68] 77 Eng. Rep. 72 (1583).

enforcement of a covenant against the successor-in-interest of the covenanting party. Only covenants that touched or concerned the land would
be enforceable against successors.

Towards the middle of the nineteenth century, New York courts
applied the touch and concern doctrine to permit lease assignees to avoid
leasehold obligations undertaken by their predecessors. Dolph v. White[69]
illustrates the doctrine. Jeremiah White and Stevenson executed a prom-
issory note obligating them to pay $100 to Gilbert. At that time, White
owned a saw mill. Subsequently, White leased the saw mill to Stevenson
and another. As partial consideration for the lease, Stevenson agreed to
pay the note he and White had previously executed. Stevenson later
assigned his interest in the lease to Samuel White. When the note was
not paid, Gilbert's assignee, Dolph, brought an action against Samuel
White to recover on the note. In holding that Samuel White was not
liable on the covenant, the Court of Appeals distinguished the covenant
to pay the note (which the court deemed "collateral") from the covenant
to pay rent which, in the court's view ran with the land. The covenant to
pay the note did not touch or concern the land, and therefore Samuel
White could be liable on the covenant only if he himself had promised to
pay the note; assignment of the lease did not carry with it the obligation
to perform a covenant personal to the original tenant.

The Court of Appeals decided Dolph v. White in 1855. During the
succeeding 83 years, not once did the court invoke—or even discuss—the
touch and concern doctrine. The court had never applied the doctrine to
any covenant outside the landlord-tenant context. Several Appellate
Division cases had, however, discussed the doctrine[70], and in one of
those—Lawrence Park Realty v. Crichton[71]—the Second Department
held that a covenant to pay a proportionate share of maintenance costs
did touch and concern the land. The Association's lawyers must have
concluded that they had nothing to lose by briefing the doctrine and
contending that the assessment covenant met the doctrine's requirements.

2.   The Prohibition on Enforcement of Affirmative Covenants

Although, in the decades before Neponsit, "touch and concern" had
largely slipped from the judicial vocabulary of the New York courts,

---

[69] 12 N.Y. 296 (1855).

[70] Buffalo Academy of Sacred Heart v. Boehm Bros., Inc., 241 App.Div. 578, 272
N.Y.Supp. 578 (1934); St. Regis Restaurant, Inc. v. Powers., 219 App.Div. 321, 219
N.Y.Supp. 684 (1927); Lawrence Park Realty v. Crichton, 218 App.Div. 374, 218 N.Y.Supp.
278 (1926); Rhinelander Real Estate Co. v. Cammeyer. 216 App.Div. 299, 214 N.Y.Supp.
284 (1926); Storandt v. Vogel & Binder Co., 140 App.Div. 671, 125 N.Y.Supp. 568 (1910);
Munro v. Syracuse, L.S. & N.R. Co., 128 App.Div. 388, 112 N.Y.Supp. 938 (1908).

[71] 218 App.Div. 374, 218 N.Y.Supp. 278 (1926).

those courts had frequently discussed and sometimes applied another restriction on the content of covenants "running with the land": affirmative covenants could not bind successors-in-interest.[72] The leading case was Miller v. Clary[73], decided in 1913. Phoenix Mills promised, for itself and its assigns, to construct and maintain a wheel and shaft for the purposes of supplying power to neighboring landowners. Miller, who succeeded to the interest of the neighbors, brought an action to enforce the covenant against Clary, who had acquired the Phoenix Mills property. The Court of Appeals held the covenant unenforceable, endorsing the English rule that "affirmative or positive" covenants are not enforceable against successors-in-interest. The court acknowledged that the rule was subject to exceptions, both in England and in New York, but concluded that Miller v. Clary did not fall within the scope of the exceptions.

What is an affirmative covenant? In Miller v. Clary, the Court of Appeals wrote that an affirmative covenant "compels the covenantor to submit not merely to some restriction in the use of his property, but compels him to do an act thereon for the benefit of the owner of the dominant estate."[74] That definition created a problem for the Association. Although some of the deed covenants imposed by Neponsit Realty Co., such as the limitation to single-family residential use, would qualify as restrictive covenants, the assessment covenant might not. That covenant required the lot owners "to do an act"—to pay the annual fee. Unless the Association could persuade the court that the covenant was not an affirmative covenant, or fell within an exception to New York's prohibition on affirmative covenants, the Association might be in trouble.

The Association's brief relied largely on precedent—but not from the Court of Appeals. Instead, the Association relied on two then-recent Appellate Division cases dealing with assessment covenants, one of them involving another litigation brought by the Association to enforce the same covenant against another recalcitrant landowner.[75] The Association quoted heavily from the other Appellate Division opinion, in which the court stressed that to treat the assessment as an affirmative covenant

> "would enable the defendant to accept the benefits of the covenants in the deed on the part of the plaintiff, the grantor in the deed, and

---

[72] See, e.g., Morgan Lake Co. v. N.Y., N.H & Hart. RR Co., 262 N.Y. 234, 186 N.E. 685 (1933); Greenfarb v. R.S.K. Realty Corp., 256 N.Y. 130, 175 N.E. 649 (1931); Crawford v. Krollpfeiffer, 195 N.Y. 185, 88 N.E. 29 (1909); Sebald v. Mulholland, 155 N.Y. 455, 50 N.E. 260 (1898).

[73] 210 N.Y. 127, 103 N.E. 1114 (1913).

[74] Id. at 132, 103 N.E. at 1115.

[75] Neponsit Property Owners' Assn v. Mayer, 250 App.Div. 738, 294 N.Y.S. 735 (1937); Lawrence Park Realty Co. v. Crichton, 218 App.Div. 374, 218 N.Y.Supp. 278 (1926).

to enjoy free of expense ... the enhanced value of the premises by reason of having it located in a park with all these benefits and appurtenances.''[76]

The Association then cited a trial court case upholding an assessment covenant,[77] and closed by emphasizing the similarity of the covenant at bar to those upheld in the three cited cases.[78]

Although the Association prevailed in the Court of Appeals, its treatment of the prohibition on affirmative covenants, and of the reasons the assessment covenant should fall outside of that prohibition, could have been stronger. The problem with enforcement of affirmative covenants against successor landowners is two-fold. First, affirmative covenants, like restrictive covenants, can become obsolete over time, leaving title burdened by an obligation to which subsequent landowners would never agree.[79] Second, unlike restrictive covenants, affirmative covenants are generally unnecessary to accomplish the landowners' mutual objectives. Miller v. Clary is a case in point. The landowners who wanted to arrange for construction and maintenance of a shaft could easily have done so without imposing an obligation on subsequent owners of the burdened land. The landowners could have purchased the services of shaft-makers and shaft-maintainers on the market; the landowner on whose the land the shaft would be located enjoyed no special advantage in providing those services.

Thus, New York courts declined to enforce most affirmative covenants because these covenants imposed clogs on title, and were unnecessary to accomplish legitimate landowner objectives. Restrictive covenants, by contrast, often are necessary to accomplish landowner objectives. If a homeowner wants to assure that his neighbors use their lots for single-family homes only, the only way the homeowner can obtain that assurance is to extract a promise from his immediate neighbors that will bind the neighbors' heirs and assigns.[80] A comparable promise from someone who owns land across town simply will not do. There is, then, no ordinary market available to a landowner seeking the benefit of a restrictive covenant. As a result, New York courts enforced restrictive covenants.

---

[76] Lawrence Park Realty Co. v. Crichton, 218 App.Div. at 377, 218 N.Y.Supp. at 278.

[77] Kennilwood Owners Association v. Jaybro Realty & Development, Inc., 156 Misc. 604, 281 N.Y.S. 541 (1935).

[78] Respondent's Brief at 8.

[79] See, e.g. Stewart E. Sterk, Freedom from Freedom of Contract: The Enduring Value of Servitude Restrictions, 70 Iowa L Rev 615, 619–20, 648 (1985).

[80] See *Id.* at 646–47.

The assessment covenants in Neponsit, when taken in conjunction with the promises made by Neponsit Realty that the assessments would be used to maintain the common facilities, were designed to avoid the freerider problems that would otherwise have plagued efforts to maintain those facilities. Why should any landowner pay if he can avoid paying and still benefit from his neighbors' expenditures? To prevent freeriding, Neponsit Realty had to bind the all of the beneficiaries of maintenance—landowners in the subdivision, and their successors-in-interest, to the assessment covenant. That objective would have been unattainable unless the covenant were enforceable. In this sense, then, the assessment covenant was akin to the restrictive covenants that New York courts had routinely enforced.

3. Equitable Enforcement

Having argued that the assessment covenant met all the requisites for enforcement as a real covenant, the Association then hedged its bets. The brief argued that even if Emigrant were to succeed on its "technical defense" that the covenant "does not run with the land", the covenant was nevertheless enforceable in equity.[81] The Association emphasized a clear intent to establish the restrictions for its benefit, together with "constructive, if not actual notice" by Emigrant, and compliance with the covenant's terms by the Association and its assignor, Neponsit Realty. "Under such circumstances," the brief contended, "a court of equity will enforce the covenant in favor even of a stranger to the conveyance."[82] The Association then cited, and quoted, four Court of Appeals opinions, starting with Trustees of Columbia College v. Lynch, in which the court had first embraced the rule that covenants not enforceable at law might still be enforceable in equity.[83]

Each of the cases the Association cited, however, involved restrictive covenants, not assessments or other affirmative obligations. Needless to say, the Association did not emphasize that distinction. Instead, the Association asserted that it was not seeking a money judgment against Emigrant, but instead was seeking only to enforce a charge that was already in existence at the time Emigrant took title to the premises.[84]

---

[81] Respondent's Brief at 11.

[82] *Id.* at 12.

[83] Vogeler v. Alwyn Improvement Corp., 247 N.Y. 131, 159 N.E. 886; 247 N.Y. 131, 159 N.E. 886 (1928) Equitable Life Assurance Society v. Brennan, 148 N.Y. 661, 43 N.E. 173; 148 N.Y. 661, 43 N.E. 173 (1896); Hodge v. Sloan, 107 N.Y. 244, 17 N.E. 335; 107 N.Y. 244, 17 N.E. 335 (1887); Trustees of Columbia College v. Lynch, 70 N.Y. 440 (1877).

[84] Respondent's Brief, at 19.

C. The Court's Opinion

The Court of Appeals affirmed the Appellate Division's order up-holding the Association's complaint. Writing for a unanimous court, Judge Irving Lehman started by noting that Neponsit Realty had a clear intent to bind successor landowners to the assessment covenant. As Judge Lehman put it, "[t]he language of the covenant admits of no other construction."[85] But Judge Lehman then acknowledged that intent alone was not enough to permit a covenant to "run with the land." He summarized three "age-old essentials of a real covenant": (1) intent that the covenant should run with the land; (2) the covenant must be one " 'touching' or 'concerning' the land with which it runs," and (3) privity of estate between the parties.[86] These age-old essentials, however, were derived not from earlier New York cases (recall that the Court of Appeals had not invoked the touch and concern doctrine in more than 80 years), but from Professor Clark's then-recent treatise on Covenants and Inter-ests Running With the Land.[87]

This new-found focus on "touch and concern" enabled Judge Leh-man to downplay the affirmative aspects of the assessment covenant. Instead of a categorical rule that affirmative covenants cannot run with the land, the court's opinion adopted a touch and concern limitation that by the court's own admission was "too vague to be of much assistance."[88] Whether a covenant was affirmative became a factor to consider in determining whether the covenant touched or concerned the land, but the court went out of its way, at several points in the opinion, to reject a formalistic approach to the question; for Judge Lehman, the binding effect of the covenant should not rest on technical distinctions.

The court's own efforts to articulate a rule or standard for determin-ing whether a particular covenant would touch or concern the land was hampered by the court's apparent inability to construct (or to articulate) any rationale for the doctrine. Indeed, at one point in the opinion, the court appeared to suggest that touch and concern is largely a matter of intent (after starting its opinion by emphasizing that intent alone was insufficient unless the covenant touched or concerned the land)![89]

---

[85] 278 N.Y. 248 at 254, 15 N.E.2d 793 at 795.

[86] *Id.* at 255, 15 N.E.2d at 795.

[87] Charles E. Clark, Real Covenants and Other Interests Which "Run With Land" (1929).

[88] 278 N.Y. 248 at 256, 15 N.E.2d at 795.

[89] Thus, the court wrote:

> ". . . [S]tressing the intent and substantial effect of the covenant rather than its form, it seems clear that the covenant may properly be said to touch and concern the land of the defendant and its burden should run with the land."

With respect to the Neponsit covenant itself, the court emphasized the close connection between the easement to use the common facilities and the covenant that the landowners should bear the burden of paying to maintain those facilities. In Judge Lehman's words, "[i]t is plain that any distinction or definition which would exclude such a covenant from the classification of covenants which 'touch' or 'concern' the land would be based on form and not on substance."[90]

Having disposed of the touch or concern requirement, the court turned to Emigrant's primary argument: that the Association was not entitled to enforce the assessment covenant because the Association did not own any land in the development. The court characterized the issue as one of privity, and started by acknowledging that none of the standard definitions of privity would embrace the relationship between the Association and Emigrant—largely because the Association did not own any property originally owned by the grantor. The court acknowledged that equity courts had dispensed with the privity requirement, but recognized that prior cases enforcing covenants as equitable servitudes had involved restrictive covenants, not the charges or assessments involved in Neponsit.[91] The court decided nevertheless that the Association could enforce the assessment covenant because the corporate entity was acting as agent or representative of the Neponsit property owners—who did own land within the development. As with touch and concern, the court concluded that "in substance, if not in form, there is privity of estate between the plaintiff and the defendant."[92]

The Aftermath

What impact did the Court of Appeals decision have on the Neponsit community? Almost none. The decision was not even reported in any of the local Rockaway newspapers—and there were at least three at the time.

One might surmise that this omission reflected a low level of local awareness of legal issues. That surmise, however, would be wrong. The local papers reported on a number of legal issues, including stories relating directly to the Neponsit Property Owners Association.

First, the papers reported on the Association's efforts—through litigation—to stem the conversion of single-family homes to two-family

---

Id. at 259, 15 N.E.2d at 797.

[90] Id. at 260, 15 N.E.2d at 797.

[91] Id. at 261, 15 N.E.2d at 798.

[92] Id. at 262, 15 N.E.2d at 798.

homes.[93] A number of homeowners, pressed financially as a result of the Depression, sought to generate rental income from their homes, in violation of the covenants in their deeds. Applicable zoning regulations— but not the deed covenants—permitted two-family homes in the area. The Association and most of its members, however, were intent on maintaining Neponsit's single-family character.[94] As the deed restrictions were about to expire, the Association mounted a successful campaign to have the City of New York rezone Neponsit to permit single-family homes only. The leading local newspaper reported on this campaign, and on lawsuits brought to prevent landowners from conversions before the new zoning ordinance took effect.[95]

Second, newspaper articles reported on disputes over distribution of award generated by condemnation of the beach front.[96] The disputes centered largely on whether landowners closer to the beach should receive a larger share of the award, or whether the funds should be distributed more equally. Although one article reported that the Association's president had testified that he believed lot owners who had not paid their assessments to the association should have the amounts due deducted from their share, newspaper discussion did not focus on the issue.[97]

What inferences can be drawn from local silence about the case? First, the silence undercuts the argument that the Association brought the case to settle issues about distribution of the condemnation award. If the condemnation award had been the motivating factor for the litiga-

---

[93] See Restrictions Now on Trial, Rockaway Wave, June 22, 1939 [discussing trial of case brought against Neponsit landowner who was maintaining a two-family home]; Restrictions at Neponsit are Upheld, Rockaway Wave, June 29, 1939 [discussing judge's injunction against two-family homes]; see also G–Zone Rests in City Plan, Rockaway Wave, June 8, 1939.

[94] In 1939, more than sixty percent of Neponsit landowners signed petitions asking the city to place the community in a zoning district that would permit only single-family homes. Five percent of the residents signed a petition protesting against the rezoning. Restrictions at Neponsit are Upheld, Rockaway Wave, June 29, 1939.

[95] See id; see also New G–Zone Approved by Estimate Board, Rockaway Wave, July 20, 1939 [detailing approval of the zone change over the opposition of some community members, and noting that the zone change was prompted by expiration of land restrictions, and the fact that some landowners had begun to use the property in violation of the restrictions, but in a manner consistent with existing zoning regulations].

[96] See Neponsit Owners, With $88,000 Melon, Ask Court How to Cut It, Rockaway Wave, May 25, 1939; Court Trial of Neponsit Award Opens, Rockaway Wave, June 1, 1939; Ocean Front Owners Win First Share in Neponsit Beach Award, Rockaway Wave, June 29, 1939; Bank Appeals From Court's Award Order, Rockaway Wave, August 31, 1939.

[97] Court Trial of Neponsit Award Opens, Rockaway Wave, June 1, 1939.

tion, more discussion would almost certainly have appeared in the local press.

Why, then, did the Association bring the action, and why did the bank resist? The litigation expenses incurred by the two parties through three levels of court would appear to have dwarfed the amount in controversy, which was only $340 plus interest. One explanation, consistent with the bank's weak brief, is that the bank wanted to establish the principle that assessment covenants were enforceable. During the Depression, Emigrant and other banks had foreclosed on various residential properties, some of them in areas subject to assessment covenants. Those properties might have been more valuable for resale purposes if potential purchasers could be assured that common areas would be maintained. Hence, it might have been in Emigrant's interest to establish that assessment covenants would be enforceable. From that perspective, Neponsit would have been an attractive test case. With a "cap" on the annual assessments, and a termination date within reach, the Court of Appeals was unlikely to conclude that enforcement of the assessment covenant would place an onerous and uncertain burden on the homeowners. If the bank wanted to establish the general enforceability of assessment covenants, Neponsit was a good place to start. Although the theory is a provocative one, there is little evidence to support it (or to refute it).

Equally plausible is the conclusion that the litigation was a grudge match between the Association and dissident members. Newspaper reports establish that dissidents were unhappy with the Association's efforts to maintain high standards at a time when many homeowners were in the midst of financial crises.[98] These tensions were undoubtedly exacerbated by the limited functions performed by the Association after condemnation of the beach. Although the "grudge match" explanation could account for some of the other litigation the Association pursued to enforce the assessment covenants, it seems somewhat unsatisfactory with respect to litigation against a bank.

The motivations that lie behind the Neponsit litigation, then, remain something of a mystery. What we do know is that Neponsit remained an attractive residential neighborhood even after the covenants expired.[99] In the 1940s and 1950s, it was home to judges and

---

[98] At the time the Association and most Neponsit residents were campaigning for a zoning change that would limit use to single-family homes, the Association president is quoted as saying that "[a] few of the residents were launching a derogatory campaign against the standards of Neponsit, which forbid multiple dwellings." Five percent of Neponsit residents had signed a petition opposing the zone change, and some residents had violated the existing deed restrictions, prompting legal action. Restrictions at Neponsit Are Upheld, Rockaway Wave, June 29, 1939.

[99] See e.g., Out Here Doubt Springs Eternal; Another Decade, Another Plan for Redeveloping the Rockaways, New York Times, February 4, 2002, Page B1 [contrasting

politicians (including two New York City mayors); celebrities like Judy Garland and comedian Sam Levenson were also in Neponsit.[100] We also know that the Neponsit Property Owners' Association remains active today, even without the financial role that expired in 1940.[101]

The Legacy of Neponsit

Why has Neponsit remained a staple of Property casebooks more than six decades after the case was decided? In part, Neponsit has endured as a teaching tool because of the court's restatement and application of ancient principles. But Neponsit's endurance, and increased importance, also reflects social, economic, and legal developments that the Court of Appeals could not have foreseen when it decided the case.

As we have seen, the enforceability of assessment covenants was quite unclear in 1911 when Neponsit Realty Company began imposing these covenants in deeds to Neponsit lots. Little that happened during the ensuing 35 years clarified their status. A few lower court cases in New York enforced assessment covenants.[102] A 1923 case in Maryland rejected a claim by dissident landowners seeking to avoid assessments imposed in the pioneering Roland Park subdivision.[103] None of those opinions, however, dealt as extensively with the doctrinal issues raised in Neponsit. In other areas, there were no decided cases.

The paucity of cases reflected, in part, the relative rarity of large subdivisions with assessment covenants. A few imaginative large-scale developers championed assessment covenants as a means to permit affluent homeowners to secure public services beyond those most municipalities would be willing to provide. Charles Ascher, developer of Rad-

---

million dollar homes in Neponsit with blight on the other end of the Rockaway peninsula]; About New York, New York Times, July 24, 1985, Page B1 [discussing disputes over parking in Neponsit, where on-street parking is prohibited from May 15 to September 30, making beach access difficult for non-residents]; Belle Harbor and Neponsit Protect Seashore Oasis, New York Sunday News, March 21, 1971 [discussing continued resentment that the city had made the beach public].

[100] Seyfried and Asadorian, *supra,* at 94.

[101] See, e.g., Neponsit Residents Frown on Park Plan, New York Daily News, November 6, 1998, Suburban Section, Page 2 [detailing comments of president of the Association about plans for redevelopment of the Neponsit Health Care Center (residents preferred single-family homes to a beachfront park or a hospital)].

[102] Lawrence Park Realty Co. v. Crichton, 218 App.Div. 374, 218 N.Y.Supp. 278 (1926); Kennilwood Owners Association v. Jaybro Realty & Development, Inc., 156 Misc. 604, 281 N.Y.S. 541 (1935).

[103] Wehr v. Roland Park Company, 143 Md. 384, 122 A. 363 (1923).

burn, New Jersey, was a prime example. Ascher saw "government-by-contract" as a mechanism for developing a self-contained community, including both residential and non-residential uses.[104]

When Neponsit was decided in 1938, however, the suburbanization of America was still in its early stages. The suburban development that had occurred in the 1920s slowed considerably in the face of the Depression.[105] Moreover, much early development involved the purchase of individual lots for the construction of individual homes. Financing for larger projects was difficult to come by.

Just a few years before Neponsit was decided, however, President Roosevelt and Congress created the Federal Housing Administration (FHA), whose programs and policies spawned a dramatic increase in large-scale development. First, the FHA's mortgage insurance program increased the availability of financing, both for developers and for home buyers themselves.[106] Second, the FHA's policies promoted common facilities, and also encouraged use of deed restrictions.[107]

With the post-war boom in suburban development, common facilities and community associations became more common in newly-built communities. The success of these facilities and associations depended heavily on the enforceability of assessment covenants. And it was Neponsit that reassured developers and homeowners that these covenants would, indeed, be enforced.

By 1960, suburban land was becoming scarcer and more expensive.[108] As a result, developers sought ways to increase the density of housing development.[109] In response to these concerns, Congress, in 1961, acted to make FHA mortgage insurance available to purchasers of condominium housing.[110] At that time, a few condominiums had been created on common law foundations, but these condominiums were of no

---

[104] See Charles S. Ascher, The Extra–Municipal Administration of Radburn, National Municipal Review, July 1929, at 412; Charles S. Ascher, How Can a Section of a Town Get What it is Prepared to Pay for?, The American City, June 1929 at 98.

[105] From 1920 through 1929, more than seven million housing units were started in the United States; housing starts during the 1930s fell to 2.7 million. Evan McKenzie, Privatopia (Yale University Press 1994) at 56–57.

[106] Marc A. Weiss and John W. Watts, Community Builders and Community Associations: The Role of Real Estate Developers in Private Residential Governance, in Residential Community Associations: Private Governments in the Intergovernmental System (Advisory Committee on Intergovernmental Relations 1989) at 99–100.

[107] Id. at 100.

[108] McKenzie, supra, at 81.

[109] Id.

[110] Id. at 95.

economic importance, and had not achieved statutory sanction in any state. Within six years of Congress' action, however, all fifty states had statutes authorizing condominiums.[111] Condominiums required community associations to maintain common areas, and the new statutes all provided for enforcement of assessments imposed by the association. The popularity of condominiums and other common interest developments mushroomed. In 1962, fewer than 500 residential community associations were in existence in the United States; by 1973, the number had jumped to 15,000.[112]

During the intervening 30 years, community associations have become pervasive in the United States. Neponsit was the case that first placed those associations on a solid legal foundation. With respect to condominiums, the common law rules articulated in Neponsit have been replaced by comprehensive statutes, but Neponsit continues to be influential with respect to the large number of community associations that exist outside the condominium framework.

The explosive development of community associations leads to a natural question: would these associations have developed as they have if Neponsit had been decided differently? On one theory, the answer is yes: given the market demand for common interest communities, an adverse determination in Neponsit would have led to statutory overruling of the decision, and a development pattern identical to the one we have seen over the last sixty years. Just as plausibly, however, if the Court of Appeals had refused to enforce the assessment covenants developers would have devised other mechanisms for providing and financing common facilities. All we know for sure is that the Neponsit decision was a pivotal step on the actual path to a housing market in which common interest communities play a central role.

---

[111] McKenzie at 95.

[112] Weiss and Watt, *supra,* at 100.

12

David Callies

Village of Euclid v. Ambler Realty Co.

"Zoning reached puberty in company with the Stutz Bearcat and the speakeasy. F. Scott Fitzgerald and the Lindy Hop were products of the same generation. Of all these phenomena of the twenties, only zoning has remained viable a generation later."

Richard F. Babcock, *The Zoning Game*, at 3

"The landmark case in American zoning law is Village of Euclid v. Ambler Realty Co."

Seymour Toll, *Zoned American*, at 213

Introduction

Zoning is the basis of land use controls in America, and the *Euclid* case is zoning's touchstone. Zoning touches the vast majority of most Americans, but if not for *Euclid*, there would have been no zoning. It is trendy and commonplace to denigrate both. Zoning is said to be an *ancien regime*, and the literature is filled with gleeful requiems for its passing. *Euclid* is said to be a reactionary case by a reactionary court, dedicated to preserving the status quo of residential neighborhoods and excluding minorities therefrom. While there is some truth in certain of such assertions, many are wide of the mark. Zoning is alive and well, and increasingly robust after years of neglect.[1] Local zoning never really declined except in the perception of commentators. The cities–where the

---

[1] Clifford L. Weaver and Richard F. Babcock, *City Zoning: The Once and Future Frontier*, Washington, D.C.: Planners Press, American Planning Association, 1979.

vast majority of people live and work and where, therefore, land use decisions most directly affect their way of life–never abandoned zoning, which retains much of its Euclidean character. While state and federal agencies have successfully promoted a range of regional and statewide land use control regimes to deal with regional land use issues,[2] these are added layers of land use control rather than a substitute for local zoning.

Euclid fares little better at the hands of most recent commentators. Its service and use as a vehicle for executing plans for providing attractive urban environments seems lost in a welter of post hoc commentary on the ulterior–indeed insidious–motives of its supporters and defenders.[3] To be sure, there is more than a little evidence that the *Euclid* court sustained zoning for its ability to preserve residential neighborhoods from the supposed predations of the apartment building. Nevertheless, there are other aspects and merits to the decision, including aesthetics, planning and economic stability. It is these aspects of the case to which this chapter is in part devoted. First, however, it is useful to examine the context of pre-Euclidean zoning, and second, the considerable drama which preceded the decision itself.

Euclid in Context: Zoning, Planning, and the City Beautiful

If zoning reached puberty, as Babcock suggests, in the 1920's, it was conceived in recognizable form during the latter part of the 19th century, though its antecedents predate the founding of the republic.[4] However, zoning came into its own as a method of controlling the use of land by implementing city plans in New York City in 1920. The story is well and thoroughly told in many fine historical commentaries, among them Seymour Toll's *Zoned American* and Charles Haar and Jerold Kayden's edited *Zoning and the American Dream*. What follows is a brief summary of that tale.

Zoning is a means for implementing plans: city plans, comprehensive

---

[2] See, for review and comment on such systems, Fred P. Bosselman and David L. Callies, *The Quiet Revolution in Land Use Controls* (1972); Peter A Buchsbaum and Larry J. Smith, eds., *State and Regional Comprehensive Planning*, Chicago, IL: The Association, 1993; Eric Damien Kelly, *Managing Community Growth* (1993); Cullingworth, J. Barry, *Planning in the USA*, 1997; John DeGrove and Deborah Milnes, *The New Frontier for Land Policy: Planning and Growth Management in the States* (1992); Healy, Robert G., *Land Use and the States*, Baltimore: Johns Hopkins University Press, 1976.

[3] See, e.g., Richard H. Chused, Symposium on the Seventy–Fifth Anniversary of Village of Euclid v. Ambler Realty Co.: Euclid's Historical Imagery, 51 Case Western Res.L. Rev. 597 (2001).

[4] See, e.g., Fred P. Bosselman, David L. Callies and John Banta, *The Taking Issue: a study of the constitutional limits of governmental authority to regulate the use of privately-owned land without paying compensation to the owners*, 1973.

plans, development plans, general plans. The "plan as law" theories[5] that characterize much present land use control theory and jurisprudence were but a shadow, if that, in the back of the minds of the early proponents of local land use controls that eventually culminated in the zoning ordinance. Arguably rooted in the British "garden city" concept popularized by Ebenezer Howard in his landmark *Garden Cities of Tomorrow*[6], the key was to separate uses of land by off-parcel effect. Thus, residential would be separate from commercial, and commercial from residential. As we shall see, residential areas were later to be further separated into single family and multifamily zones, with interesting consequences.

Much of the early battle for such planned separation appears to have taken place in New York. A fortuitous confluence of events and individuals produced a critical report upon which the first major municipal zoning ordinance was based. It is at least arguable that without that confluence and that ordinance, there would have been no Euclid case— and precious little municipal zoning. The events were the increasing use of the skyscraper (in part due to the perfection of the elevator) and the hodgepodge of uses that characterized late 19–century New York City, together with a reform group that seized power from the city's notorious Tammany Hall shortly after the turn of the 19th century. The individuals were Edward Bassett, late returned from an apparently eye-opening (from the perspective of city planning) trip to Germany who found himself appointed to a Heights of Buildings Commission after joining the National Conference on City Planning, and James Metzenbaum of Cleveland, who defended the Euclid zoning ordinance. Zoning became his passion.[7]

One result was the 1913 Report of the Heights of Buildings Commission. Directed principally toward preserving Fifth Avenue from perceived blight from various quarters, the 1913 Report nevertheless noted that the problems magnified there were city-wide, and therefore required a city-wide solution: mixed uses which did not mix, and the invidious invasion of the tall building which surcharged streets and sidewalks and caused both congestion and dark canyons, all contrary to the health and safety of the citizens of New York. The Report "laid down a blueprint" for the later zoning ordinances which, unlike the sporadic attempts to

---

[5] Fasano v. Board of County Commissioners of Washington County, 264 Or. 574, 507 P.2d 23 (1973); Lum Yip Kee Ltd. v. City and County of Honolulu, 70 Haw. 179, 767 P.2d 815 (1989); J. DiMento, The Consistency Doctrine and the Limits of Planning (1980).

[6] Ebenezer Howard, *Tomorrow: A Peaceful Path to Real Reform*; republished as *Garden Cities of Tomorrow*, 1965.

[7] Seymour I. Toll, *Zoned American*, New York: Grossman Publishers, 1969, pp. 144–150.

control height only as in such cities as Chicago and Philadelphia and Boston, would address setbacks and, most important, the use of land by creating use districts. These were to be created by use of the police power, and the potential for unreasonable distinctions and differences solved by reference to a nebulous comprehensive plan, which the commissioners never defined.[8]

There followed in quick succession (1914) a bill in the New York legislature to amend New York's charter to give it the power to zone, and the creation of a Commission on Building Districts and Restrictions, the latter with Bassett as chair. Relying on the 1913 Commission Report, the new Commission set to work drafting a resolution which, after public hearings and a huge advertising campaign, became law in 1916. All of New York City was divided into use districts on maps which had the force of law. Applicable to each district was a set of use, height and area restrictions. Residence districts topped the use "pyramid" with "unrestricted" uses at the bottom. Five classes of height districts regulated the height of buildings in each use district. Area districts dealt with yards and the like. Uses which did not fit into the new regulatory scheme were denominated "nonconforming" which did not necessarily require elimination. A Board of Appeals was empowered to avoid rigidity and grant variances from the strict letter of the district regulations in the event of unnecessary hardship.[9]

A parallel development was the promulgation of the Standard State Zoning Enabling Act by the Hoover Commission in draft form in 1922. Finally issued in 1926 as "A Standard State Zoning Enabling Act Under Which Municipalities May Adopt Zoning Regulations," it provided a useful boost to the concept of zoning at a critical juncture. Fueled by the migration of increasingly large portions of the U.S. population to urban areas (cities and exclusive suburbs), zoning swept into most major metropolitan areas during the 1920's on a wave of reform and the need to protect real estate values. The close association with urban planning and its goals were largely forgotten. But the initial legal problems foreseen in the 1913 New York report were not, and soon, zoning was under attack in the courts. The legal foundations for the *Euclid* case were soon laid.[10]

Village of Euclid v. Ambler Realty Co.: The Beginnings

Euclid was in many ways an atypical American village. Incorporated in 1903, the Village formed a 16–square-mile rectangle eastward from

---

[8] Toll, *supra* note 7, at 160–171; see also Charles M. Haar & Jerald S. Kayden, *Zoning and the American Dream*, Chicago, IL: Planners Press (1989).

[9] Toll, *supra* note 7, at 172–188.

[10] Toll, *supra* note 7, at 189–210.

Cleveland and along Lake Erie, with a population of about ten thousand. To the south from Cleveland ran Euclid Avenue, famous in that area during the latter part of the nineteenth century as Prosperity Street and Millionaire's Row, for its great mansions along its tree-lined precincts. North ran two railroads–the Nickel Plate and the Lake Shore, and St. Claire Avenue and Lake Shore Boulevard. Euclid Avenue was a main artery leading to Cleveland. The Ambler Realty Company of Cleveland commenced assembling its 68–acre parcel between Euclid Avenue and the Nickel Plate among the vacant farmlands which characterized that part of the Village in 1911, principally for eventual industrial development.[11]

Meanwhile, Euclid's mayor appointed a zoning commission in 1922 to investigate the passage of a zoning ordinance for the Village. Among its members was Cleveland attorney and Euclid Avenue resident James Metzenbaum, who was later to write a treatise on the law of zoning. Key resources for the commission were the 1913 New York Report and the subsequent zoning ordinance. Later that year, the Village adopted its first comprehensive zoning ordinance modeled closely on the New York ordinance: use, height and area districts. It was, of course, the use districts–running from U–1 single family residential districts through U–6 unrestricted industrial manufacturing district–that became the subject of the *Euclid* decision. Ambler's sixty-eight acre parcel was classified U–2 (single family and duplex) along Euclid to a depth of 150 feet, U–3 (apartment) for the next 40 feet, and the rest, backing onto the Nickel Plate, U–6.[12] Ambler claimed this resulted in a reduction in value from $10,000 to $2,500 per acre, a loss of several hundred thousand dollars.

Litigation commenced almost at once in federal district court. The constitutional theory was that the ordinance deprived Ambler of its property without due process of law contrary to the U.S. Constitution's 14th Amendment. Metzenbaum undertook to defend the Village. The case proceeded largely through summaries of pre-trial examination of witnesses testifying about the effect of the use classifications on the value of Ambler's land (largely unrebutted) the purpose of zoning and what it was the Village was attempting to do: preserve an aesthetic character (generally agreed to be beyond zoning's legal authority) or protect the health and safety of its citizens from undue industrial incursions.

In the end, the judge held that the ordinance unconstitutionally took Ambler's property, finding that the fine line between what the police power—through zoning—could accomplish without violating private property rights had indeed been crossed, citing the then recently-decided

---

[11] Toll, *supra* note 7, at 214–215.

[12] Toll, *supra* note 7, at 216.

Pennsylvania Coal Co. v. Mahon.[13] There, recall, Justice Holmes penned the near-immortal words which ushered in the concept of regulatory takings: "The general rule at least is that while property may be regulated to a certain extent, if regulation goes too far it will be recognized as a taking."[14] As the early proponents of zoning feared with respect to zoning's constitutionality, "[T]his is a question of degree."[15] For the district court, zoning went too far; the degree of regulation and its effect on private property was too great. As Metzenbaum observes in his treatise, "It was recognized from coast to coast, that a defeat in this case, would cause all zoning ordinances in successive order throughout the land to fall, like a row of dominoes stood end to end."[16] As a result of this widely-held view, the Village appealed to the U.S. Supreme Court. Clearly, zoning was in play.

The U.S. Supreme Court heard the case first in January of 1926. Represented by Metzenbaum, the Village's brief ran to 142 pages, much of it filled with references to zoning's national acceptance and the Hoover Commission's Model Zoning Enabling Act, and arguments and supporting statements of the New York zoning commissioners the constitutionality of whose own ordinance, of which Euclid was a virtual copy, was also at stake. Indeed, copies of both the 1913 and 1916 New York reports were sent to the Court before oral argument. Unfortunately, this national scope was not what counsel for Ambler first persuaded the Court to address. The issue, rather, was the effect of the ordinance on Ambler's 68 acres. On this ground, one might logically expect a result similar to *Pennsylvania Coal*, in which Holmes focused not on the general subsidence havoc wrought by coal company underground mining, but rather "the case of a single private house".[17] The philosophy of zoning was thus no match for the march of industrial progress and the devaluation of valuable private property for such industrial use. Oral argument went badly for the Village–so badly that Metzenbaum sought and won permission to file a reply brief to his opponent's oral argument![18]

And so it was that further briefs–after oral argument–were submitted and read by the Court. One such was that of Alfred Bettman on behalf of a variety of planning groups and associations. He presented the

---

[13] Pennsylvania Coal Co. v. Mahon, 260 U.S. 393 (1922) and Toll, *supra* note 7, at 220–224.

[14] 260 U.S. 393 (1922) at 415.

[15] *Id.* at 416.

[16] James Metzenbaum, *The Law of Zoning*, 1955, p. 111.

[17] 260 U.S. at 420.

[18] Toll, *supra* note 7, at 231–237.

Court with the many decisions–eleven state supreme courts alone[19] from around the country which had so far upheld the concept of zoning, together with a heretofore absent emphasis on the planning bases for zoning, distinguishing it from other forms of public land use controls and the law of nuisance upon which many of them purported to be grounded. Good health and safety arguments about aesthetics, particularly over what was perhaps the different and unique feature of Euclidean zoning: the exclusion of apartment buildings and businesses from single-family residential districts. Here the language of the New York reports concerning safety, health, child-rearing and so forth were most helpful.[20] The Court reheard the case.

The rest is history. *Euclid* upheld at least the theory of zoning against the 14th Amendment challenge brought by Ambler Realty Company. What follows is an examination of the case, foreshadowing its importance to land use controls in the United States.

Village of Euclid v. Ambler Realty Company: The Decision

The *Euclid* decision held that the Village ordinance "in its general scope and dominant features ... is a valid exercise of authority."[21] Obviously the Court had been successfully driven from its first inclination to find zoning unconstitutional. From the language of the opinion itself, it would certainly appear that the Bettman brief did its job. Indeed, it is only by reference to the brief that one can make sense of the Court's extensive treatment and criticism of apartment houses–neither a proposed use or argument raised by Ambler Realty Company:

> "With particular reference to apartment houses, it is pointed out that the development of detached house sections is greatly retarded by the coming of apartment houses, which has sometimes resulted in destroying the entire section for private house purposes; that in such sections very often the apartment house is a mere parasite, constructed in order take advantage of the open space and attractive surroundings created by the residential character of the district. Moreover, the coming of one apartment house is followed by others, interfering by their height and bulk with the free circulation of air and monopolizing the rays of the sun which otherwise would fall upon the smaller homes, and bringing, as their necessary accompa-

---

[19] Massachusetts, California, Minnesota, Ohio, Illinois, Oregon, Rhode Island, New York, Wisconsin, Louisiana and Kansas. See Bettman, *City and Regional Planning Papers*, at 166.

[20] Toll, *supra* note 7, at 238–241; Brief in Euclid. Village Zoning Case, in part II, Briefs, from Bettman, City and Regional Planning Papers (Comey, ed.) (1946) pp. 157 et seq.

[21] Village of Euclid v. Ambler Realty Co., 272 U.S. 365, 397 (1926).

niments, the disturbing noises incident to increased traffic and business, thus detracting from their safety and depriving children of the privilege of quiet and open spaces for play, enjoyed by those in more favored localities–*until finally the residential character of the neighborhood and its desirability as a place of detached residences are utterly destroyed.* Under these circumstances, apartment houses, which in a different environment would be not only entirely unobjectionable but highly desirable, come very near to being nuisances."[22]

It is perhaps this paragraph which both explains the outcome of the case and encapsulates the views of the majority of the Court, leading as well to some of the most trenchant criticism of the decision: its exclusionary nature by upholding a regulatory framework designed primarily to exclude both multifamily residential and commercial uses from the precincts of the presumably well-off detached residential neighborhoods. (The purple prose describing the evils of apartments and the need for quiet and open spaces would be mirrored when the Court finally revisited zoning a half-century later to extol the virtues of "A quiet place where yards are wide, people few ... [and] where family values, youth values, and the blessings of quiet seclusion and clean air make the area a sanctuary for people.")[23] But if *Euclid* is about a 68–acre vacant tract among vacant tracts, devalued by hundreds of thousands of dollars when partially-zoned for residential and commercial use rather than Ambler's preferred industrial use, why has the Court digressed into the evils of apartment buildings in single-family residential districts?

The answer, of course, is the Bettman brief and its references to the New York Reports of 1913 and 1916. The Court preceded the above language first by a discussion of height and building materials restrictions, observing that there was "no serious difference of opinion" in respect of those laws and regulations.[24] Nor did this trouble Bettman and his cohorts. As the Court surmised, the issue was the use district. Beginning with the separation of industrial from residential, the Court similarly observed it found "no difficulty" in upholding the police "power because the effect of its exercise is to divert an industrial flow from the course which it would follow, to the injury of the residential public, if left alone, to another course where such injury will be obviated."[25] Indeed, there the Court could easily have stopped, since this was all, factually, that was before it.

---

[22] *Id.* at 394.

[23] Village of Belle Terre v. Boraas, 416 U.S. 1, 9 (1974).

[24] 272 U.S. at 388.

[25] *Id.* at 390.

But it did not. It instead looked to "the serious question ... over the provisions of the ordinance excluding from residential districts apartment houses, business houses, retail stores and shops ..."[26] Here it noted that while the decisions of state courts were "numerous and conflicting ... those which broadly sustain the power greatly outnumber those which deny it ... and it is very apparent that there is a constantly increasing tendency in the direction of the broader view."[27] Score another point for Bettman, who listed a raft of such cases in his brief. And it is to the Bettman brief again that one turns for the extensive materials from the 1913 and 1916 New York reports which, recall, emphasized the very problems with the tall buildings excoriated by the Court upon which the Court seized to uphold the broad concept of zoning as opposed to its narrow application to the Ambler property:

> "The matter of zoning has received much attention at the hands of commissions and the results of their investigations have been set forth in comprehensive reports. These reports, which bear every evidence of painstaking consideration, concur in the view that segregation of residential, business and industrial buildings will make it easier to provide fire apparatus suitable for the character and intensity of the development in each section; that it will increase the safety and security of home life, greatly tend to prevent street accidents, especially to children, by reducing the traffic resulting confusion in residential sections, decrease noise and other conditions which produce or intensify nervous disorders, preserve a more favorable environment in which to rear children, etc."[28]

There you have it: the Court is persuaded to uphold zoning generally, and in particular the vulnerable use district classifications, on the strength of the New York reports brought to their attention by Metzenbaum and Bettman, and driven home by Bettman's masterful brief.

Euclid's Implications: What Hath Euclid Wrought?

Before launching into some observations about what *Euclid* did for (or to) land use planning and control, let's first have a look at what the decision meant for the Village, then and now. At first, the various sites–including the Ambler property–along Euclid Avenue remained essentially vacant. Apparently, the folks in Euclid hoped that high-end residential development would continue out of Cleveland right through the Village. It didn't happen. However, whether or not as a result of zoning, Euclid

---

[26] *Id*. at 390.

[27] *Id*. at 390.

[28] *Id*. at 394.

certainly began to thrive, at least according to Metzenbaum (hardly a disinterested observer, of course):

> Euclid has not been hampered, as was predicted by those oppose to zoning. On the contrary, it has enjoyed what is said to have been one of the most singular ratios of growth, among all municipalities in this land, from 1940 to 1950; then numbering more than 42000 population. It has become the third largest of the municipalities in its county. It has attracted the very best known industrial companies, whose names are recognized throughout the world and who have established model plants, administration buildings and landscaped surroundings. With this, has come what is said to be the largest ratio of homes increase in that same decade. Beautiful Apartment Houses, fine Schools, new, modern Police and Fire Stations, many Churches have been constructed. Its real estate tax valuation has reached over $100,000,000. It is believed that its Zoning Ordinance–early enacted–has played no inconspicuous part in this almost unmatched development, for homes have felt safe against intrusion of factories and business; great industrial plants have abundant acreage for their fine buildings; retail business is advantageously situated. Euclid presents orderliness–good housekeeping municipally: Homes are with homes; business is with business; factories are with factories. A carefully planned, early enacted Zoning Ordinance made provision for each type, for each use.[29]

During World War II, the General Motors Corporation built a "war plant" for the manufacture of aircraft engines and landing gear on the Ambler site, which the Village rezoned for the million-square-foot plant. After the war, General Motors produced auto bodies, then auto trim, until closing the plant in 1994, joining the ranks of other industrial plants costing the Village about 7000 jobs commencing in the 1970's. Much of the rest of the area is mixed residential (high-rise apartments and bungalows) and commercial interspersed with what is left of the industrial base of the Village. Half of Euclid's 50,000 residents rent, many are elderly, and half are low-income.[30]

Zoning

Euclid's principle value, of course, was and is the validation of local land use controls beyond simply building construction and height restriction ordinances, by regulating the location and separation of uses of land on private property. While some have suggested that the failure of zoning might have thrust American land use controls into a new and

---

[29] Metzenbaum, *The Law of Zoning*, (1955) at 60–61.

[30] Knack, *Return to Euclid*, Planning Magazine (Nov. 1996) at 5–6.

better direction,[31] there is little question but that zoning was the preeminent form of local land use controls prior to the decision, and most certainly became the dominant one thereafter. By 1930, zoning enabling legislation had passed in 47 of the then 48 states, and in the 48th, courts had construed constitutional home rule provisions to authorize it, according to U.S. Department of Commerce surveys. These same surveys report that by the same year, zoning ordinances were in effect in 981 municipalities.[32]

Indeed, Euclidean zoning remains the dominant local government method for controlling the use of land today, though not necessarily in the same format as the Euclid ordinance or the New York zoning resolution upon which it was based. Whether called a land use code, a zoning ordinance, a comprehensive amendment or something more prosaic, most local governments divide their land area into zoning districts. However, rather than separate districts for height, use and area (a type of overlay district now used for site limitation such as flood hazards and steep slopes and for historic building and district preservation) most ordinances attach height, area, and a host of other bulk, parking, and other regulations to each separate zoning district. The number of use districts have also proliferated so that far from the six such districts which characterized the Euclid ordinance, most ordinances will contain 20 or more, not only further subdividing residential, commercial and industrial classifications into gradations based upon use intensity (for example, r–1 large-lot single family, r–2 medium lot single family, r–3 duplex, r–4 medium density apartment, r–5 high density apartment) but also adding districts such as wholesale warehousing, storage, agriculture, open space, institutions, and offices. Moreover, many such use districts are now "exclusive" so that housing is forbidden altogether in some commercial and industrial districts, as compared with the Euclid ordinance in which each more intensive use district permitted all or most of the uses permitted in the less intensive uses "above" it on the zoning pyramid.[33] Despite the occasional incursion and considerable research and writing,[34] innovative local land use techniques such as performance zoning have made virtually no real headway against the standard Euclidean zoning ordinance whose basis is the land use district, except occasionally in the industrial zones.

---

[31] Larry Gerckens, for example in Knack, supra, at page 8.

[32] See Haar, Charles Monroe, *Land Use Planning*, Boston: Brown, 1959, p. 165.

[33] J.F. Garner and David L. Callies, *Planning Law in England and Wales and in the United States*, 1 Anglo–Amer. L. Rev. 292 (1972).

[34] E.g. Lane Kendig *Performance Zoning*, Washington, DC: Planners Press, 1980.

Exclusion and the Protection of the American Home

To claim that zoning was not meant to be exclusionary in some sense is, of course, to ignore both history and reality. The segregation of uses is by definition exclusionary, as the Metzenbaum quote in the preceding section clearly demonstrates: "Homes are with homes; business is with business; factories are with factories."[35] Indeed, in one of the more famous pre-*Euclid* decisions upholding early zoning, the California Supreme Court said:

> In addition to all that has been said in support of the constitutionality of residential zoning as part of a comprehensive plan, we think it may be safely and sensibly said that justification for residential zoning may, in the last analysis, be rested upon the protection of the civic and social values of the American home. The establishment of such districts is for the general welfare because it tends to promote and perpetuate the American home. It is axiomatic that the welfare, and indeed the very existence, of a nation depend upon the character and caliber of its citizenry. The character and quality of manhood and womanhood are in a large measure the result of home environment. The home and its intrinsic influences are the very foundation of good citizenship and any factor contributing to the establishment of homes and the fostering of home life doubtless tends to the enhancement, not only of community life, but the life of the nation as a whole.[36]

Well, then! Nor is this an exceptional statement. According to Bettman, of the eleven state high court decisions upholding zoning prior to the *Euclid* decision, "Every one of these decisions upheld the creation of exclusively residential districts and the exclusion of non-nuisance industries and businesses therefrom, and many of them upheld the creation of exclusively single family home districts from which apartment houses were excluded."[37]

That such districting could lead to segregation and exclusion on the basis of race and class was certainly a concern of the early proponents of zoning. Use controls fed into a concern of many commentators at the time over barriers to "middle groups in the urban populations. Use controls which set up different kinds of residential arrangements tended to reinforce class segregation."[38]

---

[35] Metzenbaum, *supra*, at 60.

[36] Miller v. Board of Public Works, 195 Cal. 477, 234 P. 381, 387 (1925).

[37] Bettman, City and Regional Planning Papers, at 166.

[38] Toll, *supra* note 7, at 260.

In the short run, zoning was often used as an exclusionary tool, both racially and economically. As one contemporary (with *Euclid*) commentator put it:

> City planning and zoning experts were appealing to their clientele with promises that the new controls would protect them from " 'undesirable neighbors.' In fact, all the arguments adduced to show that zoning protects property values are meaningless unless they imply this important element in the determination of values. No height restriction, street width, or unbuilt lot area will prevent prices from tottering in a good residential neighborhood unless it helps at the same time to kept out Negroes, Japanese, Armenians, or whatever race most jars on the natives."[39]

Again, a prominent zoning consultant in Atlanta allegedly prepared a zoning ordinance in which residential districts were divided into three types: white, colored and undetermined, for the reason that "race zoning . . . is simply a common sense method of dealing with facts as they are."[40] The same consultant was equally happy with the economic segregation which zoning might perpetuate. While the Supreme Court made relatively short work of explicit zoning by race in *Buchanan v. Warley*[41], upholding a contract right to sell to a willing black buyer despite zoning restriction of that part of St. Louis to whites only, there left the matter of economic discrimination among residential classifications.

If minorities could not afford to live in particular communities, it would not be due to racial discrimination per se, but to the inherent constraints of wealth, or lack thereof. Thus, in the 1940's and 50's, local governments began touting the importance of preserving community character and controlling growth, and implemented ever-expanding requirements for minimum floor space, setbacks, and lot sizes.[42] As housing requirements became more demanding, low-and moderate-income housing became less viable. The effects of "exclusionary zoning," that is, zoning practices which tend to segregate people along economic, social, and racial lines, became increasingly common. Nevertheless, courts overwhelmingly upheld these ordinances as legitimate exercises of the general welfare police power, particularly in the Northeast, where judges were

---

[39] Toll, *supra* note 7, at 261–262, quoting Lasker.

[40] Toll, *supra* note 7, at 262.

[41] Buchanan v. Warley, 245 U.S. 60, 38 S.Ct. 16 (1917).

[42] Lionshead Lake, Inc. v. Township of Wayne, 10 N.J. 165, 89 A.2d 693 (1952) (minimum floor space); City of Dallas v. Lively, 161 S.W.2d 895 (Tex. 1942) (minimum setbacks); Caruthers v. Board of Adjustment, 290 S.W.2d 340 (Tex. 1956) (minimum lot size).

known to cite the "quiet and beauty of rural surroundings"[43] and the value of "nice houses."[44] In New Jersey, the state court approved a residential five-acre minimum lot size on such grounds.[45] The conflict between planning the "city beautiful" and the (everlasting) nature of zoning becomes particularly acute as a comparison of this section and the following section demonstrates.

Ironically, it was the New Jersey Supreme Court that later struck the hardest blow to exclusionary zoning tactics, with its landmark decision in *Southern Burlington County NAACP v. Township of Mount Laurel*.[46] In Mount Laurel, over half of the township was restricted to single family homes, with minimum lot sizes of one-half acre, one acre, or three acres. "Garden apartments" and multi-family housing, which had been highly anticipated by poor, mostly black, residents in the area, were expressly prohibited.[47] The New Jersey court first analyzed the state's police power, which must further the public's general welfare and conform to state constitutional standards.[48] Because housing is one of "the most basic human needs," the availability of housing is an essential element of the general welfare, and must therefore be promoted by the state and its municipalities.[49] Furthermore, the court declared that New Jersey's state constitution, which is stricter than its federal counterpart, requires local governments to provide equal protection for the poor and substantive due process protection for housing.[50] Mount Laurel's zoning ordinances did not meet either of these requirements, and its stated interest, to collect enough property taxes to cover municipal governmental and educational costs, was not sufficient to overcome these constitutional limitations and avoid these constitutional duties.[51]

In the end, the New Jersey court imposed a duty on each developing municipality, such as Mount Laurel, to:

"affirmatively ... plan and provide, by its land use regulations, the *reasonable opportunity* for an appropriate variety and choice of

[43] Simon v. Town of Needham, 311 Mass. 560, 42 N.E.2d 516, 518 (1942).

[44] Flora Realty & Investment Co. v. City of Ladue, 362 Mo. 1025, 246 S.W.2d 771 (1952).

[45] Fischer v. Township of Bedminster, 11 N.J. 194, 93 A.2d 378 (1952).

[46] 67 N.J. 151, 336 A.2d 713 (1975).

[47] David L. Kirp, *Our Town: Race, Housing, and the Soul of Suburbia*, 2. (1995).

[48] South Burlington County NAACP v. Township of Mount Laurel, 67 N.J. 151, 336 A.2d 713, 725 (1975).

[49] *Id.*, at 727.

[50] *Id.*, at 725.

[51] *Id.*, at 731.

housing, including ... low and moderate cost housing, to meet the
needs, desires and resources of all categories of people who may
desire to live within its boundaries."[52]

Thus, developing municipalities would be required to "make all
reasonable efforts to encourage and facilitate" their "fair share" of low-
and moderate-income housing.[53] This concept was later codified in the
New Jersey Fair Housing Act of 1985.[54]

In the years following Mount Laurel, several other courts interpreted their state constitutions to require affordable housing on a regional
basis.[55] Other states took a different approach, adopting "inclusionary"
zoning ordinances to combat the longstanding history of exclusionary
practices; these were either voluntary or mandatory, with or without
incentives.[56] A prime example is California's Density Bonus Statute,
which grants developers an automatic bonus if their plans set aside
certain percentages of the property for low-income, very-low-income, and
senior citizen housing.[57] By statute, the inclusionary units are required
to maintain exterior designs consistent with surrounding non-inclusion-
ary units, so low-income residents are less identifiable and less stigma-
tized than they might be otherwise.[58]

Thus, while some courts and legislatures recognize the need to
provide for affordable housing, courts continue to take a hands-off
approach to local zoning ordinances, especially where the municipality
asserts preservation of family and community, along with the "city
beautiful," as the following section demonstrates.

Zoning and Planning the City Beautiful

Recall that an early rationale for zoning was the enforcement of
plans and planning in order to contribute to the workability and attrac-

---

[52] *Id.*, at 728 (emphasis added).

[53] *Id.*

[54] N.J. Stat. Ann. 52:27D–311 to 329 (2001). Compare this to federal Fair Housing Act,
42 U.S.C.A. § 3601; first enacted in 1968, interpreted in Acevedo v. Nassau County, 500
F.2d 1078 (2d Cir. 1974); Smith v. Town of Clarkton, 682 F.2d 1055 (4th Cir. 1982); Jaimes
v. Toledo Metropolitan Housing Authority, 758 F.2d 1086 (6th Cir. 1985).

[55] Berenson v. Town of New Castle, 67 A.D.2d 506, 415 N.Y.S.2d 669 (1979) (court
struck ordinance excluding multifamily use, but declined specific "fair share" quota);
Surrick v. Zoning Hearing Board of Upper Providence, 476 Pa. 182, 382 A.2d 105, 108
(1977) (court struck township ordinance excluding multifamily dwellings).

[56] 89 Calif. L. Rev. 1847, 1857 (Dec. 2001).

[57] Id., at 1860.

[58] Id., at 1878.

tiveness of the city. This was the thrust of the early arguments before the U.S. Supreme Court in the *Euclid* case and it was the city beautiful as a result of such planning that impressed the early proponents of zoning like Basset.

However, plans and planning were early set aside, not to arise again until well into the 20th century. In the 1920's, piecemeal zoning was rampant and usually without any reference to plans and planning, or if at all, only as an afterthought.[59] Indeed, the zoning ordinance was often equated with the plan. Thus in *Kozesnik v. Township of Montgomery*[60] the court held that the standard statutory requirement that zoning proceed in accordance with a comprehensive plan was met by the fact of a zoning ordinance. Plans have come into their own, however, in the 1980's, in a series of court decisions which considerably boosted the stock of plans with respect to zoning.

Perhaps the most famous of these is *Fasano v. Board of County Commissioners of Washington County*[61] holding that reclassification of land under the county zoning ordinance must be just what the legislature in its enabling legislation said: in accordance with its designation in the county comprehensive plan. Also typical, both in terms of court language and the extensive use of comprehensive plans, is the Hawaii case of *Lum Yip Kee v. City and County of Honolulu*[62] well worth quoting:

> Lum Yip Kee has not demonstrated that "low density apartment" is not in accord with the comprehensive plan. The council made findings that the development plan amendment was consistent with the objectives and policies of the County General Plan.

Case law in California likewise requires that zoning be undertaken in conformance with plans. According to *Neighborhood Action Group v. County of Calaveras*[63], the general plan is atop the hierarchy of local government law regulating land use.

> It has been aptly analogized to a constitution for all future developments ... Subordinate to the general plan are zoning laws, which regulate the geographic allocation and allowed uses of land. Zoning laws must conform to the adopted general plan. Thus, the validity of

[59] Toll, *supra* note 7, at 258–261.

[60] 24 N.J. 154, 131 A.2d 1 (1957).

[61] 264 Or. 574, 507 P.2d 23 (1973).

[62] Lum Yip Kee, Ltd. v. City & County of Honolulu, 70 Haw. 179, 767 P.2d 815, 823 (1989).

[63] Neighborhood Action Group v. County of Calaveras, 156 Cal.App.3d 1176, 1183, 203 Cal.Rptr. 401 (1984).

a conditional use permit, which is governed by the zoning regulations, depends (derivatively) on the general plan's conformity with statutory criteria.

Similarly, courts in New York have also found that zoning must be in conformance with comprehensive plans. In *Udell v. Haas*[64], the court overturned zoning ordinances that were not in conformance with legislatively adopted plans and stated:

> Zoning may easily degenerate into a talismanic word, like the "police power," to excuse all sorts of arbitrary infringements on the property rights of the landowner. To assure that this does not happen, our courts must require local zoning authorities to pay more than mock obeisance to the statutory mandate that zoning be "in accordance with a comprehensive plan."

This requirement of conformance is mirrored by case law and statutes around the country. In *Webb v. Giltner*[65], an Iowa court overturned the rezoning of property due to a failure to be consistent with the comprehensive plan as required by statute and said:

> Where a county has enacted a written comprehensive plan, we hold the requirement of Iowa Code section 358A.5 (that zoning be "in accordance with a comprehensive plan") contemplates the zoning ordinance will be designed to promote the goals of that individualized plan. The Board did not consider "The Plan."

The comprehensive plan gives guidelines and a basis for the formulation of zoning regulations and their amendments. A Texas court stated in *Mayhew v. Sunnyvale*[66] that "the law is settled that the adopted comprehensive plan must, by statutory mandate, serve as the basis for subsequent zoning amendments" according to § 1011c and cited the earlier decision of *City of Pharr v. Tippitt*[67]:

> The duty to obey the existing law forbids municipal actions that disregard not only the pre-established zoning ordinance but also the long-range master plans and maps that have been adopted by ordinance.

Often zoning that is enacted without thought of or conformance with the comprehensive plan will result in spot or piecemeal zoning, as the court found in *Pharr*, spot zoning is "piecemeal zoning, *the antithesis of planned zoning.*"[68]

---

[64] Udell v. Haas, 21 N.Y.2d 463, 470, 288 N.Y.S.2d 888, 235 N.E.2d 897 (1968).

[65] Webb v. Giltner, 468 N.W.2d 838, 841 (Iowa 1991).

[66] Mayhew v. Sunnyvale, 774 S.W.2d 284 (Tex. 1989).

[67] City of Pharr v. Tippitt, 616 S.W.2d 173, 176–77 (Tex. 1981).

[68] Id. at 177.

Virtually from the beginning of the movement, the supporters of zoning maintained a somewhat schizophrenic attitude towards the use of nuisance as a basis for zoning. On the one hand, it made a good analogy, adding to the comfort level of the courts in upholding zoning. On the other hand, zoning needed to go beyond nuisance suppression if it were to be wholly successful. Bettman recognized this tension in his papers, in the process noting an early U.S. Supreme Court case supporting this view:

> The [*Euclid*] opinion contains considerable use of the word "nuisance" and some reference to the common law of nuisances, and, while the Court seemed to feel it necessary to relate the police power to the nuisance concept, even going so far as to state that apartment houses in a single-family residential neighborhood come very near to being nuisances, still the Court carefully refrained from treating the scope of the police power as coterminous with the power to suppress or prevent nuisances and expressly states that the law of nuisances was "consulted not for the purpose of controlling but for the helpful aid it its analogies in the process of ascertaining the scope of the police power." This is a mild affirmation of the principle set forth in *Bacon v. Walker*, 204 U.S. 311 (1907), that the police power "is not confined to the suppression of what is offensive, disorderly, or unsanitary. It extends to so dealing with the conditions which exist in the State as to bring out of them the greatest welfare of its people."

Nevertheless, the "city beautiful" aspect of zoning, whether or not related to a comprehensive plan, is, of course, alive and well–post-Euclid, particularly in federal courts. One need look no further than the U.S. Supreme Court's famous eminent-domain-cum-aesthetics 1954 decision in *Berman v. Parker*[69], and its return to the land use controls fray after half a century of silence (after *Euclid and* Nectow v. Cambridge) in the oddly-reasoned *Village of Belle Terre v. Boraas*[70] in 1974.

Berman v. Parker was perhaps the most unusual of the cases from a doctrinal perspective. Cited in virtually every case in which zoning is used for some aesthetic purpose, the case has, of course, nothing whatsoever to do with zoning. It is, rather, an eminent domain case, standing for the proposition that courts ought not to inquire into legislative motives with respect to the establishment of the public purpose which the Fifth Amendment requires (along with just compensation) of its otherwise unbridled exercise by a sovereign unit of government. Originally confined to urban renewal cases based on the facts of the case (condemnation of unblighted commercial land by a District of Columbia

---

[69] Berman v. Parker, 348 U.S. 26, 75 S.Ct. 98 (1954).

[70] Village of Belle Terre v. Boraas, 416 U.S. 1 (1974).

redevelopment authority in accordance with a redevelopment plan), the opinion's ringing endorsement of the "application of the police power to municipal affairs" in language more applicable to zoning then eminent domain:

> "Miserable and disreputable housing conditions may do more than spread disease, crime and immorality [shades of Bettman and Metzenbaum!]. They may also suffocate the spirit by reducing the people who live there to the status of cattle. They may indeed make living an almost insufferable burden. They may also be an ugly sore, a blight on the community which robs it of charm, which makes it a place from which men turn. The misery of housing may despoil a community as an open sewer may ruin a river.... The concept of public welfare is broad and inclusive. The values it represents are spiritual as well as physical, aesthetic as well as monetary. It is within the power of the legislature to determine that the community should be beautiful as well as healthy, spacious as well as clean, well-balanced as well as carefully patrolled. In the present case, the Congress and its authorized agencies have made determinations that take into account a wide variety of values. It is not for us to reappraise them. If those who govern the District of Columbia decide that the Nation's Capital should be beautiful as well as sanitary, there is nothing in the Fifth Amendment that stands in the way."[71]

The Supreme Court followed *Berman* twenty years later with a zoning case articulating largely the same principles in it first foray into land use controls in the half-century since *Euclid* and *Nectow*. In *Village of Belle Terre v. Boraas*[72] the Court upheld zoning ordinances limiting one-family dwelling occupancy to a maximum of two persons unrelated by blood or marriage in an attempt to regulate the "unsuburban" aspects of college student housing. This time the Court addressed the actual use of the police power for aesthetic purposes, again largely in the same terms as it had in *Berman,* commencing again with a most *Euclid*-like attack on multiple-family housing, this time of any sort or variety rather than only the ubiquitous (and iniquitous) apartment building:

> "The regimes of boarding houses, fraternity houses, and the like present urban problems. More people occupy a given space; more cars rather continuously pass by; more cars are parked; noise travels with crowds. A quiet place where yards are wide, people few, and motor vehicles restricted are legitimate guidelines in a land-use project addressed to family needs. This goal is a permissible one within Berman v. Parker, supra. The police power is not confined to

---

[71] Berman, 348 U.S. at 32.

[72] 416 U.S. 1 (1974).

elimination of filth, stench and unhealthy places. It is ample to lay out zones where family values, youth values, and the blessings of quiet seclusion and clean air make the area of sanctuary for people."[73]

Thus emboldened, both lower federal and state courts rapidly followed the lead of the US Supreme Court in holding that the city beautiful trumps equal housing opportunity. Thus, the Ninth Circuit Court of Appeals held in two cases from the mid–1970's that minimum one-acre lots and stringent growth controls based in part on aesthetic considerations were constitutional regardless of any discriminatory housing effects in the respective communities. In *Ybarra v. City of Los Altos Hills*,[74] the court held that preservation of a town's rural environment justified single-family residential zones with one-acre minimum lot sizes. Although expressly recognizing that such restrictions would, as a practical matter, prevent poor people from living in Los Altos Hills, the court had no difficulty in finding that the ordinance was rationally related to a legitimate governmental interest–the preservation of the town's rural environment–and thus withstood a 14th Amendment equal protection challenge. Again in *Construction Industry Association of Sonoma County v. City of Petaluma*,[75] the Ninth Circuit upheld a growth restriction ordinance that it recognized would not only severely restrict available housing options in Petaluma, but that such ordinances could easily "affect the needs and [housing] resources of an entire region." Nevertheless, the court held that "the City's interest in preserving its small town character and in avoiding uncontrolled and rapid growth falls within the broad concept of 'public welfare'," relying specifically on the *Berman* and *Belle Terre* opinions. Note that both of the Ninth Circuit opinions relied heavily as well on the existence of local and detailed comprehensive plans as bases for the exercise of local zoning regulations for such aesthetic purposes. This continued reliance on the comprehensive plan continues to be a hallmark of decisions upholding the use of local land use controls–especially zoning–for a range of welfare-based "city beautiful" purposes including most particularly historic preservation.[76] However, even in the absence of a plan, state courts have had little difficulty in

---

[73] Village of Belle Terre, 416 U.S. at 9. See, e.g., Charles M. Haar and Michael Allan Wolf, *Euclid Lives: The Survival of Progressive Jurisprudence*, 115 Harv. L. Rev. 2158 (June 2002); Richard H. Chused, *Euclid's Historical Imagery*, 51 Case W. Res. L. Rev. 597 (Summer 2001).

[74] 503 F.2d 250 (9th Cir. 1974).

[75] 522 F.2d 897 (9th Cir. 1975).

[76] See, e.g., A-S-P Associates v. City of Raleigh, 298 N.C. 207, 258 S.E.2d 444 (1979); Reid v. Architectural Board of Review of City of Cleveland Heights, 119 Ohio App. 67, 192 N.E.2d 74 (1963).

upholding aesthetic or historic preservation restrictions on the use of land.[77]

In sum, the conclusion is well-nigh inescapable that when push comes to shove, the purposes of zoning to preserve residential neighborhoods and attractive suburban, small-town character conflicts with the exclusionary aspects of zoning, the former generally wins, hands down. Euclidean zoning lives.

Zoning to Protect Property Values

Zoning finds its legitimacy in the police power: government's authority to regulate the health, safety, and welfare (and at one time morals) of the people. Even prior to *Euclid*, however, courts interpreted this definition to include economic welfare, more specifically, the preservation of property values.[78] Today, "[c]onservation of property value is a legitimate governmental interest well within the broad scope of the police power."[79]

Throughout the 1990s, preservation of property values was yet another justification courts relied upon to uphold zoning ordinances that keep residential districts residential. Restricting mobile homes to mobile home parks is one such example. In 2001, the Court of Appeals of Kentucky held that a zoning administrator properly refused to approve the placement of a manufactured home in residential district to prevent a decline in property values.[80] In 1997, the District Court of Colorado upheld several city ordinances that prohibited manufactured homes in any residential area after "[m]unicipal officials testified that the objectives of the various ordinances include the compatibility of housing and preservation of both the tax base and market values of site-built homes."[81]

Courts have also considered neighboring property values to uphold ordinances that regulate placement of adult establishments. The city of

[77] See, e.g., New York v. Stover, 12 N.Y.2d 462, 240 N.Y.S.2d 734, 191 N.E.2d 272 (1963) and State ex rel Stoyanoff v. Berkeley, 458 S.W.2d 305 (1970).

[78] See Saier v. Joy, 198 Mich. 295, 164 N.W. 507 (1917), granting an injunction to prevent defendant from operating a funeral home in a residential district.

[79] Texas Manufactured Housing Ass'n v. City of Nederland, 101 F.3d 1095, 1105 (5th Cir. 1996). See also McCollum v. City of Berea, 53 S.W.3d 106 (Ky. App. 2000) and Harrison v. Upper Merion Township Zoning Board of Adjustment, 45 Pa. D. & C. 2d 452 (1968).

[80] City of Berea, 53 S.W.3d at 112.

[81] *Id.*, citing Colorado Manufactured Housing Ass'n v. City of Salida, 977 F.Supp. 1080 (D. Colo. 1997).

Rochester, Minnesota enacted a zoning ordinance that prohibited the placement of adult establishments within 750 feet from any residential district, church, school, youth facility, or another adult establishment after the Planning Department published a report entitled, "Adult Entertainment: Land Use and Legal Perspectives."[82] The report listed adverse secondary effects of adult entertainment businesses, including diminished property values, both commercial and residential, when located close to such businesses:

> "The concentration of adult entertainment uses in commercial areas or the location of adult entertainment uses in close proximity to residential uses, churches, parks and schools will result in devaluation of property values and decreases in commercial business sales, thereby reducing tax revenues to the City and adversely impacting the economic well-being of the citizens of this City."[83]

In 1992, Rochester issued two Notices of Violation to advise an adult bookstore owner that it was violating the ordinance by doing business within 750 feet of the Rochester Public Library, a youth facility.[84] The bookstore owner challenged the ordinance on First Amendment and due process grounds. The Eight Circuit reversed the lower court's preliminary injunction against enforcement of the ordinance, holding that the ordinance served a substantial governmental interest by lessening the adverse effects accompanying adult entertainment businesses: increased crime rates, lowered property values, and increased transience.[85]

Similarly, in 2002, the Eleventh Circuit upheld the Huntsville, Alabama Board of Zoning Adjustments' decision to deny a special exception and variance to American Tower, a company that wanted to build a wireless communications tower in a residential neighborhood.[86] The court found that the Board had the requisite substantial evidence to support its decision, including testimony from a local realtor who said that the proposed tower cost her potential buyers for her own property in the area.[87]

Besides preserving property values, zoning has been used to constrain property values for the same purposes of preserving the middle-class character of a residential neighborhood. Due to the rise in noise, partying, inadequate parking, and underage drinking as a result of

---

[82] ILQ Investments, Inc. v. City of Rochester, 25 F.3d 1413, 1415–16 (8th Cir. 1994).

[83] Id. at 1417.

[84] Id. at 1415.

[85] Id. at 1417.

[86] American Tower LP v. City of Hunstville, 295 F.3d 1203, 1206 (11th Cir. 2002).

[87] Id. at 1208.

student tenants, Lower Merion Township, Pennsylvania adopted an ordinance to prohibit renting property to a group of more than three students in a residential district.[88] The residents also feared landlord-investors would buy "up properties to rent to students, thus driving up property values, pricing middle-class families out of the local housing market and changing the character of their community."[89] The District Court upheld the ordinance despite the economic hardships to landlords and inconvenience to students who suffered from scarce on-campus housing.[90]

Conclusion

If *Euclid* had been decided differently–as the U.S. Supreme Court originally intended–the local control of land use would in all likelihood look very different today. Certainly the "exclusive" residential zone would have been impossible to maintain, and with it, much of zoning and the local zoning ordinance. Without zones, what need for administrative processes like the variance? Why worry about nonconformities? Whither the relationship to comprehensive planning? One suspects local government might have been left with some sort of nuisance-based controls, perhaps of the so-called "performance" variety popular with some communities in the industrial zone. The use of covenants would have assumed greater importance, and perhaps the common interest community might have become more popular, sooner.

With the upholding of local zoning in principle, however, the local zoning ordinance became–and remains–the principle method of local land use control. The increasing importance of subdivision codes (and in particular the ubiquitous land development exaction or condition attached to plat approval) and selected state-wide controls are mere addenda, important as they are in their respective spheres. It is the local zoning ordinance which first linked plans to land use controls in any significant manner, contributing often to the implementation of plans as laws, though lately this linkage is perhaps more often associated with subdivision and land development codes. While it is true that a certain degree of exclusivity results from the application of the standard Euclidean zoning ordinance, it is likely that the more egregious forms of exclusion would have found other avenues of expression without zoning. On the whole, local zoning has served local government–and its citizens–pretty well. Once again, as Richard Babcock observed in his classic commentary on zoning:

[88] Smith v. Lower Merion Township, 1992 WL 112247 (E.D. Pa. 1992).

[89] Id.

[90] Id.

F. Scott Fitzgerald and the Lindy Hop were products of the same generation. Of all these phenomena of the twenties, only zoning has remained viable a generation later.

And, indeed, for at least one generation beyond that.

Biographies of *Property Stories* Contributors

Vicki Been is the Elihu Root Professor of Law at New York University School of Law, where she has been a member of the faculty since 1990. She teaches courses in Land Use Regulation, Property, and State and Local Government, as well as seminars on The Takings Clause, Environmental Justice, and Empirical Issues in Land Use and Environmental Law. She also co-teaches an interdisciplinary Colloquium on the Law, Economics and Politics of Urban Affairs. Professor Been received a B.S. with high honors from Colorado State University in 1978 and a J.D. from New York University School of Law in 1983, where she was a Root–Tilden Scholar. After graduation, Professor Been served as a law clerk to Judge Edward Weinfeld, United States District Court for the Southern District of New York from August 1983 to July 1984 and as a law clerk to Justice Harry Blackmun, United States Supreme Court from August 1984 to August 1985. She was an Associate at the firm of Debevoise & Plimpton in New York City for one year, then served as an Associate Counsel at the Office of Independent Counsel: Iran/Contra in Washington, DC. She joined Rutgers University School of Law in Newark as an Associate Professor in August 1988. Professor Been has written extensively on the Fifth Amendment's Just Compensation Clause, Environmental Justice, "Smart" Growth, and other land use topics, and is a co-author of Land Use Controls: Cases and Materials (with Robert C. Ellickson) (2000, Aspen Law & Business).

Patricia A. Cain is the Aliber Family Professor of Law at the University of Iowa. Professor Cain's teaching and scholarly interests include federal taxation, wills and estates, property, feminist legal theory, and lesbian and gay legal issues. She served on the board of directors of Lambda Legal Defense and Education Fund for seven years and is a Past President of the Society of American Law Teachers. She is also a member of the American Law Institute. Recent publications include *Rainbow Rights: The role of lawyers and courts in the lesbian and gay civil rights movement* (Westview Press 2000), and numerous articles on tax law, feminist legal theory, and the rights of unmarried couples.

Professor Cain thanks University of Iowa law students Annette Stewart and Jim Burgess (class of 2004), for their timely research assistance in the preparation of this chapter.

David Callies is Benjamin A. Kudo Professor of Law at the University of Hawaii's William S. Richardson School of Law where he teaches land use, state and local government and real property. He is a graduate of DePauw University, the University of Michigan Law School (J.D.) and the University of Nottingham (LL.M.), and a life member of Clare Hall, Cambridge University. He is past chair of the Real Property and Financial Services Section of the Hawaii State Bar Association; past chair of the American Bar Association Section of State and Local Government Law; past chair, Academics Forum, and member of Council, Asia Pacific Forum, of the International Bar Association; a member of the American Law Institute (ALI); a Fellow of the American Institute of Certified Planners (FAICP), and co-editor of the annual Land Use and Environmental Law Review (with Dan Tarlock). Among his books are Bargaining for Development: A Handbook on Development Agreements, Annexation Agreements, Land Development Conditions and Vested Rights (with Curtin and Tappendorf) (ELI, 2003); Taking Land: Compulsory Purchase and Land Use Regulation in the Asia–Pacific (with Kotaka) (U.H. Press, 2002), Property and the Public Interest (with Hylton, Mandelker and Franzese) (Lexis Law Publishing, 2d ed., 2003); Preserving Paradise: Why Regulation Won't Work (Univ. of Hawaii Press, 1994); Regulating Paradise: Land Use Controls In Hawaii (Univ. of Hawaii Press, 1984), and (with Robert Freilich and Tom Roberts), Cases and Materials on Land Use (West, 3d ed., 1999). His book, Land Use Controls in the United States was recently published in Kyoto and Shanghai. Prof. Callies would like to thank his research assistants, Josh Medeiros, Tricia Nakamatsu and Summer Kupau for their considerable help in researching the background for the Euclid chapter.

Richard H. Chused is Professor of Law at Georgetown University Law Center where he has taught for thirty years. He is the author of a number of books and articles on property law and history, gender and law in American history, and the hiring, retention and treatment of women and minority members of law school faculties. His major works include an innovative interdisciplinary textbook, CASES, MATERIALS AND PROBLEMS IN PROPERTY (1999), a property reader for first year students, A PROPERTY ANTHOLOGY (2d Ed. 1997), a history of divorce in the first half of the nineteenth century, PRIVATE ACTS IN PUBLIC PLACES: A SOCIAL HISTORY OF DIVORCE IN THE FORMATIVE ERA OF AMERICAN FAMILY LAW (1994), a series of four widely read articles published between 1983 and 1992 on the history of married women's property law, and recent articles on the history of Euclid v. Ambler, Euclid's *Historical Imagery*, 51 Case Western Res. L. Rev. 597 (2001) and landlord-tenant court in New York, *Landlord-*

Tenant Court in New York City at the Turn of the Nineteenth Century, in
WILLIBALD STEINMETZ (ED.), PRIVATE LAW AND SOCIAL INEQUALITY IN THE
INDUSTRIAL AGE (2000). Professor Chused is a member of the American
Historical Association, the Organization of American Historians, the
American Society for Legal History and the Society of American Law
Teachers (SALT). He sat on SALT's Board of Governors from 1982 to
1994 and is now the webmaster for the organization's site at www.salt-
law.org. His avocations include an abiding interest in American architec-
ture and constant engagement with Jewish life and ethics.

A number of people gave of their time and knowledge to help me
write this history. Katherine Emig, Georgetown University Law Center '04 did stellar work as a research assistant. Gene Fleming, Esq.,
Professor Florence Wagman Roisman, Professor Monroe Freedman, Professor Myron Moskowitz, The Honorable Patricia Wald, Charles Duncan,
Esq. and Richard Cotton, Esq., all provided me with information about
their roles in the *Javins* drama. Florence Roisman and Gene Fleming, as
well as my colleagues Dan Ernst, Sheryll Cashin, Lisa Heinzerling and
Bill Vukowich, were gracious enough to read and comment upon an
earlier draft. Many of my colleagues also made remarks about the paper
when I presented it in November 2002 at one of the weekly lunch
sessions my faculty devotes to discussion of scholarly projects. Finally,
Georgetown University Law Center provided me with a summer writer's
grant in 2002 as well as funds to gather a large collection of legal
documents in the *Javins* case. Thanks to all.

Susan French practiced law in Seattle, Washington for eight years
before joining the law faculty at the University of California at Davis in
1975. Since 1989 she has been a member of the UCLA law faculty, where
she teaches property, wills and trusts, community associations law, and
land use. She is a graduate of Stanford University and the University of
Washington Law School. She was the Reporter for the Restatement
(Third) of Property, Servitudes (2000), an engagement that grew out of
her 1982 article, *Toward a Modern Law of Servitudes: Reweaving the
Ancient Strands*, 55 So. Cal. L. Rev. 1261. In addition to numerous
articles about servitudes and the Restatement, Professor French has
written about powers of appointment, *Exercise of General Powers of
Appointment: Should Intent to Exercise Be Inferred From a General
Disposition of Property?* 1979 Duke L.J. 747, perpetuities, *Perpetuities:
Three Essays in Honor of My Father*, 65 Wash. L. Rev. 101 (1990), lapse
and survival problems, *Imposing a General Survival Requirement on
Beneficiaries of Future Interests: Solving the Problems Caused by the
Death of a Beneficiary Before the Time Set for Distribution*, 27 Ariz. L.
Rev. 801 (1985), *Antilapse Statutes Are Blunt Instruments: A Blueprint
for Reform*, 37 Hast. L.J. 335 (1985), *Application of Antilapse Statutes to
Appointments Made by Will*, 53 Wash. L. Rev. 405 (1978), and protecting

the rights of residents in common interest communities, *The Constitution of a Private Residential Government Should Include a Bill of Rights*, 27 Wake Forest L. Rev. 345 (1992). She is co-author, along with Gerald Korngold and Lea Vandervelde, of the recently revitalized, classic, Casner & Leach Property casebook and co-author, with Wayne S. Hyatt, of a casebook on Community Association Law. She continues to work with the ALI, serving as an Adviser to the Restatement (Third) of Property, Donative Transfers.

Professor French would like to express her appreciation to Michael Gruen, Victor Muskin, and Paul S. Whitby for taking the time to talk with her about the *Gruen* case. Without their contributions, this would have been a dull chapter, indeed!

Richard Helmholz currently serves as the Ruth Wyatt Rosenson Distinguished Service Professor in the University of Chicago Law School. He is the editor of *Fundamentals of Property Law* (Lexis 1999) (with Barlow Burke and Ann M. Burkhart) and *Itinera Fiduciae: Trust and Treuhand in Historical Perspective* (Duncker & Humblot 1998) (with Reinhard Zimmermann). His most recent book is Volume One in the Oxford History of the Laws of England (Oxford UP 2004), dealing with the history of ecclesiastical jurisdiction. He is a member of the American Law Institute, a Fellow of the American Academy of Arts and Sciences, and a Corresponding Fellow of the British Academy.

Gerald Korngold is Dean and the Everett D. and Eugenia S. McCurdy Professor of Law at Case Western Reserve University School of Law. He is the author of three books: *Real Estate Transactions: Cases and Materials on Land Transfer, Development and Finance* (Foundation Press, 4th edition, 2002) (with Paul Goldstein); *Cases and Text on Property* (Aspen, 4th edition, 2000) (with A. James Casner, W. Barton Leach, Susan F. French, and Lea Vander Velde); *Private Land Use Arrangements: Easements, Real Covenants, and Equitable Servitudes* (1990; new edition forthcoming with Juris Publishing). His articles include *The Emergence of Private Land–Use Controls in Large–Scale Subdivisions: The Companion Story to Village of Euclid v. Ambler Realty Co.*, 51 Case Western Reserve L. Rev. 617 (2001); *Whatever Happened to Landlord–Tenant Law?*, 77 Nebraska L. Rev. 703 (1998); *Enforcement of Restrictions by Homeowners Associations: Balancing Individual Rights and Community Interests*, 13 Colloqui: Cornell J. of Planning & Urban Issues 71 (1998); *Seller's Damages from a Defaulting Buyer of Realty: The Influence of the Uniform Land Transactions Act on the Courts*, 20 Nova L. Rev. 1069–1089 (1996); *Resolving the Flaws of Residential Servitudes Associations: For Reformation Not Termination*, 1990 Wisconsin L. Rev. 513–535; *Single Family Use Covenants: For Achieving a Balance Between Traditional Family Life and Individual Autonomy*, 22 U.C. Davis L. Rev. 951–990 (1989); *For Unifying Servitudes and Defeasi-*

ble Fees: Property Law's Functional Equivalents, 66 Texas L. Rev. 533–576 (1988); and *Privately Held Conservation Servitudes: A Policy Analysis in the Context of In Gross Real Covenants and Easements*, 62 Texas L. Rev. 433–495 (1984). Dean Korngold is an elected member of the American Law Institute and the American College of Real Estate Lawyers and served as an Adviser to the Restatement of Property (Third)–Servitudes.

Max Mehlman is the Arthur E. Petersilge Professor of Law, Director of the Law–Medicine Center, Case Western Reserve University School of Law, and Professor of Biomedical Ethics, Case Western Reserve University School of Medicine. He received his J.D. from Yale Law School in 1975, and holds two bachelors degrees, one from Reed College and one from Oxford University, which he attended as a Rhodes Scholar. Prior to joining the faculty at CWRU in 1984, Professor Mehlman practiced law with Arnold & Porter in Washington, D.C. In addition to writing numerous articles, Professor Mehlman is the co-author of the first casebook on genetics and the law, published by West; author of *Wondergenes: Genetic Enhancement and the Future of Society* (Indiana University Press 2003); co-author (with Jeffery Botkin MD) of *Access to the Genome: The Challenge to Equality* (Georgetown University Press 1998); and co-editor, with Tom Murray, of the *Encyclopedia of Ethical, Legal and Policy Issues in Biotechnology*.

Andrew Morriss is Galen J. Roush Professor of Business Law & Regulation at Case Western Reserve University School of Law, Cleveland, Ohio, where he directs the Center for Business Law and Regulation, and Senior Associate at PERC–The Center for Free Market Environmentalism, Bozeman, Montana. Prof. Morriss has a Ph.D in Economics from the Massachusetts Institute of Technology as well as law and public policy degrees from the University of Texas at Austin. Morriss also regularly teaches at Universidad Francisco Marroquín in Guatemala. He is the author of a number articles and book chapters on the role of common law property rights theories in environmental protection, including *Quartering Species: The 'Living Constitution,' The Third Amendment, and the Endangered Species Act* (with Richard L. Stroup), 30 ENVIRONMENTAL LAW 769–810 (2000) and *The Technologies of Property Rights: Choice Among Alternative Solutions to Tragedies of the Commons* (with Bruce Yandle), 28 ECOLOGY LAW QUARTERLY 123–168 (2001). He also edited THE COMMON LAW AND THE ENVIRONMENT (Rowman & Littlefield, 2000) with Roger E. Meiners. He teaches property, business associations, and a variety of seminars. Other interests include the history and jurisprudence of the nineteenth century American codification debate, second-best theory, private legal systems, and empirical law and economics. Morriss also regularly writes for *Ideas on Liberty*, published by the Foundation for

Economic Education, including articles on property rights on the play-ground, Harry Potter, dog pounds, and cyberspace. He knows first hand about cows, which feature prominently in the *Spur Industries* case, and what they smell like because he owns some, as well as horses, dogs, and cats, and is married to a veterinarian. Having lived near feedlots in the past, he keeps his cows in Texas, far away from his house in Ohio. He thanks Jared Oakes for excellent research as-sistance and Jonathan Adler, Carol Akers, DVM, Tom Bogart, Gerry Korngold, Roger Meiners, and Bruce Yandle for comments.

Carol Rose is the Gordon Bradford Tweedy Professor of Law and Organization at Yale Law School. She is a graduate of Antioch College; she has a Ph.D. (History) from Cornell University, and a J.D. from the University of Chicago. She writes and teaches in the history and theory of property, environmental law, and resource-related issues. She is the author of the book Property and Persuasion (1994), and co-author (with Robert Ellickson and Bruce Ackerman) of Perspectives on Property Law (3rd ed. 2002). Among her more recent articles are Romans, Roads, and Romantic Creators: Traditions of Public Property in the Information Age, 66 L. and Contemp. Prob. 89 (2003); and Scientific Innovation and Environmental Protection, 32 Envtl. L. 755 (2002). She is also the author of a number of other articles, including Canons of Property Talk, or, Blackstone's Anxiety 108 Yale L. J. 601 (1999); The Several Futures of Property: Of Cyberspace and Folk Tales, Emission Trades and Ecosys-tems, 83 Minn. L. Rev. 129 (1998); The Shadow of The Cathedral, 106 Yale L. J. 2175 (1997); Property as the Keystone Right? 71 Notre Dame L. Rev.329 (1996); Women and Property, 78 Va. L. Rev. 421 (1992); Rethinking Environmental Controls, 1991 Duke L. J. 1; Energy and Efficiency in the Realignment of Common–Law Water Rights, 19 J. Legal Stud. 261 (1990); Crystals and Mud in Property Law, 40 Stan. L. Rev. 577 (1988); The Comedy of the Commons, 53 U. Chi. L. Rev. 711 (1986); Possession as the Origin of Property, 52 U. Chi. L. Rev. 73 (l985); and Mahon Reconstructed: Why the Takings Issue is Still a Muddle, 57 So. Cal. L. Rev. 561 (l984). Professor Rose served as an advisor to the American Law Institute's Restatement of Property (Servitudes), and she is on the Board of Editors of Foundation Press, as well as of the Land Use and Environmental Law Journal. She is a member of the American Academy of Arts and Sciences.

Professor Rose would especially like to thank Michael Soules and Chris Stevens for their valuable research assistance, as well as the workshop participants at the Yale Law School and University of North Carolina Law School for helpful comments on earlier versions of this chapter.

Peter Salsich is the McDonnell Professor of Justice in American Society at Saint Louis University School of Law. He holds a joint appointment in the Department of Public Policy Studies and is a fellow of the American College of Real Estate Lawyers. He is a former editor of the ABA Journal of Affordable Housing and Community Development Law, a former chair of the ABA Commission on Homelessness and Poverty, a former member of the Council of the Section of Real Property, Probate and Trust Law of the American Bar Association and a former member of the Governing Committee of the ABA Forum on Affordable Housing and Community Development Law. He is a member of the American Planning Association, Association of American Law Schools, Missouri Bar and the Bar Association of Metropolitan St. Louis. He received his A.B. from the University of Notre Dame (1959) and his J.D. from Saint Louis University (1965).

Prof. Salsich was the first chair of the Missouri Housing Development Commission and chaired the board of directors of Legal Services of Eastern Missouri Inc. and the Ecumenical Housing Production Corp. He is author of *Missouri Landlord–Tenant Relationship,* and is co-author of *Land Use Regulation, Property Law, State and Local Government in a Federal System,* and *State and Local Taxation and Finance in a Nutshell.* He is the author of chapters in a casebook on housing law and a treatise on state and local government financing. He has published numerous articles and has been an active participant in CLE programs at the local, state and national levels. He has been a recipient of the Thompson and Mitchell faculty scholarship award and the Student Bar Association teacher of the year award. He teaches Property, Land Use, Legal Profession, Real Estate Transactions, State and Local Government, and Housing.

Professor Salsich would like to thank Maureen Lober for taking the time to talk with him about the *Lober* case. He also appreciates the excellent research assistance of Kevin Etzkorn and Brian Nolan, 3Ls at Saint Louis University School of Law.

A.W. Brian Simpson is the Charles F. & Edith J. Clyne Professor of Law at the University of Michigan Law School, where he teaches Property Law, and English Legal History, and gives seminars on aspects of Human Rights and Legal Theory; a recent seminar was entitled The Boundaries of the Market. Before moving to Michigan he has taught in Oxford, Canterbury, Halifax, Ghana and Chicago. His published books include *Cannibalism and the Common Law, Leading Cases in the Common Law,* and *Human Rights and the End of Empire. Britain and the Genesis of the European Convention on Human Rights.* He is a Fellow of the American Academy of Arts and Sciences and of the British Academy, and an Honorary Queen's Counsel.

Stewart Sterk is Mack Professor of Law at the Benjamin N. Cardozo School of Law, where he regularly teaches Property. His articles on servitude law include *Minority Protection in Residential Private Governments*, 77 B U L Rev 273 (1997), *Foresight and the Law of Servitudes*, 73 Cornell L Rev 956 (1988), and *Freedom from Freedom of Contract: The Enduring Value of Servitude Restrictions*, 70 Iowa L Rev 615 (1985). Professor Sterk also served as an Advisor for the Restatement (Third) of Property (Servitudes).

Professor Sterk's other scholarship relating to Property and Land Use includes *Restraints on Alienation of Human Capital*, 79 Virginia L Rev 383 (1993), *Competition Among Municipalities as a Constraint on Land Use Exactions*, 45 Vanderbilt L Rev 831 (1992), *Nollan*, *Henry George, and Exactions*, 88 Columbia L Rev 1731 (1988), and *Neighbors in American Land Law*, 87 Columbia L Rev 55 (1987). He has also co-edited (with Joel C. Dobris and Melanie B. Leslie) a leading Trusts and Estates casebook. Elliot Gardner provided valuable research assistance in the preparation of this chapter.

†